CB128316

B1

TEACHER'S BOOK PACK

PREMIUM

BEYOND

MACMILLAN

Anna Cole
Michael Terry

Macmillan Education
4 Crinan Street
London N1 9XW
A division of Macmillan Publishers Limited

Companies and representatives throughout the world

ISBN 978-0-230-46135-2

Written by Anna Cole and Michael Terry

First published 2014

Designed by emc design ltd.

Cover design by emc design ltd.

Cover photographs by Alamy/Losevsky Pavel, Alamy/Ian Nolan

Printed and bound in Thailand

2019 2018 2017 2016 2015
11 10 9 8 7 6 5 4 3 2

CONTENTS

LISTENING & VOCABULARY	GRAMMAR (2)	LANGUAGE & BEYOND	SPEAKING	WRITING
Leaving home ***Recognise informal speech*** **Vocabulary (2):** Adjectives for describing objects	Past tenses review ***Talk about past actions***	Get organised ***Collaborate to organise a group activity***	Invitations ***Make and react to invitations*** I'd love to	A special object (description) ***Make a writing plan***
Around the world ***Listen for the information you need*** **Vocabulary (2):** Travel	The future ***Talk about events in the future***	Respect others ***Respect other people's personal space***	At the airport ***Check in at the airport*** I'd like to check in	Wish you were here (postcard) ***Use correct verb tenses***
Talking music ***Transfer spoken information to a table*** **Vocabulary (2):** Adverbs of degree	Comparison of adverbs ***Compare how people do things***	Get organised ***Stay on task and avoid distractions***	My sister thinks … ***Present other people's opinions*** What's your opinion?	My music profile (profile) ***Link contrasting ideas***
Back from the future ***Use stress and intonation to help you understand*** **Vocabulary (2):** Extreme adjectives	Second conditional ***Talk about imaginary situations in the present and future*** PRONOUNCE stressed words and phrases	Know yourself ***Decide what's important to you***	Do you mind? ***Make and react to requests*** Go ahead	A poem about true friends (poem) ***Use a dictionary***
The power of colour ***Follow a conversation*** **Vocabulary (2):** Colour idioms	*(In order) to … , so (that) …* ***Talk about the purpose of doing things***	Communicate & cooperate ***Recognise non-verbal communication***	At the chemist's ***Ask for help with words*** What's the difference?	A place I really like (description) ***Link similar ideas***

WELCOME TO THE *BEYOND* TEACHER'S BOOK

Beyond is an exciting 6-level course for teenagers, covering CEFR levels from A1+ to B2. Its scope & sequence is meticulously mapped to the CEFR and international exams. The course offers comprehensive coverage of the four language skills through the incremental and cumulative development of subskills. It equips students with transferable linguistic strategies to use in the English classroom and beyond. The inclusion of age-appropriate 21st century skills adds an inspiring new dimension to language teaching. The life skills lessons create a learning environment that's relevant and accessible to teenagers.

The course is flexible and works in a number of teaching contexts. Lessons are clearly labelled so that you can choose to prioritise material that's relevant in your teaching contexts. The extensive online materials present you with a variety of teaching and practice alternatives to enrich the learning experience.

With 6 levels, your school's needs can be met with one single course – be it for streaming, multi-level entry or a programme that takes your students from A1+ all the way up to B2.

The material has a creative and dynamic approach to topics which motivates students and makes language learning more meaningful and successful. Units provide constant opportunities for students to express themselves, while the pages are brought to life through a series of specially produced videos. Throughout the course, language is recycled and reviewed, allowing students to assess and consolidate their progress.

The course's combination of language skills, life skills and motivating material prepares students for success in and beyond the classroom.

A message from the authors

“Secondary teaching is a rewarding but demanding profession. With this course we have aimed to make your role as a teacher as easy as possible, with material that is clearly organised and can be taught with little or no preparation time. We have also provided resources to help you deal with mixed-ability classes, test and evaluate progress and review material.

Having enthusiastic and interested students also makes the teaching role easier, so throughout the writing process we have considered the teenagers' perspective on learning and come up with materials that teach them about the world and allow them to express their own inner worlds.

When producing the course we used the following key principles to guide our writing.”

10 KEY PRINCIPLES OF *BEYOND*

1 Subskills: learning how to read, listen, speak and write

All reading, listening, speaking and writing lessons have an integrated subskills focus that teaches students linguistic strategies to maximise their learning. This comprehensive subskills syllabus is a key part of *Beyond*'s aim to develop literacy.

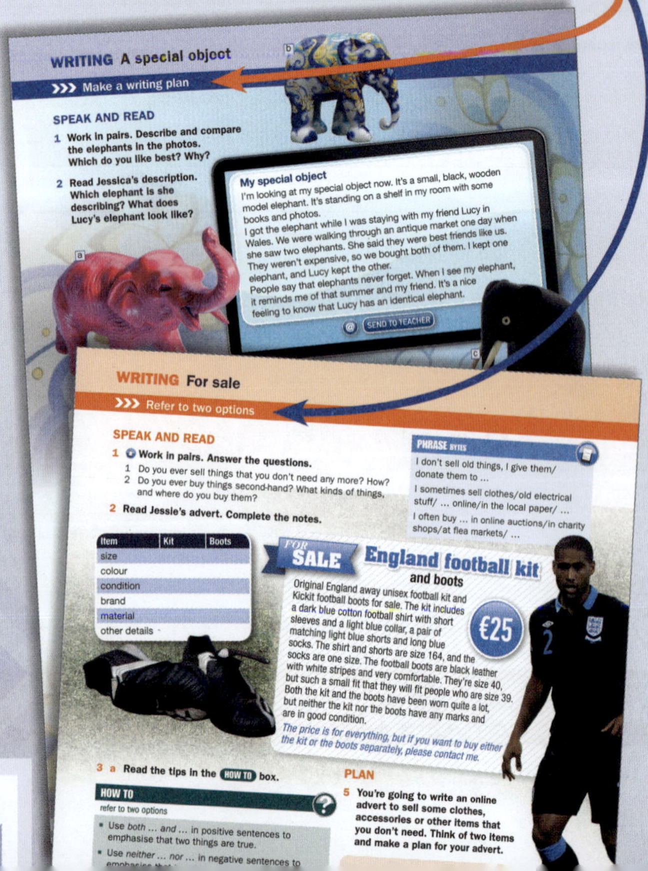

2 Life skills: learning for life

To be successful at school and in life, students need to learn skills that go beyond pure academic knowledge. In order to thrive in today's global market, they need to become aware of and acquire a range of life skills, such as learning to deal with stress, communicating effectively and understanding different cultures. One lesson in every unit is dedicated to developing a life skill under one of five umbrella headings: Get organised, Get thinking, Respect others, Know yourself and Communicate & cooperate.

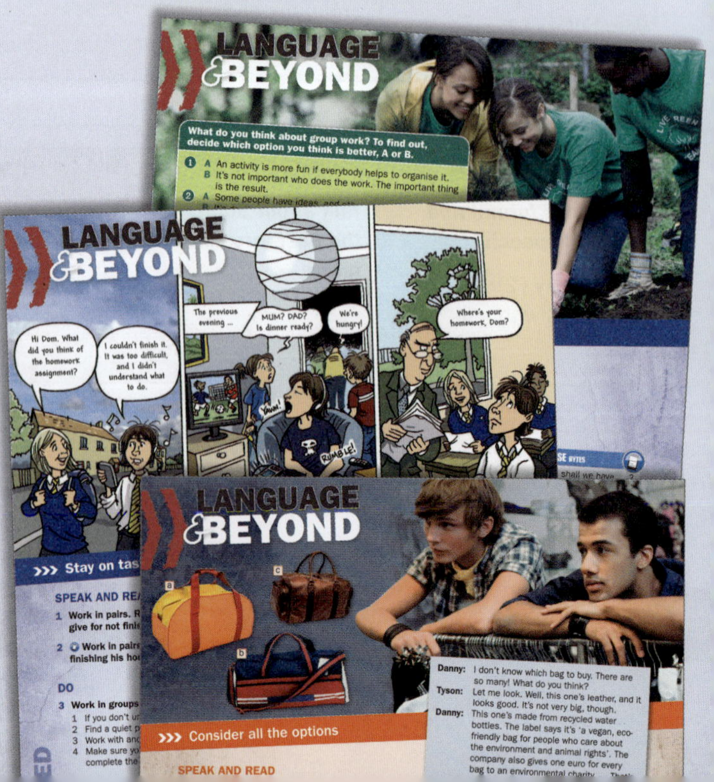

3 Original content and striking images

The cross-curricular focus of *Beyond* helps students learn about the world around them and the original material sustains students' interest. The striking images create a strong visual impact and engage students with the content.

4 Varied and adaptable approach

Beyond caters for students' differing learning styles and levels, with ideas and prompts for students who need more help and a varied approach to dealing with topics and language. To help with differentiation in the classroom, the Teacher's Book suggests alternative procedures for stronger or weaker students and for fast finishers.

5 Clear and easy to use

All lessons in *Beyond* are easy to teach directly off the page, with clear aims and stages, so students see what they will be learning and progress in a structured way.

6 Opportunities for personalisation

Throughout the course, students are encouraged to relate what they have learned to their own experiences. This personal investment in the course is motivating and rewarding, and makes the learning process more memorable and the content more relevant.

7 Strong communication focus

Beyond's pairwork discussions, functional speaking tasks, presentations and variety of writing tasks all encourage students to produce meaningful and real communication.

8 Language in context

All new language in *Beyond* is contextualised for students to see its functional purpose and a situation for use before it is studied.

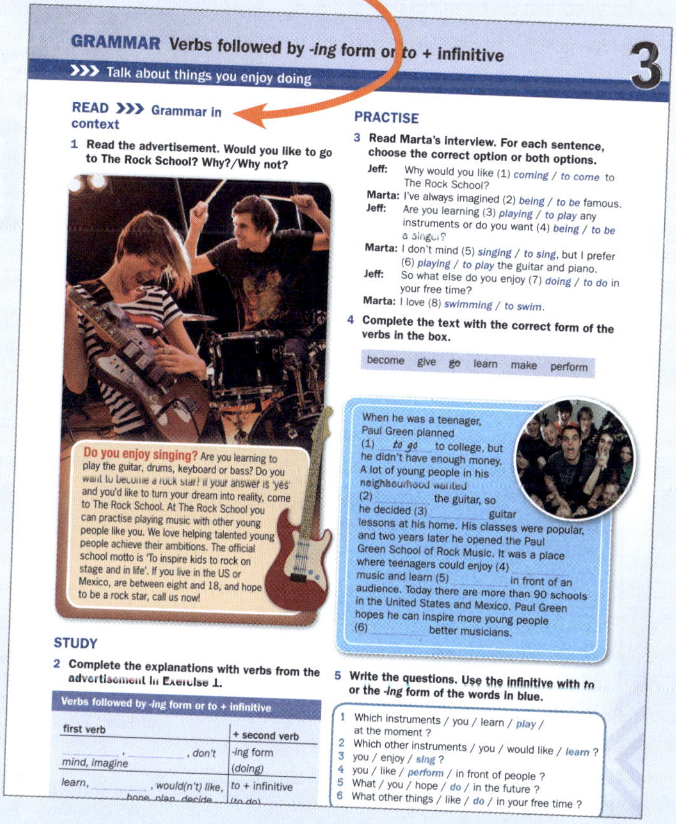

GRAMMAR **Verbs followed by *-ing* form or *to* + infinitive** **3**

>>> Talk about things you enjoy doing

READ >>> Grammar in context

1 **Read the advertisement. Would you like to go to The Rock School? Why?/Why not?**

Do you enjoy singing? Are you learning to play the guitar, drums, keyboard or bass? Do you want to become a rock star? If your answer is 'yes' and you'd like to turn your dream into reality, come to The Rock School. At The Rock School you can practise playing music with other young people like you. We love helping talented young people achieve their ambitions. The official school motto is 'To inspire kids to rock on stage and in life'. If you live in the US or Mexico, are between eight and 18, and hope to be a rock star, call us now!

STUDY

2 **Complete the explanations with verbs from the advertisement in Exercise 1.**

Verbs followed by *-ing* form or *to* + infinitive	
first verb	+ second verb
_____, _____, *don't mind, imagine*	*-ing* form (*doing*)
learn, _____, *would(n't) like, hope, plan, decide*	*to* + infinitive (*to do*)

PRACTISE

3 **Read Marta's interview. For each sentence, choose the correct option or both options.**

Jeff: Why would you like (1) *coming* / *to come* to The Rock School?
Marta: I've always imagined (2) *being* / *to be* famous.
Jeff: Are you learning (3) *playing* / *to play* any instruments or do you want (4) *being* / *to be* a singer?
Marta: I don't mind (5) *singing* / *to sing*, but I prefer (6) *playing* / *to play* the guitar and piano.
Jeff: So what else do you enjoy (7) *doing* / *to do* in your free time?
Marta: I love (8) *swimming* / *to swim*.

4 **Complete the text with the correct form of the verbs in the box.**

become give go learn make perform

When he was a teenager, Paul Green planned (1) *to go* to college, but he didn't have enough money. A lot of young people in his neighbourhood wanted (2) _____ the guitar, so he decided (3) _____ guitar lessons at his home. His classes were popular, and two years later he opened the Paul Green School of Rock Music. It was a place where teenagers could enjoy (4) _____ music and learn (5) _____ in front of an audience. Today there are more than 90 schools in the United States and Mexico. Paul Green hopes he can inspire more young people (6) _____ better musicians.

5 **Write the questions. Use the infinitive with *to* or the *-ing* form of the words in blue.**

1 Which instruments / you / learn / *play* / at the moment ?
2 Which other instruments / you / would like / *learn* ?
3 you / enjoy / *sing* ?
4 you / like / *perform* / in front of people ?
5 What / you / hope / *do* / in the future ?
6 What other things / like / *do* / in your free time ?

9 Learner autonomy

Students are encouraged to work independently in a variety of ways from a carefully graded inductive approach to grammar to self-study worksheets on the Online Resource Centre. This approach makes learning more memorable and furthers learner autonomy.

10 Flexible multi-media material

Beyond can be used by teachers with limited or no access to technology. But for those wanting to use technology, both inside and outside the classroom, the course includes a digital version of the Student's Book and Workbook as well as a huge bank of additional materials and tests in the Online Resource Centre. Every *Beyond* unit contains two original videos to supplement the lessons.

> We hope you enjoy teaching and your students thrive learning with *Beyond*. We wish you a successful and productive academic year. We are always interested to know your thoughts on the course, so please get in touch at www.macmillanbeyond.com
>
> *The Beyond Team*

"The first two pages are a single **vocabulary lesson** which serves as an introduction to the unit and its central theme."

Unit themes appeal to teenagers and provide interesting, quirky and informative material.

1 The lesson starts with a Recall activity that activates prior knowledge. Recall words are listed in the Words & Beyond section at the back of the book, where students learn and practise a related vocabulary tip.

2 New vocabulary is clearly visible in a word box and is presented and practised with the support of the images on the pages. Lexical sets are recorded for ease of presentation. Once introduced, vocabulary is recycled throughout the unit and reviewed in the Unit Review and every two units in a Progress Check.

UNIT 8

SHE SAID, HE SAID

IN THE PICTURE In the news

>>> Talk about people working in the media

WORK WITH WORDS

1 RECALL **Work in pairs. Do the tasks. You have three minutes.**

a Complete the names of things we read.

1	___ ___ rtoon	8	___ ___ em
2	___ ___ cipe	9	___ ___ ofile
3	___ ___ port	10	___ ___ ticle
4	___ ___ tter	11	___ ___ ory
5	___ ___ cture ___ ___ ption	12	___ ___ iz
6	___ ___ og	13	___ ___ les
7	___ ___ terview	14	___ ___ rvey

b Find an example in this book of three of the things in the list.

2 3.01 **Write the media jobs in the correct category. Listen and check. Then listen and repeat.**

author blogger cartoonist designer editor gossip columnist graphic artist journalist photographer printer publisher reporter

People who write	People who work with visuals	People who work behind the scenes

3 Choose the correct people from Exercise 2 to complete the sentences about a newspaper.

1 The *printer* / *publisher* owns the newspaper and employs a lot of people.
2 The *reporter* / *journalist* reports the news while the *reporter* / *journalist* investigates the news.
3 The *designer* / *photographer* takes pictures to illustrate the stories. The *graphic artist* / *cartoonist* creates other visuals, like graphs and diagrams.
4 The *author* / *editor* decides which stories to include in tomorrow's paper.
5 The *designer* / *photographer* creates the final pages.
6 The *printer* / *cartoonist* adds some visual fun to the news while the *gossip columnist* / *blogger* writes funny things about famous people. Today he's writing about the famous *author* / *reporter* of a bestselling book.
7 When the newspaper is ready to print, it goes to the *printer* / *publisher*.
8 While the paper is being printed, the *designer* / *blogger* is writing for the digital edition of the paper.

82

USING THE *BEYOND* STUDENT'S BOOK

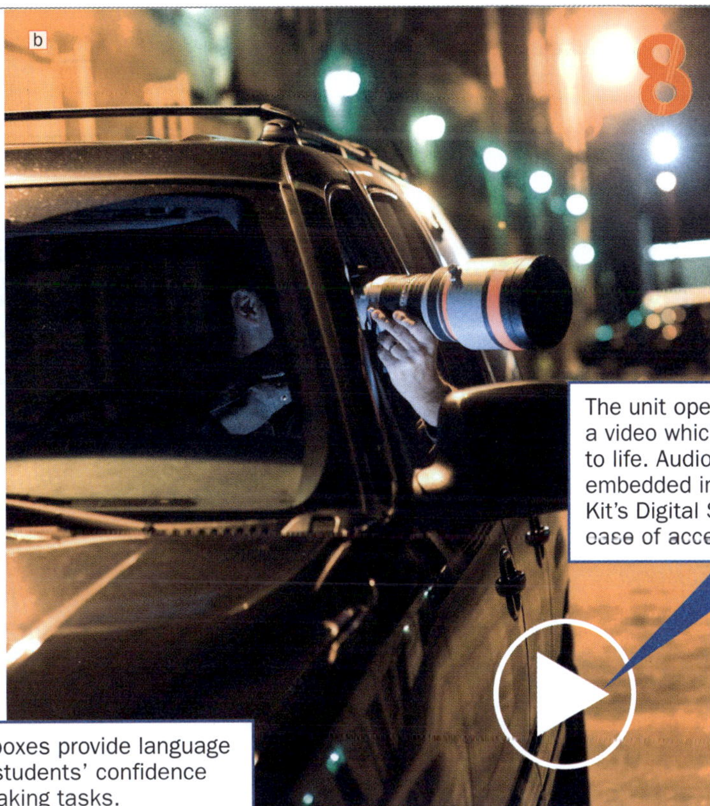

The unit opener is supported by a video which brings the pages to life. Audio and video are embedded in the Presentation Kit's Digital Student Book for ease of access in the classroom.

The Phrase Bytes boxes provide language support and build students' confidence when planning speaking tasks.

4 **Which of the people in Exercise 2 can you see in the photos?**

5 3.02 **Listen to a designer talk about the photos. Which photos is she talking about?**

1 .... 3 .... 5 ....
2 .... 4 .... 6 ....

6 a 3.03 PRONOUNCE **Listen and repeat the word. Pay attention to the stressed syllable and the /ə/ sound in the unstressed syllable.**

/ə/ author

b 3.04 **Listen to the other words in the box in Exercise 2. Underline the stressed syllables, and circle the syllables that have the /ə/ sound. Then listen and repeat.**

7 THE MOVING PICTURE **Watch the video. Which of the people from Exercise 1 do you see?**

PHRASE BYTES

I hardly ever/rarely/occasionally …
I was looking for … / I wanted to find …
I'd prefer to be the … because … / Being a … must be …
Really? But surely …
I'd want to publish …

A pronunciation section focuses on the common misunderstandings when English is used between speakers of different first languages. Pronunciation sections can appear in any lesson, depending on the content, and focus on key sounds and stress patterns in words and sentences.

Media habits

1 Which magazines or comics do you read?
2 Which cartoons or cartoonists do you like?
3 When was the last time you looked at a newspaper? What part(s) did you look at (eg sports, TV, news)?
4 What was the last book or story you read? Who is your favourite author and why?
5 Which media job would you most like to do? Why?
6 If you were a publisher, what type of magazine would you like to publish and why?

SPEAK

8 **Work in pairs. Ask and answer the questions in the survey on media habits.**

GO BEYOND

Do the Words & Beyond exercise on page 137.

Workbook, page 88

5 The Go Beyond extras provide material for fast finishers, homework or additional class activities and refer students to the additional exercises on the Words & Beyond pages at the back of the Student's Book.

3 The Moving Picture feature on the opening pages brings a dynamic feature to the spread by introducing a video connected to the lesson and an accompanying task.

4 The final exercises consolidate language with a communicative activity in a personalised context.

> After the double-page opening spread, each individual page is one complete lesson. The **reading and listening** lessons include an integrated but explicit subskills focus, designed to teach students how to read and listen successfully to a variety of text types over the course of a level.

1 The first exercise gives students the opportunity to say what they know or think about the lesson's topic. This increases confidence and helps students to focus on the lesson.

2 Students read a variety of text types and learn the subskills they need to apply to each type. Reading texts include unusual and original perspectives on familiar syllabus topics.

3 The How To box provides tips for putting the subskill into action. Students read the tips, carry out a related task and then reflect on which tips they used to complete the task.

4 The React exercises encourage students to share opinions on the text and relate to it in a personal way.

5 The Go Beyond task provides a further activity related to the content of the reading text.

Subskills are clearly identified.

READING Media culture

»» Recognise formal and informal writing

All texts are recorded to provide extra classroom and self-study opportunities.

SPEAK AND READ

1 Work in pairs. Answer the questions.

1 Which famous people do you like in music, television, sport or film?
2 What facts do you know about their lives?
3 Where did you find the information?

2 a Read the tips in the HOW TO box.

b 3.05 **Read each text then match it to the correct publication (1–3).**

1 A showbiz blog 2 A celebrity magazine 3 A serious newspaper

A

A young Hollywood celebrity has spoken about being a victim of the paparazzi. In an interview with the *Los Angeles Times*, the 26-year-old actor said: 'Today's media culture is a dangerous monster.' Currently promoting his latest film, the star has also been in the news for personal reasons. Separating public and personal life has always been difficult for film and music stars. On the one hand, they want media attention in order to help promote their careers. On the other hand, they want the media to respect their privacy.

One magazine has suggested that the actor should move to France, where there are stricter privacy laws. In the United States however, the paparazzi can take photographs of anyone if they are in a public place, including the children of celebrities.

Sue Jakes, the respected journalist, told me that some photographers often scare celebrity children to make them cry. She said that an emotional or embarrassing photograph was easier to sell.

Maybe it's time to stop this form of 'journalism'. It's easy to do – just stop buying celebrity magazines.

B

Hot young star ████ has told a newspaper that I am a monster! What did I do?! Did I hurt his feelings when I suggested that the 26-year-old actor's relationship was over? Or was it last week's embarrassing photo in our 'They're only human' feature?

If you don't like being famous, go to France, *chéri*! But please stop saying terrible things about the people who helped to make you a star.

By the way, an anonymous source told me that she had seen ████ having dinner with a famous singer at one of the city's top restaurants. Hello? If you don't want to be photographed, eat at home!

We ... resp ... this ... Let's ... stops appearing in print!

Reading texts contain examples of the next lesson's grammar point in context.

3 Choose the best title for each of the texts.

1 'Celebrity children complain about paparazzi'
2 'Star tells me to leave him alone!'
3 'Can public figures have private lives?'
4 'Anonymous monster attacks Hollywood star!!'

HOW TO

recognise formal and informal writing

In formal writing, look for ...
- ☐ longer sentences with formal words and phrases (*on the one hand, however*).
- ☐ full verbs (*I will, do not*).
- ☐ correct use of punctuation.

In informal writing, look for ...
- ☐ shorter sentences with spoken English phrases (*well, By the way*).
- ☐ contractions (*I'll, don't*).
- ☐ extra punctuation to add emphasis, especially exclamation marks.

4 Which tips in the HOW TO box did you use for help with Exercises 2b and 3? Tick (✓) them.

5 Read the sentences and circle *A* (text A) or *B* (text B).

1 A / B includes a quote by the actor.
2 A / B includes the views of an expert.
3 A / B includes a fact that is wrong.
4 A / B includes information given by an anonymous person.
5 A / B says that the actor should move to France.
6 A / B thinks we can do something to change the situation.

REACT

6 Work in pairs. What do you think? Tell your partner.

1 Which of the texts is more interesting? Give reasons for your answer.
2 Why is text A probably more accurate than text B?
3 Why do people like reading about the lives of famous people?
4 How can famous people have private lives?

GO BEYOND

Read the two texts again and find two more differences between them.

84

»» Workbook, page 89

There are links to the corresponding Workbook page at the bottom of each page.

Lesson 3 – Grammar (1)

> The target **grammar** is always presented in context and students are encouraged to work out rules from examples.

GRAMMAR Reported speech

8

>>> Report what people say

READ AND LISTEN >>> Grammar in context

1 3.06 **Read and listen to the conversation. Who is Lucy's new photographer?**

Harry: Jack! I'm surprised to see you. Where's Lucy? I told her that I'd meet her here at seven. We're doing a story for the school magazine.
Jack: Lucy told me she didn't want to see you. I told her that I could talk to you.
Harry: I don't understand. We arranged to meet here yesterday. I've brought my camera.
Jack: She said that she'd found another photographer. She said she was going to do the story with him. Hello? … Yes, I'll tell him … Yes, I can be there in five minutes.
Harry: Was that Lucy?
Jack: Yes. She said she was sorry. She also said that she was waiting for her new photographer.

STUDY

2 **Complete the explanations. Use Exercise 1 to help you.**

Reported speech

Use:
To report something that somebody said.
Direct speech: *She said: 'I'm sorry.'*
Reported speech: *She said she was sorry. / She told me/him, etc (+ that) she was sorry.*

Form:
Tense changes
Use the past forms of the verbs:
'I'm sorry.' > She said (that) she was sorry.
'I don't want to see him,' > Lucy told me (that) she ________ to see you.

Other changes
Pronouns and possessive adjectives change in reported speech:
'I'm surprised to see ________.'
*Harry said that he was surprised to see **him**.*

See GRAMMAR DATABASE, page 127.

PRACTISE

3 **Write the sentences from Exercise 1 in reported speech with *said*.**

1 Harry: 'I'm surprised to see you.'
He said that he was surprised to see him.
2 Harry: 'We're doing a story for the school magazine.'
3 Harry: 'I don't understand.'
4 Harry: 'I've brought my camera.'
5 Jack: 'I'll tell him.'
6 Jack: 'I can be there in five minutes.'

4 **Write the sentences from Exercise 1 in direct speech.**

1 Lucy told me that she didn't want to see you.
Lucy to Jack:
'*I don't want to see him.*'
2 I told her that I'd meet her here at seven.
Harry to Lucy:
'________.'
3 I told her that I could talk to you.
Jack to Lucy:
'________.'
4 She said that she'd found another photographer.
Lucy to Jack:
'________.'
5 She also said she was going to do the story with him.
Lucy to Jack:
'________.'
6 She also said that she was waiting for her new photographer.
Lucy to Jack:
'________.'

5 **Complete the sentences about yourself.**

Your life in six sentences

1 Food: For breakfast, I usually have …
2 Entertainment: The last film I saw was …
3 Plans: Next weekend, I'm going to …
4 Dreams: One day I hope I'll …
5 Now: At the moment I'm feeling …
6 Skills: I can't …, but I can …

SPEAK

6 **Work in pairs. Read out your sentences from Exercise 5. Take notes about your partner and then tell the class what she or he said.**

She said that she usually had … for breakfast.

She told me that the last film …

>>> Workbook, pages 90–91

85

1 Target grammar is always presented in context. Students either read or read and listen to a conversation or short text that expands on the unit's theme.

2 In the Study section, students are guided to notice grammar structures from the text and then to complete explanations in the Study box.

3 The target grammar is typically practised in a meaningful context that regularly provides opportunities for personalisation.

4 Practice exercises start with more controlled task types and then become progressively freer, helping students to talk about their own lives and experiences in the Speak exercise at the end of the lesson.

5 The final tasks focus on speaking and/or writing for accuracy of the target structure.

Lesson 4 – Listening and Vocabulary

> **Listening** comprehension tasks are designed to support understanding and not to test. They work from a focus on global understanding to an understanding of specific details. Students are also asked to react personally to what they hear.

1 As on the Reading page, the first exercise ensures that students access their relevant knowledge and experiences before they listen.

2 Listening texts contain examples of the next lesson's grammar point, allowing students to hear the language in context before looking at it in depth.

3 The How To box provides tips that help students.

4 The React exercise encourages students to give their personal opinion on the listening text.

5 In the Work with Words section, students focus on the second lexical set of the unit. In some units the Work with Words comes before the listening in order to establish new target vocabulary first.

6 The Go Beyond task allows students to do a further task related to the new vocabulary set.

LISTENING AND VOCABULARY Picture stories

»» Infer meaning

SPEAK AND LISTEN

1 **Work in pairs. Describe what you can see in the pictures.**

2 3.07 **Listen and tick (✓) the correct picture to answer each question.**

3 a **Read the tips in the HOW TO box.**

b 3.07 **Listen to the scenes again and choose the correct option in the sentences.**

1 The police officer is *happy* / *unhappy* that the reporter called.
2 The actor *likes* / *doesn't like* talking about her next project.
3 The reporter *is* / *isn't* sure the witness remembers what she saw.
4 The athlete feels *very happy* / *a bit disappointed* after the race.
5 The reporter and his source *trust* / *don't trust* each other.
6 In the same scene, the *reporter* / *reporter's source* switches off the recorder.

c **Which tips in the HOW TO box did you use for help with Exercise 3b? Tick (✓) them.**

1 When will the journalist meet the police officer?

2 What type of film is the star going to make next?

3 What did the witness see?

4 In which place did the athlete finish the race?

5 Where's the letter?

REACT

4 **Work in pairs. Act one of the scenes in Exercise 2 in your own words, reflecting the feelings of the characters.**

HOW TO
infer meaning

People often don't say directly what they think and feel.

- ☐ Listen to <u>how</u> people talk. How people say things often tells you what they really think.
- ☐ Identify the <u>relationship</u> between speakers. People often don't say things directly when they don't know or don't trust the other person.

WORK WITH WORDS

5 3.08 **Complete the sentences with the correct form of the reporting verbs in the box. Then listen and check.**

add admit claim confirm deny promise

Police officer: You said you wouldn't call me again, remember?
Reporter: I know. It's the last time. I (1) ________ .

Reporter: Can you (2) ________ the stories about you and rap star Dustin Dredd?

Reporter: In your original statement you (3) ________ that you saw three men?
Witness: That's right. I (4) ________ it sounds strange.

Athlete: Can I just (5) ________ one more thing? I couldn't have done this without the support of everyone back home.

Source: If you use my name, I'll (6) ________ I ever spoke to you.

6 3.09 **Complete the sentences. Then listen and repeat the verbs from Exercises 5 and 6.**

1 The police officer **suggested** that they meet at …
2 The witness **insisted** that she saw …
3 The athlete **explained** how she felt …
4 The reporter **agreed** to switch off …

GO BEYOND
Do the Words & Beyond exercise on page 137.

86

»» Workbook, pages 92–93

Lesson 5 – Grammar (2)

> The second **Grammar** lesson follows the same structure as the first **Grammar** lesson of the unit – see page 13.

GRAMMAR Reported questions

8

>>> Report what people ask

READ >>> Grammar in context

1 **Read the news report. What kind of job does Johan have?**

When I met Johan after the game, I asked him why he was leaving the club. He explained that it was for personal reasons. I then asked him how the other players had reacted. At first, he denied that there had been any problems on or off the pitch, but when I asked him if he was still friends with Pepe, he refused to comment. I asked him whether he had any immediate plans and he said that he was talking to a club in Spain. I asked him which club he was talking to, but he wouldn't say. As he was leaving, I asked him if he could say something to his fans. He promised that he'd come back one day.

STUDY

2 **Complete the explanations with examples from Exercise 1.**

Reported questions

Use:
To report a question that somebody asked.
Direct question: *'Why are you leaving the club?'*
Reported question: *I asked him why he was leaving the club.*

Form: *wh-* questions
asked + person + question word + *I/you*, etc + verb:
I asked him how __________.
I asked him which __________.

Form: *yes/no* questions
asked + person + *if/whether* + *I/you*, etc + verb:
I asked him if __________.
I asked him whether __________.

Other changes:
Change verb tenses, pronouns, possessive adjectives, time expressions and adverbs of place if necessary (see page 85).

See GRAMMAR DATABASE, page 127.

PRACTISE

3 **Write the reported questions in orange in Exercise 1 as direct questions.**
'Why are you leaving the club?'

4 **Read the journalist's notes and write her questions in reported speech.**

1 *Janet Mills (politician): 'Have you spoken to the minister?'* *I asked her if she'd spoken to the minister.*
2 *Justin (singer): 'Can you play any instruments?'*
3 *Cyclops (pop group): 'When will you play in Britain again?'*
4 *Mrs Mills (witness): 'Did you see what happened?'*
5 *Jeff Manners (athlete): 'How are you feeling?'*
6 *Mary Webb and Jack Landon (actors): 'Are you excited about the film?'*

5 a **Look at the information you were asked for in an oral exam. Write the direct and reported questions.**

1 Where / from?
'Where are you from?' / They asked me where I was from.
2 What / school / go to?
3 How long / study English?
4 ever / visit / the UK?
5 like / go to the cinema?
6 What / do / next weekend?

b **Answer the questions in reported speech.**
I told them I was from Mexico City.

6 **Complete the tasks. Choose the type of reporter you'd like to be.**

- sports reporter
- entertainment reporter
- news reporter

Write the name of a famous person you'd like to interview. Write five questions you'd like to ask the famous person.

SPEAK AND WRITE

7 **Work in pairs. Complete the tasks. Your partner is the famous person you chose in Exercise 6. Ask your partner the five questions you prepared. Make a note of their answers. Write a short report of the interview using reported questions and reported speech. Read your report to the class.**

>>> Workbook, page 94

87

Target vocabulary is recycled throughout the unit.

There are frequent opportunities for students to talk about themselves and to express their views.

The Grammar Database is a useful reference section where all of the level's grammar points are covered in further detail. You can find additional tips and suggestions for using the Grammar Database in the Online Resource Centre.

Lesson 6 – Language & Beyond

> The **Language & Beyond** page is the life skills lesson. The aim of these lessons is to equip students with the necessary transferable skills for life beyond the classroom, especially at college/university and in the workplace. The life skills lessons are grouped under five umbrella headings: Know yourself, Get organised, Get thinking, Respect others, and Communicate & cooperate.

1 A wide range of texts and images is used to raise students' awareness of a particular issue or challenge in their everyday lives.

2 Students are then directed to carry out a practical task in the Do stage. Often working in small groups, they put themselves in the situation described and think about what they would do.

3 The Reflection Point feature encourages students to pause and think about what they've just done and guides them towards drawing their own conclusions.

4 The life skills in *Beyond* are transferable to other situations and contexts. The exercises in the Extend section enable students to transfer the skills learned, building a classroom-to-real-life bridge.

Useful phrases help students to discuss issues and carry out tasks in English.

Working with other students is a key part of the life skills lesson.

LANGUAGE & BEYOND

Anonymous
is a student in another class at the school. 'A friend told me that Laura had been excluded from school. Another friend said that Laura had used a phone camera to take photos of Beth's homework and copied it at home. I heard a long time ago that she'd copied other people's homework.'

Chris
is Laura's best friend. 'I know Laura better than anyone. She told me that she didn't copy Beth's homework, and I believe her. She admitted that she'd copied some school work from the internet in the past, but she said she'd never copy another student's work.'

Stefan
is Beth's friend. 'Beth told me that she'd seen Laura copying her homework in the break. She asked me if I could tell the teacher. She said that the teacher wouldn't believe her. Last year, someone said Beth had stolen a phone. Beth denied it, but no-one found the phone.'

Maite
is in Laura's class. 'I don't know Laura very well, but I think she's a good person. People claim that she stole someone's homework, but why would she do it? She helped me last month when I was having problems with history. She knows a lot. She's clever. She doesn't have to cheat.'

»» Compare and evaluate information that you read or hear

SPEAK AND READ

1 3.10 **Work in pairs. Read and listen to the four people. What's th[e] …**

2 **After reading and listening … guilty? Why? Discuss your opinions.**

DO

3 **Work in groups. Answer the questions. Which speaker(s) …**
1 share the same opinion?
2 might be influenced by their relationship with the people involved?
3 don't agree about some facts?
4 don't give their name or the name(s) of their sources?
5 include information that is possibly out of date?

4 **Order the speakers from the *least* to the *most* reliable, giving reasons for your choices.**

PHRASE BYTES
I don't believe much of what … says because …
She/He isn't very reliable because …
… is much more reliable than …

REFLECT

5 **Discuss the questions with your class. Do you agree with the REFLECTION POINT?**
1 Why was it important to have more than one source for information in the situation in Exercise 1?
2 Why are multiple sources important when you look for facts?
3 How often do you use the internet to find information for school work? How often do you compare the information from different sources?

REFLECTION POINT
It's important to find more than one source for information in order to compare and evaluate the different sources and information.

EXTEND

6 **Work in groups. Write five tips for using the internet to find factual information. Use Exercise 3 to help you.**
Always check your information at more than two different sites.

GET THINKING

88

Workbook, page 97

Lesson 7 – Speaking

> Using real life scenarios, the **speaking** page provides students with the language they need to communicate effectively in a range of everyday situations. Every speaking page features a video in which teenage members of a drama group act out scenes illustrating the speaking function/situation.

SPEAKING Excuse me … 8

»» Interrupt someone

SPEAK

1 **Work in pairs. Describe the picture. What's the situation?**

WATCH OR LISTEN

2 3.11 **Watch or listen to the first scene and check your answer to Exercise 1.**

Dad: What time do you call this?
Leo: I …
Mum: You promised you'd be back by eight.
Dad: We've been worried.
Leo: (1) __________ ?
Dad: You should've phoned us and …
Leo: (2) __________ I did phone you. I got voicemail.
Mum: What? Where's my phone?

3 3.12 **Watch or listen to the second scene. Where was the phone?**

Ethan: Then what happened?
Ruby: My mom and dad are just the same.
Leo: (3) __________ , let me finish.
Ruby: If I'm late home, they get real mad.
Leo: (4) __________ . I haven't finished the story.
Ethan: My dad is always losing his phone. It drives Mum up the wall.
Leo: (5) __________ . Will you let me tell the story?
Ruby: OK. Keep your shirt on.
Leo: Thanks. The phone was …

4 a 3.13 **Watch or listen to both conversations again and write the correct phrases in the spaces.**

b 3.14 **Listen and repeat the phrases. Pay attention to intonation.**

5 **Read the sentences. Match them [to] the conversations with the same [meaning].**

1 It makes Mum extremely angry.
2 I heard the answering machine.
3 They get very angry.
4 You're very late.
5 Calm down.

> Teachers can choose to use the video or the audio version of the scene.

6 **Work in groups of three. Practise saying the conversations.**

PHRASEBOOK 3.15

Interrupting phrases

Can I say something?
Excuse me …
Hang on a second/minute/moment.
(I'm) sorry to interrupt, but …
(I'm) sorry for interrupting, but …
Wait a second/minute/moment.

ACT

7 **Work in groups of three. Complete the tasks. Read the conversation in Exercise 2 and decide what happens next. What do the people say? How do they find the phone? Write the conversation and include at least three interrupting phrases. Give each person in the group one of the parts and perform the scene for the class.**

»» Workbook, page 95

> The drama group context reflects the classroom situation in which students often role-play scenes, and having teenage actors makes it easier for students to relate to the scene.
> Students feel more confident about role-playing the situations after watching the drama group video.

1 The lesson starts with speaking exercises, giving students the opportunity to describe pictures and speculate about a situation.

2 Specially-commissioned videos, and photos from the videos, help students understand the context by showing facial expressions and body language, as well as the key functional language. Students watch or listen and complete an initial gist exercise before focusing on the speaking function or subskill.

3 A variety of exercise types focuses students' attention on the speaking function.

4 Each lesson ends with an Act section in which students prepare a scene of their own to present in groups or to the rest of the class.

5 A useful Phrasebook with relevant functional phrases is provided for use with the Act section of the lesson. This is part of the audio material provided and also serves as revision for speaking functions.

Lesson 8 – Writing

> The **writing** lesson in each unit allows students to put everything they've learned in the unit into practice. Students are systematically guided to plan, write and check their writing in order to produce a final draft.

1 The lesson opens with a short reading and speaking exercise to establish the topic. Students read a model text and complete a task to check they have understood it.

2 The How To feature offers tips about the lesson aim.

3 After practising the subskill, students follow a step-by-step writing plan to help them prepare for writing.

4 Students are encouraged to check and reflect on their writing to help them assess their work.

5 Sharing work for peer review helps students identify the areas where they need to improve.

WRITING School news

»» Use correct punctuation

SPEAK AND READ

1 Work in pairs. Put the words in order to make newspaper headlines.

2 Match the news story to the correct headline in Exercise 1.

3 Complete the punctuation rules with the words in the box.

apostrophes   capital letters   commas   exclamation marks   full stops   question marks

1 Use ____________ for names, nationalities, titles, days of the week and professions, titles of books, etc.
2 Use ____________ at the end of sentences.
3 Use ____________ for short forms of verbs and possessive s.
4 Use ____________ at the end of direct questions.
5 Use ____________ in lists, to separate phrases and with direct speech.
6 Use ____________ to indicate surprise or to add emphasis.

4 a Read the tips in the HOW TO box.

HOW TO
use correct punctuation

- Use a colon (:) to start a list or a quote.
- Use a semicolon (;) to separate longer phrases in a list.
- Use dots (...) to show that a sentence or quote isn't complete.
- Use single (' ') or double (" ") quotation marks for direct speech.

b Work in pairs. Find examples of the punctuation in the news story and explain how it is used.

1 IMPROVE / RESULTS / EXAM / SPANISH

2 TEACHER / WELCOMES / SCHOOL / NEW

3 PROBLEMS / BICYCLE / CONTINUE

This term a new Spanish teacher has started working at the school. Rosa Martínez, from Granada in Andalucía, has a lot of exciting interests: going to the cinema, the theatre and museums; taking photos of people, buildings and wildlife; and improving her English! When I met her yesterday, I asked her if she was looking forward to meeting her new students. 'Of course,' she said, 'I'm really excited to be here.'

PRACTISE

5 Check and correct the punctuation and spelling in another news story from the school magazine.

This year the drama group is going to perform a musical version of William Shakespeares play *romeo and juliet*. Are you intrested in acting if you are, come to the auditions on friday. Mrs jones the director of the show told me i am looking for poeple who luv doing all these things singing in the shower dancing to diffrent types of music and performing in public,

PLAN

6 Work in pairs. You're going to write a news story about your school for the school magazine. Choose a topic and make a plan for your story.

WRITING PLAN

1 **Write a short news story**
Explain the main points of your news story at the beginning.
Use direct and indirect speech.

2 **Use examples of different punctuation.**
Include some of the punctuation from Exercise 3 and the HOW TO box.

3 **Give your news story a headline.**
Look at the sample headlines in Exercise 1 and write a similar headline.

4 **Check the punctuation and spelling.**
Read your story carefully, then give it to another person to check.

WRITE AND CHECK

7 Use your plan and write your news story. Then check it. Tick (✓) the things in the plan.

SHARE

8 Swap your story with other students.

90

»» Workbook, pages 96–97

> **The Unit Review page allows students to check and assess their own progress in vocabulary and grammar.**

UNIT REVIEW 8

VOCABULARY Print and digital media jobs

1 Complete the text with the missing words.

Meet Bill Hearst. He's the (1) p__________ of the *Billington Post*. Bill also writes for the paper. In fact, he's the paper's top (2) r__________ . Actually, he's the paper's only real (3) j__________ . Bill is also the paper's award-winning (4) p__________ . When Bill has written a story, he gives it to his (5) e__________ , who's called Bill. Bill then gives the story to Bill, the (6) d__________ , who prepares the page. If the story needs some other visuals, he contacts Bill, the (7) g__________ a__________ .

Write the missing letters in some of Bill's other jobs.

8 c_rt__n_st
9 g_ss_p c_l_mn_st
10 pr_nt_r
11 bl_gg_r
12 __th_r

___ /12

Reporting verbs

2 a Choose the correct options in each newspaper story.

1 'It's not me!' Yesterday Hearst *admitted* / *denied* that he was the thief.
2 'OK. It was me!' Today Hearst *admitted* / *suggested* that he'd stolen his dad's biscuit.
3 'I'll do it soon.' Last week, Hearst *added* / *promised* that he'd do the washing-up soon.
4 'You're right!' Today Hearst *agreed* / *denied* that he still hadn't done the washing-up.
5 'It's true! I don't like them.' Hearst also *confirmed* / *explained* that he didn't ...

b Match the verbs in the box ... correct definitions.

add claim decide explain insist suggest

1 __________ : to help somebody understand something
2 __________ : to offer an idea or a plan
3 __________ : to say something more about the same thing
4 __________ : to say something is true
5 __________ : to continue saying that something is true

___ /10

GRAMMAR Reported speech

3 a Write the quotes in reported speech.

1 The President: 'I will make the world a better place.'
2 Actor: 'I'm making a film in Brazil now.'
3 Policewoman: 'I saw the thief here yesterday.'
4 Pop group to Bill: 'We're going to play six concerts next week.'
5 Mum to Bill: 'You're the best editor in the world.'
6 Athletes to reporters: 'We love your country.'

b Choose the correct option to complete the sentences.

1 I *said* / *told* Bill that he needed to find more reporters.
2 But Bill *said* / *told* he enjoyed writing all the stories.
3 His mum and dad *said* / *told* him he should do a sport.

___ /18

Reported questions

4 Report the questions, using pronouns in place of names.

1 Bill to his parents: 'Can I go out tonight?'
2 Dad to Bill: 'Have you done your homework?'
3 Mum to Bill: 'Where are you going?'
4 Bill to Mum: 'Do I have to tell you?'
5 Mum and Dad to Bill: 'What time will you be home?'

___ /10

Your score: ___ /50

SKILLS CHECK

✓✓✓ Yes, I can. No problem!
✓✓ Yes, I can. But I need a bit of help.
✓ Yes, I can. But I need a lot of help.

I can recognise formal and informal writing. ______
I can infer meaning when I listen. ______
I can compare and evaluate information that I read or hear. ______
I can interrupt someone. ______
I can use correct punctuation when I write. ______

Workbook, pages 98–99

91

1 The Unit Review starts with two exercises to assess both lexical sets covered in the unit. Each exercise has a space for students to record their score.

The exercises in the Unit Review are all set in a single context and reflect the way language is used in real life.

2 Two grammar exercises test both grammar points covered in the unit.

3 Students then calculate their total score. Each review has the same overall score so that students can assess their progress across units.

4 Students are encouraged to self-assess their progress using CEFR 'can do' statements that refer directly back to the aims of the skills pages.

Progress Check

> After every two units there is a two-page skills-based **Progress Check** that allows students and teachers to see how well the class aims in the preceding two units have been taken on board. Tasks on these pages reflect those that students will meet in official English examinations. The Progress Checks also include tips on how to deal successfully with the various tasks.

1 Progress Check tasks consolidate the language from the preceding two units.

2 The Exam Tips help students prepare for standard exam-style tasks.

3 Students see how the skills they've already learned in the units will help them in an exam situation, which helps build confidence.

PROGRESS CHECK

READ

1 Read the text and the questions below. For each question, choose A, B, C or D.

1 In the essay, the style of writing is …
- **A** all formal.
- **B** all informal.
- **C** informal with a few formal sentences.
- **D** formal with a few informal sentences.

2 What does Tara say about health?
- **A** Around the world, people live longer than they used to.
- **B** People live longer than they used to in some parts of the world.
- **C** In some countries, people live shorter lives than in the past.
- **D** In the United States, people live shorter lives than in most countries.

3 Her grandfather thinks that teenagers …
- **A** don't have as much fun as in the past.
- **B** have too many possessions.
- **C** aren't as grateful as they used to be.
- **D** are more anxious about work.

4 Tara has written the essay …
- **A** based on her personal knowledge.
- **B** after reading a magazine article.
- **C** using a variety of sources.
- **D** using just one main source of information.

5 How might Tara end her essay?
- A In conclusion, in most aspects, life was much better in the past than it is today.
- B My conclusion is that life isn't as much fun as it was in the past.
- C In conclusion, life was better in the past in some ways but much worse in others.
- D To conclude, people are more satisfied with life today than in the past.

EXAM TIPS

answer multiple-choice questions
- Read all the questions carefully and then read the text.
- Read each question again and read all the choices.
- Decide which choices are definitely wrong.
- Look at the text again to help you choose the correct answer.

recognise formal and informal writing
See page 84

Tara

People often claim that life was better in the past. But is this true? In this essay I'm going to look at how things have changed in different areas of life.
In my opinion, health is much better than it used to be. Statistics confirm that, in general, people live longer today than they used to. According to the United Nations, here in the United States, the average man and woman live until they are about 75 and 80 years old. In 1900, they lived until they were about 46 and 48. However, there are still countries today where life expectancy is as low as around 45 and 47.
I asked my granddaddy if he thought life was better for teenagers in the past. He said that he felt sorry for young people today. He admitted that life was much harder when he was a boy – his family lived on a farm, used gas lights and grew their own food – but he suggested that people were happier, partly because they made their own entertainment.
I'm not sure my younger brother would agree with him. When I suggested to him that life was more fun in the past, he said: 'You've got to be joking. Look at all this stuff – my laptop, phone. Can you imagine how life was before the internet? Boring!'
What about the environment? There didn't use to be so much pollution in the past because there were fewer people. However, we are more aware of how important it is to protect the environment today.

Reading: ______ /10

92

PROGRESS CHECK 7&8

LISTEN

2 3.16 **You will hear a radio reporter presenting a news story. Listen and write the missing information in the spaces.**

NEWS REPORT

REPORTER: Karen White
LOCATION: Paris, France

SUMMARY:

Film star Veronica Payne denies giving up her career, giving money to charity and going to live (1) ________ close to Venezuela.

OTHER NAMES AND FACTS:

Veronica has signed a contract to make a new (2) ________ film called *Beyond.*

Heidi Williams is a Hollywood gossip columnist and (3) ________ .

New biography claims Veronica wants to live a simple life, making furniture, baking bread and (4) ________ .

Veronica plans to take legal action against the (5) ________ of *My Life.*

Listening: ______ /10

EXAM TIPS

- listen and complete notes
  See page 27
- understand the situation
  See page 76
- infer meaning
  See page 86

WRITE

3 **Write a story (about 100 words) with the following first sentence:**

I had just got off the bus when my phone rang.

Writing: ______ /10

Progress check score ______ **/30**

EXAM TIPS

- write a story
  - Read the task carefully.
  - Think of the main events in your story.
  - Use the past simple, past continuous and past perfect to tell your story.
  - Use time expressions to order the events in your story.
  - Check punctuation and the number of words.
- say how and when things happen in a story
  See page 80
- use correct punctuation
  See page 90

Download extra speaking activities from www.macmillanbeyond.com

Other features

At the back of the Student's Book you'll find the following resources:

Grammar Database
The Grammar Database provides detailed, additional explanations of the grammar points of each unit, as well as grammar tables and common mistakes to watch out for, and is a valuable reference section for students.

Words & Beyond
On these pages you can find vocabulary lists for each unit comprising the main lexical sets and other important unit vocabulary, as well as vocabulary tips and tasks.

Irregular verbs
A useful list of irregular verbs is provided for students' reference.

Extras
The material for pairwork activities (with Student A and Student B) from the units is provided here as well as answers to quiz questions.

Projects
An outline of the five step-by-step projects which students can download from the Resource Centre (one for every two units) is provided. Comprehensive teacher's notes are provided online for setting up and supporting the projects.

4 Overall scoring is the same in every Progress Check, so students can monitor both their overall progress and their progress in specific skills.

Each Progress Check has an optional speaking section complete with teacher's notes and supporting material which can be downloaded from the Resource Centre at www.macmillanbeyond.com

USING THE *BEYOND* WORKBOOK

The *Beyond* Workbook lessons re-contextualise, review and recycle target items from the corresponding lesson pages of the Student's Book, and offer comprehensive practice for homework and class use.

- Two vocabulary pages per unit practise the target lexis in new contexts.
- Intuitive rubrics.
- Puzzles and games add an element of fun and variety.

UNIT 8

SHE SAID, HE SAID

VOCABULARY 1 ››› Talk about people working in the media

1 Match the sentence parts.

1 An author ___
2 A journalist ___
3 An editor ___
4 A photographer ___
5 A graphic artist ___
6 A gossip columnist ___

a writes articles.
b creates visuals.
c takes pictures.
d writes about celebrities (famous people).
e writes books.
f decides which articles to publish.

2 Label the parts of the magazine with the words in the box.

cartoon interview letter news article picture caption quiz recipe survey

TIP
Use your dictionary to look up words you don't know, as you did in Unit 4.

1 ______
LOCAL BAND WINS CONTEST
A local music band has won the first prize in an international ...

2 ______
Who's your perfect friend?
1 Your friends are usually
- outgoing.
- quiet.
- sympathetic.

3 ______
Easy Carrot Cake
Ingredients: 1 kilo fresh carrots ...

4 ______

5 ______

6 ______
What's the capital of Spain?
a) Barcelona b) Madrid c) Portugal
Answer correctly and you can win a top prize!

7 ______
Dear Annie,
I'm having a problem with my boyfriend ... he only talks about sport ...

8 ______
A day in the life of ... Jessica Valentine
What do you eat for breakfast? Black coffee and toast.

3 Complete the sentences with the best job in the box.

author blogger cartoonist designer editor photographer printer reporter

1 You're good at choosing colours. You should be a(n) ______.
2 You love writing stories. You should be a(n) ______.
3 You love travelling to different countries. You should be a(n) ______.
4 You're good at planning pages. You should be a(n) ______.
5 You like choosing good articles and deciding where to put them in your school magazine. You should be a(n) ______.
6 You like writing articles on the internet. You should be a(n) ______.
7 Your drawings are really good! You should be a(n) ______.
8 You take really good pictures. You should be a(n) ______.

4 a Choose the correct option to complete the sentences.

1 I saw a really funny ***cartoon / blog*** in the newspaper today. It made me laugh!
2 Look – there's a(n) ***profile / article*** of my favourite film star in this week's magazine.
3 Why don't you try this ***poem / recipe*** for apple pie? It looks delicious!
4 Did you hear the ***interview / report*** with the film director? What did he say?
5 The ***reporter / designer*** who wrote this article is really excellent.
6 Have you read this ***cartoon / report***? It says that most people read the news online.
7 The ***publisher / editor*** has sold a million copies of this book.
8 This travel ***journalist / artist*** writes articles from countries all over the world.

b Which media job do you like best? Why?

88

GRAMMAR 1 Reported speech

››› Report what people say

1 Complete the grammar table.

	Direct speech	Reported speech
present → past	'I'm a bit nervous,' she said.	She said (that) she was nervous.
	'I (1) ______ an interview at 5pm,' she said.	She said she (that) had an interview at 5pm.
	'Oh, no! We're going to be late,' she said.	She said (that) they (2) ______ going to be late.
	'I don't have a camera,' she said.	She said (that) she (3) ______ have a camera.
will → *would*	'I'll bring my camera,' he said.	He said (that) he (4) ______ bring his camera.
can → *could*	'I (5) ______ get there by 6,' she said.	She said (that) she could get there by 6.
simple past / present perfect → past perfect	'They asked a lot of questions,' he said.	He said (that) they (6) ______ a lot of questions.

Note:
Remember to use a pronoun after *tell*.
Example:
*He told **me** that he was sorry.*

2 Complete the grammar table.

Subject	Object	Possessive
I	(1)	my
you	you	your
she	her	(2)
he	(3)	his
it	it	its
we	(4)	our
they	them	(5)

3 Complete the text with the correct form of *say* or *tell*.

Sally (1) ______ Kate that she was going to have a party. Kate (2) ______ me that Sally had invited her, and she (3) ______ that Sally didn't want to invite me. I (4) ______ Sally that Kate had (5) ______ me about the party. I didn't (6) ______ that I knew she hadn't invited me. And Sally (7) ______ she had sent me an email to (8) ______ me about the party. I (9) ______ her that I hadn't received her email. But then later I found it in my junk folder, and I (10) ______ her I was sorry.

4 Choose the correct option to complete the sentences. Then rewrite the sentences.

1 Parents to son: 'We won't give you any more money.'
He / They said they ***wouldn't / won't*** give ***him / them*** any more money.
They said they wouldn't give him any more money.
2 Man to friend: 'The newspapers printed a story about me that wasn't true.'
He / They said that they ***had printed / print*** a story about ***them / him*** that wasn't true.
3 Woman to friend: 'The newspapers are going to interview me about my book.'
He / She said that ***they / he was / were*** going to interview ***me / her*** about ***his / her*** book.
4 Daughter to parents: 'I can phone you from the station.'
She / They said ***she / they could / can*** phone ***them / her*** from the station.

90

- The Workbook contains three pages per unit for practising target grammar.
- Grammar Study boxes revise the form and use of key grammar.
- Students then practise through contextualised grammar exercises.
- Exercises on the Grammar pages are presented in order of difficulty, shown by chevrons (› = easiest, ›› = medium challenge, ››› = most difficult).

LISTENING

››› Infer meaning

1 Complete the tips with the words in the box.

REMEMBER HOW TO ...
infer meaning

directly how relationship tells think

- Listen to (1) ______ people talk. How people say things often (2) ______ you what they really (3) ______.
- Identify the (4) ______ between speakers. People often don't say things (5) ______ when they don't know or don't trust the other person.

2 (34) Listen to the conversation. What is the relationship between the speakers? Tick (✓) the correct answer.

A film star and ...
some fans. ☐
some friends. ☐
some newspaper reporters. ☐

3 (34) Listen again and choose the correct option to complete the sentences.

1 The film star is ***excited about / disappointed with*** her new film.
2 She ***got on well / didn't get on well*** with her co-star.
3 She ***got on well / didn't get on well*** with the director.
4 She ***always / sometimes*** does her own stunts.
5 The film star is ***excited about / disappointed with*** her last film.
6 She's ***happy / not happy*** to talk about her boyfriend.
7 She probably ***is / isn't*** breaking up with her boyfriend.
8 She ***trusts / doesn't trust*** newspapers to tell the truth.

4 Read the interview and decide if these statements are correct (*C*) or incorrect (*I*).

Interviewer: The newspapers said you didn't like your co-star – correct?
Holly Finnie: Not true. He did a great job.
I: Yes, everyone agrees. But that wasn't my question. Did you get along OK?
H: I really admire him as an actor. William Robbins is amazing.
I: There were no fights?
H: He's one of the most talented actors around. Everyone knows that. Next question ...

1 Holly Finnie doesn't think William Robbins is a good actor. ___
2 She probably doesn't like William Robbins as a person. ___
3 She answers the interviewer's questions directly. ___

5 Complete the table with the words in the box.

her boyfriend her co-star her last film her new film her private life her stunts the director

The film star wants to talk about	But she doesn't want to talk about

6 Complete the sentences with the past tense form of the words in the box.

add admit claim confirm deny promise

1 **Mary:** It's true! Angus and I have split up!
Mary ______ that she had broken up with her boyfriend.
2 **Director:** Mary is great! We didn't have any problems.
The director ______ that they had had problems.
3 **Johnny Best:** This is my best film!
The co-star ______ that this was his best film.
4 **Mary:** Yes, and Johnny is my favourite actor.
Mary ______ that Johnny was her favourite actor.
5 **Director:** My next film will be even better!
The director ______ that his next film would be even better.
6 **Mary:** I didn't really do all of the stunts. I had a double!
Mary ______ that she hadn't done all of the stunts herself.

92

- Key listening subskills from the Student's Book are reintroduced and re-examined.
- Exercises put these skills into practice and revise target language.
- Additional listening exercises focus on the unit's theme, often through exam-style tasks related to the lesson's subskills.

USING THE *BEYOND* WORKBOOK

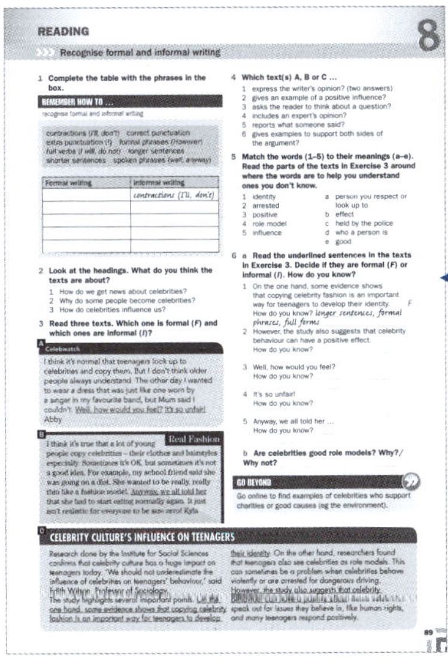

- REMEMBER HOW TO boxes focus on key subskills from the Student's Book lesson.
- Texts build on the themes introduced in the Student's Book.
- Tasks focus on putting reading subskills into practice, recycling key language and exposing students to exam-style tasks.

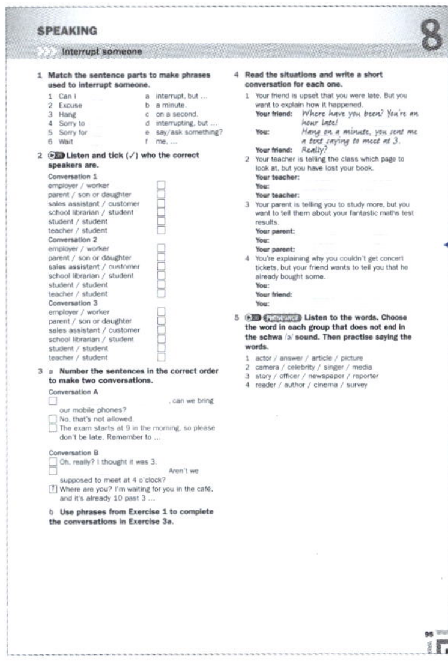

- The Speaking lesson focuses on revising key lexical items.
- Target items are presented in context and recordings are frequently used to focus on important aspects of speaking, such as register, stress and intonation.

- Key writing subskills from the Student's Book are developed in carefully chosen exercises which exemplify the skill.
- Emphasis is put on the planning and structuring of texts, and final productive exercises prepare students with exam-type tasks, giving them guidance on important elements to include.

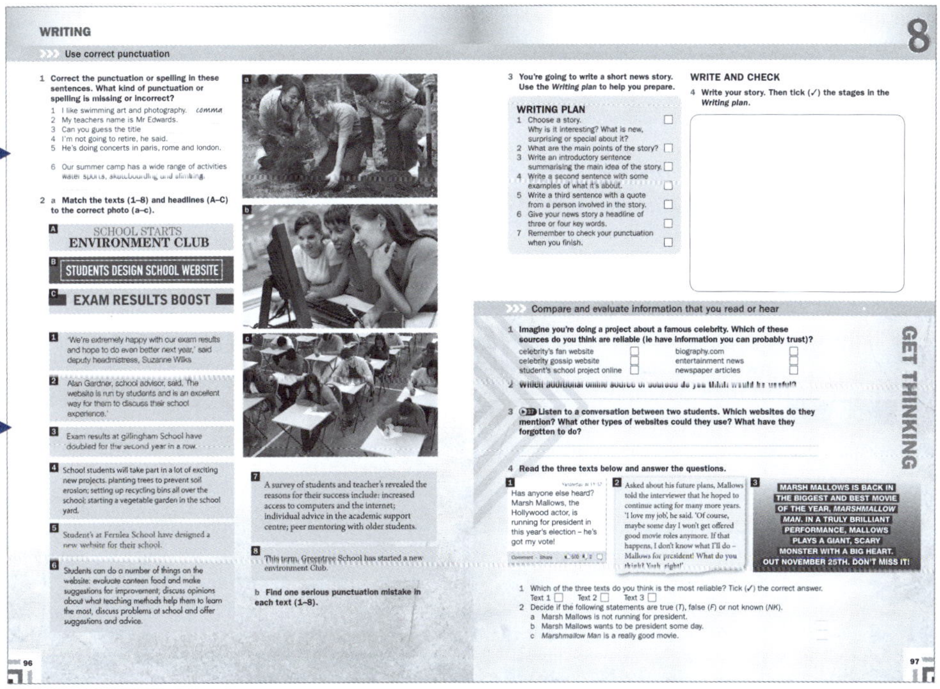

- The unit life skill is revisited and students are challenged to apply the learned skill in a personalised new context.

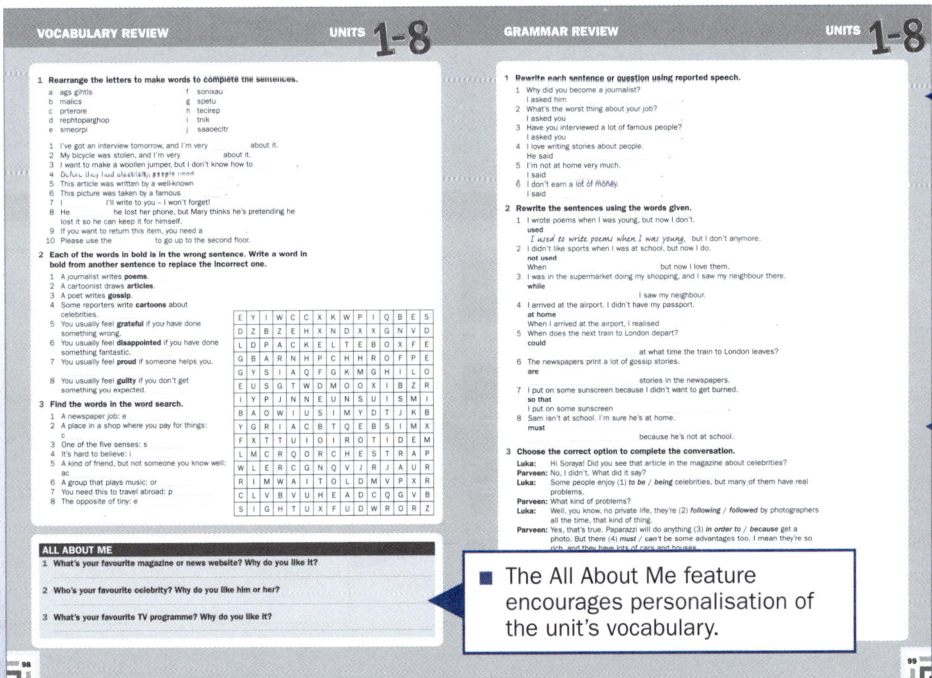

- Target vocabulary and grammar taken from any units of the Student's Book covered to date are re-contextualised and revised here, allowing students to monitor their own progress.
- The review pages offer cumulative assessment, with exercises combining two or more grammar points or vocabulary sets.
- The All About Me feature encourages personalisation of the unit's vocabulary.

BEYOND DIGITAL

Beyond's digital components are easy to integrate into live class and lesson preparation. The range of multimedia resources gives teachers a great opportunity to digitise their lessons and present the material in different ways. This varies the pace and dynamics in the classroom. Classwork, homework and testing are all accommodated at ***Beyond*** online, where plenty of flexible additional materials for both online and offline use can be found.

Go to www.macmillanbeyond.com to access:

- *Beyond* B1 Online Workbook.
- *Beyond* B1 Presentation Kit, consisting of a digital Student's Book designed for classroom presentation.
- *Beyond* B1 Student and Teacher Resource Centres, for extra materials, tests, videos and downloadable audio.

Online Workbook

The ***Beyond*** Online Workbook is the fully interactive digital version of the ***Beyond*** Workbook, with embedded audio, for students to use on their personal devices. It's powered by Macmillan's Big Tree platform. Instant feedback and multiple attempts keep students motivated as they work through the activity screens. Teachers can use the platform to manage multiple classes, using different levels of *Beyond*, in one place. The teacher version of the Online Workbook automatically collates students' results into the Gradebook.

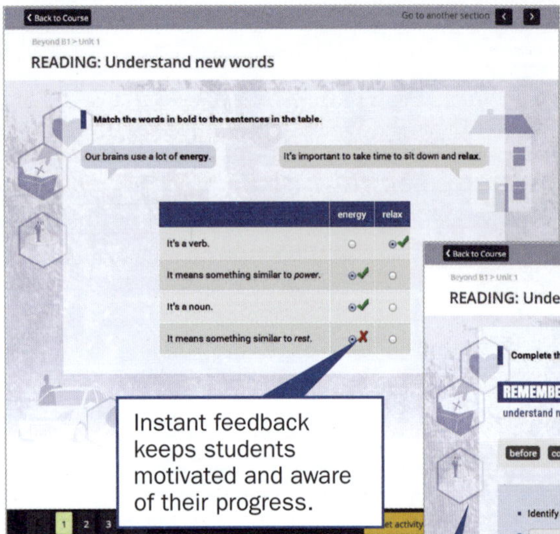

Instant feedback keeps students motivated and aware of their progress.

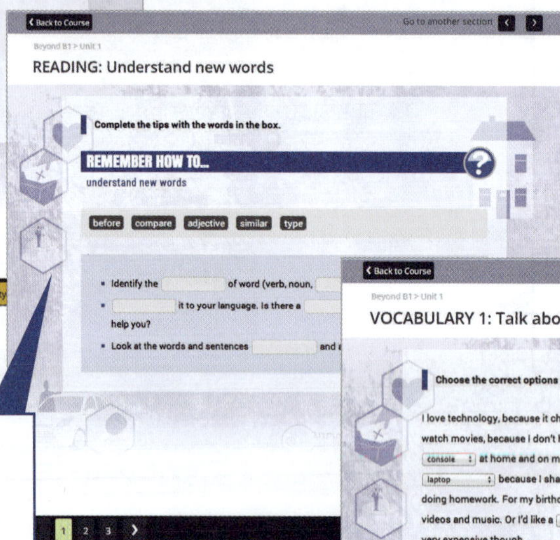

Display the ***Beyond*** Online Workbook on a projector or interactive whiteboard to check students' work in open class.

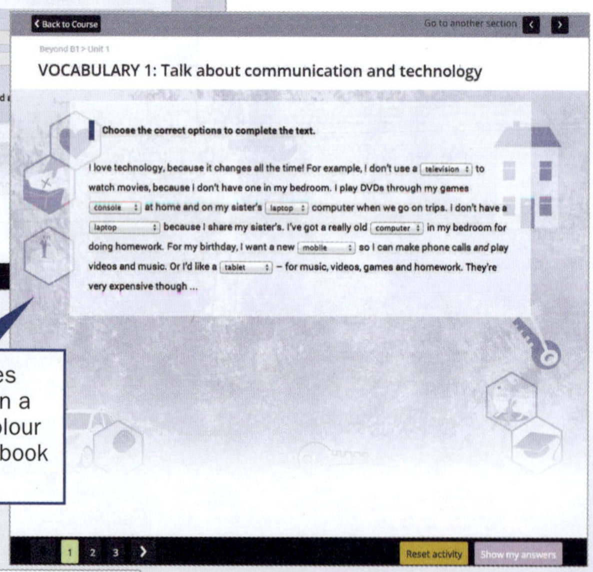

The Online Workbook features flexible content that works on a variety of devices with full colour versions of the ***Beyond*** Workbook artwork and illustrations.

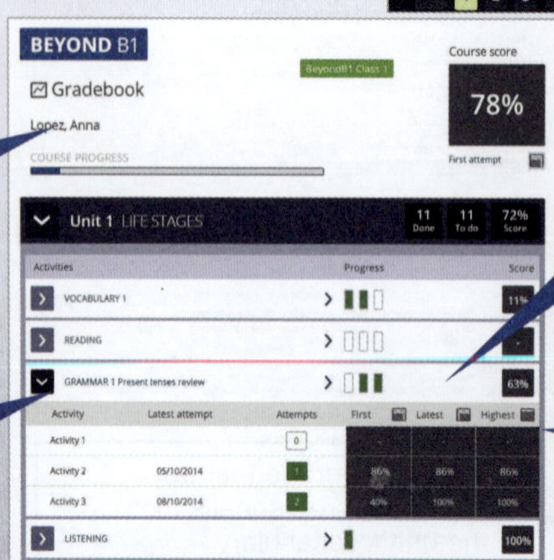

The Gradebook is part of an LMS and accommodates multiple classes, and multiple courses, in a single location.

The Gradebook shows students' FIRST attempt results, along with their BEST attempt, for accurate representation of their work.

Activities are marked instantly, and results are displayed in an easy-to-read, easy-to-compare way.

You can automatically gather data on your students' progress throughout the course.

Presentation Kit

A digital version of the ***Beyond*** print Student's Book for teachers to use in class to promote 'eyes-up' learning and student interaction. Easily downloadable to multiple devices from www.macmillanbeyond.com, the Presentation Kit can also be used for lesson preparation at home. Once downloaded, the Presentation Kit can be used offline. Audio, videos and answer keys are embedded in the pages for easy reference, as are the interactive versions of many exercises to work through as a class. The Resources section of the product contains downloadable PDFs of the Audio Script, Video Script and complete Student's Book Answer Key.

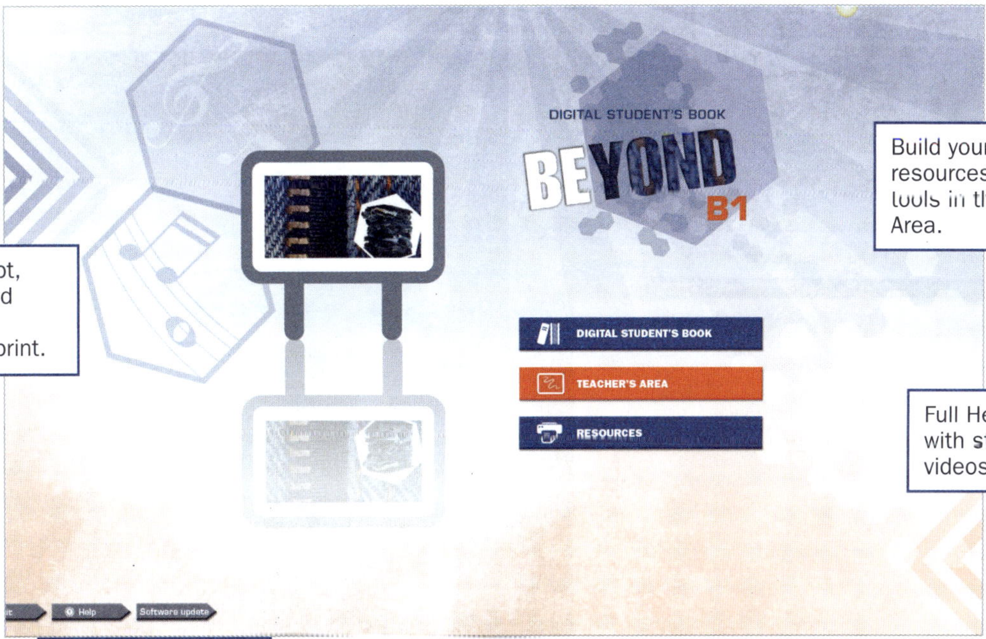

PDF Audio Script, Video Script and Answer Key to download and print.

Build your own resources using IWB tools in the Teacher's Area.

Full Help section with step-by-step videos and notes.

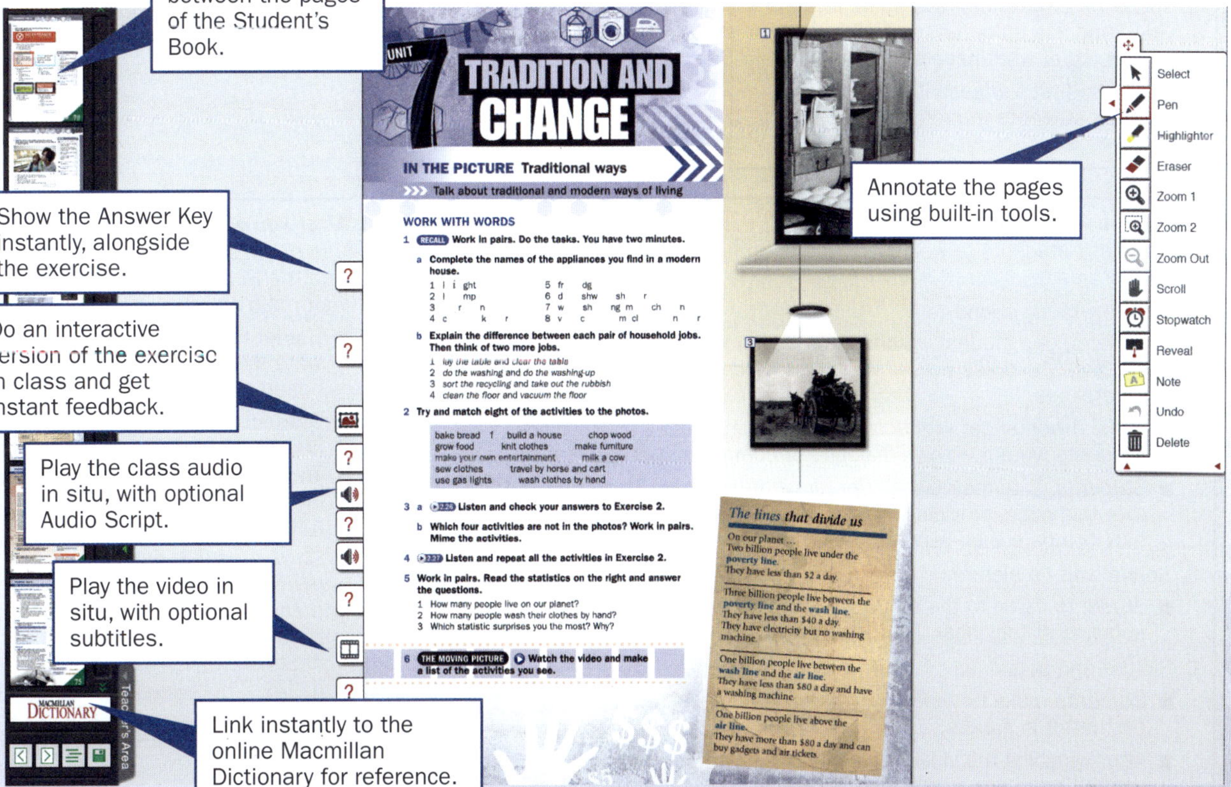

Move easily between the pages of the Student's Book.

Show the Answer Key instantly, alongside the exercise.

Do an interactive version of the exercise in class and get instant feedback.

Play the class audio in situ, with optional Audio Script.

Play the video in situ, with optional subtitles.

Link instantly to the online Macmillan Dictionary for reference.

Annotate the pages using built-in tools.

Beyond videos

There are two videos for every ***Beyond*** unit, adding richness and variety to the material. The Moving Picture videos from the opening spread bring global experiences into the classroom. The videos include documentary clips, vox pops, slideshows, digital animation and YouTube™- style videos. The Speaking videos facilitate speaking through role-plays and model conversations. The ***Beyond*** videos are embedded in the Presentation Kit, and supplied on a DVD in the back of this book. Students and teachers can also access them at home via the Resource Centres.

From The Moving Picture video, Unit 6.

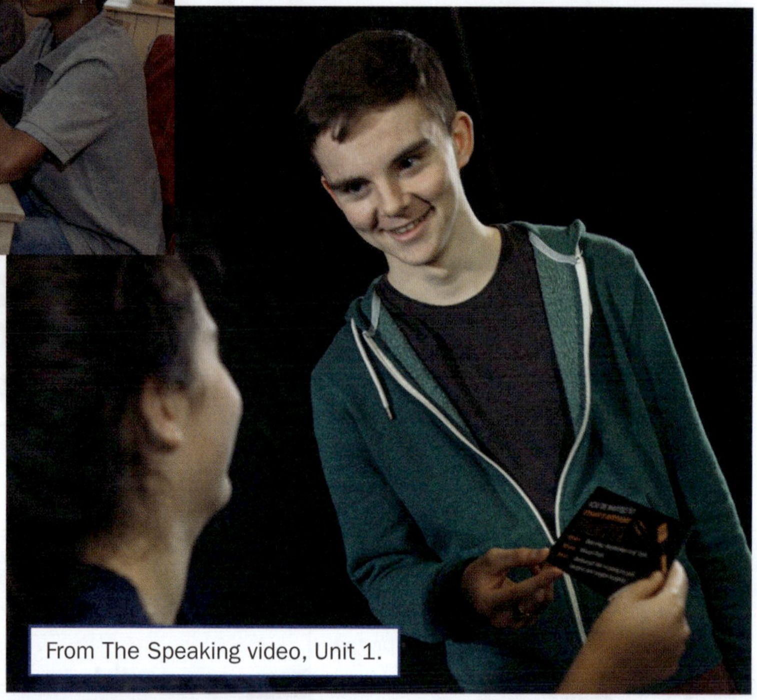
From The Speaking video, Unit 1.

Video Tips

You can extend the activities or use the videos separately by using some of these video tips.

Before you watch
Students can predict what they'll see and hear in the video.

- Show students the title of the video or give them the topic and ask them to brainstorm vocabulary they think will come up.
- Show the video using the 'Fast forward' option or show one or two stills from the video and ask students to predict what is happening or what people are saying.
- Show the first few seconds of the video and ask students to predict what will happen next.

While you watch
You can ask students to watch the videos normally or just using the picture or audio.

A Picture with no sound
- In pairs, one student watches and describes what they see to their partner, who takes notes. They then watch together and discuss differences.
- Make a worksheet with screen shots from scenes in the video. Students write their own dialogue or complete speech bubbles.
- Students write their own script for what they see. They then speak over the video, providing the narration or character voices. Finally, they compare their version to the original.

B Sound with no picture
- Students listen to the sound only and speculate in pairs/groups about what they hear. They then watch to see if they were right.

C Picture and sound
- Students make notes as they watch and then compare notes with a partner or in groups.
- After watching the video a first time, give students cards with key words or phrases from the video and ask students to hold them up when they hear them.

After you watch
Use these activities in conjunction with the *Before/While you watch* or as your main activity.

- Students create a fictional story, write a news story or do a role-play based on the video or part of it.
- Students write an email or a text message to somebody in the video. They can also make a brochure, advert, fact file or poster related to a theme or place in the video.
- Show students still photos of people from the video and ask them to make a brief biography for that person – name, age, nationality, family, likes and dislikes, hobbies, favourite food, etc.

BEYOND DIGITAL

Online Resource Centres

The Online Resource Centres are loaded with additional resources to support the ***Beyond*** course material. The Resource Centres are accessed by a single sign-in and contain a wide range of media for streaming and downloading.

Student's Resource Centre

For students, the ***Beyond*** Resource Centre provides a reference bank for media and vocabulary and additional downloadable ***Beyond*** materials to practise the main Student's Book content.

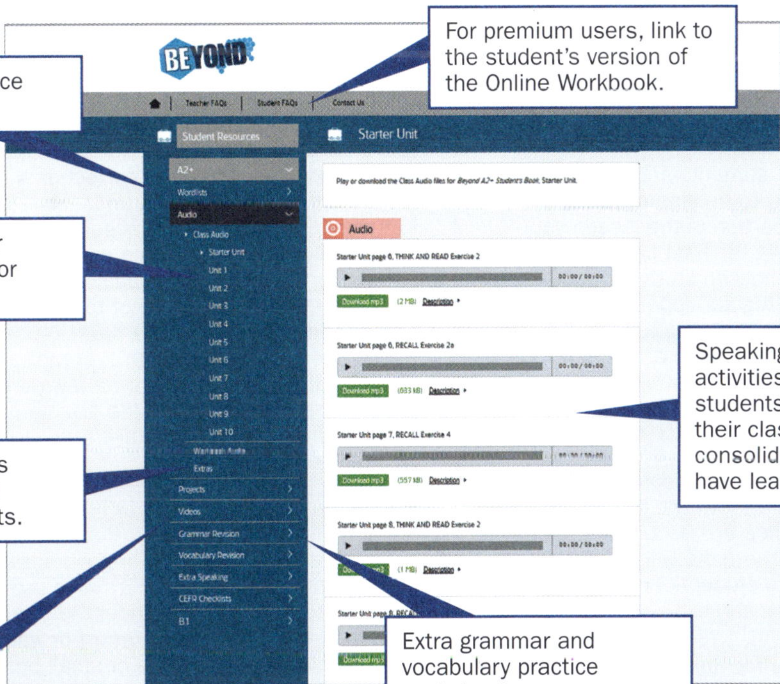

Wordlists for reference and personal study.

Full course audio for students to stream or download.

Additional recordings of Phrase Bytes and conversation prompts.

Full course video.

For premium users, link to the student's version of the Online Workbook.

Speaking Database activities to encourage students to go beyond their classwork and consolidate the skills they have learned.

Extra grammar and vocabulary practice worksheets.

Teacher's Resource Centre

The Teacher's Resource Centre provides teachers with downloadable extra worksheets, tips and testing material to support the course. It contains a whole range of additional ***Beyond*** materials to be used in the classroom or assigned for homework as well as access to everything on the Student's Resource Centre.

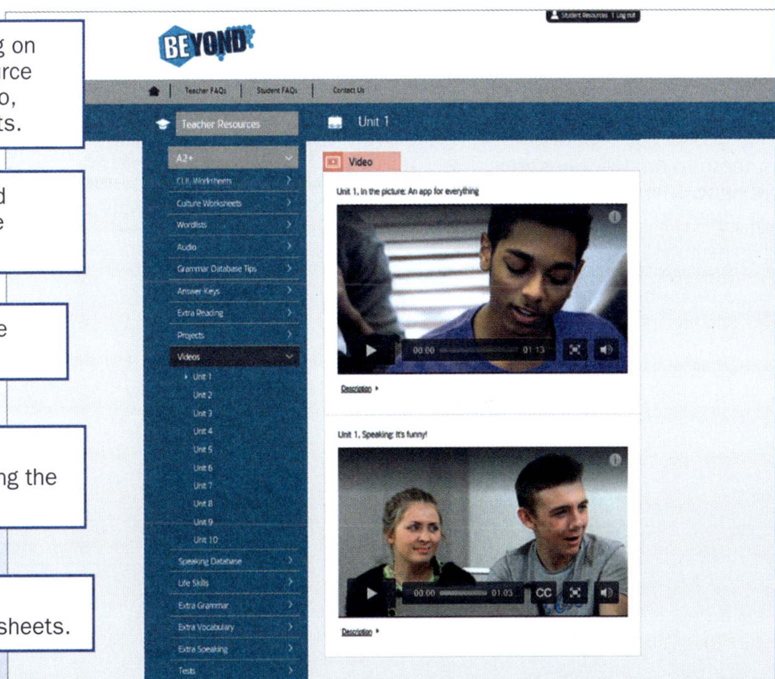

Access to everything on the Student's Resource Centre – audio, video, wordlists, worksheets.

Full answer keys and scripts for all course components.

Culture, CLIL and life skills worksheets.

Further ideas and activities for exploring the ***Beyond*** videos.

Teacher's notes to accompany all worksheets.

Tips and model answers to accompany the Student's Book and Workbook writing tasks.

A teacher-delivered Speaking section to accompany every Student's Book Progress Check.

Static PDF tests for each unit and the beginning, middle and end of each level.

Tests you can generate yourself with the customisable Test Generator.

Link to special ***Beyond*** materials on www.onestopenglish.com, as well as access to other useful onestop resources.

TEACHING TIPS

To optimise your teaching experience with ***Beyond*** we've put together some tips for the following key areas:

- Classroom management
- Teaching vocabulary and grammar
- Teaching skills
- Teaching pronunciation

Classroom management

Managing a classroom of teenagers is not always easy, and good classroom management, including organising resources, creating an effective learning environment, monitoring student progress and anticipating potential obstacles to learning, is crucial to keep students on track. The following tips will help you maximise the time in the classroom and ensure a productive learning environment.

Set time limits

Realistic time limits challenge students and engage them in the task. They are less likely to be disruptive. Use the as a guide for what proportion of the lesson you should spend on each task. Set the time limit after you have explained the task and checked students understand the instructions. You can give regular updates on the time remaining for a task. For example, during a three-minute task you might give a *One minute to go* warning, then *Only thirty seconds left …* , etc.

Encourage peer checking

Students appreciate the opportunity to look at their partner's answers to make sure they have the right idea. By letting students compare their answers, they'll have more confidence in them and therefore will be more likely to volunteer them. It also gives students an opportunity to develop their ability to compare and explain in English why they chose their answers.

At this age, students are often frightened of making mistakes in front of their peers. Point out to students, whenever possible, that making mistakes is positive, reminding them that the most successful learners are usually the ones who are not afraid to experiment and make mistakes.

Vary nomination techniques

Keep students alert by varying the ways you nominate them to answer questions. Alternate between nominating students to give answers and asking for volunteers in order to involve all students in the process of checking answers.

Another option is to nominate a student and let them decide which question to answer. This is good for less confident students, as it allows them to answer questions that they are more likely to have right. This student can then choose who will answer the next question. Alternatively, if you have closely monitored students while they were doing the exercise, 'randomly' call on the students who have the correct answers. Both of these techniques are good for giving students confidence to speak and offer up their answers in class.

Correct errors effectively

It is important not to over-correct as this can make students lose confidence. However, under-correcting leads to students developing bad language habits and decreases their ability to communicate in the long term. When students are carrying out pairwork exercises, the focus is on fluency and it's better not to correct errors. However, monitor students and note down important errors and good use of language to go over at the end of the exercise in a feedback session. Allow a few minutes of class time for error correction. Write the errors on the board without saying who made the mistake and elicit correct answers from the class.

Reward students

You can reward students for good answers or improvement with instant feedback, but it's also useful to create a system to be used throughout the term where points are awarded for improvement, effort or work in a particular skill or area. Award certificates or small prizes for students at the end of term. Longer-term goals can help keep students motivated throughout the year.

Be aware of different learner styles

Different students have different ways of learning. Ensure each student is catered for: vary approaches and activities to include a combination of visual (pictures, presentations, writing), auditory (listening, pair and group conversation activities) and kinesthetic (moving, computer work) activities.

Be sensitive

Some students may not want their problems shared in open class. Use your discretion when discussing any personal topics in class and be prepared to have an alternative task ready if students are not willing to join the discussion.

Teaching vocabulary and grammar

The following tips give you some ideas for teaching vocabulary and grammar as well as some reminders about commonly confused words and forms.

Remembering words

Encourage students to practise vocabulary by saying words in English when they go to various places. Recommend to students that they spend 10–15 minutes every day writing lists of vocabulary and saying these words out loud. The more they repeat this procedure, the more they will familiarise themselves with the words. Students can surround themselves with English by labelling their home with stickers or Post-it notes. Ask students to think of their own method for remembering vocabulary and to try it for a month. At the end of the month ask them to feedback to the class on whether their method was successful.

Words in context

In ***Beyond*** students always meet new language within a context first, so they can see how they use the target word and in what situation. Encourage students to learn in this way outside the classroom too by choosing three students each month to be 'Culture reporter', 'Music reporter' and 'News reporter'. Ask them to spend one hour researching their area on the internet and report anything interesting they find back to the class.

Test before you teach

Starting a grammar lesson with a *test-before-you-teach* type activity helps you find out how much students already know. If students have problems with form and use at the initial stage, you may need to provide more guidance during the lesson. However, if students are familiar with form and use, you can move more quickly through the lesson.

Make students grammar experts

Each Student's Book contains a Grammar Database at the back, with a reference of all grammar points from that level. As a revision activity, when you are coming to the end of the level, put students in groups of three or four and assign each group a grammar point from the database that they have studied. Tell them that they have 10 minutes to become 'experts' on this grammar and that they should prepare a mini presentation of this point and a couple of examples to demonstrate it. Give the groups 10–15 minutes to prepare their presentations. Then re-form into new groups, with each of the different grammar points re-presented. They then peer-teach their grammar points to their groups.

Recall, recycle, review

The ***Beyond*** course is structured so that students have the opportunity to recall previously learned vocabulary, recycle new language throughout the unit and review what they have learned.

Look for other ways to incorporate these three stages, for example by using games to review language or having short conversations at the beginning of the lesson to recycle language in a different context.

B1 Adjectives ending in *-ed* and *-ing*

In Unit 4, students study extreme adjectives. Point out to students that adjectives ending in *-ed* describe how you feel. Adjectives ending in *-ing* usually describe the effect that something has on your ideas and feelings.

Like all adjectives, *-ing* and *-ed* adjectives can be used in front of a noun and can be modified by adverbs such as *very* and *really*. They can also be used in the comparative and superlative forms, eg *… are always more exciting than other games.*

B1 *See, look* or *watch* and *hear, listen* or *sound*

The verbs *see, look* and *watch* are all connected to sight but they have important differences in meaning. *See* means to use your eyes and notice things, eg *There's so much to see in the city. Watch* means to look at something for a period of time, *eg I like watching the sea. It's so blue under the sky. Look* means to have a particular appearance, eg *Wow, that looks fantastic.*

Hear, listen and *sound* are connected to the act of hearing – when we *hear* something the sound comes into our ears without any effort on our part, eg *I could hear a loud banging noise outside. Listen* means to try to hear a sound, eg *I like to listen to music when I'm doing my homework. Sound* is similar to *look* above and means to have a particular sound, eg *Their new album sounds amazing.*

B1 *When* and *while*

When students are revising past tenses in Unit 1, remind them of how *when* and *while* are used. We use *when* to talk about something that interrupts a longer action or event: *John was cooking in the kitchen when the phone rang.*

We usually use *while* to indicate that during the time that an action was in progress, another event occurred. However, *when* can also be used in this case: *When John was cooking in the kitchen, the phone rang.*

B1 *Funny* or *fun?*

In Unit 8, students come across the words *fun* and *funny*. These are often confused, so it's worth pointing out the difference:

fun is both a noun, eg *We had fun at the party*, and an adjective, eg *We had a fun time at the party.*

Suggest to students that if they are talking about something that makes them laugh, they should use *funny*. If they are talking about something that they enjoy, they should use *fun*.

B1 *Lend* or *borrow?*

The difference between *lend* and *borrow* can be difficult for some students as one word covers both transactions in many languages. A short role-play can help make the words more memorable. Put students in groups of four, with one person being a bank manager and the others being customers. Ask them to write a short dialogue where the customers ask to borrow an amount of money for something and the bank manager declines and makes another offer, eg: Customer 1: *Can I borrow 50,000 euros for a Porsche?*

Bank manager: *I'm sorry, we can only lend you 20,000 euros for that.*

Give the students five minutes to write their dialogues and then ask each group to perform theirs. If possible, bring in some paper money for the 'bank manager' to use, so the lending part is acted out.

B1 State verbs

All verbs in English are classified as either state verbs or action verbs. State verbs refer to the way things are, whereas action verbs refer to things we do. The most important difference between state and action verbs is that action verbs can be used in continuous tenses and state verbs are rarely used in continuous tenses. Generally, state verbs fall into four groups: verbs describing thought or opinions, eg *know*, *understand*; verbs showing emotions, eg *love*, *hate*, *want*, *need*; verbs showing possession, eg *have*, *belong*; and verbs showing senses, eg *hear* and *smell*.

B1 Present continuous tense

When studying future tenses in Unit 2, remind students that the present continuous is especially common with the expressions *tonight*, *tomorrow*, *this weekend*, etc and with these verbs: *go*, *come*, *meet*, *see*, *leave* and *arrive*. English teachers often call the present continuous for future the 'diary form' because you can use it for anything that you can write in your diary, eg *On 23rd October I'm seeing my doctor.* Try to incorporate this use into informal classroom conversation, asking students: *What are you doing this Saturday? Where are you going this evening?*

B1 Countable and uncountable nouns

Countable nouns can be used in both the singular and the plural form, eg *one egg*, *four eggs*. Uncountable nouns, on the other hand, generally do not divide into separate units and cannot be easily counted. Make sure your students understand that nouns such as *luggage/baggage* are uncountable. Other commonly confused words that are uncountable include *advice*, *news*, *information*, *furniture* and *travel*. Many nouns can be both, depending on whether we're using them as units or as a mass, eg *glass* (the material used for windows) is uncountable but *a glass* (something you drink from) is countable.

Like many other grammar points, you can review countable and uncountable nouns in the reading texts during the course. When students have finished reading, you can ask them to find as many examples as they can of both types of noun in the text.

B1 Articles

Choosing the correct article (*a*, *an*, *the* or (-)) can be difficult for learners of English at any stage. Remember to always teach new nouns with *a* or *an* so that the use becomes natural for students. The following activity can help students learn one of the differences between *a* and *the* usage.

Place some real objects (eg books) around the room. Drill two simple sentences: *Could you pass me the book, please?* and *Could you pass me a book, please?* Whenever they say *the*, they must point at the specific object they want. When they use *a*, they lift both hands in a general 'asking' gesture. The listener now gives them what they asked for (ie either a specific book or any book). This student then makes a new request.

B1 Adjectival phrases

Students often want to know why certain prepositions are used with certain adjectives or verbs. Unfortunately there is no simple formula, so memorising the dependent prepositions is often the only answer.

Some ideas which can help students to memorise adjective + preposition combinations are:

- to use them in sentences that mean something personal to students, eg *My grandmother's scared of spiders.*
- to group adjectives according to the prepositions that go with them, eg *of* with *tired*, *scared* and *full*.

Teaching skills

Writing

Make it a group activity

Try to incorporate group work into writing lessons so that it is not always a solitary activity. Put students into small groups to work on the processes of writing: brainstorming, planning, structuring, drafting and reviewing.

Ask students to write to or email you

Set a task once a month where students email or write to you with a response to a set question. This could be anything from *What is your favourite lesson from the unit so far? Why?* to *What are your goals in English?* Remember to indicate to them whether you expect a formal or informal email/letter. This is a really effective way to get feedback from your students and to get them into the routine of regular writing.

Dictation activities

Dictation activities are very useful to practise listening and writing accuracy. Try to avoid just reading out long chunks of text and instead work on using shorter but engaging dictation activities. This suggestion can work well and can incorporate recently studied vocabulary sets:

- Read out a numbered list of descriptions of words (eg *Number 1, a type of music; Number 2, an extreme adjective.*)
- Students should write down their own answers.
- When they've finished their lists, dictate a short story that you've written, but with gaps where students will write their own chosen words. For example, *Last night I went to a [Number 1] concert. It was [Number 2].*
- Ask one or two students to read out their versions at the end.

Speaking

Keep topics interesting and relevant

The topics in ***Beyond*** are all designed to be relevant and engaging to teenagers. When you are doing any speaking task, make sure it will be something your class will want to talk about so that students will put effort into trying to communicate on the topic.

Be patient

Don't be tempted to interrupt or to start talking when students hesitate. Remember to give some time after asking students a question as they need to assimilate the language and prepare how they will respond. Try not to keep asking the question in a slightly different way as this will disrupt their train of thought.

TEACHING TIPS

Manage class discussions

In class discussions, it is common for the more confident students to dominate, but it is important for you to act as a facilitator and encourage everyone to speak. The following technique can be used to ensure everyone spends time on each question, and the physical movement helps maintain interest.

- Put students in pairs and label them A or B. The As stand in a circle facing outwards. The Bs stand in a bigger circle around them facing inwards, each facing their partner.
- Read out the first discussion question and give students two minutes to discuss with their partner.
- Clap your hands as a signal for the B students to move one place to their right and either discuss the same question or the next one.
- After four or five turns, ask students to sit back down, and you can then nominate one or two students to give their opinions.

Disappearing conversation

Write a short, six-line conversation on the board and ask the students to read it out loud and then to practise it in pairs. Start erasing one or two words at a time and ask students to read it aloud again. Soon they will be able to remember the whole conversation unsupported.

Listening

Encourage prediction

Predicting content is something that we all do in our first language before and while we are listening.

- **Predict the topic.** Where possible, draw students' attention to any images on the Student's Book page and ask them what they think the topic will be.
- **Predict the speakers.** Hand out printouts of the audio script for a chosen conversation in the Student's Book. Ask students to cover the speakers' names with a piece of paper, then ask them to read the conversation and guess the age, gender and relationship between the speakers. Write their ideas on the board and after you have listened to the audio, check if any of their guesses were correct.
- **Predict the word.** While playing the audio track, press the pause button mid-sentence and ask students if they can predict the next word. Repeat this process throughout the track. At the end of the exercise ask students if any of their guesses were correct and if so why they chose that word. Remember not to comment on the accuracy of their guesses during the exercise – the goal isn't to get everything right, but to concentrate on the language and topic in order to make guessing possible.

Loop dictation

Loop dictation is a technique which you can use in reading lessons. It gives students the chance to listen more intensively, and can be used to introduce a reading text.

- Select the first paragraph (or small section) of the reading text from the lesson. Make sure students have their books closed.
- Start reading aloud at a natural, but steady, speed and ask them to write down what they hear.
- When you get to the end, go straight back to the start and read again so you are repeating the text in a continuous 'loop'.
- When a student thinks they have a perfect version of the text, they shout 'Stop!' Put students into groups of 3–4 to allow them to compare what they have. Then allow them to open their books and check against the original.

Make students active listeners

In most listening exercises, students take a passive 'eavesdropping' role which doesn't really prepare them for all situations where they will be expected to both listen and react. To give them some practice at reading then responding, choose a dialogue from the Student's Book or Workbook and read out the first line. Ask the students to take on the other role (without looking at the audio script). Once they have heard your line, they should respond. Continue the process (either by using the next line of the dialogue or by responding to what the students have said). At the end, hand out copies of the audio script.

Reading

Jigsaw reading

For longer pieces of reading, put students in pairs and give them a section each to read. When they have finished reading, encourage the students to tell each other what they have read and to ask each other questions. Then allow time for them to read the full piece.

Encourage prediction

As with listening, being able to predict what's coming can help understanding. Tell the students they are going to read a particular type of text, eg a recipe, a letter of complaint or some instructions on how to drive a car. Have these texts ready on handouts, but don't give them to students yet. Put students in pairs and give them five minutes to write down five words or phrases they think they will read in the text. Then, hand out the texts and ask them to circle the words and phrases if they find them.

What's the context?

Knowing the context of a text can help students with the content and aim. Put students in pairs and give each pair a set of decontextualised words and sentences for them to read. Give them five minutes to answer the following questions:

- Where does the word/sentence/text come from?
- Who might be reading it and when?
- What does it mean?

Some ideas to use are:

- *Danger! This animal can bite!*
- *Click Start and Run.*
- *No smoking in the waiting room.*
- *Turn left at the first set of lights and take the second turning on the right.*

Teaching pronunciation

Be aware of how sounds are made

Pronunciation can often be overlooked in the classroom, but it is a key part of students' ability to communicate effectively, and in a more passive sense to listen and understand language. When approaching pronunciation tasks, make sure that students are aware of all the factors involved in making sounds (the position of the tongue, lips, etc) and that *you* can explain how to make them. Remember the primary goal is not to sound like a native speaker, but to produce the sounds in a way that allows them to communicate effectively.

TEACHING TIPS

Vary drilling techniques

Drilling can be a useful technique if employed in the right way. Make sure you vary the type of drilling you do with your class, so that it does not become monotonous and meaningless repetition. Choral drilling (the whole class repeating a word or phrase together after you) works well when students are saying new language for the first time, and you can then move to individuals. Back-chaining (starting at the end of the phrase or word and building up a syllable or chunk at a time) works particularly well with longer sentences. You can alter your delivery (eg to a 'whisper drill') if your class is becoming a bit noisy.

Stressed and unstressed articles

Articles and prepositions are often unstressed when we speak. This means they are produced more rapidly and with a glide. Drill the stressed (strong) and unstressed (weak) forms:

of /əv/ (weak),/ɒv/ (strong)

a /ə/ (weak), /eɪ/ (strong)

an /ən/ (weak), /æn/ (strong)

Content words are the important words that carry the meaning or sense in a phrase and are therefore usually stressed (these are usually nouns, main verbs and adjectives).

Sentence stress

Function words are not usually stressed in English. When these words are unstressed, a weak form of the word is used:

you /jə/ (weak) /juː/ (strong)

the /ðə/ (weak) /ðiː/ (strong)

will /wəl/ (weak) /wɪl/ (strong)

Raising awareness of sentence stress will not only help to improve students' pronunciation, but will help their listening skills as they will become used to listening for the content words and to hearing the weak forms of function words.

Stressed and unstressed form of *was*

Counting the number of words in a sentence and sentence dictations are useful activities which can help raise awareness of weak forms. Point out to students that the pronunciation of *was* changes according to its position in the sentence. At the beginning or end of a sentence it is stressed. In the middle of a sentence it is often unstressed:

Was the bird carrying something? Yes, it was. /wɒz/

It was flying. /wəz/

B1 Consonant clusters

Consonant sounds that occur together are known as consonant clusters. These can be difficult for students, particularly if the consonants are not normally pronounced together in their own language(s). If your students are having particular difficulty with any of the clusters try isolating the cluster and ask them to repeat the two sounds a number of times without a pause, eg /brbrbrbr/, or /stststst/. You could also try back-chaining, ie building up the sounds in the word from the end to the beginning, eg *bridge*: /dʒ/, /ɪdʒ/, /rɪdʒ/, /brɪdʒ/.

B1 Past forms

In the past simple and past participle forms, the regular verb ending *ed* is pronounced /d/ after all voiced consonant sounds and /t/ after all voiceless consonant sounds. Remind students that we do not pronounce the preceding *e* in either of these cases – the extra syllable is only pronounced on verbs that end in a *t* or *d*.

Point out to students that the difference between the /d/ and /t/ is very small and it is much more important to remember to pronounce /ɪd/ after verbs that end in *t* and *d*. In fact many teachers do not insist on the distinction between the /t/ and /d/ endings on past tense regular verbs (eg *opened* vs *walked*), preferring to focus simply on whether or not there is an extra syllable (eg *started*, *ended*, *visited*).

The important thing is to make sure that students differentiate between the present simple and these past tenses by clearly pronouncing the /t/, /d/ or /ɪd/ ending.

B1 Adjectives ending in *-ed*

Remind students that they follow the same pronunciation rules as the *-ed* endings in the past simple:

/d/ after a voiced sound, eg *surprised*

/t/ after an unvoiced sound, eg *relaxed*

/ɪd/ after *t* or *d*, eg *excited*

Drill the *-ed* adjectives in Unit 4, page 42 chorally to practise the pronunciation.

B1 Spelling *g* sounds → /g/, /dʒ/

In the travel vocabulary in Unit 2, two sounds for the letter *g* are represented.

- In *passenger,* the letter *g* is pronounced as /dʒ/.
- In *gate, g* is pronounced as /g/.

A general rule is:

- when *g* is followed by *e*, *i* or *y*, it is pronounced /dʒ/.
- when it is followed by *a*, *o*, *u*, *l* or *r,* it is pronounced /g/.

However, there are many exceptions to this rule, such as *get*, *give*, etc.

B1 /ʧ/ sound

The /ʧ/ sound is made by raising the middle of the tongue to the hard palate behind the teeth and blowing air through forcefully to create a small explosion. The most common spelling for the /ʧ/ sound is *ch*. However, as you will see in the example of *departure* in Exercise 6 on page 20 of the Student's Book, the combination of /t/ + /j/ can also result in /ʧ/. Other examples are *picture* or *furniture*. In the exercise above the /ʧ/ sound is contrasted with /ʃ/ as in *share*. If your students are having difficulty with /ʧ/, ask them to repeat the minimal pairs *share/chair* or *wash/watch*. Tell them that /ʧ/ is an abrupt sound whereas /ʃ/ can continue as long as they have enough breath!

GAMES

Used judiciously, games can be a really useful tool in the classroom. Not only can they inject a bit of energy and a change of tempo, they can also be used to practise and consolidate target language. The games below can be adapted for use with different target language.

The Book Quiz

The book quiz is a good way of starting the course and familiarising students with the Student's Book but it can also be used as a way of revising topics later in the term. Have 10 questions about the book ready (eg *How many units are there? What's the topic of Unit 5? On what page can you find a list of irregular verbs?*). Read out the questions and the student who is quickest at finding the answer wins.

Hot Seat

Divide the class into three or four teams. Place three or four chairs separately, each facing the class with the board or a screen behind them. Each team elects one person to sit in the hot seat. Each team has two minutes to describe as much vocabulary as they can for their team member in the hot seat to guess the word. Explain that teams can't: say the word, act out the word, draw the word, spell the word or point to the word.

Write the first word on the board or screen. If the first person in the hot seat guesses, another student comes to the front, and so on. If the word is too difficult for the person in the hot seat, they can 'pass' to the next person.

Example: *cycling*. Possible clues: *It's an activity. You do it in your free time. There are two wheels. You use your legs.*

Broken Telephone

Divide the class into groups of about 10 students, from the front to the back of the classroom.

Give one student in each group a present continuous sentence to memorise, eg *Dave's cousin is coming to stay at 10 o'clock on Friday morning.*

Each student whispers the sentence to the next student, and so on, until it reaches the last person in the group.

The last person in the group then says the sentence out loud. The first person says how the original sentence has changed.

Kim's Game

- Show students about 10 everyday objects (or objects related to the lesson vocabulary, eg travel items) one by one, eg backpack, hairbrush, passport, scissors, shampoo, toothbrush, toothpaste, wallet, ticket. Check they know the name of each one.
- Place them on the table and cover them with a cloth.
- Encourage students to work in pairs to remember what's there and where the objects are, eg *the hairbrush is next to the shampoo.*
- To make sure students speak in English, write the sentence prompt: *There's a* .... *and a* ....

Snowman

To elicit a word or phrase or to give extra practice at spelling, write short lines for each letter of the word or phrase on the board and invite students to guess letters. For each incorrect guess draw a part of a snowman: one circle for the head, one for the body then two arms, three buttons, a hat, two eyes and a smile.

Mystery Word

This game can be used to introduce students to some of the techniques they will be using in Unit 3, where they look at the subskill of understanding new words when reading.

- On the board, write a nonsense word like *flib.*
- Tell the students that *flib* is a mystery word and that to guess the word they will need some more information.
- Now write *a flib* and ask students what they now know about the word, ie that it is a noun. Prompt them by underlining the article.
- Next add: *We use a flib to eat ...* Elicit ideas for the meaning of *flib.* Prompt students by asking: *What do we use to eat?* and miming someone eating with cutlery. Write students' suggestions on the board.
- Finally write: *We use a flib to eat soup.* Hopefully students will come up with *spoon,* or possibly *bowl.* Either could be correct.
- Remind students how important it is to think about the meaning of the words which come before and after the mystery word, as well as to recognise what *type* of word the mystery word is.

If you have time, play the mystery word game again with *flib* as a verb, eg *flib / I flib / I flib English ... / I flib English because it is a useful language in the world today.*

Three in a Row

This can be used to revise vocabulary or grammar.

- Divide the class into two teams and draw a 3x3 grid on the board.
- In each cell write words from a vocabulary set or verbs in the infinitive.
- One team chooses a cell and has to form a correct sentence using that word. If the word is a verb, the sentence must also use the target tense(s), eg past simple or past continuous.
- If they get it correct they 'take' the cell and it's the other team's turn.
- The aim is to get three cells in a row. The game can be adapted for use with many of the language items, and a larger grid can be used to make it last longer and improve the opportunities for tactical game play.

Twenty Questions

This is a good game to practise question formation as well as other vocabulary.

- Ask one student to think of an object, a person or a place.
- The rest of the class can ask 20 questions, but the student can only answer *yes* or *no*.
- After 20 questions the class has to make a guess at what the object, person or place is.

Categories

Group students in teams of four or five and ask them to write the names of three or four recently studied vocabulary sets, each at the top of a separate column (eg travel, music, shopping). Choose a letter of the alphabet and give students two minutes to come up with as many words beginning with that letter as they can that are connected to the categories and write them in the correct column. After two minutes choose another letter. When the students have tried with three letters, count up the number of correctly spelled words, and whichever team has the most wins.

USING THE *BEYOND* TEACHER'S BOOK

This Teacher's Book is a valuable and practical resource. With its clear and comprehensive teaching notes, it's audio scripts and answer keys, background notes and extra features, it will help you plan and deliver impactful, well-paced and memorable lessons.

The unit topic, content and lesson aims of each unit are clearly presented.

6 SELLING POWER

The target language, functions and stages of each lesson are outlined, with suggested timings for each stage shown visually to help you pace your lesson. The darker grey shading shows the part of the lesson already completed and the lighter grey shows the amount of time allocated for each stage.

IN THE PICTURE In a shop

Talk about shopping

Pages 60–61

STAGE	TIME	FOCUS
GET STARTED		Talk about something you've bought recently.
WORK WITH WORDS		Recycle vocabulary for shops and phrases to do with shopping. Listen to two conversations in a shop. Match phrases from the conversations to definitions.
SPEAK		Do a questionnaire about shopping habits.

The Get started feature provides an activity to start the lesson and is an opportunity to recycle language and prepare students for the lesson. These warmers are designed to not require additional preparation or materials.

Activities that recycle language are labelled with the recycle icon.

Clear and concise procedural notes maximise the Student's Book material.

Get started

Write these question prompts on the board: *What? Who? Where? Why? How much? Happy?* Ask students to think about something they've bought recently, either for themselves or for someone else. Divide the class into pairs to ask and answer questions about the item they are thinking of. Set a time limit of three minutes. Before they start, indicate the prompts on the board and elicit full questions.

WORK WITH WORDS

1a and 1b RECALL

- Elicit from students what you buy at a baker's, eg bread, cakes.
- Ask students to make a list of at least eight more types of shop. Set a time limit of one minute.
- Invite students to call out their answers, writing any unusual ones on the board.
- If students are unsure of the meaning of any of the words, ask others to say what you can buy there, eg
  Student A: What's a butcher's?
  Teacher (to class): What can you buy at a butcher's?
  Student B: Meat.
  Student C: Sausages.
  Student A: Ah … OK.
- Focus students on the phrases in Exercise 1b and ask them to complete them with the words in the box. Allow two minutes.
- As students finish, ask them to compare their answers in pairs before you check them in open class. Encourage students to explain the meaning of the phrases and how they differ, eg *save money* means you keep it but *spend money* means you use it to buy things.
- Ask students to do the Work with Words task on page 135.

ANSWERS
Exercise 1b
1 ask the price 2 be cheap / expensive
3 buy / pay for / sell an item 4 cost / save / spend money

2

- Focus students on the shop in the big picture and ask them what sort of shop it is and what it sells. Ask them if the shop in the picture is like the ones they buy clothes in. Invite them to say which clothes shops they like and why they like them.

ANSWER
It's a clothes shop. It sells clothes, bags, sunglasses and jewellery.

3 2.12

- Ask students to listen to two conversations in the shop and to fill in how much the two people pay.
- Play the track for students to listen and read. Ask them to fill in the amounts mentioned.
- Elicit answers from different students in open class.

ANSWERS / AUDIO SCRIPT 2.12
1 €31.97 2 €18
See Student's Book page 60 for audio script.

4 2.13

- Play the track for students to listen and repeat the phrases in orange in Exercise 3.
- Ask them to match these phrases to the definitions, drawing their attention to the example before they start. Set a time limit of four minutes.
- Encourage students to compare their answers in pairs before you nominate different pairs to each give an answer that they are confident of.

ANSWERS / AUDIO SCRIPT 2.13
2 exchange an item 3 try on clothes 4 keep the receipt
5 pay in cash 6 return an item 7 on special offer
8 in the sale 9 get a discount 10 get a refund

on special offer in the sale try on clothes
keep the receipt exchange an item return an item
get a refund get a discount pay in cash pay by card

USING THE *BEYOND* TEACHER'S BOOK

Activity suggestions for fast finishers are provided throughout the lessons.

Answer Keys and Audio Scripts are embedded within the teaching notes.

Fast finishers
Ask students to test each other by taking it in turns to read out some of the definitions for their partner (with book closed) to say the phrase.

5a 2.14 PRONOUNCE

- Play the track for students to listen to the sounds /æ/and /ɑː/ in the words and say which one is longer.
- Play the track again for students to listen and repeat.

ANSWER / AUDIO SCRIPT 2.14
/ɑː/ is longer
See Student's Book page 60 for audio script.

5b 2.15

- Focus students on the pairs of words and ask them to circle the one they hear. Play the track for students to listen and choose.
- Encourage students to compare their answers in pairs.
- Take a poll on each pair of words before giving the answer.
- Play the second part of the track for students to listen and repeat both words.

ANSWERS / AUDIO SCRIPT 2.15
1 aren't 2 chart 3 had 4 jars 5 pack
1 ant / aren't 2 chat / chart 3 had / hard 4 jazz / jars
5 pack / park

6 THE MOVING PICTURE

- Introduce the video by explaining to students that they are going to watch the four people in the photo talking about shopping.
- Ask students which of the names are boys' names (Sebastian and Tyler) and which are girls' (Shay and Roisin). Identify the names of the people, as students will need this information to complete the listening task.
- Ask students to write each person's name in their notebooks and leave space under each one to write the answers.
- Play the video for students to note their answers as they watch.
- Encourage students to compare their answers in pairs and ask if they would like to watch the video a second time.
- Play the video again if necessary and then check answers in open class.

ANSWERS / VIDEO SCRIPT
Shay: Doesn't like shopping and gets stressed out at the shops. Prefers to shop online.
Sebastian: Doesn't mind shopping and often goes shopping with his friends, so that they can hang out and get food at the same time.
Roisin: Prefers shopping online. When going to the shops, she loves vintage shops and market stalls. Sometimes goes shopping with her mum.
Tyler: Loves going to big shops because of the variety. Doesn't like online shopping because he prefers to see the merchandise before buying anything.

Complete scripts for the Moving Picture videos are embedded in the lesson notes.

SPEAK

7

- Write the word *shopaholic* on the board and elicit its meaning (*someone who is addicted to, or can't stop shopping*).
- Underline the suffix *aholic* and tell students that this suffix means 'addicted to'. Ask them if they know any other words with this suffix. Elicit or teach: *workaholic* and *chocoholic*.
- Ask students to read the shopaholic questionnaire and think about their answers. Set a t[...]
- Divide the class into pairs to ask [...] questions. Encourage them to giv[...] with their answers.
- Circulate and monitor to make co[...] students on task.

The optional extra activities provide ideas for extending the lesson and offering additional practice.

GO BEYOND
Ask students to do the Go Beyond task on page 135.

Extra activity
Ask students to complete these gapped sentences with a preposition:
Where can I pay ________ *this scarf, please?* (for)
Excuse me, is this jacket ________ *the sale?* (in)
These socks are ________ *special offer at the moment – you can get two pairs for the price of one.* (on)
Is there somewhere I could try this top ________ *, please?* (on)
I don't have a credit card, so I'll have to pay ________ *cash.* (in)
I'm going to ask ________ *a discount on these shoes – there's a dirty mark on them.* (for)
I hate shopping ________ *clothes … it's so boring!* (for)
I think it's dangerous to pay ________ *card all the time – you forget how much you're spending!* (by)

Homework
Ask students to choose five of the questions from the shopaholic questionnaire and to write their answers, giving reasons or examples.

Task-based homework is provided at the end of every lesson and connects to the lesson's topic or skill.

Other features

The Teacher's Book also contains:

Procedural notes for the Unit Reviews and Progress Checks
Full and detailed notes are given for the Unit Reviews and Progress Checks from the Student's Book.

Workbook answer keys and audio scripts
At the back of the Teacher's Book, Answer Keys and Audio Scripts are given for the corresponding Workbook.

Teaching Tips
Pages 28–33 of the Teacher's Book provide useful tips on classroom management, teaching, vocabulary, grammar, skills and pronunciation and using games in the classroom.

Alternative procedures
Alternative procedure suggestions are provided for selected exercises, offering a different approach to teaching the Student's Book content. These alternatives appeal to different learner styles and abilities.

Background information
Useful and interesting background information on specific lesson topics is provided to help with the presentation of the content.

1 LIFE STAGES

IN THE PICTURE Special days

Talk about special days in your life

Pages 6–7

STAGE	TIME	FOCUS
GET STARTED		Introduce yourself and the theme of the lesson. Talk about students' special days.
WORK WITH WORDS		Recycle vocabulary to describe the stages of life and learn new words. Talk about important life events and when they happen in your own country. Do a quiz and compare ages you need to be to take part in different life events in different countries. Pronounce words with /e/ and /ɜː/ sounds. Watch a video and describe the people and what they are doing.
SPEAK		Do a survey to talk about the age or experience you need to take part in different life events in your own country.

Get started

Introduce yourself to students as a lead-in to the theme of the lesson and to provide them with extra listening practice. Explain that you are going to talk about yourself and that they should think of questions to ask you afterwards.

> **MODEL LIVE LISTENING**
> *My name's Joe and I'm 36 years old. I've got two children, they are both boys. They both love sport. I love being with them and it's great having a family. The two days when my children were born were the most special days of my life. Another special day was the day I got married. My wife's name is Julie.*

Invite questions from students and answer them, eg *What are the names of your children? How old are they? Where did you get married?* etc.

Write the title of the lesson, *Special days*, on the board and encourage students to work in pairs or small groups to ask each other *What was a special day in your life*? Elicit interesting examples from the class.

WORK WITH WORDS

1a and 1b RECALL

- Divide the class into pairs to do the tasks. Draw students' attention to the instructions to both Exercises 1a and 1b and the photos on pages 6–7. Ask students to do both tasks, matching the stages of life to the photos and then completing the sentences. Point out that some photos may match more than one word/phrase. Set a time limit of three minutes.
- Encourage students to check their answers in pairs and then nominate one pair to say their answers in open class.
- Ask students to do the Work with Words task on page 130.

> **SUGGESTED ANSWERS**
> **Exercise 1a**
> baby – 7 child – 1 teenager – 2, 3, 4, 6, 9 university student – 9 young adult – 8, 9 adult – 5, 7, 10 parent – 1, 7, 8
> **Exercise 1b**
> 1 pensioner – photo 10 2 middle-aged person – photo 8

Fast finishers

Ask fast finishers to write down what ages (approximately) go with each stage of life, eg *baby 0–3, child 4–12, teenager 13–19, university student 18–22, young adult 20–30, adult/parent 30+ years.* Encourage students to compare their ideas in pairs.

2

- Focus students on photo 4 and ask them what they think is happening. Point out the example answer.
- Divide the class into pairs to match photos (1–10) to the actions in the box. Don't check answers at this point.

3 1.01

- Play the track for students to listen and check their answers to Exercise 2.

ANSWERS / AUDIO SCRIPT 1.01

get a driving licence - 6 get a job - 2 get married - 5
go on a first date - 4 go to university - 9 have children - 7
leave home - 8 retire - 10 start school - 1 vote - 3

1 Today I start school. Um ... that's all I can think of to say.
2 Check out the uniform. Well, you can't really see it in the photo. I got this job through a friend and I started today. I don't really like fast food but that's OK. It's a job!
3 This is a special day for me because it's the first time I can vote in an election. I think it's important for young people to vote.
4 Hi. I'm Johnny.
And I'm Kirsten. And today's special because we're going on our first date.
5 My best friend got married today. I made a video and took some photos ... at the wedding – obviously.
6 What do you think? Isn't this the worst driving licence photo ever? I got it today. Finally. And this is the key to Dad's car!
7 Um ... This is my wife, Rosa, and this is little Marc. It's a very special day. Now we have a baby I suppose we're a family.
8 Well, as you can see, I'm leaving home. That's Dad in the blue shirt. It's kind of scary but exciting at the same time.
9 These are some of the other students ... It's our first day at university so we're all very serious and a bit nervous.
10 This is the first day of the rest of my life. Now I'm retired, I can relax, take things easy and spend time with my friends.

4

- Ask students to write the life events in Exercise 2 in the order people usually do them in their country.
- Encourage students to compare their answers in pairs before you discuss them in open class.

5a 1.02 PRONOUNCE

- Point to the words *get* and *first* and to the phonemes. Play the track for students to listen and repeat the sounds.

5b 1.03

- Before you play the track, invite students in pairs to say the words out loud in order to distinguish between the two sounds.
- Play the track for students to listen and confirm their answers.

ANSWERS / AUDIO SCRIPT 1.03

/e/ friend, Net /ɜː/ person, work, university
See Student's Book page 6 for audio script.

5c 1.03

- Play the track again for students to listen and repeat.

Extra activity

Dictate words from the list below in a different order and ask students to write them next to the correct sound, /e/ or /ɜː/.

/e/ bread, breakfast, heavy, head

/ɜː/ third, perfect, nurse, dirty

6a

- Refer students to the quiz and ask them to complete the sentences and then check their answers in pairs.
- Encourage the students to guess the correct words to complete the sentences.

6b 1.04

- Play the track for students to listen and check their answers. Ask students if they think any of the facts are surprising or interesting.

ANSWERS / AUDIO SCRIPT 1.04

1 In some parts of the USA, you can get married at 14.
2 Children in Finland don't start school until they're 7.
3 In Brazil and Austria, you can vote in an election when you're 16.
4 In Niger, you can't get a driving licence until you're 23.
5 People in Saudi Arabia can't go on a date before they get married.
6 Most people can only have one child in China.

Extra activity

Ask students to recycle nationalities and languages for each country, eg American (English), Finnish, Brazilian (Portuguese), Austrian (German), Nigerien (French, Hausa, etc), Saudi Arabian (Arabic), Chinese (Mandarin, Cantonese, etc).

7 THE MOVING PICTURE

- Tell students they are going to watch a video about special days for some people. Play the video.
- Divide the class into pairs to describe the people and say what they are doing.
- Choose different students and elicit answers in open class.

SPEAK

8

- Ask students to work in the same pairs to ask and answer the questions in the survey. Before they start, draw their attention to the expressions in the PHRASE BYTES box.
- Monitor and note good use of language and errors to go over in a feedback session.
- Check students' answers in open class.

Extra activity

Ask students if they remember questions to ask for: meaning, pronunciation, spelling, repetition or clarification, eg *What does X mean? How do you pronounce/say this word? How do you spell X? Could you say that again, please? Could you speak more slowly, please?*

You could ask students to make posters of these questions and display them in the classroom for the first month of the course.

GO BEYOND

Ask students to do the Go Beyond tasks on page 130.

Homework

Ask students to write a short report of approximately 200 words on what they can and can't do in their country, using the questions in the survey and the expressions in the PHRASE BYTES box to help structure their texts.

READING Coming of age

Find specific information

Page 8

STAGE	TIME	FOCUS
GET STARTED		Recycle vocabulary to describe stages of life and introduce the theme – coming of age.
SPEAK AND READ		Compare coming-of-age ceremonies where you live to those in other countries. Read an article about coming-of-age traditions and rituals around the world. Discuss tips on how to understand main ideas and find specific information.
REACT		Give your opinion on which celebration and ritual you found the most interesting and say why.

Get started

Recycle vocabulary from the previous lesson by writing the words to describe stages of life in a jumbled order on the board: *middle-aged person, baby, teenager, child, pensioner, young adult, university student.* Ask students to work in pairs to put the stages in a logical order.

Invite different students to number the stages from 1–7 on the board.

Elicit the stressed syllable of each word and then have a quick drilling session. Also recycle the /e/ sound in *p**e**nsioner* and the /ɜː/ sound in *p**er**son* and *univ**er**sity*. (See Tips for drilling techniques page 31)

Ask students if there are any important ages or celebrations within any of the life stages on the board.

SPEAK AND READ

1

- Elicit the meaning of *coming of age* (the age when a person becomes an adult). Divide the class into pairs to ask and answer the questions. Set a time limit of two minutes.
- Invite different students to report their partner's responses.

GO BEYOND FOR TEACHERS

Coming of age

Coming of age in Australia, New Zealand, the United Kingdom and Ireland is celebrated at either 18 or 21. The age of legal majority is 18 and means you can vote, get married without parental consent and sign contracts. In comparison, turning 21 has few legal effects.

Alternative procedure

For this speaking activity do question 1 as a pair work activity. For question 2 divide the class into small groups.

2 1.05

- Tell students they are going to read the results of a survey. Ask students to read the texts quickly in order to answer the questions. Don't play the audio at this point. It is an extra feature and suggestions for making use of it in class are included at the end of the lesson.
- Encourage students to compare their answers in pairs before you check them in open class.

ANSWERS

1 Students in class 3B at a school.
2 Students' own answers.

3a

- Ask students to discuss in pairs what skills they use to understand the main ideas and specific information in a text. Prompt their discussion by asking them: *What parts of a newspaper page can help you with main ideas?* (headlines, photos, etc) *How do you find out what a book is going to be about?* (Read the back cover, look at the cover illustration, etc)
- Refer students to the tips in the HOW TO box, inviting some more confident students to read the tips out loud.
- Ask students if their strategies are the same or different from the ones in the HOW TO box.

3b

- Ask students to read the texts again, this time in more detail, to complete the table. Point out that if a text doesn't include the information, they should write *doesn't say*.
- Walk round and monitor, helping students if necessary.
- Write the table on the board and nominate different students to come up and write their answers.

ANSWERS

Name	Type Party? Ritual?	Boys/ Girls	When	Age	Clothes	Activities
Seijin no Hi	*Special Day*	Both	*Second Monday of January*	20	A special kimono for girls; a suit for boys	A ceremony at the local city offices called Seijin-Shiki, then a party with friends and family
Satere-Mawé	Ritual	Boys	Doesn't say	12 or above	Gloves with ants inside them	Boys have to wear gloves with hundreds of ants in them for ten minutes and they mustn't scream
Quinceañera	Party	Girls	On their 15th birthday	15	Usually a pink dress and crown	A church ceremony, then a big party

- Ask some comprehension questions to check full understanding of the texts:
  – Seijin no Hi: *What is a kimono*? (a traditional form of dress in Japan, like a long dress with sleeves);
  – Satere-Mawé: *What's special about the bullet ant*? (Its bite hurts more than any other insect bite in the world); What mustn't boys do when they are wearing the gloves? (They mustn't scream.) *How many times do they have to do this ritual*? (20 times).
  – Quinceañera: *What present does the birthday girl get*? (A doll called *la última muñeca* – 'the last doll') *What does she do with it*? (She dances with it and then gives it to a younger girl.)

4

- Elicit from students which tips in the HOW TO box they used to help them in Exercise 3b and ask them to tick them.

Extra activity

Write these definitions on the board: *a party or special event that you celebrate* (celebration /ˌseləˈbreɪʃ(ə)n/), *something you do regularly and always in the same way* (ritual /ˈrɪtʃuəl/), *a formal, public event with special traditions* (ceremony /ˈserəməni/)

Ask students to match the definitions to the words in the text. Chorally drill the pronunciation.

REACT

5

- Divide the class into pairs to discuss the questions.
- In open class, choose different students to give their point of view and say why. Try to develop a class discussion on the different points. Start by asking some questions such as *Do you think that the Satere-Mawé ritual is dangerous? Do you think that coming-of-age celebrations should be fun or serious events? Should they be different for girls and boys?*

Extra activity

Books closed. Write these sentence prompts on the board and ask students to complete them from memory:

1 In Japan, you can't vote until you're …
2 The bite of the bullet ant …
3 During the ritual, the boys …
4 At a Quinceañera, the birthday girl dances with …
5 Now she's 15, the girl can …

Ask students to look at the texts again if necessary to check their answers.

ANSWERS

1 20
2 hurts more than any other insect bite in the world
3 have to wear gloves with hundreds of ants inside them
4 a doll
5 go on her first date

GO BEYOND

Books closed. Ask students to each choose one of the rituals and write down whatever they remember about it.

Encourage them to read out their notes to a partner to see if he/she can remember any further details. Finally, invite students to check their notes by reading the texts again.

Recorded reading text 1.05

The reading text is recorded as an extra audio track which can be exploited for various purposes.

In this lesson, use the audio as part of the checking process in Exercise 3b. Ask students to raise their hands when they hear the specific information they used for the table.

Homework

Ask students to write about how coming-of-age is celebrated in their own country or in another one of their choice. Encourage students to make notes and present their information in the next class in groups of five or six.

GRAMMAR Present tenses review

Talk about present actions

Page 9

STAGE	TIME	FOCUS
GET STARTED		Brainstorm ideas for having a low-cost or an expensive party.
READ AND LISTEN		Read and listen to a conversation about a coming-of-age party.
STUDY		Use the conversation to study the use of the present simple and the present continuous.
PRACTISE		Complete exercises with the correct form of the present simple or the present continuous.
SPEAK		Ask and answer questions about habits and routines and what is happening now.

Get started

As a class, brainstorm things that are important for a party. Write students' ideas on the board, eg *music, food, decorations, clothes, activities, entertainment, theme, drink, invitations*, etc.

Divide the class into pairs to think of ideas for a low-cost party and an expensive party. Draw two columns on the board with the headings: *Low-cost party* and *Expensive party*. Invite students to come up and write their ideas in the columns. Discuss which party students think they would enjoy most and why. Use the opportunity in this discussion to pre-teach *to afford* (to have enough money for) as this comes up in Exercise 1.

READ AND LISTEN Grammar in context

1 1.06

- Refer students to the photo and ask students what they think the conversation is going to be about.
- Play the track for students to read and listen to the conversation. Ask students where the girls are and what they are doing.
- Ask a few comprehension questions to check full understanding of the text: *What is the name of the typical coming-of-age party in the USA?* (a Sweet 16); *Why is Tina unhappy about her sister's coming-of-age party?* (Her sister wants a big party but Tina thinks it is too expensive.)

ANSWERS / AUDIO SCRIPT 1.06

They're at the home of one of the girls. They're celebrating her 16th birthday.
See Student's Book page 9 for audio script.

STUDY

2a

- Refer students back to the conversation in Exercise 1 and ask them to underline eight examples of the present simple and circle four examples of the present continuous. (See Tips page 29)
- Nominate students to say the examples.

ANSWERS

Present simple: They're, It's, do people (usually) do, They do, My sister wants, she talks, The problem is, I don't think
Present continuous: are these girls doing, This girl's celebrating, she isn't wearing, She's preparing

2b

- Ask students to read and complete the grammar explanations with words and expressions from the conversation.
- Nominate a student to read out the grammar explanation.

ANSWERS

usually every day at the moment want think

Extra activity

Students may not remember the spelling rules for the *-ing* form. Write these verbs and the spelling rules on the board and ask students to make present continuous sentences using these verbs:

lie (we change the *-ie* to a *-y* and add *-ing*, ie *lying*)

get, run, swim, set (verbs with one syllable, ending in one vowel and one consonant, double the final consonant and add *-ing*, ie *getting*)

have (verbs ending in *-e*, remove the *-e* and add *-ing*, ie *having*)

PRACTISE

3 1.07

- Refer students to the photo and the conversation. Ask them to circle the correct options to complete the conversation.
- Play the track for students to listen and check their answers.
- Ask students extra questions to check their understanding of the grammar, eg: *Why is the answer to 2 in the present simple?* (because it is a state verb) *Why is the answer to 3 in the present continuous?* (because she is describing an action that is taking place now) *Why are the answers to 4, 5 and 6 in the present simple?* (because they are describing a tradition that is repeated every year).

ANSWERS / AUDIO SCRIPT 1.07

2 don't know 3 's preparing 4 do the girls dance
5 lasts 6 dance
See Student's Book page 9 for audio script.

Extra activity

Divide the class into pairs to practise reading out the conversation.

4

- Ask students to complete the questions with the present simple or present continuous form of the verbs in brackets. Before they start, draw students' attention to the example and elicit why the present continuous is used.
- Walk round and monitor, helping students if necessary.
- Encourage students to compare their answers in pairs before you check their answers in open class.

ANSWERS

2 Do you think 3 are most teenagers wearing
4 Do adults usually wear 5 does a person really become
6 are they doing

Fast finishers

Encourage fast finishers to look at the texts on page 8 and find an example of the present continuous tense (*the girls are wearing traditional kimonos*).

SPEAK

5

- Divide the class into pairs to ask and answer the questions in Exercise 4. Remind students to ask each other follow-up questions to ask for examples, details and reasons.
- Ask a more confident pair of students to demonstrate this activity before students continue in pairs.

Homework

Ask students to find a photo of a celebration or a ceremony and write notes to prepare a presentation for the next class. Encourage students to describe it using the present simple and the present continuous. For less confident students, write a short plan on the board: *Describe where the photo is taken; Describe what is happening; Describe what the people are doing; Describe this ritual or celebration (time of the year, traditions); Say what you think about it.*

LISTENING AND VOCABULARY Leaving home

Recognise informal speech

Page 10

STAGE	TIME	FOCUS
GET STARTED		Play a game to recycle the present simple and present continuous tenses.
SPEAK AND LISTEN		Describe objects from your childhood. Listen to a conversation about Aidan leaving home and sorting out objects he has stopped using. Learn how to recognise informal speech.
REACT		Discuss what is going to happen when Aidan leaves home.
WORK WITH WORDS		Order adjectives to describe objects.
SPEAK		Talk about an interesting present you gave and one you received.

Get started

Play a game of *Three in a Row* (See Games page 33). To win a square, teams take it in turns to choose a square and make a question with the present simple (PS) or the present continuous (PC) using the indicated verb.

PS: study	PC: wear	PS: think
PC: prepare	PS: think	PC: dance
PS: know	PC: do	PS: celebrate

SPEAK AND LISTEN

1

- Refer students to the photos. Divide the class into pairs to discuss the questions. Encourage students to use adjectives and add as much extra detail as possible for the descriptions in question 1.

2 1.08

- Explain to the students that they are going to listen to a conversation between Aidan and his sister, Katie, about him leaving home. Play the track for students to listen and put photos a–d in the order they hear them mentioned.

ANSWERS / AUDIO SCRIPT 1.08

1 d 2 b 3 c 4 a

Katie: What's in this box?
Aidan: Nothing. Just stuff I'm throwing out. Take anything you want.
Katie: Look at this. It's enormous!
Aidan: Hey, don't laugh. That was my first mobile phone. Mum gave it to me when I started school.
Katie: Does it still work?
Aidan: I dunno.
Katie: So it's not very useful. Who does this tiny blue shirt belong to?
Aidan: That's my Chelsea football shirt.
Katie: I don't think it fits you any more. Why have you still got it?
Aidan: It's ... kinda ... you know ...
Katie: Colourful?
Aidan: No.
Katie: Unusual?
Aidan: Special.
Katie: Why?
Aidan: It was a present from Uncle Harry. He gave it to me on my eighth birthday when he took me to see a match – my first.
Katie: So if it's special, why are you throwing it out?
Aidan: I dunno. I've got too much stuff. I can't keep everything. You have it.
Katie: No thanks. I don't want your old cotton football shirts. ... Ahah! Here's something really embarrassing. Big brother's plastic doll.
Aidan: It's not a doll. It's an action figure. It's antique.
Katie: Old-fashioned, you mean.
Aidan: It's probably valuable.
Katie: Hello? It's broken. Anyway, they're only worth money if they're in the original packaging. Can I keep these?
Aidan: What? I can't see.
Katie: Here's a clue. They're round plastic things you keep in a kind of square case?
Aidan: Are you talking about my CDs? I thought you didn't like my music.
Katie: I don't. But I can play them when I miss you.
Aidan: Hey, that's a really nice thing to say.
Katie: Not really. When I hear your terrible music, I'm gonna remember how lucky I am that you're not here.
Aidan: Very funny.
Dad: Aiden! Are you ready to go?
Aidan: Coming Dad!
Katie: Got everything?
Aidan: Think so.
Katie: So ... see ya.
Aidan: Yeah. See ya.

3 1.08

- Focus students on the sentences. Play the conversation again for students to decide if each sentence is correct (C) or incorrect (I).
- Encourage students to compare their answers in pairs and ask them to correct the incorrect sentences. Check answers in open class.

ANSWERS

1 I (his mother gave him the phone) 2 I (the shirt is tiny) 3 C
4 I (Aidan thinks it's probably valuable) 5 C
6 I (she says she doesn't like his music)

4a

- Encourage students to think of how they can recognise informal speech when they listen.
- Ask students to read the tips in the HOW TO box and compare them with the ideas they thought of.

4b 1.09

- Play the extracts from the conversation and ask students to complete them with words from the HOW TO box.
- Ask students to find six contractions in the extract.
- Give students extra practice with the new informal words and phrases to help them sound natural. Chorally drill them and then ask students to practise the conversation in pairs.

ANSWERS / AUDIO SCRIPT 1.09

1 Hey 2 kinda 3 you know 4 dunno 5 stuff 6 Um
7 ya 8 Yeah

Contractions: don't, It's, it's, I've, can't

See Student's Book page 10 for audio script.

REACT

5

- Divide the class into pairs to discuss the questions.

WORK WITH WORDS

6 1.10

- Point out to students that when they see more than one adjective before a noun, the adjectives follow the order of the table. Give and elicit some more examples, eg *a beautiful, old, wooden chair*.
- Ask students to complete the table with the adjectives in the box.
- Play the track for students to listen and check their answers.
- Play the track again for students to listen and repeat.

ANSWERS / AUDIO SCRIPT 1.10

Opinion: useful, old-fashioned, unusual, valuable;
Size: enormous, tiny;
Shape: square;
Age: antique;
Colour: colourful;
Material: cotton

Fast finishers

Ask students to write another adjective in each column.

SPEAK

7a

- Ask students to work individually to write a few sentences about an interesting present they gave and one they received, using more than one adjective. Before they start, invite a volunteer to read out the model sentences.

7b

- Divide the class into pairs to talk about their presents. Encourage them to use and respond with informal language, looking back at the extracts in Exercise 4b if necessary.

Alternative procedure: less confident classes

Disappearing conversation: create the conversation together on the board, eg:

A: Hey! What interesting present did you receive?
B: I got a kinda interesting present for my last birthday.
A: What was it?
B: It was an enormous lion for my bedroom.
A: Yeah, kinda interesting.
B: What interesting present did you give?
A: I gave my brother a pet frog. He loves frogs, you know.
B: Yeah, that's definitely different!

Erase the middle part of the conversation. Ask students to try to reconstruct the conversation in pairs, each one saying their part. Then erase almost all of the conversation and ask students to swap roles and try to remember as much as they can. Walk round and monitor. Invite a pair who can remember it all to say the conversation to end the activity.

GO BEYOND

Ask students to do the Go Beyond task on page 130.

Homework

Ask students to cut out pictures from magazines or newspapers and write sentences with more than one adjective to describe them, eg *An interesting, old, Spanish politician, A fast, red sports car, A small, round, black box.*

GRAMMAR Past tenses review

Talk about past actions

Page 11

STAGE	TIME	FOCUS
GET STARTED		Play a game to recycle irregular past tense forms.
READ AND LISTEN		Read and listen to a conversation about a mystery object to discover what it is.
STUDY		Read the grammar explanations about past tenses and complete them.
PRACTISE		Practise the target language in written exercises. Complete a conversation and questions with the past simple or the past continuous.
SPEAK		Talk about things you lost.

Get started

Play a game of *A–Z List*. Divide the class into small teams to write an A to Z list of irregular past tense verbs. Point out that there are no irregular verbs that begin with *j, n, q, v, x, y* or *z*. Set a time limit of three minutes. Invite students to write the verbs on the board. Then encourage students, in the same groups, to ask each other and answer three questions starting with a question word, eg *When did you … ? What did you … ?*, choosing from the irregular verbs on the board. Remind them of the question order if necessary, question word – auxiliary – subject – verb (infinitive form), and ask them to answer with full sentences.

READ AND LISTEN Grammar in context

1 1.11

- Refer students to the photo and ask them *How do you think the girl is feeling? Can you describe her?* (She looks excited. She is a teenager with long, brown, wavy hair. She is carrying shopping bags.)
- Play the track for students to read and listen to the conversation and guess what type of object they are talking about.
- In open class, invite different students to share their ideas.

ANSWER / AUDIO SCRIPT 1.11

They're talking about a musical instrument.
See Student's Book page 11 for audio script.

STUDY

2

- Ask students to read and complete the grammar explanations with *continuous*, *simple* and words and expressions from the conversation.
- Check answers in open class.

ANSWERS

sounded bought were simple continuous

PRACTISE

3

- Refer students to the text and ask them to choose the correct options. (See Tips page 29)
- Encourage students to compare their answers in pairs before you check them in open class.

ANSWERS

1 met 2 was visiting 3 became 4 occasionally came
5 were sitting 6 saw

4 1.12

- Ask students to complete the conversation with the past simple or past continuous form of the verbs in brackets.
- Play the track for students to listen and check their answers.

ANSWERS / AUDIO SCRIPT 1.12

1 did you see 2 saw 3 was staying 4 were talking
5 noticed 6 took 7 weren't looking 8 saw 9 was doing
10 put
See Student's Book page 11 for audio script.

Extra activity

Ask students to practise saying the conversation in pairs. First, ask them to prepare the conversation by underlining all the stressed words. You can play the track again if necessary.

When they read the conversation, ask them to 'glide' over the unstressed words. Encourage them to put more emphasis and volume on the stressed words to reproduce the 'rhythm' in English speech.

5

- Ask students to write questions with the past simple, past continuous or both, if necessary. Focus students on the prompts and the example question.
- Ask students to compare their answers in pairs before you check them in open class.

ANSWERS

2 When and where did you lose it?
3 What were you doing when you lost it?
4 How long did you look for it?
5 While you were looking for it, did other people help you?
6 Did you ever find it?

6

- Ask students to think of something they lost in the past and write answers to the questions in Exercise 5.
- Walk round and monitor, helping students if necessary.

SPEAK

7

- Divide the class into pairs to talk about the things they lost. Encourage them to ask follow-up questions, as well as the questions they wrote in Exercise 5, in order to have a more natural conversation and get more information from their partner. Refer students to the model conversation for some examples of follow-up questions.
- Ask them to make notes about their partner's lost item and invite them to share their information in open class.

Extra activity

Ask students to swap partners and repeat the activity without using their notes.

Homework

Ask students to write a short text of approximately 150 words about a dream they had. Tell students a dream you had or make one up and ask them to listen to the key points of the dream whilst taking notes. Ask students to include at least one sentence with *while* and another with *when*.

LANGUAGE &BEYOND GET ORGANISED

Collaborate to organise a group activity — Page 12

STAGE	TIME	FOCUS
GET STARTED		Introduce the theme of working in a group and talk about personal strengths.
SPEAK AND READ		Discuss the last time you organised an activity and complete a survey about organising activities. Make a list of tips for organising activities to discuss in a group.
DO		Work in groups to plan a sale of second-hand things.
REFLECT		Reflect on which tips were useful and how you performed in the group activity.
EXTEND		Plan an end-of-term trip in groups.

LIFE SKILLS

COLLABORATE TO ORGANISE A GROUP ACTIVITY
Group work can motivate students and help them develop problem-solving and decision-making skills. It also helps students to identify their own strengths and weaknesses and to discover if they are good negotiators, leaders or motivators. Acknowledging the strengths and talents of others helps students develop the social skills they need for life, such as cooperation and respect. The skills students learn by taking part in group tasks make them highly valued in the workplace. Employers are very keen to hire people who can work well with others to analyse arguments and complete tasks on time.

Get started

Play a game of *Talent Party*. Explain to students that they have all been invited to a party but instead of bringing food to share, they are going to bring the strengths they think they contribute to this group. Brainstorm a few ideas, eg *a creative thinker, a good note-taker, can motivate others, a good listener, very organised*.

Ask students to write down two strengths or talents that they're going to bring to the party. Encourage students to compare with a partner what they are going to bring to the party. Then ask them to join up with another pair to see what strengths they now have as a four. Invite students to write their strengths on the board and to read what other people have written. Explain to the students that today they are going to look at ways of working together. Elicit whether they think the party would be better if they organised it alone or as a group. Do not erase the strengths. Review them at the end of the lesson to see if students have discovered new talents.

SPEAK AND READ

1

- Divide the class into pairs to answer the questions.
- Invite different students to tell the class about their discussion.

2

- Refer students to the photo at the top of the page and ask when they work in groups in class (projects, discussions, presentations, problem-solving activities, etc).
- Ask students to do the survey about group work individually.

3

- Divide the class into groups to compare their answers before you elicit them in open class.
- For each question, invite students to raise their hands for either the A or B options to see which option most people chose. For each answer, read out the following comments and discuss the different options in open class.

1 A – You prefer a fair division of work where everyone is responsible.
B – You are interested in completing the task and think the result is more important than the organisation.

2 A – You think control and organisation are the most important things.
B – You think it's a good idea to explore ideas and take it in turns to listen to the views of others.

3 A – You like to appoint a leader in a group.
B – You prefer everybody's opinion to be equal.

4 A – You prefer to take on a role.
B – You prefer things to be open and unstructured.

4

- Encourage students to write a list of tips for organising a group activity.
- Ask them to compare their lists with the tips on page 141 and discuss the differences in pairs or small groups.

DO

5

- Explain to students that they're going to organise a sale of second-hand things to make money for an end-of-term trip. Divide the class into groups and ask a student to read out the tasks to make sure they understand the instructions. Explain to them they're going to give a short presentation to the class on what they have discussed. Before they start, draw students' attention to the PHRASE BYTES box and encourage students to use these expressions to structure their answers.
- Monitor and help students with any language difficulties.

6

- Invite each group to present its decisions to the class.
- Then ask students to pool their ideas and, as a class, decide how they are going to organise the sale.
- You could ask students to vote by raising their hands for the best decision for each category (day, place, etc).

REFLECT

7

- Focus students on the REFLECTION POINT and ask them whether they agree or not. Invite students to discuss the questions one by one in open class.

GO BEYOND FOR TEACHERS

Collaboration

Emphasise the importance of exploring ideas together and agreeing on a set of 'talk rules' to make sure everyone takes it in turns to speak, takes on a role and collaborates to complete the task.

You could read out this case study of a group of teenagers who didn't enjoy a group work activity and ask students to recommend ways for them to work better in the future:

We argued a lot in our group and we didn't get anywhere. We all had different ideas and we couldn't agree on anything at all. Some people in the group didn't say anything and one person talked all the time. When I said something, someone laughed at me.

Suggestions:

- All group members should feel a sense of personal responsibility for the success of their team mates and realise that their individual success depends on the group's success.
- Assign different roles to the group members so that they are all involved in the process (eg recorder, spokesperson, timekeeper, etc).
- Specify clear objectives.
- Don't make fun of each other, and accept everyone's ideas.

EXTEND

8

- Ask students to get into groups to plan their end-of-term trip.
- Give them a few minutes to note down where they're going, what needs to be done and who's going to do what.
- Point out to students that they are going to write up their plan for the end-of-term trip for homework. They should take careful notes at this stage to help them complete the homework task.
- Ask students to present their ideas and discuss which idea is the best in open class.

Extra activity

Ask students to review the strengths they talked about at the beginning of the lesson and add any more important qualities for working together successfully in groups.

Homework

Ask students to write up their plan for an end-of-term trip.

SPEAKING Invitations

Make and react to invitations *Page 13*

STAGE	TIME	FOCUS
GET STARTED		Introduce the theme of the lesson, what to put in an invitation and collocations with the word *invitation.*
SPEAK		Discuss the last time you went to a party and recycle talking about events in the past.
WATCH OR LISTEN		Watch or listen to teenagers talking about who can come to a birthday party. Work with phrases to accept and refuse an invitation and ways of saying thank you.
ACT		Role-play inviting someone to a party and accepting or refusing the invitation.

Get started

Recycle vocabulary for celebrations and talk about a party you went to, using different collocations with the word *invitation*, eg *Last year, I got a wedding invitation from my best friend in the UK. He wanted me to be the best man and make a speech. I didn't want to refuse the invitation, but it was on Friday so I had to take the day off work. I accepted the invitation and it was a great wedding.*

Ask students to say the verbs that go with *invitation*. Ask: *Can you think of any others?* (*send, decline, turn down, say no to*, etc). Elicit the kind of events they would receive an invitation for and what information is usually included in an invitation. Refer students to the invitation on page 13 to see if it has the same information they thought of.

SPEAK

1

- Divide the class into pairs to ask them to look at the invitation and answer the questions.
- Elicit answers from different students and encourage them to explain their answer.

WATCH OR LISTEN

2 1.13

- Refer students to the photos and ask them to predict what the conversations are going to be about.
- Play the scenes for students to watch or listen to find out who can't come to the party and why not.
- Ask students to read the conversation to check their answers before you confirm in open class.

ANSWERS / VIDEO/AUDIO SCRIPT 1.13

Leo, because he's visiting his grandparents that day.

Ethan: Hi Alice. Can you come to my birthday party?
Alice: When is it?
Ethan: It's next Saturday, the 6th. I'm having a barbecue.
Alice: Sure. That sounds great. Thanks for inviting me.
Ethan: Great. See you there!

Ethan: Hey, Leo. I'm having a birthday party next Saturday. Are you free?
Leo: Sorry. I'd love to come, but I can't. I'm visiting my grandparents that day.
Ethan: That's too bad.
Leo: Yeah. But thanks for the invitation!

Ethan:	Max, would you like to come to my birthday party?
Max:	Yes, I'd love to. When is it?
Ethan:	It's next Saturday.
Max:	I'm sorry, but I can't. I'm going to a barbecue in Wilson Park.
Ethan:	A barbecue in Wilson Park?
Max:	Yeah. Alice is going, and she invited me.
Ethan:	Max, that's my party!
Max:	Really? Well, I guess I'll see you there!

3 1.13

- Ask students to complete the questions in the conversation.
- Play the scene again for students to listen and check their answers.

ANSWERS
1 Can you 2 Are you 3 would you

4 1.14

- Play the track for students to listen and repeat the invitations. Drill the questions chorally.

AUDIO SCRIPT 1.14
1 Can you come to my birthday party?
2 I'm having a birthday party next Saturday. Are you free?
3 Would you like to come to my birthday party?

Extra activity
Ask students to read out the conversations in pairs. Remind them to pay special attention to the rising intonation in the invitations.

5a

- Ask students to underline the sentences for accepting and refusing an invitation and for saying thank you.

5b 1.15

- Play the track for students to listen and check.
- Play the track again for students to listen and repeat.

ANSWERS / AUDIO SCRIPT 1.15
1 Sure. That sounds great. 2 Yes, I'd love to.
3 Sorry. I'd love to come, but I can't. 4 I'm sorry, but I can't.
5 Thanks for inviting me. 6 Thanks for the invitation!

Extra activity
Recycle the present continuous for future use. Refer students back to the conversation and ask them to use a different colour to underline all the sentences they can find with the present continuous for future use. Ask them to also underline a time expression. Ask students to discuss in pairs what they have in their diary for next Saturday. Nominate a few students to answer.

ACT

6 1.16

- Ask each student to write an invitation to a party, using Ethan's invitation to help them.
- Divide the class into A/B pairs. Student A should invite Student B to his/her party. Student B should accept or refuse the invitation, giving a reason as necessary. Before they start, play the track of the expressions in the PHRASEBOOK box and encourage students to use them in their conversation.
- Ask students to swap roles and act out the situation again with Student B's invitation.

7

- Encourage students to work in the same pairs and write out their conversation. Monitor as they work, helping as necessary.
- Then invite pairs to join up with another pair to present their conversations.

Homework

Ask students to imagine that they've been invited to spend a weekend with their English e-pal's family. Ask them to write a short email to say why they can't go and give a reason why not. Remind them that this is quite a formal piece of writing and they should remember to say thank you for the invitation.

WRITING A special object

Make a writing plan

Page 14

STAGE	TIME	FOCUS
GET STARTED		Discuss memory and facts about elephants.
SPEAK AND READ		Describe and compare model elephants. Read a description of a special object. Discuss the difference between *remember* and *remind*. Talk about how to make a writing plan.
PRACTISE		Make a writing plan for another description.
PLAN		Plan a description about a special object or a special day.
WRITE AND CHECK		Write the description and check you have covered the points in the plan.
SHARE		Swap your description and compare with other students' descriptions.

Get started

Play the game *What's the Question?* Write this short, famous poem about elephants on the board:

I have a memory like an elephant.
In fact, elephants often consult me.
(Noel Coward 1899–1973)

Ask students if they think it is true that elephants have long memories.

Write these words in clouds on the board: *Mammoth*; *Asian and African elephant*; *ivory*; *5kg*; *16 hours a day*.

Ask students to think of five questions to ask that would give them these answers (*What is the prehistoric ancestor of the elephant called? What two species of elephant are left in the world? What is the elephant hunted for?* or *What are its tusks made of? How much does an elephant's brain weigh? How many hours a day does an elephant spend eating?*) Set a time limit of three minutes.

Nominate different students to read out their questions for you to write the correct parts on the board until you have constructed the correct questions.

Elicit any other facts students know about elephants.

SPEAK AND READ

1

- Refer students to the photos. Divide the class into pairs to describe and compare the elephants.
- Encourage students to tell their partner which elephant they like best and say why.
- Nominate different students to share their descriptions and opinions in open class, and use the opportunity to recycle comparative and superlative adjectives.

2

- Ask students to read Jessica's description and decide which elephant she is describing and what Lucy's elephant looks like.
- Nominate a student to give the answer in open class.
- Ask students to read the **Get it right** box. Ask them to underline the example in the text, *When I see my elephant, it reminds me of that summer and my friend.* Point out that the elephant helps Jessica remember.

ANSWER

Jessica is describing elephant c. Lucy's elephant looks exactly the same.

Extra activity

If students have problems understanding the difference between *remember* and *remind,* teach them this sentence: *You remember something and you remind somebody to do something.*

Ask students to complete these sentence stems in pairs:

I remember the first time I …; Can you remind …; I can't remember …; To remind me of things, I …; Do you remember … ?; I can remember … .

Divide the class into groups to compare their answers.

Choose different students to read out their sentences.

3a

- Ask students to read the tips in the HOW TO box. Invite a volunteer to read them out.

3b

- Focus students on Jessica's plan and encourage them to find the answers to the questions in Jessica's description.
- In open class, elicit the sentences that answer the questions in each section.
- Ask them if she followed all the steps and answered all the questions. (There were some questions she didn't answer in the corresponding paragraph, eg *Is it old or new?*)

ANSWERS

Paragraph 1: It's a small, black, wooden model elephant. It's standing on a shelf in my room …
Paragraph 2: I got the elephant while I was staying with my friend Lucy in Wales. She said they were best friends like us.
Paragraph 3: When I see my elephant, it reminds me of that summer and my friend. It's a nice feeling to know that Lucy has an identical elephant.

PRACTISE

4

- Ask students to make a writing plan for another description called 'A special day'.
- Walk round and monitor students, helping as necessary.

PLAN

5

- Explain to students that they are going to write a description of a special object or a special day.
- Direct students' attention to the **Writing plan** to help them prepare. (See Tips for writing lessons page 30)
- Give students a few minutes to brainstorm ideas and take notes.
- Walk round the class, helping students if necessary.
- Ask students to check that they followed all the steps and answered all of the questions.

WRITE AND CHECK

6

- Ask students to use their plan to write their description. Set a time limit of 10 minutes.
- When students have finished writing, encourage them to check their texts.

SHARE

7 Ask students to swap their descriptions with one or two classmates and discuss the similarities and differences.

Homework

Ask students to write the other description about a special day or a special object.

Introduction

Unit Reviews bring together all the grammar and vocabulary seen in the unit. Students can refer to the Grammar Database and Words & Beyond pages first and then try to do the exercises. Alternatively, they can try the exercises first and then study the reference material if necessary. Unit Reviews can be used in the classroom or for self-study at home. Procedural notes are provided here for their use in the classroom.

As in an exam, in the Unit Reviews students can clearly see how many points they can score for each exercise. When they have finished, encourage students to swap their books with a partner and mark each other's work, totalling up the score.

VOCABULARY Special days

1

- Focus on the title of the text and ask students what things could be included in a life plan, eg *going to university*, *getting married*, etc.
- Ask students to read Tony's life plan and complete it with the words and phrases in the box.
- Check answers in open class.

ANSWERS
1 school 2 driving licence 3 first date 4 home
5 university 6 job 7 married 8 children 9 vote
10 Retire

Adjectives for describing objects

2

- Explain to students that they are going to read a list of things for sale. Ask students to read the introductory text and say why these things are on offer. (Tony needs money to buy a car.) Elicit the three items for sale (watch, carpet, MP3 player).
- Set a time limit of three minutes for students to complete the adjectives in the descriptions. Point out that the first and the last letter of each adjective is given.
- Encourage students to compare answers in pairs before you check them in open class.

ANSWERS
1 antique 2 useful 3 fashioned 4 valuable
5 enormous 6 coloured 7 cotton 8 square
9 tiny 10 unusual

GRAMMAR Present tenses

3

- Explain to students that they are going to read a conversation between two men who haven't seen each other for a long time. Focus on the options and ask students to say what the two tenses are (present simple and present continuous), and when we use them.
- Ask them to complete the conversation by choosing the correct options.
- Circulate and monitor as they do the task. If you feel they are having difficulty, stop them mid-task and do a quick review of the use of the present simple and present continuous, as well as state and dynamic verbs.
- Check answers in open class.

ANSWERS
1 are you doing 2 'm not working 3 usually spend
4 'm looking 5 Do you ever see 6 don't know
7 'm making

Past tenses

4

- Explain to students that they are going to read an email from Tony to an old school friend.
- Ask students to complete the email with the past simple or past continuous form of the verbs in brackets.
- Ask fast finishers to think of two more ways to start and sign off an email, eg *Hi! Hi there! Hello! Best wishes, Speak to you soon.*
- Check answers in open class. If students have the wrong answers, guide them towards the correct answers by asking questions like: *Did the action happen once or over a period of time? Was Stan in the middle of an action?*

ANSWERS
1 was looking 2 found 3 spoke 4 phoned
5 were doing 6 saw 7 was shopping 8 got

Extra Resources

Go to the Teacher's Resource Centre at www.macmillanbeyond.com for:

- downloadable audio and audio scripts for the Student's Book and Workbook
- videos and video scripts
- extra vocabulary at two levels of difficulty
- extra grammar at two levels of difficulty
- CLIL lessons, with full teacher's notes
- a life skills lesson, with full teacher's notes
- Speaking Database materials
- the *Beyond* B1 wordlist
- test generator for Unit 1 testing materials (all skills)
- tips for using the Grammar Database
- and more!

Go to the Workbook pages 4–15 for further practice material

2 UNIT PACK YOUR BAGS

IN THE PICTURE Travel

Talk about travel items

Pages 16–17

STAGE	TIME	FOCUS
GET STARTED		Introduce the theme of the lesson and think about words related to travel.
WORK WITH WORDS		Recycle methods of transport and associated prepositions and verbs. Describe travel items and talk about which items you can take on a plane. Pronounce words with /p/ and /b/ sounds. Watch a video of an airport scanner and say the items you see.
SPEAK		Plan what to pack for a school camping trip in your area.

Get started

Write the unit title *Pack your bags* on the board and elicit what it means (to put your possessions into a bag, case or box so that you can take or send them somewhere). Write *She told him to pack his bags!* on the board and say that it is an informal expression. Ask if students can work out what it means (tell someone to leave a place and not return).

Ask the class what they think the unit is going to be about (*travel*) and write synonyms or partial synonyms for the theme of travel in a jumbled order for students to work out, eg *pirt* (trip), *yegova* (voyage), *yonurej* (journey). Ask students to work in pairs to say what the difference is between these words and the word *travel*.

ANSWERS

travel: a verb to say you go from one place to another
trip: when you go somewhere and come back again (the word we most often use in this context.)
voyage: long distance travel by sea
journey: a longer or more adventurous trip, or the time you spend travelling

WORK WITH WORDS

1a, b and c RECALL

- Refer students to the instructions for each of the three exercises. Divide the class into pairs to do the three tasks. Set a time limit of two minutes.
- Copy the table onto the board and invite different students to add methods of transport under the headings. Then check the answers to the other tasks in open class.
- Ask students to do the Work with Words task on page 131.

ANSWERS

Exercise 1a
See table on page 131.
Exercise 1b
by
Exercise 1c
drive a *bus*, car, coach, train, tram, taxi
fly a helicopter, plane
ride a bike, horse, motorbike; ride a bus, tram (as a passenger)
sail a boat, ferry, ship

Fast finishers

Ask fast finishers to think of unusual forms of transport to write in their list, eg *hot-air balloon*, *racing car*, *canoe*, *yacht*, *rowing boat*, *barge*, *donkey*, etc.

Extra activity

Ask students to underline the stressed syllables in the multi-syllable words in the table.

Extra activity

Recycle the structure of the present simple with adverbs of frequency. Divide the class into pairs and ask students to find out what type of transport his/her partner often uses and one kind of transport he/she never uses. If necessary, elicit questions and write them on the board. Nominate different students to report their partners' answers.

2a 1.17

- Refer students to the pictures of items a–l. Focus them on the categories, *luggage/baggage*, *personal items* and *money and documents*, and point out the example. Divide the class into pairs to put the items in the correct categories.

- Play the track for students to listen and check.
- Refer students to the **Get it right** box and invite a volunteer to read it out loud.

ANSWERS / AUDIO SCRIPT 1.17

Luggage/baggage: suitcase, backpack, sleeping bag
Personal items: toothbrush, toothpaste, shampoo, hairbrush, scissors
Money and documents: passport, visa, boarding pass, wallet

2b

- Ask students which item(s) in the backpack you *can't* take on a plane in your hand luggage, and elicit why not.
- Ask students if they know of any more items that you can't take on a plane (any sharp items, items that can explode, large amounts of money, etc)

3a 1.18 PRONOUNCE

- Play the track for students to listen to the words and repeat. Ask them to pay particular attention to the /p/ and /b/ sounds. Drill any sounds they have problems with.

AUDIO SCRIPT 1.18

See Student's Book page 16.

3b 1.19

- Play the track for students to listen to the words and circle the one they hear.
- Play the track again for students to listen and repeat both words.

ANSWERS / AUDIO SCRIPT 1.19

1 back 2 peach 3 pen 4 bear 5 big
back / pack, beach / peach, Ben / pen, bear / pear, big / pig

4

- In their pairs, ask students to take it in turns to describe and guess the objects in Exercise 2a. Before they start, draw students' attention to the model conversation.

Alternative procedure: less confident classes

In less confident classes, give students time to prepare their descriptions. Recycle ways of describing objects and write model sentences on the board to help students structure their own sentences:

It's something that/which you use to keep your hair tidy.
People use it to keep their hair tidy.
It's used for keeping your hair tidy.

5

- Refer students to the pictures and ask them work in the same pairs to make a list of the other objects in the backpack and suitcase.

ANSWERS

suitcase: some batteries, a hat, a pair of shoes, some sunglasses
backpack: a mobile phone, a phone charger, a book, a pen, a bottle of water, an iPod with headphones, a plug

Extra activity

Point out to students that *backpacking* is a noun to describe a way of travelling that is very popular, especially with young people. Ask students to think of the advantages and disadvantages of backpacking and travelling with a suitcase, eg

Backpacking: *it is easier to get on and off a train or a bus with a backpack; it's lighter; you wear it on your back so it's easy to move around*, etc.

Travelling with a suitcase: *you can fit more things in; it's safer if you lock it with a key; your things are more protected because they are in a harder case*, etc.

Point out to students that the verb *to backpack*, eg *We backpacked around India*, is as common as *We went backpacking around India.*

6 THE MOVING PICTURE

- Explain to the students that they are going to watch a video of an airport scanner. Discuss what they think this is.
- Ask students if they have ever had a problem going through airport security (eg carrying too much liquid or sharp objects).
- Play the video and ask students to shout out the names of the items they see.

AUDIO SCRIPT

(The following is heard on the tannoy in the video)
This is a special announcement. For security reasons please keep your luggage and all packages with you at all times, until they are checked. Unattended baggage will be removed immediately for inspection, and may be damaged or destroyed.

Extra activity

Recycle *There's/There are … , a/an* and *some*. In their pairs, ask students to try to remember all the items that were in the video. Set a time limit of two minutes. The pair with the most items on their list wins the game.

SPEAK

7

- Explain to students that they are going on a school camping trip in their area. Divide the class into pairs to decide the five most important things to pack.
- Invite them to look at the pictures for ideas and think of other items, eg *a camera, a first aid kit, a torch, a box of matches, a compass*. Draw students' attention to the expressions in the PHRASE BYTES box and encourage them to practise using these in their conversation.
- Monitor and note good use of language and errors to go over in a feedback session.
- Ask each pair to compare their ideas with another pair.

Extra activity

Ask the same groups to eliminate some of their items so they have only five items to pack. Then ask groups to come up to the board and write their items.

Encourage students to discuss similarities and differences between each group's list.

Finally, tell the class that they can only take five of these items, as a class. Lead a class discussion to decide which ones they are going to eliminate from the board.

GO BEYOND

Ask students to do the Go Beyond tasks on page 131.

Homework

Ask students to write a short story of approximately 150 words about the school camping trip and include all of the objects in their list in their story. They should say why they were important or what they used them for. In the next lesson, choose a few students to read their stories out.

READING Be a voluntourist

Identify the purpose of a text *Page 18*

STAGE	TIME	FOCUS
GET STARTED		Recycle vocabulary to describe methods of transport and find the odd one out.
SPEAK AND READ		Talk about your best holiday. Read a text from a website about voluntourism. Discuss tips on how to identify the text type, the reader, the writer and the writer's aim.
REACT		Give your opinion on voluntourism and talk about communities in need.

Get started

Write these words to describe methods of transport on the board in groups of four: *bike, motorbike, car, horse; plane, helicopter, balloon, coach; train, bus, underground, tram; boat, ferry, ship, kayak*

Explain that three words in each group have something in common and one is the 'odd one out'. Ask students to work in pairs to say which word is the odd one out and why.

Ask students to come up to the board and circle the odd one out in each group. Have students say why they chose each odd item and ask each other why they have chosen different options.

SPEAK AND READ

1

- Divide the class into pairs to answer the questions and talk about their best holiday. Set a time limit of two minutes.
- Nominate different students around the class to report on what their partner has said.

Alternative procedure: less confident classes

In a less confident class, model this activity first yourself. Tell students about your best holiday and then ask them to answer questions 1–3. This will give students a clearer idea of what is expected of them in this activity and help familiarise them with the questions. Give students time to note down their answers to the questions before they do this as a speaking activity.

2a

- Ask the same pairs to discuss how they can identify the text type, who the text is written for and by, and the writer's aim. Prompt their discussion by asking them: *How do you know what a text is going to be about before you read it? Is it important to know who is writing a text? How do you know if a text is going to be interesting before you read it?* etc.
- Refer students to the tips in the HOW TO box, asking some more confident students to read the tips out loud.
- Elicit whether the ideas they had are the same or different from the ones in the HOW TO box.

2b 1.20

- Ask students to read the first part of the text and identify the text type, the reader and the writer's aim. Set a 30-second time limit for this to encourage students to skim over vocabulary they do not know. Don't play the audio yet. It's an extra feature and ideas for using it are given at the end of the lesson.

ANSWERS

Text type: website
Reader: students aged 14–18 who would like to be a voluntourist
Writer's aim: to persuade readers to do one of the company's voluntourist programmes

3

- Ask students which tips in the HOW TO box they used to help them in Exercise 2b and encourage them to tick them.

4 1.20

- Ask students to read the text again more closely and complete the report form for Molly and Alex.
- Circulate and monitor students, helping if necessary.
- Copy two report forms onto the board and nominate different students to come up and write their answers.
- Find out from students if they have heard of similar voluntourist programmes.
- Ask some comprehension questions to check full understanding of the texts: *How old do you have to be to be a voluntourist?* (14–18); *How long do you usually go for?* (2–4 weeks); *What did Molly like best about her time in South Africa and why?* (the people because they were always cheerful and ready to share food or tell stories); *What does she miss most?* (the children in the school where she worked); *Why was Alex nervous?* (he had never been abroad); *Why didn't he feel homesick?* (He made lots of new friends.)

ANSWERS

Molly
Area: Mtubatuba, South Africa
Project: Worked in an activity centre
Project length: 4 weeks
How the programme has helped you: I learned that you don't need a lot of money or material goods to enjoy life.
Alex
Area: Boston, USA
Project: Helped elderly people with housework and shopping
Project length: 2 weeks
How the programme has helped you: I made new friends and have become much more confident.

Fast finishers

Ask fast finishers to find words in the text to match these definitions: *in or to a foreign country* (abroad); *people who let you stay in their home* (host family); *someone's feelings about something, shown by their behaviour* (attitude); *happy, friendly* (cheerful); *feeling sad and alone because you are far from home* (homesick).

REACT

5

- Divide the class into pairs to discuss the questions.
- Lead an open-class discussion by inviting students to share their point of view and explain their reasons.

GO BEYOND

Ask students to underline the names of the six continents in the text and say which continent is missing.

> **ANSWERS**
> North America, South America, Africa, Asia, Europe and Australia.
> The missing continent is Antarctica.

GO BEYOND FOR TEACHERS

Continents

Depending on the convention used, there are six or seven continents. In some countries, students are taught to consider North and South America to be a single continent. Australia is sometimes referred to as Oceania, but not by its inhabitants.

Recorded reading text 1.20

The reading text is recorded as an extra audio track which can be exploited for various purposes.

In this lesson, you could use the audio to support less confident students the first time they read the text. Encourage them to read at the same speed as the audio then, if necessary, allow them to read again at their own pace.

Homework

Ask students to research a voluntourist programme they would like to go on and write about why it is interesting for them. In the next lesson, put students in small groups to share their ideas.

GRAMMAR Present perfect

Talk about how long something has happened *Page 19*

STAGE	TIME	FOCUS
GET STARTED		Talk about natural disasters to introduce the theme of the lesson.
READ		Read an article about a family on a voluntourist holiday.
STUDY		Use the article to study and recycle knowledge about the present perfect with *ever/never, just/yet/already* and *for/since*.
PRACTISE		Complete an interview with the correct present perfect forms of verbs and adverbs. Answer the questions in the interview using *already*, *not yet* and *never*.
WRITE AND SPEAK		Ask and answer questions about activities you do regularly and say how long you have done these activities.

Get started

Write these questions on the board and ask students to discuss them in pairs. Set a time limit of two minutes and give regular updates (one minute to go, etc):

What are some different kinds of disasters?
Do some natural disasters occur repeatedly in the same area?
What's the difference between a hurricane and a typhoon?
What's the difference between a hurricane and a tornado?
Can you think of any famous natural disasters?

Ask students to discuss the questions in pairs.

Nominate different students to say their answers.

> **SUGGESTED ANSWERS**
> Avalanche, famine, tsunami, drought, earthquake, hurricane, tornado, typhoon
> Natural disasters often occur repeatedly in the same area.
> If a storm forms in the Atlantic (ie the USA) or eastern North Pacific Ocean, it's called a hurricane. A typhoon is generally any storm that begins in the western North Pacific.
> A hurricane is a large weather system and a tornado is a column of rotating air.
> The earthquake near Fukushima, Japan in 2012; Hurricane Katrina 2005 in New Orleans, USA; Cyclone Yasi in Australia in 2011; Hurricane Wilma in Mexico and USA in 2005, etc.

READ Grammar in context

1

- Refer students to the photo and elicit what has happened. (The photo shows hurricane damage.)
- Ask students to read the article and say what volunteer activities the Rawlins family are doing and why.
- Elicit the American English word for *holiday* (vacation).
- Ask a few comprehension questions to check full understanding of the text: *How many homes were destroyed?* (300,000); *How many hours a day are they working?* (Eight hours a day); *Are they enjoying their holiday?* (They are having a fantastic time.)

> **ANSWER**
> They're rebuilding places in New Orleans that were destroyed by Hurricane Katrina.

STUDY

2

- Focus students on the explanations for the present perfect and ask them to underline examples of the three different uses of the present perfect in Exercise 1.
- Nominate students to read out the sentences.
- Read out the explanation of the form of the tense, referring students to the past participles in the list of irregular verbs on page 140 of the Student's Book.

ANSWERS
For past actions when we don't know the exact time: Since we've arrived ... I've had a fantastic time.
With *ever/never* for experiences in your life: I've never been on a trip like this before. Have you ever worked on vacation?
With *just/yet/already* for recent events: the city hasn't completed rebuilding work yet. We've already finished a playground and we've just started on a park project.

Extra activity
Students often get confused with the meanings of these common time adverbs. This is usually because in L1 a different structure from the present perfect is used to express these ideas.

Ask students to think about their timetable for the day and write sentences using *just/yet/already*, eg *I've just had maths. I haven't had science yet. I've already had English twice this week.*

3
- Ask students to underline *for* and *since* in Exercise 1.
- Ask them to complete the explanations with *for* and *since*. Then nominate a student to read out the completed grammar explanations.

ANSWERS
since for

Extra activity
To give students more practice understanding the difference between *for* and *since*, ask them to write two columns in their notebook with the headings *for* and *since*. Read out this list of time expressions and ask students to write them in the correct column:

20 minutes, three days, 9am, four years, January, I left school, two centuries, 1600, Monday, a long time.

Point out that *for* can be used with all tenses, whereas *since* can only be used with the perfect tenses.

Ask students to think of two more examples for each column and compare them in pairs before they write their examples in the correct columns.

ANSWERS
For: 20 minutes, three days, four years, two centuries, a long time
Since: 9am, January, I left school, 1600, Monday

PRACTISE

4a
- Ask students to complete Ben's interview with the present perfect form of the verbs and the adverbs in brackets.
- Invite two students to read out the completed conversation. The rest of the class can listen and check their answers.

ANSWERS

1 Have you ever been	2 've already visited
3 Have you ever stayed	4 've never been
5 've slept	6 Have you ever worked
7 haven't done that yet	8 've just changed

Extra activity
Divide the class into pairs to practise the conversation.

4b
- Ask students to write their own answers to the three questions in Exercise 4a using *already*, *just*, *not yet* or *never*.
- Circulate and monitor, helping students if necessary.
- Encourage students to compare their answers in pairs before you check them in open class.

Fast finishers
Ask fast finishers to look at the text on page 18 and find seven examples of the present perfect tense.

Ask students to identify the different uses of the present perfect for each sentence and explain why they are used.

ANSWERS
You've probably heard of volunteers. Since 2001, *Holiday Help* has offered voluntourist programmes ... I've learned you don't need a lot of money or material goods to enjoy life. Since the trip I've felt much more confident. (past actions, don't know exact time)
I've just spent four weeks in Mtubatuba. I've been home for a week now but I haven't got used to it yet. (recent events)
I've never been abroad. (experience in life)

5
- Ask students to complete the visitor's form by writing the questions and completing the answers with *for* or *since*.
- Go through the first one in open class to check they understand, and point out the example answer.
- Encourage students to compare their ideas in pairs before you check them in open class.

ANSWERS
1 have you spent your holidays in Westbourne?; *since*
2 have you stayed at the Beach Campsite?; for
3 have you been here?; since
4 have you had good weather?; since
5 have you looked forward to this holiday?; for

WRITE AND SPEAK

6a
- Ask students to work individually to write five activities they do regularly. Before they start, draw students' attention to the example sentences. Then divide the class into pairs to exchange lists with their partner.

6b
- Encourage students to ask each other how long their partner has done the activities on the list and take it in turns to answer each other's questions. Before they start, invite one pair to read out the model conversation.

6c
- Invite students to tell the class one interesting thing about their partner.

Homework
Ask students to write six sentences about themselves with *already*, *just* and *yet*. Ask them to write one false sentence. At the beginning of the next class, students read out their six sentences to their partners for them to decide which sentence is false.

LISTENING AND VOCABULARY Around the world

Listen for the information you need

Page 20

STAGE	TIME	FOCUS
GET STARTED		Play a game to recycle the present perfect with *already*, *yet*, *just*, *since*, *for*, *ever* and *never*.
SPEAK AND LISTEN		Talk about favourite ways to travel and the positive and negative aspects of travelling by sea. Listen to a video blog about a boy who is sailing around the world with his parents. Practise understanding the main ideas and extracting specific information when listening.
REACT		Discuss the good and bad things about living on a boat and homeschooling.
WORK WITH WORDS		Complete a map and an online ticket with travel words. Create your own online ticket and ask questions to find out the details of your partner's journey.

Get started

Play a game of *Three in a Row* (see Games page 33) with the grid below. To win a square, teams take it in turns to choose a square and make either a positive sentence (✓), a negative sentence (✗) or a question (?) with the indicated adverb and the correct form of the present perfect.

already ✓	yet ?	just ✓
never ✗	ever ?	since ✓
for ✗	not yet ✗	for ✓

SPEAK AND LISTEN

1

- Divide the class into pairs to take it in turns to ask and answer the questions. Set a time limit of three minutes.
- Invite different students to report their partner's answers.

2 Refer students to the photo and the start of Oscar's blog. Ask them to read it quickly to find out why he's writing it.

ANSWER

His family are sailing around the world on a boat for two years.

3a

- Elicit ideas from students about how they can understand main ideas and specific information when they do a listening activity in class.
- Ask students to read the tips in the HOW TO box. Invite a volunteer to read them out.

3b 1.21

- Explain to the students that they are going to listen to Oscar's video blog.
- Before you play the track, ask students to read the questions. Remind them that in the first listening, they should listen for the main ideas only and note down answers to the questions. In the second listening, they should then add details to their answers.
- Play the track twice for students to listen and answer the questions as indicated.

ANSWERS / AUDIO SCRIPT 1.21

1 They're getting ready for their departure to Australia. They're buying food and getting fuel for the boat and the cooker.
2 He's looking forward to it. He thinks it's amazing to see water everywhere, but he thinks a boat can be a bit small when you can't get away from the other people.
3 He does homeschooling with his dad; he reads something and writes about it.
4 He fishes and then he helps with dinner.
5 He's meeting his friend Callum and his family.
6 They're going to take the train to Sydney with Callum's parents and they're going to spend a few days there.

'Hi everyone. We're in a harbour in Tahiti now but our next destination is Australia. Tomorrow we leave for Brisbane, so we're getting ready for our departure. Today we're going to buy food and get fuel for the boat and the cooker.
I'm looking forward to being on the ocean again. It's always amazing to just see water everywhere you look. Especially when you sit outside on deck at night and there's a full moon ... that's so cool. But it's also great to just go on land when you want. A boat can be a bit small when you spend *all* your time ... you know, 24/7 ... with your family and you can't get away. Sometimes I just need a bit more personal space!
We'll probably be at sea for nearly two weeks this time. We've had good weather for weeks but unfortunately the hurricane weather starts soon, so we're likely to have some storms. That might mean a change in the route that we take and a delay in our arrival date. I'll keep you posted. Bye!'

'Hi everyone. Now I'm at sea, I have homeschooling with my dad every morning as usual. Basically he just gives me some books, tells me to read something and then write about it. In the afternoon I usually fish and then help with dinner. I like cooking but I hate doing the washing up. People forget that when you're on a boat, you still have to do stuff like that. And we don't have a dishwasher!
We'll be in Brisbane in five days. We're meeting my friend Callum and his parents who are going to be on holiday there. I've known Callum for years, so it'll be great to see him. Sometimes I really miss my old friends. Callum, his parents and I are going to take the train down to Sydney and spend a few days there ... it'll be cool to be a train passenger for a change!
OK, time to go! Check back soon!'

4

- Ask students which tips in the HOW TO box they used to help them in Exercise 3b and encourage them to tick them.

REACT

5

- Divide the class into pairs to ask and answer the questions. Encourage students to explain their reasons.
- Invite students to share their ideas with the class. Start a class discussion by asking other students if they agree or have anything to add to the answers.

WORK WITH WORDS

6 1.22

- Encourage students to complete the labels on the map and the online ticket with words from the box.
- Play the track for students to listen and check their answers.
- Play the track again for students to listen and repeat.

ANSWERS / AUDIO SCRIPT 1.22

a route b destination c departure d arrival e connection f delay g passenger h reservation i seat j fare

7a

- Ask students to work individually to make an online ticket like the one in Exercise 6, changing the journey details. They can add as much artistic detail as they like! They shouldn't show their partners at this point.

7b

- Divide the class into pairs to ask and answer questions about the details of their partner's journey and make notes.
- Ask students to join up with another pair to tell them about their partner's trip and say whether they think it's interesting, expensive or complicated.

Alternative procedure: less confident classes

In a less confident class, brainstorm all the questions that students will need to ask and write them on the board: *What is the destination? What is the route to get there? What is the departure time? What time do you arrive? Do you have to make a connection? Are any delays expected? How many passengers are there? What are your seat numbers? How much does the trip cost?*

Ask students to do the activity first with the partner they are sitting next to and then repeat the activity with a different partner. The second time, erase the questions from the board.

Extra activity

Ask students to make a mind map with the key word *travel*. Encourage them to include the travel words from the unit so far with these different headings: *verbs, sailing, types of trip, travel items, methods of travel* and *words associated with travelling*.

GO BEYOND

Ask students to do the Go Beyond task on page 131.

Homework

Ask students to imagine they have been on the journey they planned in Exercise 7. Ask students to write a short text of about 100 words to describe the journey details and what happened on their journey.

GRAMMAR The future

Talk about events in the future — *Page 21*

STAGE	TIME	FOCUS
GET STARTED		Play a game to recycle travel words from the unit so far.
READ		Read a chat message and define an InterRail trip.
STUDY		Read explanations about future forms and find examples in a text.
PRACTISE		Practise the target language in written exercises and distinguish between the different future forms.
WRITE AND SPEAK		Talk about your plans and dreams for the future.

Get started

Play a game of *Hot seat* (see Games page 33). Use ten words from the unit so far, eg *backpack, voyage, crew, luggage, fare, route, vacation, sleeping bag, voluntourism, delay.*

READ Grammar in context

1

- Refer students to the photo and ask them to describe what they see.
- Ask them to read the chat message quickly to find out what an InterRail trip is. Set a time limit of one minute. Then nominate a student to say the answer.
- Ask some comprehension questions to check full understanding of the chat message: *Who is going on an InterRail trip?* (Dan's big sister) *What is her first destination?* (Paris) *What time does she leave?* (12 o'clock) *How long is she travelling for?* (a month)

ANSWER

A trip by train around Europe, using a ticket which allows you to travel in 30 countries for one month.

STUDY

2

- Ask students to read the explanations about future forms and underline examples in the text in Exercise 1.
- Check answers in open class. As you do so, point out that in positive sentences with *will*, the adverb (eg *probably, definitely*) comes AFTER *will*. In a negative sentence, the adverb comes BEFORE *won't*.

ANSWERS

Present continuous: *My big sister's starting her InterRail trip, she isn't travelling alone*

Present simple: *Her train to Paris leaves at 12 o'clock*

be + going to + infinitive: *she's going to travel around Europe, What countries are they going to visit?*

will/won't + infinitive: *that'll be amazing, Will she be OK?, my parents will definitely phone her, They probably won't remember*

be + likely to + infinitive: *she isn't likely to have any problems, it's likely to be a lot*

Extra activity

Ask students to write full positive and negative sentences with *will*, the verb *rain* and the given word.

It / probably ✓ ✗ — *It / definitely* ✓ ✗

It / likely to ✓ ✗ — *It / possibly* ✓

Then ask students to complete the table matching the approximate meaning of these future phrases.

ANSWERS

It'll definitely rain.	100% chance of rain
It'll probably rain. It's likely to rain.	80%–95%
It'll possibly rain.	50%–80%
It probably won't rain. It isn't likely to rain.	5%–20%
It definitely won't rain.	0% chance of rain

PRACTISE

3 1.23

- Explain to students that they are going to hear Sam telling a friend about the holiday he's going on. Elicit anything students may already know about the Trans-Siberian Railway.
- Ask them to choose the correct options to complete the conversation.
- Play the track for students to listen and check their answers.

ANSWERS / AUDIO SCRIPT 1.23

1 're going 2 does your train leave 3 It arrives
4 Are other people going to sleep 5 likely to be
See Student's Book page 21 for audio script.

GO BEYOND FOR TEACHERS

The Trans-Siberian Railway

This is the world's longest railway and is about 10,000km long. Stretching from Europe to Asia, it crosses 16 rivers and spans eight time zones. It is an example of tremendous human effort. It was built between 1891 and 1916 by convicts, soldiers and peasants who risked their lives in the extreme climate. It was an incredibly challenging project, cutting through forests, swamps and permafrost without the modern technology we have today.

4

- Ask students to read the quotes by students about their plans and dreams and write the correct future forms.
- Encourage them to compare their answers in pairs before you check them in open class. Elicit why each form was used for each question to help consolidate the rules.

ANSWERS

2 starts 3 'm going to learn 4 'll/will definitely be
5 isn't likely to come 6 'll/will probably get

WRITE AND SPEAK

5a

- Divide the class into pairs. Ask students to write three sentences about their plans and dreams using the time phrases given, without showing their partner.
- Circulate and monitor students, helping them if necessary.

5b

- Ask students to write three sentences predicting their partner's future, using their own ideas.

5c

- Draw students' attention to the model conversation. Ask them to take it in turns to tell their partner their ideas.
- Ask students to exchange sentences from Exercise 5a to see if any of their predictions were correct.
- Elicit some examples of correct predictions in open class.

Homework

Ask students to write sentences with different future forms including these words or phrases: *Polar bears / become extinct*; *School / Friday*; *Marry*; *Fish for supper / tonight*; *Pass / English exam*; *Use mobile / tomorrow*; *Dark sky / rain*; *Party / this weekend*; *Watch TV / internet*. At the beginning of the next class, students compare their sentences with a partner.

LANGUAGE & BEYOND — RESPECT OTHERS

Respect other people's personal space Page 22

STAGE	TIME	FOCUS
GET STARTED		Introduce the theme of personal space and differences between cultures.
READ		Read an article about personal space and compare your feelings about being in closed spaces with the class.
DO		Carry out a task to test your awareness of personal space.
REFLECT		Reflect on your own ideas about personal space and how you protect it.
EXTEND		Talk about your own behaviour and if personal space is important to you.

LIFE SKILLS

RESPECT OTHER PEOPLE'S PERSONAL SPACE

Speaking good English does not always guarantee effective communication because non-verbal factors such as an awareness of personal space also affect communication. Between different cultures, ideas about personal space can vary. What's polite and acceptable in one culture can be considered rude, unacceptable or confusing in another.

In this lesson, students are made aware of their own behaviour and they reflect on how different people have different ideas about personal space. This is important when establishing good relationships at both a social and professional level. By interpreting body language correctly, they can increase their comprehension and expression, hold their listener's attention and be more successful in the communication process.

Get started

Write the words *personal space* on the board and ask students to think of situations where there is a small amount of personal space (*on a crowded train*, *in a queue*, *in a lift*, *in crowds at concerts*, etc). Ask students how they feel in these situations.

Write these statements on the board: *Two boys usually get closer together when they talk than two girls. People in China and India need a lot of personal space. People in South America or Southern Europe need less personal space than people in North America and Northern Europe.*

Divide the class into pairs to discuss if they think these statements are correct or incorrect and say why. Set a time limit of two minutes. Put some expressions on the board to help students, eg *I think that the first statement is correct/ incorrect because ...* ; *I agree/don't agree with you; I'm not sure.*

Invite students to share their ideas in open class. Then ask them to check their answers in the article on page 22.

READ

1

- Ask students to look at the picture and say what they think it shows. Refer them to the introduction to the article to check their answer.

2

- Ask students to read and choose the correct options for themselves. Review the meaning of *I don't mind* (I don't feel upset or unhappy about something).
- Invite students to raise their hands for their chosen option to compare their answers with the rest of the class.
- Encourage students to think of recent examples when they have been in these situations and describe how they felt.

DO

3

- Divide the class into groups of three to read and follow the instructions in order to measure their own personal space.
- Invite groups to share their findings in open class in order to compare them with the rest of the class.

GO BEYOND FOR TEACHERS

Social distances

Social distances vary from person to person, but there is a good general rule that Hall (1966) identified for Americans:

Public Zone: 3 metres – When we are walking behind someone in town, we try to keep a 3m distance from them.

Social Zone: 1.5m–3m – When someone moves into the social zone, we start to feel a connection with them.

Personal Zone: 0.5m–1.5m – In the personal zone, the conversation gets more direct.

Intimate Zone: 0.5m or less – When a person is within arms' reach or closer, we can look them in their eyes. This can be either romantic or threatening!

REFLECT

4

- Focus students on the REFLECTION POINT and have a class vote on whether they agree or not. Draw students' attention to the expressions in the PHRASE BYTES box and encourage them to use these to help structure their discussions.
- Lead a class discussion of the questions one by one, nominating different students to share their answers.

GO BEYOND FOR TEACHERS

Personal space

By respecting personal space, students can create a positive impression. Remind students that within the first 60 seconds of meeting somebody, you have formed an impression about what type of person that person is, and 55% of this will be based solely on body language. This is important when students go to a job interview when the interviewer is judging what kind of employee you would make from the minute you walk in the door.

In the classroom, as teachers, we also need to be aware of personal space. Bend down to the student's level as much as possible and always try to speak to students eye to eye. In a student-centred classroom, we should be moving around the classroom listening, making sure students are on-task and clarifying any questions or concerns.

Extra activity

Write these quotes on the board. Divide the class into pairs to discuss what advice they would give.

1. My friend gets too close when she talks to me. I don't know what to do.
2. Every morning I get on a crowded train. My hands sweat and I feel nervous.
3. I have a Japanese friend who doesn't like me standing close to her.
4. At an interview, I shake hands with the person who's interviewing me but then I'm too close.

EXTEND

5a 1.24

- Explain to students that they are going to listen to sentences about areas of personal space and they should write *agree*, *disagree* or *not sure* for each statement.
- Play the track, pausing after each sentence for students to write their response.

AUDIO SCRIPT 1.24

1. My bedroom is my space. My family should only come in when I allow them.
2. My diary or journal is for my eyes only. Nobody else should read it.
3. My phone messages are private. Nobody should read them.
4. My social media page is for me and my friends – not for my parents.
5. My parents don't need to know where I go and what I do with my friends.

Alternative procedure: less confident classes
Less confident students will probably feel uncomfortable discussing these sentences if they don't see them written down. Ask students to note down any words they hear the first time they listen. Encourage them to compare their answers in pairs to try and reconstruct whole sentences. Play the track again for students to try to complete their sentences. Ask five students to come up and write the sentences on the board to check.

5b

- Divide the class into pairs to compare their answers and explain any differences to each other.
- Ask students to present their opinions to the class and hold a class discussion to close the lesson. You could ask some opening questions to start the discussion, eg *Do you keep a diary? Do you feel that your bedroom is your own private space? Is it right for parents to look at their children's emails and messages? Do you tell your parents where you are going when you are going out?*

Homework

Ask students to write a short text of approximately 150 words on personal space, based on their answers in Exercise 5b. In the next lesson ask them to compare their texts with a partner.

SPEAKING At the airport

Check in at the airport *Page 23*

STAGE	TIME	FOCUS
GET STARTED		Recycle vocabulary and present new words for talking about travelling by plane.
SPEAK		Discuss the best way to get to the airport near your home and talk about your experiences at an airport. Learn words to describe places in an airport.
WATCH OR LISTEN		Watch or listen to a scene at an airport. Work on important phrases when you check in at the airport and recycle ways to check you understand.
ACT		Role-play a conversation at a check-in desk.

Get started

Write the following sentences on the board. Point out that they are all associated with travelling by plane and ask students to complete them with the correct verb.

1 The plane ________ at your destination.
2 You ________ your luggage if you haven't done this electronically.
3 The plane goes down the runway and ________ .
4 You ________ your seat belt and switch off your mobile phone.
5 You ________ at the airport at least two hours before your flight.
6 You ________ passport control and ________ your passport.
7 You ________ the correct gate and then you ________ your flight.

Nominate different students to come up to the board and complete the sentences.

Divide the class into pairs to put the sentences in a logical order. Check answers in open class and encourage students to think of other words associated with flying and being at an airport.

ANSWERS
1 arrives/lands 2 check in 3 takes off 4 fasten
5 arrive 6 go through/pass through; show
7 go to/walk to; get on/board
Correct order: 5, 2, 6, 7, 4, 3, 1

SPEAK

1

- Divide the class into pairs to discuss the questions.
- Choose different students to explain how to get to the nearest airport from their homes and say how many times they have been to the airport.

2

- Refer students to the airport signs for them to match with the correct activities 1–6.
- Encourage them to compare their answers in pairs before you check them in open class.

ANSWERS
2 c 3 a 4 f 5 d 6 b

WATCH OR LISTEN

3 1.25

- Play the scene for students to watch or listen and decide where Bella is and what other places in an airport are mentioned.
- Play the scene again for students to check their answers. Nominate a student to say the answers.
- Ask some comprehension questions to check full understanding of the conversation: *Where is Bella flying to?* (Rome); *How many bags is she checking in?* (One suitcase); *Does she have any sharp objects in her hand luggage?* (Yes, she has a pair of scissors); *What does she do with them?* (She puts them in her suitcase).

ANSWERS / VIDEO/AUDIO SCRIPT 1.25
Bella is at the check-in desk.
Departures and Gate 30 are also mentioned.
See Student's Book page 23 for audio script.

4 1.26

- Refer students back to the conversation in Exercise 3 and ask them to underline the sentences and phrases for situations 1–4.
- Play the track for students to listen and check.
- Play the track again for students to listen and repeat. Ask students to underline the stressed words in each sentence.

ANSWERS / AUDIO SCRIPT 1.26

1 I'd like to check in for the flight to ...
2 Here you are.
3 I have a backpack.
4 Which gate number is it?

Extra activity 1.25

Ask students to read out the conversation in pairs. Play the scene again for students to listen and pay special attention to the intonation and to stressed and unstressed words. Drill the sounds as a class.

5a

- Ask students to read the tips in the HOW TO box. Invite a volunteer to read them out.

5b 1.27

- Ask students to cover the conversation and try to complete phrases 1–4 from the conversation.
- Encourage students to compare their answers in pairs before you play the track for them to listen and check.
- Play the track again for students to listen and repeat.

ANSWERS / AUDIO SCRIPT 1.27

1 Sorry, I don't understand.
2 Sorry, I didn't hear that.
3 Could you repeat that, please?
4 Can you say that again, please?

ACT

6 1.28

- Divide the class into pairs to role-play the situation as described in the instructions: Student A is at the check-in desk (Assistant) and Student B wants to check in (Traveller).
- Ask the 'travellers' to first decide where they are flying to, how much luggage they have and if they have any sharp objects in their hand luggage.
- Play the track with the phrases from the PHRASEBOOK box and encourage students to use these phrases when acting out their conversation.
- Suggest to the 'travellers' that they check their understanding at different points in the conversation by using the PHRASEBOOK expressions.
- Invite students to join up with another pair to present their conversations.

Alternative procedure: Less confident classes

In less confident classes, students may need to practise the conversation in a more structured way. Copy this structure onto the board and elicit key sentences for each stage, writing them on the board. Ask students to act out the conversation in pairs. Then ask them to form different pairs and try to perform the conversation without looking at the board.

Traveller	Assistant
Greet / Say destination	Passport?
Give passport	Check in luggage?
Describe luggage to check in	Hand luggage?
Describe hand luggage	Sharp objects?
Say yes/no	Yes – in suitcase. Give boarding pass
Gate number?	Say gate number
Check you understand	Repeat gate number

Homework

Ask students to investigate different ways to get to the airport(s) in their town or area and write a short text about the different methods of transport and how much each one costs. Have a class vote on the best method in the next class.

WRITING Wish you were here

Use correct verb tenses Page 24

STAGE	TIME	FOCUS
GET STARTED		Brainstorm words connected to holidays and holiday activities and play a game to introduce the theme of the lesson.
SPEAK AND READ		Talk about when you send postcards and who you receive them from. Read a postcard and match pictures to the text. Discuss how to use correct verb tenses in a postcard.
PRACTISE		Write sentences in another postcard in the correct tense.
PLAN		Make a plan to write a holiday postcard.
WRITE AND CHECK		Write the postcard and check you have covered the points in the plan.
SHARE		Swap your postcard with a partner to decide whose trip sounds most interesting.

Get started

Play a game of *A–Z List*. Divide the class into small teams to write an A to Z list of words connected to holidays and holiday activities (except *u* and *z*). To make this game more challenging, tell students that in order to get a point, they must say both a word with the correct letter and identify the part of speech (noun, verb, or adjective). Set a time limit of five minutes. Use this opportunity to recycle vocabulary students will need in the lesson. Invite the teams to say their words beginning with the successive letters in the alphabet. Teams win an additional point if they say a word that no other group has written.

Alternative procedure: more confident classes
Play the *A–Z List* game in the same way but ask them to say a noun, a verb *and* an adjective for each letter, and give them a point for each one they can say successfully.

SPEAK AND READ

1

- Divide the class into groups to answer the questions.
- Nominate different students to share their answers.

2

- Ask students to read Vik's postcard and tick the correct picture for each category.
- Encourage students to compare their answers in pairs before you check them in open class.
- Focus students on the **Get it right** box and ask them to write an example sentence for each word.

ANSWERS
Journey: c   Campsite: a   Weather: b   Food: a

3a

- Encourage students to read the tips in the HOW TO box. Invite a volunteer to read them out loud.

3b

- Ask students to look at Vik's postcard and underline examples of seven different tenses. Encourage them to identify the tenses. (See Tips page 29)
- Encourage them to compare their answers in pairs before you elicit them in open class.
- Ask different students around the class to read out their sentences to peer check their answers. Point out that there are several different sentences for most of the tenses.

SUGGESTED ANSWERS
We've been in Spain for three days now. (present perfect)
I'm having a fantastic time. (present continuous)
The journey was terrible. (past simple)
I was getting really tired of waiting. (past continuous)
But our campsite is brilliant. (present simple)
We're going to do some sightseeing. (*going to* future)
I think it'll be exciting (*will* future)

PRACTISE

4

- Ask students to write the sentences in the correct tenses, using the tips in the HOW TO box to help them.
- Circulate and monitor students.
- Check answers in open class.

ANSWERS
1 got   2 play   3 haven't played   4 are going to watch
5 is raining   6 will stop

PLAN

5

- Explain to students that they're going to write a holiday postcard. Ask them to think about their ideal holiday.
- Focus their attention on the **Writing plan** and go through the structure of the postcard with them.
- Give them 10 minutes to write their ideas for their plan. Circulate and help students if necessary.

WRITE AND CHECK

6

- Ask students to use their plan and the model to help them write their postcard using as wide a variety of tenses as possible. Remind them to make sure they are using the correct form of each verb. Set a time limit of 10 minutes.
- When students have finished writing, encourage them to check their work.

SHARE

7 Ask students to swap their postcard with a partner and decide whose trip sounds most interesting.

Alternative procedure: more confident classes
Ask students to write their postcards on separate sheets of paper. Then ask them to draw a picture that represents the description of their ideal holiday. Collect in the postcards and pictures and redistribute them in groups of six. Ask students to read the postcards and match the descriptions to the pictures.

Homework

Draw students' attention to the first part of Vik's postcard and elicit what went wrong at the beginning of the holiday. Ask students to write a postcard about the worst holiday they can imagine. Ask them to describe what went wrong on the journey, at the campsite/hotel and with the weather and food. Ask students to swap their postcards with a partner at the beginning of the next lesson and decide whose trip sounds worst.

VOCABULARY Travel items

1

- Refer students to the picture and ask them to describe where the boy is and what his problem is (*he is picking up his luggage from baggage claim and his suitcases are very heavy*). Ask students if they know what the maximum weight is for luggage on most flights (about 23kg) and elicit which items can be very heavy (*books, toiletries, shoes*, etc). Explain to students that the conversation is between the boy and the teacher and they're going on a school trip.
- Ask them to complete the conversation with the correct words, pointing out that the first letter of each word is given.
- Check answers in open class.

ANSWERS
1 suitcases 2 backpack 3 sleeping bag
4 toothpaste/toothbrush 5 toothbrush/toothpaste
6 hairbrush 7 shampoo 8 boarding pass(es)
9 visa 10 scissors 11 passport 12 wallet

Travel

2

- Explain to students that the travel plan gives details on how to get to Berlin. Ask students what they know about Berlin and what they can visit there, eg The Berlin Wall, The Brandenburg Gate, Checkpoint Charlie, the Riechstag, Berlin Zoo, Pergamon Museum, etc.
- Ask students to choose the correct options to complete the travel plan. Allow three minutes.
- Encourage students to compare their answers in pairs as they finish. Then nominate different students to read out their answers.
- Encourage fast finishers to underline the stressed syllables in the nouns.

ANSWERS
1 de<u>lays</u> 2 reser<u>va</u>tion 3 seat 4 de<u>par</u>ture
5 <u>pass</u>engers 6 a<u>rri</u>val 7 con<u>nec</u>tion
8 destin<u>a</u>tion 9 route 10 fare

GRAMMAR Present perfect

3

- Ask students where Luke and his classmates are. (They're visiting the Egyptian section of a museum.)
- Write the words *for* and *since* on the board and elicit when we use each one (*for* = period of time, *since* = a specific point in the past).
- Ask students to complete the conversation by writing the verbs in brackets in the present perfect and choosing *for* or *since*.
- Check answers in open class.

ANSWERS
1 's/has been 2 since 3 've/have worked 4 for
5 For 6 has wanted 7 've/have just decided
8 hasn't taken

The future

4

- Ask students to read the initial sentences and choose the teacher's next sentence (A or B) in each case.
- Nominate different students to read out their answers, inviting the rest of the class to help you correct any errors.

ANSWERS
1 A 2 A 3 B 4 B 5 A 6 B

Extra Resources

Go to the Teacher's Resource Centre at www.macmillanbeyond.com for:

- the Speaking section of the Progress Check 1&2
- a downloadable Project linked to Units 1–2
- downloadable audio and audio scripts for the Student's Book and Workbook
- videos and video scripts
- extra vocabulary at two levels of difficulty
- extra grammar at two levels of difficulty
- culture lessons, with full teacher's notes
- a life skills lesson, with full teacher's notes
- Speaking Database materials
- the *Beyond* B1 wordlist
- test generator for Unit 2 testing materials (all skills)
- tips for using the Grammar Database
- and more!

Go to the Workbook pages 16–27 for further practice material

PROGRESS CHECK UNITS 1&2

Preparing for the Progress Check

The Progress Check can be done either as a revision of the two preceding units or as a formal test. For the first Progress Check, it is a good idea to get students to prepare as thoroughly as they can so that they get into the habit of regularly revising what they have learned. Reassure the class that the Progress Check contains material that they have covered in Units 1 and 2.

Vocabulary review

- Write the following on the board and ask students which words are needed to compete the phrases for life experiences:
  get ________ (married; a job; a driving licence; a degree)
  start ________ (school; university)
  go on ________ (a first date)
  leave ________ (school; university; home)
  go to ________ (school; university)
  have ________ (children)
  ________ *from your job* (retire)
- After a few suggestions, ask students who can find the rest from the Words & Beyond section on page 130 (suggested answers are given in brackets above).
- To review adjectives for describing objects, ask the class to turn to Exercise 6 on page 10. Remind them of the work they did on word order there. Explain to students that they are going to play a quick memory game and they have to try to remember what was said before.
  - Begin by asking Student A: *What have you got?* Student A should then answer with a noun described by two adjectives (eg *I've got a valuable old watch.*)
  - Encourage Student A to ask Student B the same question. Student B then repeats the item and adds one more, eg *I've got a valuable old watch and a new red bag*. Student B then asks Student C, who repeats the previous two items before adding a third.
  - Keep going round the class until someone makes a mistake or fails to think of a new item. If the chain is broken, start again with the next student and continue until all the members of the class have had a turn.
- Put students in pairs to review travel items. Give them exactly one minute to look at the vocabulary on pages 16 and 17. Next, pairs should see how many items they can remember with their books closed. Students then look in the book to see if they forgot any words. Ask several pairs to tell you if they forgot anything important.
- Working individually, students call out other words related to travel that they can remember from the book. Write these on the board as you hear them. When suggestions begin to slow down, or if they seem to be coming from the same students each time, ask the class to look at Unit 2 and the Unit Review on page 25. This time, aim to get suggestions from students who have contributed the least so far.

Grammar review

- To remind the class of the grammar they have studied in the previous two units, start a 'race', where students check the book and tell you the main grammar points from each unit. The grammar for this Progress Check is:
  - Unit 1: Present tenses review; Past tenses review
  - Unit 2: Present perfect; The future
- Write these on the board, asking for example sentences as students call the grammar points out. Deal with any problems by correcting mistakes and referring students to the grammar explanations on pages 9, 11, 19 and 21.

Optional warm-up activities

These activities are suitable when you are not using the Progress Check as part of a formal test.

READ Exercise 1

- Tell students that they are going to practise skimming a text. Explain that skimming will give them a good idea of what the text is about, what the main points are and how the text is organised. Give them one minute to read the text for gist. Remind students that they are not expected to read it in detail.
- After a minute, ask them to close their books and tell you what they remember. Elicit the main points about the text, correcting anything students have misunderstood.
- Point out how useful it can be to skim a reading text. Explain that they will have to read more closely when they need to answer the questions in the task but that this will be easier because they will now be able to find the relevant sections of the text quickly.

LISTEN Exercise 2

- Refer students back to the listening activities and the HOW TO boxes they covered on pages 10 and 20. Ask some students to tell you which tips they thought were the most useful.
- Remind them of the importance of reading ahead before they listen. Point out that listening activities, especially in tests, are not an opportunity to sit back and rest. They need to use all the time available to predict what they will hear. If they do this, what they hear will make more sense to them.
- Put students in pairs and ask them to look at the gaps in the form in Exercise 2 and say which one requires the following (answers are given in brackets): a number (3), a period of time (1), a place (5), a noun (4).
- If students are worried about the LISTEN section, you could ask them to suggest what the answers might be. Do not, however, give any indication of the actual answers. Instead, respond by saying *It could be that* or pointing out why a suggestion is unlikely (eg because the student suggests an adjective and that wouldn't fit syntactically).
- Finally, point out to students how much useful information they have gathered *without* listening. They will now be much more focused when they do listen.

WRITE Exercise 3

- Students following the *Beyond* course have done transformation exercises before. However, some students might not be familiar with them, so make sure they understand that they cannot use more than three words, and the second sentence must have the same meaning as the first.
- You should also remind students that the gaps usually depend on the grammar that they have studied in the two previous units (see *Grammar review* above).
- Write the following on the board:
  I have been here since 9 o'clock.
  I was a student in 2010.
  Do you want a drink?
  I'm still waiting for my test results.

- Ask the class how they could write these sentences differently but with the same meaning. Accept suggestions, dealing with any problems that might occur. You can then write some of the following on the board and explain that they say the same thing but in a different way:
  - I have been here for (three) hours. I came here at 9 o'clock. I came here (three) hours ago.
  - I have been a student since 2010. I started studying in 2010.
  - Would you like a drink? Can I get you something to drink?
  - I haven't got/had my test results (yet). My test results haven't come out (yet). My teacher hasn't given me my test results (yet).
- Point out that there is sometimes more than one way to transform a sentence. Remind students that the meaning has to be the same after the transformation.

WRITE Exercise 4

- Refer students back to the HOW TO box on page 24, and remind them that they have been reviewing tenses in these two units.
- Ask students to look at the bullet points in Exercise 4 and ask them which tenses they will use for each bullet point. Elicit the following:
  - First bullet point: present continuous
  - Second bullet point: present perfect
  - Third bullet point: *going to*

  In addition, students could use:
  - present simple to say what day it is today or tomorrow;
  - past simple to say what happened yesterday, on Monday, etc, or to add details after a present perfect;
  - present continuous for future plans
- Put students in pairs and ask them to note down some of the things they could write for each bullet point. They do not have to write complete sentences.

Doing the Progress Check

READ

1

- Ask students to look at the HOW TO boxes that they have studied (on pages 8 and 18). Make sure they remember that they have several different strategies to choose from in order to do this kind of task.
- Go through the first tip for how to do a true/false activity in the **Exam tips**. Then give the students a minute or two to read sentences 1–10. Prompt them with some very basic questions, eg:
  - *Where in the world are we talking about?* (Liverpool)
  - *Who do you think Paul McCartney and John Lennon are?* (members of a group)
  - *Who were the Beatles?* (a music group)
  - *What do you think Mendips and Forthlin Road are?* (places where the musicians lived)
- If you have decided not to do the full warm-up, tell students that a good thing to do next would be to read the text quickly to understand how it is organised (and where they might find the answers).
- Go through the remaining tips for how to do a true/false activity. Ask if the headings or the picture help them with more information. Then ask them to read the text carefully, checking details and answering the questions. Allow 15 minutes for this section.

ANSWERS

1 B 2 B 3 B 4 B 5 A 6 A 7 B 8 A 9 A 10 A

LISTEN

2 1.29

- If you have decided not to do the full warm-up, encourage students to spend a minute or two looking at the gaps and predicting what they might hear. Make sure that they understand that they have to write a word, number or short phrase in each gap.
- Go through the **Exam tips** for the listening task, briefly referring students back to the work they did on pages 10 and 20.
- Point out that they will hear everything twice. Students should aim to fill each gap the first time but they must be careful not to lose their place and miss the answer to one of the questions. The second listening should be for checking and filling in any gaps they have left.

ANSWERS / AUDIO SCRIPT 1.29

1 12 years 2 working together 3 €30 4 boarding pass 5 (the) station

Organiser: Hi, everyone. Can I just say a few words before you get ready to leave? First of all, I'd like to say how much we've enjoyed our time with you over the last week. We've been organising our Adventure Weeks for 12 years and you've been one of our best groups. On a personal level, I hope you'll keep in touch with your new friends. I also hope you remember what you've learnt here. Working together to organise things is one of the most important skills you'll ever need. It'll help you at school and when you leave home and get a job.
I'd just like to run through a few practical things next. For those of you who are travelling back home by plane, the coach to the airport leaves at ten. Please don't be late. We can't delay your plane's departure! If you miss the coach, you'll have pay for a taxi to the airport, and the fare is €30.
Remember to put your passport in your hand luggage, not in your suitcase. And have you all printed your boarding passes? No? OK, if you *haven't* printed your boarding pass, could you please go to reception when I finish talking and they'll do that for you. It'll save you time at the airport and you can also reserve the seat you want. And when you've printed it, remember to keep your boarding pass with your passport.
If you're travelling by train, a different coach is going to take you to the station. It leaves at 11, so you have a bit more time to fold up your sleeping bags and get all your belongings into your backpacks.
That's it. It's 9 o'clock now, so I'll see some of you down here in an hour.

WRITE

3

- Read through the **Exam tips** for this task. Make sure students understand that they can write one, two or three words in the gaps, but no more.
- Remind students that this type of task is often grammar-based. They should expect present, past and future tenses to be included.
- Explain that spelling is important in this type of task because in a real exam they will lose marks for spelling mistakes, so checking is very important.

ANSWERS

1 were studying 2 you like 3 for two weeks
4 hasn't answered

4

- Spend a few minutes going through the task with students and eliciting who they have to write to and what their message must include (*the three bullet points*).
- Remind them that, even if their writing is excellent, they won't get full marks if they do not include all the points in the task.
- Refer students back to the work they did and the postcard they wrote on page 24. Point out that this message is similar to a postcard, only here they have to write fewer words.
- Explain that they shouldn't spend too long on their beginnings and endings. Suggest that they begin with *Hi Neil,* and end with *Write soon, [name]*.
- Stress that the correct tenses are important. Briefly remind them of the work they did on tenses on page 24 and the optional WRITE warm-up activity above.
- Finally, remind students of the word limit and the importance of checking their spelling, grammar, etc.

MODEL ANSWER

Hi Neil,
How are things? It's Friday after school and I'm reading my messages. It's been a hard week. I've had exams every day since Monday. But tomorrow's Saturday. We will probably go to a theme park, but it's likely to rain.
Write soon,
Jim

After the Progress Check

Optional game

This game follows up on the past, present and future tenses, as well as the travel vocabulary that students have been reviewing and will help to lighten the atmosphere after the test.

- Ask students to have their books open at Unit 2.
- Put students in pairs. Explain that they are going to write conversations together. On a clean sheet of paper, each pair writes the first two lines of a dialogue about two people getting ready for a journey. Ask students to include at least one example of the present perfect in their conversations.
- Pairs then pass their piece of paper to the pair on their right, who read the beginning and add two more lines of dialogue. They continue in this way, adding two lines each time until they have finished. Remind students to refer to Unit 2 if they need help with any grammar or vocabulary. Then ask pairs to act out the dialogue they started.
- Ask the class to listen carefully while the dialogues are read out. When all the dialogues have been heard, ask them to vote for the best one.

Feedback and extension

After the Progress Check has been marked, provide feedback to the class as a whole and individually as far as possible. Ask students which parts they found the most difficult and how they think they could improve their marks next time.

READ

- Review sentences 1–10 one at a time, reminding students that all of the details in each question must be found in the text for it to be marked as *correct*. For example, in sentence 1, you could point out that paragraph 1 clearly states that Woolton is now a part of Liverpool but in 1957 it was a separate village.
- Ask students where they found the answers each time. If they made mistakes, make sure they understand why.
- Emphasise to students the importance of reading English, either online or in magazines, etc. The more they can read, the better it will be for them. Ask students what kinds of things they read in their own language and suggest suitable English equivalents (eg, pop or sport magazines, websites about hobbies, or more general interest magazines and sites such as *National Geographic Kids* or *Focus (www.sciencefocus.com)*). If students have a hobby or interest, they might be motivated to read about it in English.

LISTEN

- Handing out photocopies of the audio script is a good way to provide feedback. Deal with any mistakes in this way. You could make one photocopy per pair and ask students to discuss where they went wrong. Seeing the dialogues written down will help students to recognise if they have misheard something.
- As with reading, every opportunity students have to listen to English is valuable because most exams have a listening component. Through the internet, students can readily get access to lyrics, for instance, if they enjoy listening to songs in English. Radio and television are also excellent sources of spoken English. If you know of any stations, channels or programmes that are suitable for their age group, encourage students to listen, even if only for five minutes. This could become an ongoing project, with students reporting back on what they have heard or seen.

WRITE

- Students who had difficulty with Exercise 3 need to focus on the grammar points from the unit. Write one or two example sentences which use the grammar point in question on the board and then put students in groups of four to come up with more examples of their own. If necessary, ask students to write more sentences for homework.
- For students who had difficulty with Exercise 4, do a similar task, building up a model on the board. Write the following, asking different students for ways to fill in the gaps:

  Hi Ben,

  I am having a good/bad week because ....

  This week, I have .... *and* ....

  At the weekend, I ....
- When the model is complete, ask other students to suggest alternatives. You could then rub out the previous suggestions and fill in the gaps with new ones.

GO BEYOND FOR TEACHERS

The Beatles

The reading text in this Progress Check is about The Beatles. If students enjoyed reading about them, you could ask them to search online for more information about the group. For example, divide the class into two and give them the names of the other two Beatles. Half of the class could then look online for information about George Harrison, while the other half looks up Ringo Starr. If you think your students would be more interested in contemporary bands or musicians, ask them to choose one and find out more by searching for the name online. Remind them that they will find difficult words, but that they should try to understand the general meaning. They should aim to find between six and ten main points and report back in the form of a mini-presentation in the next lesson.

3 MY MUSIC

UNIT

IN THE PICTURE Live music

Talk about music and music events

Pages 28–29

STAGE	TIME	FOCUS
GET STARTED		Introduce the theme of the lesson and talk about music.
WORK WITH WORDS		Recycle different genres of music, types of group, musician and instrument. Learn new music vocabulary and listen and complete sentences with the new words. Pronounce words with /ɔː/ and /ɒ/ sounds. Watch a video of a concert and describe what you see.
SPEAK		Ask and answer questions in a music survey.

Get started

Ask students to work individually to write three personal statements about music – two true statements and one false one. Divide the class into pairs to read out their statements to their partner and take it in turns to ask questions and find out which statement is false. Model this activity first with students so that they have a clear idea of what types of things to say, eg *I have seen Rihanna in concert. I play the guitar. Music was my favourite subject at school.*

Refer students to the title of the lesson (*Live music*) and ask them to say what it means (live music can be watched or listened to at the same time as it happens). Practise the pronunciation of *live*. Remind students that the pronunciation is /laɪv/ when it is an adjective and /lɪv/ when it is a verb. If necessary, revise the difference in meaning. Read out these two gapped sentences and ask students to call out the correct word: *We found a bar that has ______ music on Friday nights. Barcelona is a nice place to ______ .*

WORK WITH WORDS

1a and 1b RECALL

- Divide the class into pairs to do both tasks. Set a time limit of three minutes.
- First students refer to the photos and make lists of words under the headings. Then they match the verbs *listen* and *play* to the correct categories.
- After three minutes, nominate different students to say their answers. Note that several categories use both *listen* and *play*.
- Ask students to do the Work with Words task on page 132.

2

- Ask students to match two words from the box to each of the photos a–f and add them to the table, if they do not already have them there.

ANSWERS

a *band, venue* b audience, opera c jazz, trumpet
d folk, performance e conductor, orchestra f brass band, flute

Types of music	Instruments	People	Types of group	Places & events
folk jazz opera	flute trumpet	audience conductor	*band* brass band orchestra	performance venue

Alternative procedure: less confident classes

For less confident students, write definitions of the more difficult vocabulary on the board for students to match to words from Exercise 1. Chorally drill the pronunciation.

the place where an activity or event happens (venue /ˈvenjuː/)

the act of entertaining someone (performance /pəˈfɔrməns/)

someone who directs the musicians of an orchestra or other musical group (conductor /kənˈdʌktər/)

a group of musicians who play brass instruments such as trumpets (brass band /bræsbænd/)

a musical instrument that you hold sideways to your mouth and play by blowing over a hole at one end as you press its keys (flute /fluːt/)

Extra activity

Divide the class into pairs or small groups to think of a famous musician or group which they associate with each genre in the table in Exercise 1, eg jazz – Louis Armstrong, opera – Placido Domingo, rock – Muse, classical – Beethoven, heavy metal – Led Zeppelin, reggae – Bob Marley, pop – One Direction, folk – Ed Sheeran, hip hop – Jay Z, R&B – Alicia Keys

Divide the class into groups of four and ask each pair to read out the name of the musician for the other pair to guess the music genre.

3 ▶1.30

- Play the track for students to listen and match the speakers to the photos.
- Encourage students to compare their answers in pairs before you check them in open class. Ask students which key words helped them decide on their answers.

ANSWERS / AUDIO SCRIPT ▶1.30

1 f 2 e 3 c 4 b 5 d 6 a

1 We started playing together a year ago, but I've played the flute since I was 12. I also play the trumpet in the school brass band.
2 The sound of the orchestra in the concert hall is fantastic. I've seen the conductor before, but I've never seen him conduct Beethoven.
3 Thank you for coming to the Newtown Jazz Festival. Now please welcome one of the greatest trumpet players of all time. Ladies and gentlemen, put your hands together for ...
4 I don't like opera very much, but a friend gave me tickets and I'm really enjoying it. I think the rest of the audience is having a good time too. People are shouting 'bravo!' all the time.
5 I usually perform folk songs ... a mix of old traditional songs and more modern stuff like Ed Sheeran. If I give a good performance, then people give money. ... Thank you.
6 The venue is amazing. I've never been to a concert in a place like this with all these hills and rocks. And the band is performing really well.

4a ▶1.31

- Ask students to use the words from Exercise 2 to complete the sentences.
- Play the track for students to listen and check.

ANSWERS / AUDIO SCRIPT ▶1.31

1 venue; band 2 Jazz; trumpet 3 folk; performance
4 flute; brass band 5 opera; audience 6 orchestra; conductor
See Student's Book page 28 for audio script.

4b ▶1.32

- Ask students to cover the box in Exercise 2. Play the track for them to listen and repeat the words.

5a ▶1.33 PRONOUNCE

- Play the track for students to listen to the target sounds in the words.
- Play the track again for students to listen and repeat.

AUDIO SCRIPT ▶1.33

orchestra opera

5b ▶1.34

- Play the track for students to listen and focus on the blue part of the words and repeat them. Point out the meaning of *score* (a written copy of a piece of music; music written for a film or play).
- Elicit which words have the /ɔː/ sound and which have the /ɒ/ sound.

ANSWERS / AUDIO SCRIPT ▶1.34

/ɔː/ audience performance score
/ɒ/ stop song lost
See Student's Book page 29 for audio script.

6 THE MOVING PICTURE ▶

- Play the video and ask students to describe what they see.
- Ask students what type of performance it is.

ANSWERS

They are all *live* performances.
Scene 1: an orchestra with a conductor; classical music;
Scene 2: a guitar player performing outside; folk music;
Scene 3: the audience at a rock concert;
Scene 4: a jazz band playing brass instruments;
Scene 5: a woman singing opera.

7

- Explain to students they are going to answer questions in the music survey. Divide the class into pairs. Refer Student A to the questions on page 141 and Student B to the ones on page 29. Encourage each student to answer the questions about him/herself and make notes.

SPEAK

8

- In the same pairs, Student A asks Student B the questions on page 141 and Student B asks Student A the questions on page 29, making note of their partner's answers.
- Encourage students to compare and discuss their answers in pairs.
- Circulate and monitor, noting down good use of language and errors to go over in a feedback session.
- Nominate different students to tell the class one interesting thing about their partner.

GO BEYOND

Ask students to do the Go Beyond task on page 132.

Homework

Ask the students to write about a group or a famous person who sings in English. Encourage them to use words from the lesson to describe how, where, what and when they perform, when they first discovered this music and what it means to them.

READING A dream concert

Understand new words *Page 30*

STAGE	TIME	FOCUS
GET STARTED		Recycle vocabulary used to describe different kinds of music.
SPEAK AND READ		Talk about your dream concert. Read a concert programme and talk about José Angel Salazar, 14-year-old conductor of the Symphony Orchestra of Nueva Esparta, Venezuela. Discuss tips on how to understand new words when you read.
REACT		Discuss the characteristics a conductor needs and if you possess these qualities.

Get started

Play a game of *Twenty questions* (see page 33). Divide the class into two teams and explain that they have twenty questions to guess the name of a famous musician.

Write this list of words on the board: *singer, conductor, concert, venue, guitar, keyboard, alive, dead, drums, piano, rock, hip hop, reggae, classical, jazz, trumpet, pop, star, performance, band, group*. Point out to students that if they use this vocabulary from the previous lesson, they can 'win' an extra question (eg *Is she a singer?* wins an extra question).

Keep a tally on the board of the number of questions the students have asked.

SPEAK AND READ

1

- Refer students to the poster. Divide the class into pairs to answer the questions. Set a time limit of two minutes.
- Check answers in open class. Ask different students to report on what their partner has said about their dream concert.

ANSWERS

1 The poster is advertising a series of classical music concerts with the Youth Orchestra of Nueva Esparta, Venezuela and the conductor José Angel Salazar.
2 Students' own answers.

2 1.35

- Ask students to read the concert programme and guess the answers to the questions. Don't play the audio at this point. Ideas for using the audio are given at the end of the lesson.
- Encourage students to compare their answers in pairs before you check them with the class.

ANSWERS

1 because he was the youngest conductor in the world
2 the conductor 3 He wants to study languages.

3a

- Divide the class into pairs to talk about how they can understand new words when they read. Prompt their discussion by asking them: *What do you do when you read a word you don't understand in a text? What happens if you use a dictionary all the time to look up new words? What can you do to work out the meaning of new words without a dictionary?*
- Refer students to the tips in the HOW TO box. Invite a couple of volunteers to read the tips out loud.
- Ask students if the ideas they had are the same or different from the ones in the HOW TO box.

3b

- Ask students to read the text again and try to understand the underlined words following the tips in the HOW TO box. Ask students to work in pairs if you think they need additional support.

ANSWERS

auditioned
Type of word: verb in the past simple, infinitive *audition*
Roots/cognate: *audience, audio*, ie related to the verbs *to hear, to listen to*
Context: ... to join the Symphony Orchestra

gestures
Type of word: plural noun
Roots/cognate: *gestura*, Latin root meaning 'manner of carrying the body'
Context: movements ... and expressions to communicate

tell off
Type of word: phrasal verb (informal)
Roots/cognate: *tellen* Dutch/German for 'to reckon' or 'to count'
Context: find the way to ... kids who are much older than me

convey
Type of word: verb
Roots/cognate: Anglo-French *conveyer*, Latin *conviare*
Context: ... confidence to the musicians in order to get a confident performance back from them

aware
Type of word: adjective
Roots/cognate: Old English *gewær*
Context: ... of the importance of words for a conductor

grasp
Type of word: noun
Roots/cognate: Old English *graepsen* – to touch or feel
Context: I'd have a better ... of if I spoke German

4

- Ask students to match the dictionary definitions to the underlined words in the text.

ANSWERS

1 aware 2 convey 3 tell off 4 grasp 5 auditioned
6 gestures

5

- Ask students which tips in the HOW TO box they used to help them in Exercises 3b and 4.

GO BEYOND FOR TEACHERS

José Angel Salazar and El Sistema

José Angel Salazar is one of the success stories of the Venezuelan symphony orchestra programme known as El Sistema. There are more than 285 youth orchestras serving 350,000 young people across the country and the programme has especially benefitted children from disadvantaged backgrounds. El Sistema was conceived 37 years ago by José Antonio Abreu, a retired economist and politician who was also a conductor and pianist. His objective was to make music accessible to all.

Abreu was surprised by Salazar's talents and he made sure Salazar received instruction from Gustavo Dudamel (the world-famous conductor of the Los Angeles Philharmonic Orchestra).

REACT

6

- Divide the class into pairs to discuss the questions. Before they start, draw their attention to the expressions in the PHRASE BYTES box.
- In open class invite different students to explain their point(s) of view. Try to develop a class discussion on the different points. You could start the discussion by asking a few general questions, eg: *Do you know any other unusual stories about musicians? Why did they become famous? What characteristics does a pop star need?*

GO BEYOND

Ask students to write different questions about the text on Jose Angel Salazar.

Divide the class into pairs to ask and answer each other's questions.

Recorded reading text 1.35

The reading text is recorded as an extra audio track which can be exploited for various purposes.

For more confident students you could use the audio track for a loop dictation (see page 31).

Homework

Ask students to write five quiz questions about music to test their partner at the beginning of the next class. At the start of the next class, take a few minutes to check students' questions before they test their partners in a speaking activity.

GRAMMAR Verbs followed by *-ing* form or *to* + infinitive

Talk about things you enjoy doing *Page 31*

STAGE	TIME	FOCUS
GET STARTED		Recycle words related to music and famous musicians.
READ		Read an advertisement and discuss whether you would like to attend The Rock School and say why or why not.
STUDY		Use the advertisement to study verbs followed by *-ing* form or *to* + infinitive.
PRACTISE		Complete an interview and a text and write questions with verbs followed by *-ing* form or *to* + infinitive
SPEAK		Ask and answer questions about music, free-time activities and hopes for the future.

Get started

Play a game of *Three in a Row* (see Games page 33) with the grid below. Divide the class into two teams. To win a square, teams take it in turns to choose a square and answer the question that you ask them. They should answer with one of the options given in the square.

1 baton / stick	4 Herbert von Karajan / Luciano Pavarotti	7 guitar / cello
2 saxophone / tuba	5 Mahler / Beethoven	8 88 / 76
3 six / four	6 conductor / violinist	9 guitar / flute

Questions

1 *What does a conductor use to keep time?* (a baton)
2 *Which instrument is often used in jazz?* (a saxophone)
3 *How many strings does a violin have?* (four)
4 *Who was a famous conductor?* (Herbert von Karajan)
5 *What's the name of a famous music composer from the 19th century?* (Mahler)
6 *What does Vanessa Mae do?* (She is a famous violinist.)
7 *Which instrument has four strings?* (cello)
8 *How many keys does a normal piano have?* (88)
9 *Which instrument can be acoustic or electric?* (a guitar)

READ Grammar in context

1

- Refer students to the photo and the first question in the text. Ask them what type of text they think they are going to read (a brochure advertising The Rock School).
- Ask students to read the advertisement. Elicit if they would like to go to The Rock School and why or why not.
- Ask a few comprehension questions to check full understanding of the text: *What types of instruments can you study at The Rock School?* (guitar, drums, keyboard and bass) *What is the main objective of The Rock School?* (to help young musicians achieve their ambitions) *What is their motto?* ('To inspire kids to rock on stage and in life') *What are the conditions to join The Rock School?* (You have to live in the US or Mexico and be between eight and 18.)

STUDY

2

- Focus students on the grammar explanations and ask them to complete them with verbs from the advertisement in Exercise 1.
- Nominate students to read out the completed explanations in open class.

ANSWERS

enjoy; practise want; inspire

PRACTISE

3

- Ask students to read Marta's interview and choose the correct option (or options) for each sentence.
- Check answers in open class.

ANSWERS

1 to come 2 being 3 to play 4 to be 5 singing
6 playing / to play 7 doing 8 swimming / to swim

Extra activity

Divide the class into pairs to practise reading the conversation out loud.

4

- Focus students on the text and ask them to complete it with the correct form of the verbs in the box.
- Encourage students to compare their answers in pairs before you nominate different students to read out a section each.

ANSWERS
2 to learn 3 to give 4 making 5 to perform
6 to become

5

- Ask students to write questions using the prompts and the correct form of the verbs in blue.
- Encourage students to compare their questions in pairs before you check them in open class.

ANSWERS
1 Which instruments are you learning to play at the moment?
2 Which other instruments would you like to learn?
3 Do you enjoy singing?
4 Do you like performing in front of people?
5 What do you hope to do in the future?
6 What other things do you like doing in your free time?

SPEAK

6

- Divide the class into pairs to take it in turns to ask and answer the questions in Exercise 5.
- When they have finished, invite students to tell the class one interesting thing about their partner.

Homework

Dictate these sentence prompts to students and ask them to complete the sentences about themselves for homework using verbs followed by *-ing* form or *to* + infinitive: *I love*; *I'd like*; *I don't mind*; *I imagine myself … in 10 years' time*; *I prefer*; *Last year I decided*; *I hope*; *I plan.*

At the start of the next class, students could take it in turns to read out their sentences. Encourage them to ask follow-up questions to find out more information about their partner.

LISTENING AND VOCABULARY Talking music

Transfer spoken information to a table Page 32

STAGE	TIME	FOCUS
GET STARTED		Recycle words to describe different types of music.
SPEAK AND LISTEN		Talk about the music you listen to when you are doing different activities. Read about and practise tips on how to transfer spoken information to a table. Listen to different people talking about how music affects them.
REACT		Discuss when you listen to music and if listening to music can help you study.
WORK WITH WORDS		Look at adverbs of degree and word formation of adverbs with *-ly*. Describe degrees of intensity using extreme adjectives. Listen to people being interviewed and complete sentences with adverbs.
WRITE AND SPEAK		Write and talk about whether music helps you do things better.

Get started

Divide the class into pairs or small groups to brainstorm adjectives that describe different types of music (eg *happy*, *upbeat*, *energetic*, *cheerful*, *sad*, *bluesy*, *melancholy*, *instrumental*, *easy listening*, *wild*, *danceable*, *background*, *jazzy*, etc). Set a time limit of three minutes. When eliciting the words, introduce two key words for the lesson into the discussion – *rhythm* and *beat*.

SPEAK AND LISTEN

1

- Divide the class into pairs to take it in turns to ask and answer the questions.
- Nominate different students to report on what their partner has said.

2a

- Elicit ideas from students about how they can transfer spoken information to a table.
- Ask students to read the tips in the HOW TO box. Invite a volunteer to read them out.

2b 1.36

- Explain to students that they will hear different people talking about the music they listen to. Ask them to complete the missing information in the table for each person. Remind them that, in the first listening, they should listen for the main ideas only and note down brief answers to the questions. In the second listening they should add details to their answers. (See Tips page 31)
- Play the track twice for students to listen and answer the questions.
- Encourage students to compare their answers in pairs before you check them in open class.

ANSWERS / AUDIO SCRIPT 1.36

1 doing homework 2 running
3 helps her run further 4 rap 5 working
6 doesn't help her work better as it distracts her

Presenter: So, today's question is about music and how much music can help us to do things better. Does music help you do things better?
Marty: Hi. My name's Marty. Does music help me do things better? Sure it does. I always listen to rock music while I'm doing homework. It helps me to think much more creatively.
Presenter: Did you know that music has a positive effect on memory? It's extremely good for your brain.
Marty: Really? Seriously? No, I didn't know that.
Presenter: It depends on the music, of course. Apparently, baroque classical music works the best.
Marty: Rock music?
Presenter: Baroque. It's a type of classical music. It has a very steady rhythm of 60 beats a minute.
Marty: That sounds terribly boring.
Jeannine: My name's Jeannine and music doesn't help me run faster but it helps me run further. As you can probably hear, I'm listening to music now. It's pretty extreme.
Presenter: What is it?
Jeannine: Don't laugh. It's heavy metal. There's something about the beat. It helps me get into the rhythm really quickly and it keeps my energy levels up.
Salva: Rap songs. They're incredibly good to listen to before an exam.
Presenter: Can you tell us your name?
Salva: Oh, right. Sorry. I'm Salva. Yeah – rap songs. They help me get totally focused and when I go into the exam, I'm ready for anything.
Presenter: Do you have any favourite rap artists?
Salva: Jay-Z and Kanye West. They're quite powerful.
Sheera: My name's Sheera. I work weekends here in the mall and sometimes I listen to music while I work but it doesn't help me work a lot better.
Presenter: Why not?
Sheera: I find it a bit distracting. I enjoy listening to pop songs that I can sing along to. But I can't sing and work at the same time.

GO BEYOND FOR TEACHERS

Baroque music

Research reveals that Baroque music (eg classical music composed by Bach, Handel, Vivaldi or Corelli) has about 60 beats per minute and stabilises mental, physical and emotional rhythms. People who study with Baroque music in the background say that they concentrate more deeply and learn information better.

3

- Ask students which tips in the HOW TO box they used to help them in Exercise 2b, and encourage them to tick them.

REACT

4

- Divide the class into pairs to answer the questions.

WORK WITH WORDS

5 1.37

- Focus students on the table and go through the examples with them. Ask students to write the remaining adverbs of degree in the correct columns according to their intensity.
- Play the track for students to listen and check.
- Play the track again for them to listen and repeat.

ANSWERS / AUDIO SCRIPT 1.37

1 *a bit*, pretty, quite 2 *a lot*, really, very
3 *extremely*, incredibly, terribly, totally

6 1.38

- Focus students on the interview extracts in the box. Play the track for students to listen and complete the extracts with the adverbs from Exercise 5.
- Check answers in open class.
- Play the track again for students to listen and repeat.

ANSWERS / AUDIO SCRIPT 1.38

1 extremely 2 very 3 terribly 4 pretty 5 really
6 incredibly 7 totally 8 quite 9 a lot 10 a bit
See Student's Book page 32 for audio script.

Alternative procedure: more confident classes
Ask students to complete the extracts before you play the track. Then play the track for them to listen and check.

WRITE AND SPEAK

7

- Ask students to work individually to write their answers. Remind them to use the interviews to help give them ideas and to include at least three adverbs of degree.
- Walk round, monitoring and helping students.
- Ask students to tell their partner their answer. Encourage them to compare their answers and find at least one similarity and one difference.

Fast finishers
Students who finish early could choose one of the photos and write a description of the person's appearance. They then read out their text to a partner or the class for them to guess who is being described. Encourage students to use adverbs of degree in their descriptions.

GO BEYOND

Ask students to do the Go Beyond task on page 132.

Homework

Ask students to write a music survey to interview their partner at the beginning of the next class. Ask them to write down these sentence prompts and complete them to make six questions with a variety of tenses:

Do you … (eg have a favourite band or singer?)
What are you … (eg listening to at the moment?)
When was the last time you … (eg bought a CD?)
How many … (eg MP3 tracks do you have?)
Have you ever … (eg listened to Baroque music?)
Do you ever … (eg sing in the shower?)

In less confident classes, brainstorm an example for each sentence prompt.

GRAMMAR Comparison of adverbs

Compare how people do things

Page 33

STAGE	TIME	FOCUS
GET STARTED		Talk about something you are good at and say how you can further improve.
READ AND LISTEN		Read and listen to an athlete talking about improvement through practice.
STUDY		Use a text to study comparative and superlative adverbs.
PRACTISE		Practise the target language in written exercises and complete sentences with your opinions.
SPEAK		Exchange opinions and compare your ideas.

Get started

Write this quote by jazz saxophonist James Moody on the board and ask students to say the sentence in their own words:

A wise man practises slowly; a wiser man practises even slower. (You don't get good by doing things quickly.)

Ask students to think about something they are good at (eg a sport, a musical instrument, a language, etc) and encourage them to mark on a line where they would situate themselves from *beginner* to *very good* level.

Invite students to reflect on what they have to work on to improve, noting down two main things they need to do in order to achieve this goal.

Ask students to compare and discuss their talent lines with some classmates. You could model this activity first yourself and use the opportunity to recycle comparative and superlative adverbs.

MODEL PRESENTATION

I decided last year that I wanted to take up running again. I was the best in the class at school but I wasn't as fit as I was then. I decided if I was going to get better, I had to run every day. It's difficult sometimes because it can be cold and rainy, but I go running every day. I've changed my diet to eat more nutritious food and not eat as much sugar. The most important thing for me was to learn how to keep up my rhythm and to breathe in the right way.

READ AND LISTEN Grammar in context

1 1.39

- Ask the students to read and listen to an athlete talking about his training and then answer the question.
- Nominate a student to say the answer.

AUDIO SCRIPT 1.39

See Student's Book page 33.

Alternative procedure: more confident classes

With more confident students, you could play the track for students to answer the question and then ask them to read the text to check.

STUDY

2

- Ask students to complete the explanations about comparative and superlative adverbs with the words in the box, using Exercise 1 to help them.
- Check answers in open class.

ANSWERS

-er; more   *-est; the most*   *better*

3

- Invite students to look back at Exercise 1 and complete the example.

ANSWERS

as hard as   as well as

Extra activity

To give students further practice using comparative and superlative adverbs, ask them to write two groups of six names of people (famous singers and musicians they know), six verbs and the six adverbs from the grammar box in Exercise 2.

Roll a dice to choose one item from each list. Ask students to write a sentence comparing the person in the first list with the person in the second list.

Example: You roll the dice four times. You get a 1, a 2, a 3, and a 5.

1 = Rihanna, 2 = Beyoncé, 3 = dance, 5 = bad

Rihanna dances worse than Beyoncé.

Repeat the procedure until they have made sentences with all the people. Then ask students to make sentences using superlative adverbs, eg *Rihanna dances the worst.*

PRACTISE

4

- Ask students to read the sentences and choose the correct options.
- Encourage students to compare their answers in pairs before you check them in open class.

ANSWERS

1 the fastest   2 better   3 as fast as   4 more carefully
5 the highest   6 as well as

5 1.40

- Explain to students that they are going to complete sentences about a talent show. Ask students if they have ever been in a talent show and what happens there (*singers, dancers, etc compete to show their ability*).
- Ask them to complete the conversation using comparative and superlative adverbs.
- Play the track for students to listen and check their answers.

ANSWERS / AUDIO SCRIPT 1.40

1 *the best* 2 more loudly 3 as well 4 more beautifully
5 as high 6 the hardest 7 longer 8 the fastest
See Student's Book page 33 for audio script.

Extra activity

Ask students to practise saying the conversation in pairs. Ask them to put more emphasis on the stressed words to reproduce the rhythm of English speech.

6

- Encourage students to work individually and complete the sentences with names to give their opinion.

SPEAK

7

- Divide the class into pairs to take it in turns to read out their opinions and respond saying whether or not they agree, giving reasons. Before they start, invite two confident students to complete and read out the model conversation.
- Circulate and monitor, helping students if necessary.

Homework

Ask students to research a famous sports star or team. Ask them to write a paragraph using comparative and superlative adverbs to describe their current performance. Remind them to use the sentences in Exercise 4 to help them structure their writing.

LANGUAGE &BEYOND GET ORGANISED

Stay on task and avoid distractions

Page 34

STAGE	TIME	FOCUS
GET STARTED		Write excuses for not doing homework.
SPEAK AND READ		Read a comic strip and discuss possible reasons for not doing homework.
DO		Look at tips and discuss what the character in the comic strip could do to stay on task.
REFLECT		Discuss whether you agree or disagree with the Reflection Point.
EXTEND		In groups, look at the importance of staying on task in a variety of professions.

LIFE SKILLS

STAYING ON TASK AND AVOIDING DISTRACTIONS

Learning how to stay on task and avoid distractions can have a great positive impact on your life on a personal and professional level. Effective time management, decision-making skills, discipline and determination are all key skills for the workplace.

Not staying on task can have negative effects on school results and career prospects. In a project at school or at work, everyone's actions depend on someone else's. If you are not good at staying on task, you can cause a hold-up and may be exposed as the 'bottleneck' in the chain.

All of us can be easily distracted, especially when there is something we don't really want to do. There could be negative reasons why students do not stay on task, such as a fear of failure or not understanding the task. Many people feel frustrated that they have not managed to stay on task and can feel anxious and guilty. In this lesson, students discuss if they find it difficult to stay on task and look at ways to help them modify their habits.

Get started

Tell the class about some of the excuses you have heard students use when they don't do their homework, eg *My dog ate my homework! I left it at home by accident! My computer crashed!*

Divide the class into pairs to think about a good excuse to say why you didn't do the homework and write it on a piece of paper.

Collect the pieces of paper and read them out a few at a time. Invite students to say if the excuses are believable or not.

SPEAK AND READ

1

- Divide the class into pairs to read the comic strip and say what reasons Dom gives for not finishing his homework.
- Nominate a student to say the answer.

ANSWER

He says it was too difficult and he didn't understand what to do.

2

- Ask the same pairs to think of more possible reasons for Dom not finishing his homework. Before they start, draw students' attention to the expressions in the PHRASE BYTES box and encourage them to use these to structure their answers.
- Elicit possible reasons in open class.

DO

3

- Divide the class into groups to read and discuss which tips Dom should follow.
- Ask students to talk about each tip and encourage them to say why each tip could help them stay on task.

Alternative procedure: less confident classes
For less confident classes briefly recycle the form and use of *should* and *shouldn't* for giving advice.

4

- Ask students to brainstorm other things Dom could do to stay on task.
- Invite students to write their ideas on the board.
- Discuss the ideas in open class and ask students which tips they think are the most relevant for them.

REFLECT

5

- Focus students on the REFLECTION POINT and elicit whether they agree or not.
- Lead a class discussion of the questions one by one, nominating different students to share their answers.

Extra activity
Write these quotes from interviews with students on the board. Divide the class into pairs to discuss what comments/advice they would give.

1 *I make a list of things I have to do and put stars next to the most important things.*
2 *I never know if it's better to start with the small tasks or the big one(s) first.*
3 *To get started, I open a folder, create sub-folders and add titles.*
4 *I would finish my homework quicker if I could type faster.*

EXTEND

6

- Divide the class into groups to discuss when it is important for pilots, teachers, surgeons and electricians to stay on task.
- Encourage students to do the same for some other jobs.
- Invite different groups to share their answers in open class.

Extra activity
Explain to students that there is a way to organise doing homework, called a Homework Flowchart.

Draw an example of a flowchart on the board and see if the students can tell you how they think they work (a flowchart is a drawing that represents a process by using a series of lines to show the different choices you can make).

Explain to students that all flowcharts have a start and an end point, with a series of instructions and decision boxes in between. Draw these on the board as examples:

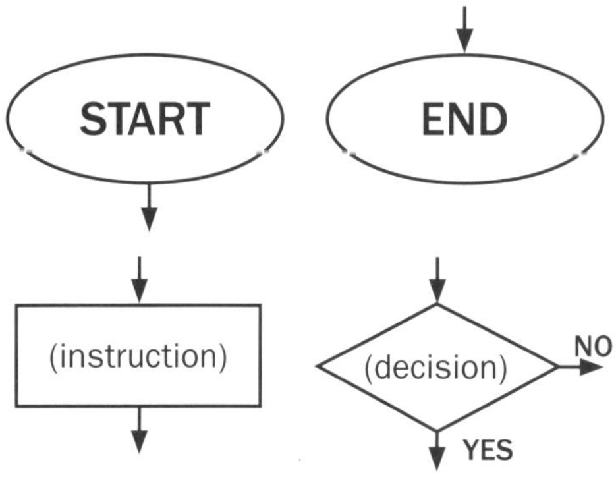

Write the Start sentence on the board: *Do you have homework to do?*

Divide the class into pairs to make a flowchart of the steps they would take to do their homework. Ask them to think about things that can distract them from their task.

Encourage students to compare their ideas with another pair and ask some students to come up and draw their flowcharts on the board.

Homework

Ask students to write a short text to describe where they usually work and distractions they have around them. Ask them to choose three of the tips from today's lesson and explain how they are going to implement changes to help them stay on task and avoid distractions.

SPEAKING My sister thinks ...

Present other people's opinions Page 35

STAGE	TIME	FOCUS
GET STARTED		Play a game to recycle adverbs of degree and comparative adverbs.
SPEAK		Discuss your favourite singers or groups.
WATCH OR LISTEN		Watch or listen to a scene with two people giving and asking for opinions. Practise sentence stress for emphasising and contrasting information.
ACT		Prepare and present a scene where you talk about different opinions.

Get started

Play a game of *Three in a Row* (see Games page 33) with the grid below. To win a square, teams take it in turns to choose a square and make a grammatically correct sentence with an adverb of degree or a comparative or superlative adverb. The sentence must be related to the topic given, eg [music] *I think Adele gave a really great concert.* [sport] *Usain Bolt runs faster than any other athlete.*

Sport	Countries	Singers/groups
Music	Films	Jobs
Food and drink	Famous people	Places

SPEAK

1

- Divide the class into pairs to complete the tasks. Set a time limit of three minutes.
- In open class, nominate different students to talk about the singers and groups on their lists and their partner's.

WATCH OR LISTEN

2 1.41

- Ask students *What do you think the couple in the photo are doing?* (Listening to music) *Do you think they like what they're listening to?*
- Books closed. Play the scene for students to watch or listen and decide what Veena wants to ask Finn's sister.
- Ask students to read the conversation and check their answers.

ANSWERS / VIDEO/AUDIO SCRIPT 1.41

Veena wants to ask Finn's sister what Finn thinks about a band because he won't say.

Veena: What do you think?
Finn: My sister thinks they're great. She's got all their albums.
Veena: You're lucky. My sister really hates them.
Finn: Why?
Veena: She says they can't sing. She says they're rubbish.
Finn: Oh, right. A lot of people didn't like their last concert.
Veena: People are always saying bad things about them.
Finn: Maybe they're right. My brother says they don't play their instruments.
Veena: I don't care what other people think. I think they're totally amazing.
Finn: Good.
Veena: So what's your opinion?
Finn: Sorry?
Veena: You've told me what everyone else thinks. What about you? What do you think?
Finn: Honestly? I don't have an opinion.
Veena: Liar. I'll have to ask your sister.

3 1.41

- Focus students on the conversation and encourage them to write in as many of the missing words as they can.
- Play the scene again for students to listen and check, or complete, their answers.

ANSWERS

1 albums 2 concert 3 instruments 4 sister

4 1.42

- Play the track for students to listen and repeat, paying special attention to the words which are stressed. You could drill the sentences chorally and individually.

ANSWERS / AUDIO SCRIPT 1.42

1 My sister thinks they're great.
2 My sister really hates them.
3 She says they can't sing.
4 She says they're rubbish.
5 People are always saying ...
6 My brother says ...

Extra activity

Divide the class into pairs to read out the conversation. Encourage them to pay special attention to the words that are stressed.

5

- Divide the class into pairs to discuss the questions.

ACT

6 1.43

- Divide the class into groups of three or four to complete the tasks.
- First, ask students to talk about things they like and find something they have different opinions about.
- Then ask students to prepare a scene similar to the one in Exercise 2. Remind them to include different opinions and other people's opinions. Before they start, play the track with the expressions in the PHRASEBOOK box and encourage students to use them.
- Invite groups to present their scene to another group.

Alternative procedure: less confident classes

In less confident classes, students may need to practise the conversation in a more structured way. Copy this structure onto the board and elicit key sentences for each stage. Ask students to act out the conversation in pairs and then ask them to form different pairs and try to perform the conversation without looking at the board.

Student A	Student B
Ask for an opinion about a band or a singer	Say what someone else thinks
Say what that person thinks	Ask why
Say why	Agree or disagree and say what other people think
Give your opinion	Give your opinion

Homework

Ask students to research opinions about a singer or group of their choice and write a short report with the results.

Give them these general guidelines: *Summarise what people have said and don't go into too much detail; Say who made each comment; Say what you have discovered and write a sentence or two to sum up your report.*

WRITING My music profile

Link contrasting ideas

Page 36

STAGE	TIME	FOCUS
GET STARTED		Discuss music you have listened to or played over the last week and recycle music vocabulary from the unit.
SPEAK AND READ		Read a music profile and talk about a famous musician. Learn how to link contrasting ideas with *but*, *although*, *even though* and *however*.
PRACTISE		Link sentences together to make them more complex.
PLAN		Plan a profile of your music hero.
WRITE AND CHECK		Write the music profile and check you have covered the points in the plan.
SHARE		Swap your profile with other students and compare them.

Get started

Ask students to work individually and write five sentences about all the different types of music they have played or listened to over the last week. Encourage them to use at least five words from this unit in their sentences.

Invite students to read out their sentences to their partner for them to write down all the words connected to music they hear.

Ask students to discuss each other's sentences and find two similarities and two differences.

SPEAK AND READ

1

- Refer students to the man in the photo. Divide the class into pairs to discuss what kind of music they think he plays. Don't confirm the answer at this point. Before they start, focus students on the expressions in the PHRASE BYTES and encourage them to use these in their answers.

2

- Ask students to read the music profile to check their answer to Exercise 1.
- Ask them if they are surprised by the answer.

ANSWER

Lang Lang is a classical pianist.

GO BEYOND FOR TEACHERS

Lang Lang

At the age of two, Lang Lang fell in love with music when he watched the Tom and Jerry episode *The Cat Concerto*, which features the Hungarian Rhapsody No. 2 by Franz Liszt. According to Lang, this first contact with Western music is what motivated him to learn piano. When Lang was nine years old, he had some difficulties with his lessons and he was expelled from his piano tutor's studio for 'lack of talent'. The music teacher at his state school and his family encouraged Lang to keep playing.

Extra activity

Write these statements on the board and ask students to say if they are true or false, correcting the false ones:

Lang Lang came from a rich background. (False. He grew up in a poor area of Beijing and his family didn't have much money.)

His piano teacher helped make Lang Lang famous. (False. His piano teacher told him that he had no talent and should stop playing.)

He practised a lot to become a star. (True. He practised night and day.)

Everybody likes Lang Lang. (False. Some people don't like his music.)

3a

- Ask students to read the tips in the HOW TO box. Invite a volunteer to read them out.

3b

- Elicit the linking words to contrast ideas that appear in the HOW TO box. Ask students to underline these words in the text and say which word appears twice.

ANSWER

however appears twice

PRACTISE

4

- Ask students to link the sentences together using the words in brackets. If necessary, go through the first one as an example with the class.
- Encourage students to compare their sentences in pairs before you check them in open class.

ANSWERS

1 Although Lang Lang's teacher said he had no talent, he managed to become successful.
2 He grew up in China. When he was fifteen, however, he moved to the United States. / He grew up in China. However, when he was fifteen he moved to the United States.
3 He normally records classical music, but he has also recorded music for video games.
4 Even though he lives a rock star's life, he finds time to help young people play music.

PLAN

5

- Explain to the students that they are going to write a profile of their music hero. Encourage them to think individually about a musician they know well.
- Focus their attention on the **Writing plan** and go through the structure of the profile with them.
- Ask them to write the ideas for their plan using the paragraph headings suggested in the box. Set a time limit of 10 minutes. Circulate and help students if necessary.

WRITE AND CHECK

6

- Ask students to use their plan and the model text to help them write their profile. Encourage them to use some of the language from this unit. Set a time limit of 10 minutes.
- When students have finished writing, encourage them to check their work.

Alternative procedure

Students need a lot of practice writing under exam conditions. It is a good idea to practise this during the year at different points. You could set up Exercise 6 as a simulation of a writing exam. Tell students they have a time limit of 18 minutes and they must write at least 80–100 words. Make sure that students have only the things allowed in a real exam and their bags are closed. If possible, give them a blank piece of paper to write on.

Collect the texts in and mark them in a similar way to how they are marked in an exam at this level. Give out the results in the next lesson and discuss the different areas students are assessed on in writing, as well as any difficulties they had when writing under exam conditions.

SHARE

7

- Ask students to swap their profiles with one or two classmates and compare them.

Homework

Ask students to research another famous person who was told they had no talent and would never succeed (eg JK Rowling, Walt Disney, Michael Jordan, Steven Spielberg). Ask them to bring their stories to share with others at the start of the next lesson. Ask them to write notes to help them present their information orally. Tell students that you will take in their written notes and mark them.

VOCABULARY Music words

1

- Divide the class into pairs to look at the words in the box and say what they mean. Encourage them to circle any words they don't remember.
- Ask students to work individually to read and complete the poster with the words in the box. Point out that they can use the pictures to help them.
- Encourage them to compare their answers in pairs and say if they now remember the meaning of any items they circled earlier. Then check answers in open class.

ANSWERS
1 audience 2 venue 3 performance 4 opera
5 Orchestra 6 conductor 7 jazz 8 trumpet
9 folk 10 flute 11 Brass band 12 bands

Adverbs of degree

2

- Invite students to look quickly at the quotes by members of the audience after Justin's concert and to say if most people thought it was good or bad (*most people thought it was good*).
- Ask students to complete the quotes with adverbs of degree. Point out that the first letter of each missing word is given.
- Nominate different students to read out each of the quotes, asking them to exaggerate the intonation on the adverb of degree.
- Check the spelling of the answers by inviting students to write them on the board.

ANSWERS
1 really 2 bit 3 lot 4 totally 5 pretty
6 extremely 7 very 8 terribly 9 incredibly
10 quite

GRAMMAR Verbs followed by *-ing* form or *to* + infinitive

3

- Explain to students that they are going to read an interview with Justin.
- Ask them to complete the interview with either the *-ing* or the infinitive with the *to* form of the verbs in brackets.
- Check answers in open class. Then divide the class into pairs to read the conversation out loud.

ANSWERS
1 coming 2 playing 3 to finish
4 working / to work 5 playing / to play
6 performing / to perform 7 being / to be
8 to spend

Comparison of adverbs

4

- Encourage students to read the news story about Justin's concert quickly and say whether he played well or badly (*badly*).
- Ask them complete the story with the correct form of the adverbs, reminding them to add *as* where necessary.
- Nominate different students to read out their answers in open class.

ANSWERS
1 faster 2 the hardest 3 as well 4 as quickly
5 longer 6 harder

Extra Resources

Go to the Teacher's Resource Centre at www.macmillanbeyond.com for:

- downloadable audio and audio scripts for the Student's Book and Workbook
- videos and video scripts
- extra vocabulary at two levels of difficulty
- extra grammar at two levels of difficulty
- CLIL lessons, with full teacher's notes
- a life skills lesson, with full teacher's notes
- Speaking Database materials
- the *Beyond* B1 wordlist
- test generator for Unit 3 testing materials (all skills)
- tips for using the Grammar Database
- and more!

Go to the Workbook pages 28–39 for further practice material

UNIT 4 VERY IMPORTANT PEOPLE

IN THE PICTURE Relationships

Talk about people you know

Pages 38–39

STAGE	TIME	FOCUS
GET STARTED		Introduce the theme of the lesson and talk about relationships.
WORK WITH WORDS		Recycle ways to describe people's appearance and character. Review the difference between *What's she like?* and *What does she look like?* Learn new words related to people and relationships. Describe relationships and personalities. Watch a video of a teenager making a relationship tree and talking about the people on it.
SPEAK		Make your own relationship tree and talk about people you know well, acquaintances and relatives.

Get started

Write the initials of these famous couples on the board: *Romeo and Juliet*, *Mickey Mouse and Minnie Mouse*, *Brad Pitt and Angelina Jolie*.

Invite students to complete their names. If they are not sure, invite them to ask you some *Yes/No* questions to help them decide.

Divide the class into pairs to think of as many famous couples as they can from history or modern day, real or fictional. Set a time limit of two minutes. The pair with the most couples on their list will be the winner. When the time is up, invite students to write their famous couples on the board. Encourage students to say if they think they are good couples together and to describe them. Prompt them with questions if necessary. Recycle *What's he/she like?* and *What does he/she look like?*

Extra activity

Display a picture of a famous person or couple. Write on the board *What does he/she look like?* and elicit answers from different students. Recycle hair colour, eye colour, height and weight, eg *He/She has blond hair and blue eyes. He/She's tall, handsome/beautiful …* . Then repeat the procedure with *What's he/she like?*, eg *He/She's funny, intelligent, friendly …* .

Show students a different picture and ask them to work in pairs to ask and answer the two questions.

WORK WITH WORDS

1a and 1b RECALL

- Divide the class into pairs to do both tasks. Refer students to the instructions and set a time limit of three minutes.
- Ask students to complete the sentences with the words in the box.
- Encourage students to make a list of four other ways to complete each answer.
- Elicit and check answers in open class.
- Ask students to do the Work with Words task on page 133.

ANSWERS

Exercise 1a

She's bad-tempered/patient/shy.

She's tall. And she's got a small nose / wavy hair.

2

- Divide the class into pairs to take it in turns to describe a person in the photos on the relationship tree for their partner to guess.

3 1.44

- Explain to students that they will hear some definitions of relationships for them to match to the words. Play the track, pausing after the first definition to point out the example.
- Encourage students to compare their answers in pairs. Don't confirm the answers at this point.

ANSWERS / AUDIO SCRIPT 1.44

See Exercise 4 for answers.

1 A really good friend
2 Somebody that lives near you
3 A friend that you've known for a long time
4 Somebody in your class at school
5 Somebody that you communicate with on the internet
6 Somebody that comes to your home to visit
7 A member of your family that doesn't usually live with you
8 Somebody you're having a romantic relationship with
9 A friend's friend, not your friend
10 Somebody that plays for the same team as you
11 Somebody that you know a little, but not a good friend
12 The opposite of a friend

Extra activity
Play the track again and ask students to note down key words. Then ask students to work in small groups and compare their notes. One person in each group acts as 'secretary' to write down the definitions. Encourage them to try to reconstruct the whole definitions. When they have finished, play the track again for students to compare their definitions to the original ones.

4 1.45
- Play the track for students to listen and check their answers. Ask students which key words helped them decide on their answers.
- Play the track again for students to repeat the words. Highlight the silent letters in *friend* and *guest*.

ANSWERS / AUDIO SCRIPT 1.45
1 close friend 2 neighbour 3 old friend 4 classmate
5 online friend 6 guest 7 relative 8 boyfriend/girlfriend
9 friend of a friend 10 team-mate 11 acquaintance
12 enemy

5 1.46
- Explain to the students they are going to listen to Louise talking about people on her relationship tree. Play the track for students to listen and write a relationship from Exercise 2 next to each name. Encourage them to describe their personality too, if the information is given.

ANSWERS / AUDIO SCRIPT 1.46
Mel: old friend Nicola: friend of a friend; shy
Jack: neighbour Matt: close friend; clever
Donna: relative; cheerful, kind, friendly

Mia: Who's that girl with the wavy hair?
Louise: That's Mel. She's a really old friend. Our mums are friends, so I've known her all my life. She's a really old friend, in fact.
Mia: And that girl? The one who looks really confident. Is she really ambitious?
Louise: That's Nicola. She's one of Marc's friend's. And she's not confident and ambitious at all. She's actually very shy.
Mia: And that boy?
Louise: That's Jack. He lives next to us, so I see him almost every day.
Mia: Is that his real hair colour?
Louise: No, he's got dark hair, but he dyes it blond.
Mia: Ooh, look. There's your boyfriend!
Louise: Matt is not my boyfriend. We're just really good friends.
Mia: He's very good looking. And so clever too!
Louise: Well, he was good-looking, but his hair's too short now. He looked better with long hair.
Mia: And that woman with the big smile?
Louise: She's my aunt Donna. She lives in Australia, but we have a video chat every month.
Mia: She looks cheerful.
Louise: Yeah, she's one of those really kind, friendly people.

6 1.46
- Play the track again for students to match the people described in Exercise 5 to the corresponding photos.

ANSWERS
Mel – picture 8 Nicola – picture 3 Jack – picture 4
Matt – picture 1 Donna – picture 5

7 THE MOVING PICTURE
- Explain to the students they are going to watch a video of Veena making a relationship tree.
- Ask students to note down the names of the people and their relationship with her.

ANSWERS / VIDEO/AUDIO SCRIPT
1 Rico – old friend
2 Anna – aunt
3 Tim – neighbour
4 Lucy – online friend
5 Samba – best friend

SPEAK

8a
- Ask students to draw their own relationship tree.

8b
- Divide the class into pairs to talk about the people on their relationship tree. Before they start, draw students' attention to the expressions in the PHRASE BYTES box and encourage them to use these in their conversations.
- Nominate different students to tell the class one interesting thing about their partner.

Alternative procedure: less confident classes
In less confident classes, you could draw a relationship tree on the board for yourself and model this activity first with students. Ask them to ask you questions about some of the people, and tell them about the others.

GO BEYOND
Ask students to do the Go Beyond task on page 133.

Homework
Ask students to write about the people on their relationship tree using the vocabulary and expressions they have learned in this lesson.

READING Close friends

Recognise examples *Page 40*

STAGE	TIME	FOCUS
GET STARTED		Tell a famous short story about two close friends to introduce the theme of the lesson.
SPEAK AND READ		Define what a close friend is and talk about how many close friends people generally have. Read a text about the important qualities of a close friendship. Discuss tips on how to identify examples when you read and find example sentences in the text.
REACT		Discuss close friends and which qualities are most important in a close friendship.

Get started

Draw these simple stick pictures on the board:

Explain to students that you are going to tell them a short story from India and they must put the pictures in order.

Two boys, Raju and Vijay, were good friends. They were on holiday together and they went for a walk in the forest. They were enjoying the walk when suddenly they saw a bear coming at them. They were frightened. Raju knew how to climb up a tree so he ran to the nearest tree and climbed up quickly. He did not think of Vijay. Vijay didn't know how to climb a tree. He thought for a second. He remembered that animals do not like dead bodies. He fell to the ground and did not move. The bear smelled him and thought he was dead so he went away.

Raju asked Vijay, 'What did the bear say to you?'

Elicit students' ideas about what they think the bear said and then tell the students the ending: *Vijay replied, 'The bear told me to keep away from friends like you', and he went on his way.*

Write the expression *A friend in need is a friend indeed* on the board. Ask students what it means (a true friend is someone who helps you when you need them). Elicit if they have similar expressions in their culture.

SPEAK AND READ

1

- Divide the class into pairs to discuss and answer the questions. Set a time limit of two minutes for this.
- Nominate different students to report on what their partner has said.

2 1.47

- Explain to the students that they are going to read an article about close friends. Don't play the audio at this point. Ideas for using the audio are given at the end of the lesson.
- Ask students to read the article and match the friendship qualities in the box to the paragraph headings 1–5.
- Encourage students to compare their answers in pairs before you check them in open class. Elicit the number of close friends we have according to the article.

ANSWERS
1 Respect 2 Honesty 3 Support 4 Good company
5 Trust
The survey says that we have just two close friends.

Fast finishers
Ask fast finishers to do a word-building exercise with the word *friend* and think of as many words as they can (*unfriendly*, *friendly*, *friendless*, *friendship*, *friendliness*, *befriend*).

3a

- Ask students why examples are important when they read a text (they make things easier to understand and help us follow the logic in arguments).
- Refer students to the tips in the HOW TO box. Invite volunteers to read the tips out loud.

3b

- Ask students to read the text again and underline the four expressions that come before examples.

ANSWERS
For instance, if you count everybody ...
... people you don't usually meet, like online friends, ...
... you don't want to hear, such as pointing out ...
... things like hobbies and interests ...

3c

- Explain to students that the first sentence in two of the sections is an example. Encourage them to compare their thoughts in pairs before you ask them to identify the two sections in open class.

ANSWERS
3 Support 4 Good company

4

- Ask students which tips in the HOW TO box they used to help them in Exercises 3b and 3c.

Extra activity
Books closed. Dictate these unfinished sentences and ask students to complete them from memory. Encourage them to read the article again to either complete or check their answers.

1 *Some people have thousands of friends if they include ...*
2 *If you respect your close friends, you don't want ...*
3 *Sometimes a close friend needs to tell you things ...*
4 *If other people are giving you problems, a close friend will ...*
5 *To be good friends with someone it isn't necessary to ...*
6 *Close friends don't talk about you ...*

ANSWERS
1 online friends 2 them to change
3 you don't want to hear 4 defend you
5 have hobbies and interests in common 6 behind your back

REACT

5

- Divide the class into pairs to discuss the questions.
- Nominate different students to share their point of view with the class, giving their reasons. Try to develop a class discussion on the different points. You could ask some general questions to open the discussion: *How many good friends do you have? How do you know you have a good friend? What can change a friendship?*

Extra activity

Write these prompts on the board: *How you met*; *How long ago you met*; *What special qualities he/she has*; *How often you see each other*; *How he/she makes you feel*; *How long you think you'll stay friends*.

Ask students to work in pairs to tell each other about a close friend. You could model this activity by telling students about a close friend of yours.

Recorded reading text 1.47

The reading text is recorded as an extra audio track which can be exploited for various purposes.

Use the audio in this lesson to help students identify where the words and phrases that come before examples are. Give students a sound or action for each word or phrase (*like*, *such as*, *for instance*) eg a clap for *like*. Play the track before Exercise 3b and ask the students to do the sound or action when they hear the relevant example words or phrases.

GO BEYOND

Ask students to do the task on page 133.

Homework

Ask students to write a short text about a close friend of theirs, based on the prompts in the extra activity. Ask students to give examples to illustrate their friend's special qualities.

GRAMMAR First conditional with *if/unless*

Talk about possible situations in the future *Page 41*

STAGE	TIME	FOCUS
GET STARTED		Talk about Murphy's Law and introduce the first conditional form.
READ AND LISTEN		Read and listen to a conversation about a girl discussing who she wants to come to her barbecue.
STUDY		Use the conversation to complete the grammar explanations about the first conditional with *if/unless*.
PRACTISE		Transform sentences in the first conditional so that they have the same meaning. Complete first conditional sentences in a conversation.
WRITE AND SPEAK		Write your ideas about friends and relationships and discuss them in pairs.

Get started

Ask students if they have ever heard of Murphy's Law. Write the following words on the board in a jumbled order and ask students to make a complete sentence that expresses the idea behind Murphy's Law.

will / can / If / wrong, / anything / wrong / go / it / go / .
(If anything can go wrong, it will go wrong.)

Explain this law in other words (if there is a possibility of several things going wrong, the one that will cause the biggest problem will be the one to go wrong) and give a couple of examples: *If you're early, the bus is late. If you're late, the bus is early.*

Write these sentence beginnings on the board and ask students to work in pairs to complete the examples of Murphy's Law: *If you wear something expensive*; *If you drop a piece of toast*; *If you are doing something stupid*; *If you go out in your worst clothes*; *If you go to a party in jeans*; *If you change queue.*

Elicit answers from different pairs around the class. Invite volunteers to create further examples.

GO BEYOND FOR TEACHERS

Murphy's Law

Murphy's Law was born at Edwards Air Force Base in 1949. It was named after Capt. Ed Murphy, an engineer working on Air Force Project. He was frustrated with a technician and famously remarked *'If there is any way to do it wrong, he will'*.

READ AND LISTEN Grammar in context

1 1.48

- Refer students to the photo and ask them to describe what is happening. (Two students/friends are talking.)
- Play the track for students to read and listen to find out who Olga wants at her birthday barbecue.

ANSWERS / AUDIO SCRIPT 1.48

Tim, Bren and Bea
See Student's Book page 41 for audio script.

STUDY

2

- Focus students on the grammar explanations and ask them to complete the information using examples from the conversation in Exercise 1.
- Nominate students to read out the example sentences from Exercise 1 for each of the grammar explanations.
- To further explain the first conditional with *if/unless*, divide the board into two halves. Write *POSSIBLE SITUATION* on the left side and *RESULT* on the right side. Then write, in the left column, two possible situations: *If I study, ... ; Unless we finish quickly, ...* .
- Explain that the *if*-clause describes a possible situation. Highlight that we use the present simple in the *if*-clause.
- Point out that we can use *unless* with a positive verb in the *if*-clause to mean 'if not', so the example on the board means 'If we don't finish quickly'.
- Complete the sentences on the right: *I will pass the exam*; *we'll be late*. Analyse the grammar, pointing out that we use the future simple with *will* + infinitive in the result clause. Alternatively we can use *may* or *might* + infinitive depending on how certain we are of the result.
- Refer students back to the conversation to find another example of the first conditional. (*If I invite Tim, he'll probably argue with Bren.*)

ANSWERS

If you talk they might stop arguing invite

Extra activity

Students may need more controlled practice with the first conditional form before doing Exercise 3. Write these sentences on the board and ask students to work in pairs to fill the gaps with the correct form of the verbs in brackets:

1 *If he ______ late (arrive) again, the trainer ______ (be) angry.*
2 *You ______ (be) sad if you ______ (not revise) for your English exam.*
3 *Unless you ______ (do) your homework now, you ______ (be) stressed.*
4 *I ______ (be) late unless the bus ______ (come) soon.*

ANSWERS

1 arrives; will be 2 will be; don't revise 3 do; will be
4 will be; comes

PRACTISE

3

- Focus students on the pairs of sentences and point out that they should mean the same thing. Invite two students to read out the first sentence and the example. Ask them to use no more than three words.
- Encourage students to compare their answers in pairs before you check them in open class.

ANSWERS

2 you don't send 3 if he can't 4 Unless you invite
5 unless we clean 6 if people don't

4 1.49

- Ask students to read the conversation and choose the correct options to complete it.
- Play the track for them to listen and check their answers.

ANSWERS / AUDIO SCRIPT 1.49

See Student's Book page 41 for the audio script.

1 won't 2 's 3 says 4 will 5 might say 6 'll stop
7 're 8 will stop

Extra activity

Ask students to work in pairs to practise reading the conversation out loud, paying attention to sentence stress and rhythm.

If you feel it would be useful before students read out the conversation, do some choral drilling and/or backchaining to practise the rhythm (see page 32).

Fast finishers

Get fast finishers to look at the text on page 40 and find as many examples as they can of first conditional sentences.

WRITE AND SPEAK

5

- Ask students to work individually to complete the sentences with their own ideas.

6

- Divide the class into pairs to take it in turns to read out their sentences from Exercise 5. Encourage students to say if they agree or not and to explain why.
- Invite students to read out some of their sentences in open class for discussion.

Homework

Ask students to write a first conditional chain of at least five sentences. Each sentence must begin with the idea expressed in the second half of the previous sentence. Ask students to help you build an example on the board, eg *If I bring an umbrella, it won't rain. If it doesn't rain, I won't get wet. If I don't get wet, I'll wear my new coat. If I wear my new coat, my mum might be happy. If my mum's happy, I may get a nice supper. If I get a nice supper, I'll sleep really well. If I sleep really well, I'll have a good day tomorrow!*

LISTENING AND VOCABULARY Back from the future

Use stress and intonation to help you understand Page 42

STAGE	TIME	FOCUS
GET STARTED		Recycle words to describe a good friend and think about words to describe the worst friend ever.
SPEAK AND LISTEN		Look at a picture and predict the situation. Listen to a podcast to see if your predictions were correct. Use stress and intonation to help you understand.
WORK WITH WORDS		Match the extreme adjectives to their definitions.
REACT		Imagine you're 34 years old and describe your situation, what you look like and how you feel.

Get started

Draw a picture of a smiling face on the board and write *Best Friend* next to the picture.

Write this sentence as a wordsnake under the face and ask students to find five important qualities in a close friendship: *A good friend accepts you the way you are, tells the truth, shares your ideas, is generous with their time and can keep a secret.*

Draw a picture of a mischievous face and write *Worst Friend Ever* next to the picture.

Divide the class into pairs to make a word snake with five undesirable qualities. Ask students to swap their word snakes with another pair for them to work out the five undesirable qualities. Ask students to discuss in groups of four which undesirable quality is the worst. Nominate different students to report on the discussion in their group.

SPEAK AND LISTEN

1

- Refer students to the picture. Divide the class into pairs to discuss the questions.
- Nominate different students to share their ideas.

2a

- Ask students to read the tips in the HOW TO box. Invite a volunteer to read them out loud.

2b 1.50

- Play the track for students to listen to a podcast and check their predictions in Exercise 1.

ANSWERS / AUDIO SCRIPT 1.50

A 34-year-old woman woke up with a memory problem and thought she was 15 again. In the picture, we see her looking at herself in the mirror. The mirror shows how she really looks and the teenager looking in the mirror shows how she thinks she looks.

Victor: Hi, this is Victor Sanchez.
Linda: And this is Linda Frantum. Welcome to this week's episode of *Stranger than Fiction*, the podcast that looks at some amazing real stories.
Victor: So what's this week's story, Linda?
Linda: Let me start with a question. What would you do if you woke up one morning and you were 34 years old?
Victor: I'd be furious! I love being 15! But that's impossible.
Linda: Naomi Jacobs thought this had happened to her.
Victor: I don't understand.
Linda: Her story starts when she woke up one morning and didn't recognise where she was. So she called out to see who was there and she didn't recognise her own voice. But things got really scary when she found the bathroom. When she looked in the mirror she was shocked to see her own face, but she looked ancient. She looked exhausted too, with huge black bags under her eyes.
Victor: That's awful. If that happened to me, I'd be terrified. But I still don't understand.
Linda: She was suffering from a really rare condition when your brain deletes all your recent memories. So it's like going back in time to before you had those memories. Naomi was 34, but when she woke up, she really thought she was 15.
Victor: That's unbelievable! So did she get her memory back?
Linda: She did, but it took a long time. And she had to learn about a whole new world. Just imagine how you'd feel if somebody told you you were actually a mother with a young child. And if you didn't know what a mobile was, or the internet.
Victor: It's hard to imagine. That really is a fascinating story.
Linda: Yep. Life really can be stranger than fiction!

3

- Ask students which tips in the HOW TO box they used to help them in Exercise 2b and encourage them to tick them.

4 1.50

- Play the track again for students to listen and choose the correct options.
- Encourage them to compare their answers in pairs before you check them in open class.

ANSWERS / AUDIO SCRIPT

1 is 2 didn't hear 3 recognised 4 an unusual
5 didn't remember 6 slowly
See Exercise 2b for audio script.

WORK WITH WORDS

5

- Ask students to match the underlined adjectives in the podcast extracts to the definitions.
- Encourage them to compare their answers in pairs before you check them in open class.
- Refer students to the information in the **Get it right** box about using *really* or an extreme adverb of degree before an adjective instead of *very*.

ANSWERS

1 very good or surprising 2 very angry
3 very surprised (in a negative way) 4 very old 5 very tired
6 very big 7 very bad 8 very frightened
9 very difficult to believe 10 very interesting

Extra activity

Read out this short text and ask students to raise their hands (or clap) to stop you every time you say *very* + adjective. Invite them to suggest an extreme adjective as a replacement.

I'm going to tell you a very interesting (fascinating) story. It's about a very old (ancient) man and his very bad (awful) experience. I think you are going to say this story is very difficult to believe (unbelievable) but it is true. He was feeling very tired (exhausted) on his daily walk in the park so he decided to sit down on park bench. He was very surprised (shocked) when the bench started to move. It was a very big (huge) man who was very angry (furious) that someone was sitting on it. At first, the very old (ancient) man was very frightened (terrified), but then he said, 'Oh my goodness me – it's George, my long-lost son'. That is the end of this very surprising (amazing) story.

If there is time, at the end, read out both texts to show students the difference and encourage them to use extreme adjectives in their writing.

6 1.51

- Play the track for students to listen and repeat the adjectives from Exercise 5.

AUDIO SCRIPT 1.51

amazing furious shocked ancient exhausted huge awful terrified unbelievable fascinating

Extra activity

Ask students to add *really* or an extreme adverb of degree to the podcast extracts in Exercise 5. Then ask them to work in pairs to read them out loud, exaggerating the extreme adjective to practise emphatic stress, eg absolutely AMAZING real stories.

You could point out that stress can also be used on the adverb of degree. Alternatively, stress could be used to emphasise the extreme adjective without the need to use an adverb of degree.

7a

- Refer students back to the adjectives in Exercise 5 and ask them to write three true sentences with different adjectives.

7b

- Divide the class into pairs to take it in turns to read out their sentences to their partner. Encourage them to ask at least one question about each sentence. Before they start, invite two students to read out the model conversation.

REACT

8

- Ask students to imagine being in Naomi's situation. Divide the class into pairs to ask each other the questions.
- Nominate different students to share their answers.

GO BEYOND

Ask the students to do the Go Beyond task on page 133.

Homework

Ask students to write a short text about The Worst Friend Ever using as many extreme adjectives with *really* and extreme adverbs of degree as they can. Ask them to read out their texts to the partner at the beginning of the next lesson. Their partner must say 'stop' every time he/she hears an extreme adjective and define it by saying *very* and the appropriate adjective.

GRAMMAR Second conditional

Talk about imaginary situations in the present and future *Page 43*

STAGE	TIME	FOCUS
GET STARTED		Race against the clock to recycle regular and irregular past tense forms.
READ AND LISTEN		Read and listen to a conversation about the type of parents two friends think they will be.
STUDY		Choose the correct options to complete the grammar explanation about the second conditional.
PRACTISE		Practise the target language in written exercises.
SPEAK		Exchange opinions and compare your ideas.

Get started

Divide the class into pairs to think of a verb in the past simple tense (not the past participle), either regular or irregular, for each of the letters of the alphabet. Set a time limit of five minutes and give regular updates on the time remaining.

Divide the board into five sections A–E, F–J, K–O, P–T, U–Z and invite students to come up to the board and write the past tense verbs they have for one of the sections.

Recycle the pronunciation of regular past simple forms, ie /t/, /d/ and /ɪd/, and check their spelling by inviting the class to point out any words that need correcting.

READ AND LISTEN Grammar in context

1 1.52

- Refer students to the picture and ask them to describe it. Ask: *Does he feel calm? What is he thinking?*
- Ask students to read and listen to the conversation and decide what type of parents Raj and Kim think they might be.
- Elicit answers in open class.

ANSWERS

Kim would be more easy-going than her parents. Raj would be quite strict.

STUDY

2

- Point out to students that the verbs in orange in the conversation in Exercise 1 are in second conditional sentences.
- Ask them to use the examples in the conversation to help them complete the grammar explanations.
- Check answers in open class.

ANSWERS
wouldn't 'd Would

Extra activity
Give students further practice of using the second conditional by asking them some questions about unlikely or imaginary situations. Ask: *What would you do if you won the lottery?* Develop some of their ideas by making follow-up questions out of their answers, eg *If you bought a new car, what kind of car would you buy?*

Write some other examples on the board and elicit answers, eg *If you lived on Mars, what would you eat? If you were an animal, which animal would you be? If you didn't live in this country, where would you like to live?*

Make sure students answer with the correct form.

Encourage students to think of three questions in the second conditional to ask their partner. They ask and answer the questions, paying attention to the form.

Extra activity
To give students extended practice with the second conditional form and the pronunciation of *'d*, ask students to make a chain around the classroom of second conditional clauses.

Write *If I had a million dollars, …* on the board and ask a student to finish the sentence in his/her own words, eg *I'd travel round the world.* The next student takes the second clause from the first student's sentence and changes it to the first clause of another sentence to continue using this clause, ie *If I travelled round the world, I'd go by ship,* etc.

Some other starting sentences could be: *I'd be happy if … ; If I lived in another country … ; If I had more money …*

PRACTISE

3

- Ask students to match the two parts of the sentences.
- Check answers by nominating different students to read out the full sentences.

ANSWERS
2 b 3 e 4 f 5 c 6 a

Extra activity
Give students 30 seconds to memorise the sentences in Exercise 3. Divide the class into pairs to take it in turns to test each other. One student closes his/her book and the other student reads out the first part of the sentence to see if his/her partner can remember the ending.

4

- Ask students to consider the sentences in Exercise 3 and say if they are true for them. If they aren't, invite students to change them to make them true.
- Circulate and monitor, helping students with any difficulties.

5

- Ask students to complete the sentences with the correct form of the verbs in brackets.
- Encourage them to check their answers in pairs before you check them in open class.

ANSWERS
1 woke 2 'd live 3 had 4 'd spend; were
5 could; 'd go 6 would give; won

6

- Ask students to write questions for the sentences in Exercise 5.
- Draw students' attention to the example question.

ANSWERS
2 Where would you live if you could study in another country?
3 If you had a special talent, what would you want to be?
4 What would you do on the extra day if there were eight days in a week?
5 If you could travel back in time for a day, where would you go?
6 What would your family do if you won the lottery?

7a 1.53 PRONOUNCE

- Ask students to read the instructions carefully.
- Play the track for students to listen and underline the stressed words or phrases in the sentences.

ANSWERS / AUDIO SCRIPT 1.53
A: If you <u>woke</u> up with <u>superpowers</u>, <u>what</u> would you <u>do</u>?
B: I'd <u>fly</u> round the <u>world</u>.
C: I <u>wouldn't</u> do <u>anything</u>. I'd <u>go</u> back to <u>sleep</u>.

Extra activity
Ask students to practise saying the conversation in pairs. Encourage them to put more emphasis on the stressed words to reproduce the rhythm of English speech.

7b 1.54

- Play the track for students to listen and repeat the sentences, paying attention to their rhythm.

AUDIO SCRIPT 1.54
See Exercise 7a for audio script.

SPEAK

8

- Divide the class into pairs to ask and answer the questions in Exercise 6 giving reasons for their answers.
- Circulate and monitor, helping students as necessary.

Homework

Ask students to use their imagination to write second conditional sentences using these beginnings: *I'd buy a new computer; I'd go to the party; If I didn't feel so ill; I'd go to the beach; If dolphins could speak; I would be rich.*

At the beginning of the next class, students can compare sentences and decide which are the most imaginative.

STAGE	TIME	FOCUS
GET STARTED		Make a human knot to introduce the theme of decision-making and how our decisions affect others.
SPEAK AND READ		Read an activity sheet and discuss a student's answers, what you think she is like and which options she may choose.
DO		Do the activity sheet and discuss the choices you made with your partner.
REFLECT		Reflect on deciding what is important for you in different areas of life and why making choices can be difficult.
EXTEND		Talk about the choices you might make in the future concerning your studies and work.

LIFE SKILLS

DECIDE WHAT'S IMPORTANT TO YOU

In this lesson, students work on decision-making – the process of choosing what to do by considering different options and thinking about their consequences. Decision-making becomes increasingly important during adolescence, as teenagers become more autonomous and encounter more choices with less and less parental or tutorial support. The choices teenagers make affect their own lives and the lives of others as well.

Get started

Invite six to eight volunteers to come to the front of the class. Ask them to get into a circle and reach across to take the hands of two different people standing on the other side of the circle, but they can't hold hands with the person next to them. When everyone has grabbed hands, you have a human knot. Now challenge students to undo the knot without letting go of each other's hands. Remind participants to take their time and make sure no one gets hurt. Ask students: *What did you do to undo the human knot? How did you make sure no one got hurt?* Tell students that today they are going to be looking at making choices.

SPEAK AND READ

1

- Refer students to the photo and invite them to say what Claire looks like and what they think she's like.
- Focus students on Claire's answers and, after they have read them, encourage them to choose two adjectives from the box to describe her.
- Ask them to compare their chosen words in pairs before you elicit some of them in open class.

2

- Divide the class into pairs to talk about Claire's answers and say which options they think she'll choose in Activity 2 and explain why. Draw students' attention to the expressions in the PHRASE BYTES box and encourage them to use these in their answers.
- In open class, nominate different students to say what they think the reasons may be.

DO

3

- Ask students to do Activity 1 on the activity sheet.

4

- Give students 30 seconds to do Activity 2, so that they don't have too much time to reflect.

5

- Divide the class into pairs to explain their choices. Ask students to explain to each other why they made these choices and if there are any choices they would change.

REFLECT

6

- Focus students on the REFLECTION POINT and elicit whether they agree or not.
- Lead a class discussion on the questions, nominating different students to share their answers.

EXTEND

7

- Ask students to repeat the procedure they used in Exercises 3, 4 and 5 for these new questions.
- Nominate different students to share their answers and develop a class discussion on the jobs they want to do.

Extra activity

As a class, brainstorm other areas where students will have to make decisions, eg Money, Relationships, Health, Where to live. Discuss what type of decisions they may have to make in the future and which ones are the most critical.

Homework

Ask students to write a sentence for each of these instructions.

Describe a decision that you made a few years ago.
Describe another decision that you made more recently.
Describe a decision that you've made that's been good for you.
Describe a decision that you've made that's been bad for you.
At the beginning of the next class, put students into pairs to ask each other questions about the decisions they've made.

SPEAKING Do you mind?

Make and react to requests

Page 45

STAGE	TIME	FOCUS
GET STARTED		Talk about personal possessions and recycle *lend* and *borrow*.
SPEAK		Discuss who you would talk to if you needed something and what their reaction would be.
WATCH OR LISTEN		Watch or listen to a scene where Leo makes requests to different people and note the reactions to these requests. Practise making requests and accepting and refusing requests in formal and informal situations.
ACT		Prepare informal and formal conversations making and reacting to requests in different situations.

Get started

Write this famous old saying on the board: *Neither a borrower nor a lender be.* Ask students if they have heard of this expression and if they know of its origin. (It is a quote from Shakespeare's *Hamlet*, Act 1, Scene 3 written in 1602.) Ask what students think the meaning may be (it's wiser to neither lend nor borrow things, especially money) and if they have a similar expression in their own culture.

Write this list of objects on the board: *toothbrush, umbrella, homework, mobile phone, MP3 player, clothes, pen*.

Ask students if they would be prepared to lend them to someone close, someone they don't know very well, or if they would never lend them to anyone. Discuss their reasons.

Write *Would you ... ?* and *Can I ... ?* on the board and ask students to complete the questions using *borrow* and *lend* + noun. If necessary, remind students that the person with the item lends it and the person without the item borrows it. Ask students to work in pairs to practise using the structures in short conversations with their partner. (See Tips page 29)

SPEAK

1

- Refer students to the photos and ask them to describe what they think is happening in each one.
- Divide the class into pairs to read the situations and discuss the questions. Set a time limit of three minutes.
- Nominate different students to share their answers.

WATCH OR LISTEN

2 1.55

- Books closed. Play the scene for students to watch or listen and decide who Leo talks to each situation and who says 'no' to his requests.
- Ask students to read the conversations to check their answers.
- Nominate a student to say the answer.

ANSWERS / VIDEO/AUDIO SCRIPT 1.55

In the first conversation, Leo talks to his dad. His dad says he can drive him to the festival but he can't come to get him afterwards.
In the second conversation, Leo talks to Jack.
In the third conversation, Leo talks to Mr Giggs. Mr Giggs says he can't drive Leo home but he can use his phone.

Leo: Dad, can you drive me to the festival?
Dad: All right. But you'll have to wait 20 minutes.
Leo: No problem. Can we take Jack too?
Dad: OK.
Leo: Thanks. And can you come and get me later?
Dad: Sorry, I can't. Mum needs the car tonight.

Leo: Jack, could you lend me some money for a drink?
Jack: Sure.
Leo: And do you mind if I use your phone to call Kate?
Jack: No, go ahead.
Leo: Thanks.

Leo: Mr Giggs, could I ask you a favour?
Mr Giggs: Of course.
Leo: Would you drive me home, please? My dad can't come and get me, and I think I've missed the last bus.
Mr Giggs: I'm sorry, but there's no space in the car.
Leo: OK. Would you mind if I used your phone to call my mother?
Mr Giggs: No, of course not. Here you are.
Leo: Thank you.

3 1.55

- Ask students to complete the conversations with the words in the box.
- Play the scene again for students to listen and check or complete their answers.

ANSWERS

1 take 2 lend 3 use 4 ask 5 drive 6 used

4

- Ask students to choose the best option for formal situations, using the conversations to help them.

ANSWERS

1 Could/Would 2 Say 3 Would 4 Of course
5 I'm afraid ...

5 1.56

- Play the track for students to listen and repeat.

AUDIO SCRIPT 1.56

1 **Leo:** Can you drive me to the festival?
Dad: All right.
Leo: Can we take Jack too?
Dad: OK.
2 **Leo:** Could you lend me some money?
Jack: Sure.
Leo: Do you mind if I use your phone?
Jack: No, go ahead.
3 **Leo:** Could I ask you a favour?
Mr Giggs: Of course.
Leo: Would you drive me home, please?
Mr Giggs: I'm sorry, but there's no space in the car.

ACT

6 1.57

- Divide the class into pairs to prepare a formal and informal conversation. Before they start, play the track with the expressions in the PHRASEBOOK box and encourage students to use these.
- Invite students to present their scenes to another pair for them to say who's talking in each conversation and if it's formal or informal.
- Invite volunteers to present their conversations to the class.

Homework

Ask students to write formal and informal requests with one of these words or phrases in each sentence: *a lift home, your calculator, €10, window, salt.*

In the next class, ask students to read out their requests to a partner to say whether the request is formal or informal and then accept or refuse appropriately.

WRITING A poem about true friends

Use a dictionary Page 46

STAGE	TIME	FOCUS
GET STARTED		Write an acrostic poem and recycle vocabulary related to friendship.
SPEAK AND READ		Talk about poems with a partner. Read the poems about friends and answer the questions. Read some tips on how to use a dictionary.
PRACTISE		Use a dictionary entry to help answer questions about the word *row*.
PLAN		Plan a poem about friends.
WRITE AND CHECK		Write the poem and check you have covered the points in the plan.
SHARE		Swap your poem with other students and discuss it.

Get started

Ask students to write an acrostic poem with the name of a close friend. Explain that acrostic poems are easy to write: they should write the name of their close friend in capital letters down the left side of the page. They then think of a word that begins with each capital letter to describe their friend. Show the class an example, eg:

J olly
O rganised
E asy-going

As students finish, ask them to read out their acrostic poems to a partner to see if their close friends have similar or different qualities. Invite some students to read out their poems.

SPEAK AND READ

1

- Divide the class into pairs to answer the questions.
- Nominate different students around the class to answer the questions and try to develop a discussion on poetry and famous poets students know and have read.

2

- Focus students on the poem and give them time to read it.
- Then ask them to answer the questions.
- Ask students which lines they agreed with and if they liked the poem and to say why or why not.

3a

- Ask students to read the tips in the HOW TO box. Invite a volunteer to read them out.

3b

- Ask students to read the poem again and answer the questions.

ANSWERS

1 Students' own answers
2 *brother* rhymes with *other*

PRACTISE

4

- Ask students to use the dictionary entry and the tips in the HOW TO box to help them answer the questions.
- Encourage students to compare their answers in pairs before you nominate different students to read out their answers.

ANSWERS

1 a noun 2 a noisy argument 3 it rhymes with *now*

PLAN

5

- Explain to students that they are going to write a poem about friends.
- Focus their attention on the **Writing plan** and go through the different stages with them.
- Give them 10 minutes to write their ideas for their plan. Circulate and help students if necessary.

WRITE AND CHECK

6

- Ask students to use their plan and the model poem to write their own poem. Encourage them to use some of the language they have studied in this unit. Allow 10 minutes.
- When students have finished writing, encourage them to check their work.

SHARE

7

- Ask students to swap their poems with one or two classmates to read and discuss if they like the poem they have read and explain why or why not.

Homework

Ask students to research a poet in their own language or in English and copy out a short section of the poem into their notebooks. If the poem is in their own language, ask students to find an English translation. If this is not possible, ask them to write down the essential ideas in the poem. At the start of the next class, ask students to work in pairs to read out their poems and discuss if they liked their partner's choice or not and say why.

VOCABULARY People and relationships

1

- Ask students what the acronym *VIP* stands for (*Very Important Person*) and invite them to tell their partner who the VIPs are in their own lives.
- Encourage students to match the people and the relationships on the notice to the definitions. Tell students there is one word in the box that isn't used (parents).
- Encourage students to compare their answers in pairs before you check them in open class.

ANSWERS
1 old friends 2 girlfriends/boyfriends 3 relatives
4 online friends 5 enemies 6 close friends
7 team-mates 8 neighbours 9 classmates
10 acquaintances 11 guests 12 friends of friends

Extreme adjectives

2

- Refer students to the pictures and ask them to describe the people. Elicit what type of person students think each one is.
- Ask them to complete the adjectives in the description of the picture. Point out that the first and last letter of each adjective is given. (See Tips page 29)
- Nominate different students to read the text out loud, sentence by sentence to check answers.

ANSWERS
1 huge 2 ancient 3 terrified 4 furious
5 fascinating 6 exhausted 7 shocked 8 awful
9 amazing 10 unbelievable

GRAMMAR First conditional with *if/unless*

3

- Explain to students that they are going to read the rules for the VIP Friends Club. Invite them to predict what they think some of the rules might be.
- Ask students to use the first conditional form to complete the club rules.
- Circulate and monitor students and stop mid-task if you feel that you need to review the form of the first conditional.
- Check answers in open class.

ANSWERS
1 become 2 won't repeat 3 won't bring
4 doesn't want 5 break 6 'll be

Second conditional

4

- Write this rule on the board: *We use the first/second conditional to talk about things in the present or the future that are not likely to happen, imaginary or impossible*. Ask students to choose which option is correct (*the second conditional*).
- Encourage students to give some examples of second conditional sentences.
- Explain that Erin is asking Matt about what he would say about the club to other people.
- Ask students to complete the interview.
- Check answers in open class before dividing the class into pairs to read the interview out loud.

ANSWERS
1 asked 2 'd say 3 would 4 wanted 5 wouldn't
6 gave 7 couldn't 8 'd find

Extra Resources

Go to the Teacher's Resource Centre at www.macmillanbeyond.com for:

- the Speaking section of the Progress Check 3&4
- a downloadable project linked to Units 3–4
- downloadable audio and audio scripts for the Student's Book and Workbook
- videos and video scripts
- extra vocabulary at two levels of difficulty
- extra grammar at two levels of difficulty
- culture lessons, with full teacher's notes
- a life skills lesson, with full teacher's notes
- Speaking Database materials
- the *Beyond* B1 wordlist
- test generator for Unit 4 testing materials (all skills)
- tips for using the Grammar Database
- and more!

Go to the Workbook pages 40–51 for further practice material

PROGRESS CHECK UNITS 3&4

Preparing for the Progress Check

Vocabulary review

- Ask students to write the letters of the alphabet, A–Z, down the left side of a page. Explain that for each letter you want them to write a word which is related to music. Students work alone initially and after about a minute, they can compare notes with a partner. After a total of two minutes, ask how many they have found. Reassure them that they will not find a word for every letter, but some letters will have more than one word (eg *opera* and *orchestra*). Go through the alphabet asking students to tell you the words they have found for each letter.
- To continue with the theme of music and to review adverbs of degree, ask some *Do you like … ?* questions about different types of music (these can include classical, piano music, rock, pop, jazz, as well as any others that your students will know). Prompt with follow-up questions to elicit adverbs of degree, eg *How much do you like it? What do you think of [singer's name]?* etc. Continue the discussion until students have used a range of adverbs of degree, reminding the class that they should expect to find them in the Progress Check.
- Put students in pairs to review the vocabulary for people and relationships. Give them two or three minutes to see how many items they can remember and note down. Students then look at the Words & Beyond section on page 133 to see if there was anything they missed. Ask different students around the class to give you examples of *old friends, online friends, acquaintances, enemies,* etc. These can be people they know or fictional characters from TV, books or films.
- Ask students to look again at Exercise 5 on page 42. In pairs, students take turns using the extreme adjectives in sentences. You could start by giving them the following example: *I had an amazing time at the party on Sunday.*
- After two or three minutes, get feedback by prompting the class with questions such as *Who can tell me something* amazing? *When was the last time you were* furious? *Tell me something you find/found* fascinating, etc.

Grammar review

- Put students in pairs and ask them to look back at the grammar pages (31, 33, 41 and 43). The grammar for this Progress Check is:
  - Unit 3: Verbs followed by *-ing* form or *to* + infinitive; Comparison of adverbs
  - Unit 4: First conditional with *if/unless*; Second conditional
- To review verbs followed by *-ing* form or *to* + infinitive, divide the board into two columns. At the top of the left column, write *ing*. At the top of the right column, write *to + infinitive*. Ask pairs to decide which student will write each form, and encourage them to write short sentences as examples of the form. For example, Student A could write *I don't mind helping in the house*. Student B could write *I'm going to learn to skate*. Allow five minutes before asking how many sentences each pair has made. Ask students to read out their sentences and, as they do so, write the verbs on the board in the correct columns.
- To review comparison of adverbs, write a list of regular and irregular adverbs (eg *loudly, beautifully, well, hard, badly, fast, carefully, long*) on the board and ask students to say comparative sentences with them. Prompt with sentences such as *I can sing beautifully* to elicit, eg *I can sing more beautifully than you*. Continue in this way until students have used all the different comparative forms.
- For the Unit 4 grammar, set a time limit of five minutes and ask pairs to write two examples of first conditional sentences and two of second conditional sentences. Ask students to read out sentences. Write a variety of these on the board, making sure to include a first conditional with *if*, a first conditional with *unless* and a second conditional.
- For a little extra practice with the second conditional, ask students to think of hypothetical questions to ask other students. Begin by asking one student, *How would you feel if you had to move to America?* The student answers (eg *I'd be very excited.*) The same student then asks someone else a different question and they continue like this until everyone has spoken.

Optional warm-up activities

READ Exercise 1

- Tell students that they are going to practise reading quickly. Give them up to one minute to look at the people's profiles and find what kind of music each person likes.
- After a minute, ask them to tell you what they have found. Point out that they can expect to find what the people *dislike* as well as what they like in this kind of task.
- Explain that they will have to read the reviews to decide which album would be suitable for each person but that this will be easier because they will now know what they are looking for.

LISTEN Exercise 2

- Remind students of the importance of reading ahead before they listen.
- Since students have recently studied stress and intonation (on page 42), ask them to practise saying the sentences in the questions out loud. Write the following on the board: *I help people with their problems. I write letters for a problem page. I tell people how to be happy.*
- Point out that students will probably hear something similar to one of these sentences in answer to question 1.
- Read out the sentences with a natural stress/intonation and ask various students to repeat. Point out that there are many different ways to stress a sentence but most people stress the nouns and verbs more.
- Try a variety of different ways of reading out the sentence, stressing different words. You could stress the word *people* in the first sentence and ask the class what they think that might suggest (*I help people and not animals*). Mention that it is unusual to stress pronouns, articles, prepositions, etc. You could reinforce this with another example – this time stressing the word *their*. Again, ask what it would imply if the pronoun were stressed (*I help people with their problems and not my/your/our problems.*)
- Ask the class to practise items 2–5 in this way with a partner. After a few minutes, ask for suggestions and discuss how the sentences change when different words are stressed.

WRITE Exercise 3

- Students sometimes have difficulty thinking of ideas about what to write. Encourage them to try to put themselves in the position suggested in the task and imagine they are that person.
- Ask students to look at the extract from their aunt's letter and to think about the main points they need to address. Elicit the following: *What do you like doing? Who are your friends? Are you studying hard?*
- Put students in pairs and ask them to note down some of the things they could write for each sentence. They do not have to write complete sentences.
- Then ask students to suggest where in their letter they would address each point (suggestions are given in brackets below).

  It's been so long since I saw you. (Perhaps just a passing comment in the opening of the letter)
  Write and tell me about yourself. (This is the general content of the letter)
  What do you like doing? (1st main point)
  Who are your friends? (2nd main point)
  Are you studying hard? (3rd main point)

PROGRESS CHECK UNITS 3&4

Doing the Progress Check

READ

1

- If you have decided not to do the full warm-up, give the students a minute or two to read the people's profiles. Then prompt them with some simple questions, eg:
  - *What kind of music does Kylie like?* (Pop and music from the charts)
  - *Does Danny like pop?* (Yes, but he prefers American rock or British folk music)
- Go through the **Exam tips**, making sure students understand the different strategies that they can choose from in order to do this kind of task.
- Remind students to be careful of negatives in the reviews. They might understand *fond of* where it actually says *isn't fond of*, for example.
- Allow 15 minutes for this section.

ANSWERS

1 D 2 G 3 E 4 H 5 F

LISTEN

2 1.58

- If you have decided not to do the full warm-up, refer students back to the work on stress and intonation that they covered on page 42. Ask them to listen carefully and to use these techniques to help them understand.
- Go through the **Exam tips** for the listening task, reminding students that these tips will help them.
- Encourage students to spend a minute or two predicting what they might hear.
- Point out that they will hear everything twice. One suggestion in the **Exam tips** is to eliminate any wrong answers when they listen for the first time. Encourage students to find a strategy that works for them.

ANSWERS / AUDIO SCRIPT 1.58

1 A 2 B 3 C 4 B 5 B

Belinda Vine: My name's Belinda Vine and I write for a weekly magazine for teens. I have a regular section called 'Ask Belinda'. Basically, people write to me with their problems and I give them advice.
Maybe I should also tell you what I don't do. I don't tell people what to do. I make suggestions. I say what I would do if I were in their situation. Ultimately, people have to make their own decisions.
Also, people really think that we write the problem letters. We don't. If someone doesn't want their name to appear in the magazine, then we'll invent a name. But we don't invent their problems. We don't need to. At the magazine, we receive hundreds of letters and messages each week.
Most of the problems we receive are about relationships. Maybe a teen's having problems with a boyfriend, a girlfriend, a close friend or a relative. I often think that writing down a problem on a piece of paper or online can be terribly helpful. Sometimes you can see things much more clearly when you write them down.
Here's an example. This is a message I received today by email. Let's see ...
Dear Belinda, I'm 14 and my best friend is ignoring me. We usually do everything together, but now she won't talk to me or even look at me. I feel awful. What can I do? Kate.
So if I decided to answer Kate's letter, I'd probably start by asking her some questions. How long have you known your friend? Has anything happened recently? For example, has your friend started to hang out with other people? Even though we often think we are the problem, quite often the problem has nothing to do with us.
I'd also probably suggest giving her friend some space. In situations like this, it's often good to find something else to do. If you spend all your time thinking about the problem, you'll only get more upset. If you start doing other things, however, you'll quickly be able to see what's really important to you.
But the best way to solve a problem is to talk about it. We often think no-one will understand us if we tell them a problem. That's simply not true. Problems usually won't go away unless you talk about them. I should know. I've had this job for more than 10 years now.

WRITE

3

- Spend a few minutes going through the task with students and eliciting who they have to write to and what their letter must include.
- Remind them that they should address all the points in the letter extract.
- Explain that they shouldn't spend too long on their beginnings and endings. Suggest that they begin and end with something straightforward such as *Dear Aunt Joan, … Love, [name].*
- Finally, remind students of the word limit and the importance of checking their own spelling, grammar, etc.

MODEL ANSWER

Dear Aunt Joan,
Thank you for your letter. I like doing a lot of things but my favourite hobby is swimming. At school I go swimming twice a week. However, I much prefer going to the beach with my friends.
I'm in a swimming club and my team-mates are all good friends. We often go out together to the cinema or to have something to eat.
I'm studying hard for my exams but there are so many other things happening, it's difficult to concentrate.
I hope you're well. If you come to the UK, will you come and visit us?
Love,
[name]

After the Progress Check

Optional game

This game, called *Snowman* (see Games page 33), follows up on the vocabulary from Units 3 and 4.

- Ask students to look at the Words & Beyond pages for Units 3 and 4 (pages 132–133). Encourage them to memorise as many words as possible in three minutes.
- Students take turns coming to the board and challenging the class using vocabulary from Units 3 and 4.
- Choose a volunteer (Student A) to come to the board first. Student A draws the required number of spaces – one for each letter of the word – on the board. He/She can then choose which students suggest letters.
- Individual students guess which letters are in the word. If they are right, Student A writes the letter in the correct place. If that letter is not in the word, Student A writes it on a different part of the board.
- Student A continues to ask other members of the class until someone guesses the word. Whoever guesses the word first scores a point. However, if no one has guessed correctly by the time there are five wrong letters on the board, Student A gets the point.
- Continue with Student B, and so on.

Feedback and extension

READ

- Review the questions one at a time, reminding students that the reviews should contain a paraphrase of what is written in the people's profiles, eg Question 1 *Kylie is a big fan of* <u>*pop music*</u>*, especially songs* <u>*in the charts*</u> matches with D – *the album from* <u>*boy band*</u> *OneStep is even better than last year's debut album. It includes* <u>*this week's number one hit*</u> *'New Acquaintance'.*
- Ask students where they found the answers each time. If they got it wrong, make sure they understand why.
- Emphasise to students the importance of reading English, either online or in magazines, etc. The more they can read, the better it will be for them. Students with an interest in music might already be reading about their favourite bands, etc. Encourage them to use the internet to learn more through the medium of English. Students can easily access lyrics, either through dedicated sites online or from lyrics which often appear alongside music videos. If students have a favourite song, encourage them to find the lyrics and bring them to class, with the song. You could then spend part of a lesson discussing the way the songwriter has used English in the lyrics.

LISTEN

- Hand out photocopies of the audio script – one for each pair of students. Ask students to find the part of the audio script which gives the correct answer to each question. Discuss these sections, asking different students to read them out with the correct stress and intonation. This will help the class understand that tone of voice often plays a part when choosing the right answers.
- You should also draw attention to sections where there are distractors, pointing out that the wrong answers sometimes appear in the audio script, but the speaker says something which shows that it is incorrect. For example, *People really think that we write the problem letters. We don't.* (question 1, option B)
- As an extension activity, students could act out the role of TV or radio agony aunt/uncle. Give students five minutes to write a fictional problem, similar to what they heard in the LISTEN section. The problems could be about relationships or related to school work, technology, etc. They should add a fictional name at the bottom of their problem. If students finish early, they can write a second problem.
- Gather all the problems into a pile and ask for some volunteers to give advice. Divide the problems between the volunteers and ask them to choose which problem they want to address.
- Tell the volunteers they can begin with *We've had an email from [name], who ...* . The volunteer should then describe the problem and offer advice.
- There should be enough problems for other students to take a turn. Keep going for as long as students are willing to volunteer.

WRITE

- For feedback with Exercise 3, ask students to focus on where they lost marks (and what they need to remember for next time). Answer any questions and make sure that students understand why they have been marked down in each case. Reassure them that it is perfectly natural to make mistakes in writing, but that they need to make an effort to avoid making *the same* mistakes each time.
- To extend the work students have done on writing (especially if there were a lot of problems), set a similar writing task for homework (see below).
- Write the task on the board and ask students to complete it for next lesson. Use this task as an opportunity to correct any mistakes that they may have made with the letter in the Progress Check. Point out that there is little difference in style between this email and the letter they wrote.

Homework

Write up this task in a style similar to Exercise 3 in the Progress Test.

Read part of an email from your cousin in America.

> *I don't know very much about you. Write and tell me something about yourself. What sort of things are you interested in? Do you enjoy studying? What do you do in your free time?*

Now write an email reply, answering the questions.

Write 90–100 words.

GO BEYOND FOR TEACHERS

The reading text in this Progress Check is about different types of music. Ask students to search online for more information about two different types of music. Suggest some genres for them to choose from, such as *hip hop, punk, indie, blues, country, folk, jazz, reggae*, etc or get them to choose their own.

They should aim to find and note down the main points about each of the two types of music and, in the next lesson, to report back to the rest of the class. Remind them that they can use comparison of adverbs (eg, *Rock musicians play more loudly than folk musicians*) or extreme adjectives (eg *[This type of music] has a fascinating history*).

If your students are not at all interested in modern music, they could do the same thing but choosing two different types of classical music (eg *opera* and *baroque*; *chamber music* and *choral music*, etc). They could also compare two classical composers (eg *Chopin, Rachmaninov, Tchaikovsky, Mahler, Mendelssohn*, etc).

UNIT 5 FIVE SENSES

IN THE PICTURE Can you feel it?

Talk about how we use our senses

Pages 50–51

STAGE	TIME	FOCUS
GET STARTED		Play *Snowman* to introduce the title of the unit and recycle pronouncing the letters of the alphabet.
WORK WITH WORDS		Recycle parts of the body. Associate sense verbs and nouns with each of the five senses. Listen to sentences to say which sense is being described. Practise saying consonant combinations. Watch a video and describe the scene using the sense verbs.
SPEAK		Write about things you love or hate and describe them to your partner.

Get started

Books closed. Play a game of *Snowman* (see Games page 33) to introduce the title of the unit: *Five Senses*.

WORK WITH WORDS

1a and 1b RECALL

- Divide the class into pairs. Allow three minutes to do both tasks.
- First ask students to write the names of parts of the body for as many letters of the alphabet as they can.
- Then ask students which words they can match to the five icons in Exercise 2a.
- Stop them after three minutes and choose different students to say their answers.
- Ask students to do the Work with Words task on page 134.

SUGGESTED ANSWERS

Exercise 1a

ankle arm back chest ear eye elbow finger foot hand knee leg mouth neck nose shoulder teeth throat thumb toe tongue

Exercise 1b

1 eye 2 ear 3 hand, finger, thumb 4 nose 5 mouth, teeth, tongue

2a

- Refer students to the names of the five senses in the box and ask them to write them next to the correct icons.

2b 2.01

- Play the track for students to listen and check.
- Play the track again for students to listen and repeat.

ANSWERS / AUDIO SCRIPT 2.01

1 sight 2 hearing 3 touch 4 smell 5 taste

3a

- Ask students to match the verbs in the box to the five senses in the table in Exercise 2a. Don't confirm the answers at this point.

3b

- Elicit which of the sense words in Exercise 2a can also be verbs.

ANSWERS

touch, smell, taste

3c 2.02

- Play the track for students to listen and check their answers to Exercise 3a.
- Play the track again for students to listen and repeat.

ANSWERS / AUDIO SCRIPT 2.02

1 sight – look, see, watch 2 hearing – hear, listen, sound
3 touch – feel, touch 4 smell – smell 5 taste – taste

Extra activity

Ask students to write their own example sentence for each of the verbs: *hear*, *listen*, *look*, *see* and *watch*, eg: *I heard a noise outside my bedroom. What kind of music do you listen to?* (See Tips for help with these verbs page 29)

Extra activity

Ask students to add vocabulary relating to the senses to the table in Exercise 2a, eg in column 4 *Smell*, they could write *odour*, *fragrance*, *perfume*, *scent*, etc. Under *Sight*, they could write *vision*, *appearance*, *stare*, etc.

4 ▶2.03

- Refer students to the photos and explain that they will hear 10 sentences and should match each of them to one of the photos.
- Play the track for students to listen and match. Point out that some of the photos will be matched with several sentences.

ANSWERS / AUDIO SCRIPT ▶2.03

1 a 2 e 3 c 4 d 5 b 6 a 7 c 8 a 9 a 10 d

1 I can't hear anything apart from amazing music.
2 A: What do you think of this one?
B: Wow! That smells fantastic.
3 It's so hot here and that water looks so cool.
4 It's so good not wearing shoes. The grass feels so soft under my feet.
5 I like Mexican food. This tastes really good.
6 There's so much to see in the city. It's huge.
7 I love watching the sea. It's so blue under the sky.
8 There's so much traffic. Everything sounds so noisy here.
9 I like listening to music while I walk. It's relaxing.
10 Sometimes I lie on the grass and imagine I can touch the clouds in the sky.

5 ▶2.04

- Ask students to use the verbs in Exercise 3 to complete the sentences.
- Play the track for students to listen and check.

ANSWERS / AUDIO SCRIPT ▶2.04

1 feels 2 sounds 3 smells 4 see 5 looks 6 tastes 7 hear 8 touch 9 watching 10 listening

See Student's Book page 50 for audio script.

Extra activity

Play a memory game in groups. Model the activity with the class first. Ask the first student to say a phrase with one of the sense verbs, eg *I see the blue sea*. The next student must repeat what the first student said, *She sees the blue sea* and add another phrase, such as *I hear the waves*. The third student must repeat what the first two students have said, eg *She sees the sea. He hears the waves,* and add another one, such as *I look at the sky*. If a student forgets a phrase he/she is out of the game. The last student to remember all phrases correctly is the winner.

6a ▶2.05 PRONOUNCE

- Play the track for students to listen to the words, paying particular attention to the consonants in blue.
- Play the track again for students to listen and repeat.

AUDIO SCRIPT ▶2.05

See Student's Book page 51 for audio script.

6b

- Point out that the letters in blue are all groups of consonants pronounced together. Ask students if they find any of these consonant combinations difficult.
- Encourage them to practise saying the consonants slowly in pairs, focusing on any that they find particularly difficult.

7 THE MOVING PICTURE ▶

- Explain to the students they are going to watch a video and they should imagine they are in each scene.
- Ask students to say something using the sense verbs.

8

- Elicit the five senses from the class. Then elicit the sense verbs they have been practising. Remind students that some sense verbs can also be nouns.
- Ask students to choose the correct option to complete each of the sentences.
- Nominate different students to read out their answers.

ANSWERS

1 smell 2 sound 3 taste 4 look

SPEAK

9

- Give students a minute to reflect and write the names of things they love or hate to complete the sentences.
- Divide the class into pairs to read their sentences to each other. Encourage them to say if they feel the same way.
- Invite some students to say one interesting thing about their partner in open class.

Extra activity

Ask students to write another sentence to explain the reason why they love or hate the things in Exercise 9. Refer them to the sentences in Exercise 5 to help as a model for their answers.

GO BEYOND

Ask students to do the Go Beyond task on page 134.

Homework

Ask students to find a picture of a city or a landscape in a magazine or on the internet. Encourage them to write a description of the scene using as many sense verbs and nouns as they can in their answer.

READING Fragrance fact file

Use pictures to help you understand Page 52

STAGE	TIME	FOCUS
GET STARTED		Discuss personal experiences and recycle vocabulary related to the five senses.
SPEAK AND READ		Name perfumes and fragrances and talk about products that use fragrances. Read a text on facts about fragrances. Discuss tips on how to use pictures to help you understand a text.
REACT		Discuss surprising facts about fragrances and if they should be banned in some public places.

Get started

Elicit the names of the five senses. Ask students which senses they think are the most and least important and ask them to explain their reasons in a brief class discussion.

Write these questions on the board and ask students to write one more question for each of the senses.

Sight: *What's your favourite colour?*

Taste: *What food didn't you like when you were young, but do now?*

Smell: *Can you remember a smell that takes you back to your childhood?*

Touch: *What don't you like to touch?*

Hearing: *What sounds don't you like?*

Divide the class into pairs to discuss these questions and take turns to ask and answer their own questions. Nominate different students to share their answers with the class.

SPEAK AND READ

1

- Ask students to brainstorm things that smell nice. Elicit answers in open class, eg *a rose*, *perfume*, *freshly-cut grass*, *Mum's cooking!*
- Divide the class into pairs to answer the questions. Set a time limit of two minutes.
- Invite different students to share their ideas with the class.

2a

- Ask students to discuss why it is useful to look at pictures and text titles before you read a text.
- Refer students to the tips in the HOW TO box to see if they thought of the same tips. Invite volunteers to read the tips out loud.

2b

- Before students start to read, ask them to look at the text and pictures quickly in order to answer the questions.
- Ask students to discuss their answers in pairs before you elicit and check them in open class.

3 2.06

- Ask students to read the text to decide if each sentence is correct or incorrect. Don't play the audio at this point. Ideas for using the audio are given at the end of the lesson.
- Ask students to correct the incorrect sentences.
- Encourage students to compare their answers in pairs before you check them in open class.

ANSWERS

1 I (The very first perfume was incense made from burning wood or plants.)
2 C
3 I (The world's first perfume maker was a woman called Tapputi. She lived in Mesopotamia.)
4 I (The first unisex fragrance appeared in 1994.)
5 I (More than 4,000 ingredients are used in the fragrance industry.)
6 C

4

- Ask students which tips in the HOW TO box they used to help them in Exercises 2b and 3.

Fast finishers

Ask students to find words in the text to match these definitions: *a scientist who studies chemistry* (chemist); *something often burnt at religious ceremonies* (incense); *something we use to make a room smell nice* (air freshener); *affected by an allergy* (allergic); *to say officially that you must not do something* (banned).

REACT

5

- Divide the class into pairs to discuss the questions.
- Invite different students to share and explain their point of view. Try to develop a class discussion.

Recorded reading text 2.06

The reading text is recorded as an extra audio track which can be exploited for various purposes.

In this lesson, use the audio for checking Exercise 3. Stop the track at each point to ask if the answer is correct or incorrect. Where it is incorrect, elicit the correct answer.

GO BEYOND

Elicit what a caption is. Then refer students to the explanation given. Focus students on the pictures in the text and ask them to write captions using information from the text.

Homework

Ask students to write a list of smells they associate with living in a flat or a house (cooking, pets, laundry, rubbish, etc) and say which smells are pleasant or unpleasant.

GRAMMAR Passives (past, present and future)

Use the past, present and future passives to talk about senses Page 53

STAGE	TIME	FOCUS
GET STARTED		Play a game to recycle vocabulary related to the five senses and pre-teach key words for this lesson.
READ		Read a text about a girl's breakfast and discuss the effect of a cold on your taste buds.
STUDY		Use the text to complete the grammar explanations about past, present and future passives.
PRACTISE		Complete a news story and sentences with the correct passive form of the verbs. Rewrite sentences using the passive form.
SPEAK		Compare information about food consumption in your country and discuss how people will eat food in the future.

Get started

Play a game of *Double your Bet.* Ask students to work in pairs to decide if the statements below are true or false. Explain that each pair has 100 points to bet on true statements. They can distribute their points as they like, but they must spend all their points and note down how they have spent them. Explain that true statements double the points they bet. However, if they get it wrong, they lose twice the points they have bet.

When they have finished betting, tell students which of the statements are true and ask them to total up the bets to see who won the game.

Statements:

The idea of there being five senses was conceived by Homer, the Greek philosopher. (False – it was Aristotle.)

Ten thousand taste buds can be found inside our mouths. (True)

Fish have the most highly developed sense of taste. (False – insects do.)

In general, girls have more taste buds than boys. (True)

Taste is the weakest of the five senses. (True)

Dogs have noses that are up to 100 times more sensitive than ours. (False – it is thought that dogs' noses are 2,000–100 million times more sensitive than ours.)

People who suffer from anosmia cannot smell at all. (True)

People who have hyperosmia are very sensitive to taste. (False – they are very sensitive to smells.)

In the US, there is a National Sense of Smell Day in April. (True)

There are four basic kinds of taste. (True – sweet, salty, sour and bitter)

READ Grammar in context

1

- Refer students to the picture and ask them to describe what is happening (*a teenage girl is about to eat an egg on toast*). Elicit if students had a similar breakfast this morning.
- Invite students to read the text about Molly's breakfast and answer the question at the end of the text.

ANSWER

When you have a cold, your nose is blocked and you can't smell the food. Without your sense of smell, the food tastes different.

STUDY

2

- Focus students on the grammar explanations and ask them to complete the information with words from Exercise 1.
- Go through the explanations with the class, nominating students to give their answers and read out example sentences from Exercise 1 for each of the grammar explanations.

ANSWERS

past participles: sent, given/received   future: will/won't

Extra activity

Students may need more controlled practice with the passive form before doing Exercise 3. Ask students to find examples of past, present and future passives in the text and write them in their notebooks. Drill the positive, negative and question form for each example.

Then ask students to change the sentences to the active form, eg *The brain sent visual messages*, etc.

ANSWERS

Past passive

Visual messages were / weren't sent to her brain / Were visual messages sent to her brain?

When all the messages were /weren't received by the brain / Were all the messages received by the brain?

She was / wasn't given the OK / Was she given the OK?

Present passive

Some cells which are / aren't found in the nose / Are some cells found in the nose?

The taste buds are / aren't located on the tongue / Are the taste buds located on the tongue?

Future passive

She'll / won't be given eggs again / Will she be given eggs again?

She'll / won't be given the OK by her brain / Will she be given the OK by her brain?

PRACTISE

3

- Focus students on the news story and ask them to complete the text with the future passive form of the verbs in brackets. Before they start, point out the example.
- Encourage students to compare their answers in pairs before you ask for a volunteer to read out the completed news story.

- Invite students to say if they would like to go to the new fast-food restaurant *Sixth Sense* and to say why or why not.

ANSWERS
2 won't be allowed 3 will be served 4 will be given
5 Will people be told 6 won't be shown

4

- Ask students to complete the sentences with the correct passive form of the verbs in brackets. Before they start, draw students' attention to the example.
- Encourage students to compare their answers in pairs before you nominate different students to read out their answers.

ANSWERS
2 were chosen 3 are sold 4 are often rejected
5 will be left 6 is grown; will be lost

5

- Focus students on the first sentence and the example answer and go through the transformation with the class.
- Ask students to rewrite the remaining sentences using the passive form of the verbs in blue.

ANSWERS
2 A product is often chosen because of the photo on the packaging.
3 However, when the food is prepared, it can look very different.
4 A lot of complaints are received by companies each year.

Alternative procedure: less confident classes

If students are still unsure about how to change an active sentence to passive, explain that they should follow these steps:

– Make the object of the active sentence the subject of the passive sentence.
– Form the passive using the correct tense of the verb to be and change the active verb to its past participle.
– Make the subject of the active sentence the object of the passive sentence (although the subject can sometimes be omitted because it is unnecessary).

Fast finishers

Ask fast finishers to look at the text on page 52 and find as many examples as they can of passive sentences.

SPEAK

6

- Divide the class into pairs to compare the information given in Exercises 4 and 5 with the situation in their own country.
- Invite students to discuss how they think people will eat in the future. Encourage them to try to include the passive form in their discussion.
- Nominate different students to explain their opinions and try to develop a class discussion to close the activity.

Homework

Ask students to write three breakfast menus: a healthy breakfast, an unhealthy breakfast and a breakfast that will be eaten in the future. Encourage the students to read out their menus to their partner at the start of the next class and discuss who has invented the healthiest, unhealthiest and most futuristic breakfast.

LISTENING AND VOCABULARY The power of colour

Follow a conversation *Page 54*

STAGE	TIME	FOCUS
GET STARTED		Recycle vocabulary related to colours to introduce the theme of the lesson.
SPEAK AND LISTEN		Talk about words you associate with different colours. Read about and practise tips on how to recognise words and phrases that develop ideas. Listen to an interview about the National Colour Wheel and find out how culture affects your choice of colour.
REACT		Discuss which colour reflects the way you are feeling now and your favourite colour.
WORK WITH WORDS		Find out the meaning of colour idioms and expressions. Discuss experiences related to colour idioms and expressions.

Get started

Write the following list on the board: *A suit for an interview, A mobile phone, Chocolate, The building we are in, Nail polish, A motorbike, The walls in your bedroom, A sports car.*

Divide the class into pairs to discuss which colour is the best for each item on the list.

Invite different students to come up and write the colours they have talked about on the board. In open class, discuss why students chose the same, similar or different colours.

SPEAK AND LISTEN

1a

- Ask students to think of what they associate with each colour in the box and write the first word they think of.
- Invite students to compare their ideas in pairs before you discuss the colour associations in open class.

Fast finishers

Ask students to categorise the colours as 'hot' (orange, red, yellow …) or 'cold' (blue, grey, green, silver …).

1b

- Focus students on the colour wheel and ask them to find the colours given in the box that are on the wheel.
- Ask them to work with a partner and take it in turns to point to a colour.

2a

- Ask students to read the tips in the HOW TO box. Invite a volunteer to read them out loud.

2b 2.07

- Tell students that they are going to listen to an interview with Amy Shore about the National Colour Wheel. Before they listen, ask them to read the list of topics.
- Play the track for students to listen and number the topics in the order they are mentioned.

ANSWERS / AUDIO SCRIPT 2.07

a 3 b 4 c 2 d 1

Presenter: So, Amy, tell us about the National Colour Wheel.
Amy: Well, basically, we're asking people to visit our website at www.nationalcolourwheel.co.uk so that they can take part in our national colour wheel survey.
Presenter: What do people have to do to take part?
Amy: It's very simple. They just have to look at our colour wheel and choose the colour that represents the way they feel and then choose their favourite colour.
Presenter: So what's the purpose of the survey?
Amy: Well, we're doing the survey in order to make people think about the importance of colour in their lives and to discover the nation's favourite colour. The thing is, our lives are full of colours, from the colours of the clothes we wear to the colours of our walls at home. But how much do we really know about what those colours mean?
Presenter: I imagine you'd get different results in different countries. I was reading on your website about how colours mean different things in different cultures.
Amy: That's right. These days, we often assume that everyone on the planet is exactly the same. But the way we all relate to colours shows how different we are. For example, in the West, we associate the colour white with peace, while in China it means death. We associate the colour green with nature and the environment, while in some parts of the world, especially countries with jungles, it means danger.
Presenter: Although I associate green with Ireland, but that's probably because I'm Irish.
Amy: That's another good example. But, even though we react to colours in different ways, they have a powerful influence on all of us. We saw this in a similar survey in Manchester. Most of the 20,000 people who took part chose yellow to describe the way they were feeling. Yellow is a happy, sunny colour. However, the city's 'favourite colour' was blue. Curiously, no-one chose white or grey as their favourite colour.
Presenter: Fascinating stuff. Well, good luck with the survey.
Amy: Thank you.

3 2.07

- Play the track again for students to listen and choose the correct answers.
- Encourage them to compare their answers in pairs before you check them in open class.

ANSWERS

1 A 2 B 3 A 4 C

4

- Ask students which tips in the HOW TO box they used to help them in Exercises 2b and 3.

REACT

5

- Divide the class into pairs to look at the colour wheel and answer the questions.
- In open class, invite students to discuss whether they chose the same, similar or different colours.
- Ask students to work in the same pairs and each choose a role, A or B. Refer Student A to the task on page 141 and Student B to the one on page 142.
- When they have finished, do a quick class survey to see if most students said the same colours.

WORK WITH WORDS

6

- Refer students to the list of idioms and phrases and ask them to match them to the definitions.

ANSWERS

1 d 2 c 3 f 4 g 5 h 6 i 7 j 8 b 9 e 10 a

Extra activity

Read out these sentences for students to complete with one of the phrases from Exercise 6.

1 I couldn't see anything in the *Sixth Sense* restaurant. It was ______ .
2 I spent too much at the weekend and now I'm ______ .
3 Do you feel all right? You look ______ .
4 I find the colour grey depressing. It makes me ______ .
5 We're waiting to ______ to go on a trip at the end of term.
6 I don't usually eat vegetables, maybe ______ .
7 The loud music started ______ and woke me up.
8 The results of the survey weren't ______ .
9 When I don't want to hurt people's feelings, I sometimes ______ .
10 It upsets me when people waste food. It makes me ______ .

ANSWERS

1 as black as night 2 in the red 3 as white as a sheet
4 feel blue 5 get the green light 6 once in a blue moon
7 out of the blue 8 black and white 9 tell a white lie
10 see red

7

- Divide the class into pairs to make a list of things that make them see red, feel blue, are black and white and only happen once in a blue moon.
- Invite students to share some of their answers in open class.

Extra activity

Tell students some colour jokes to see if they can think of the answers and find them funny.

What is black and white and 'red' all over? (A newspaper – there is a play on words on the homophone *red/read*)

What is black and white and black and white and black and white? (A penguin rolling down a hill)

You could invite students to tell the class any suitable jokes about colours that they know. Encourage them to translate them into English to see if they are funny.

GO BEYOND

Ask students to do the Go Beyond task on page 134.

Homework

Ask students to write 100 words about important colours in their country and what they represent.

GRAMMAR (*In order*) *to ...* , *so* (*that*) ...

Talk about the purpose of doing things

Page 55

STAGE	TIME	FOCUS
GET STARTED		Recycle vocabulary from the unit so far and introduce the theme of the lesson.
READ		Read about the story of Braille and say if young people still use it today.
STUDY		Read the grammar explanations and underline examples of (*in order*) *to* and *so* (*that*) in the text.
PRACTISE		Use the target language to complete sentences and a conversation. Write sentences with (*in order*) *to* and *so* (*that*).
SPEAK		Exchange opinions and compare your ideas.

Get started

Play a game of *Pictionary.* Divide the class into teams. Ask each team to send a volunteer to the front of the class. Give the students at the front of the class a word or phrase to draw on the board.

As the students are drawing, the first team to correctly shout out what it is, wins a point.

Repeat this several times with different students. Suggested words and phrases are: *fragrance*, *crisps*, *the five senses*, *taste buds*, *traffic*, *supermarket*, *shelves*, *survey.*

Invite students to think of other ways that we can communicate words, apart from saying them or drawing them. (You could introduce the idea of Braille here as well as miming words.)

READ Grammar in context

1

- Refer students to the photo and elicit what they think the boy is doing and what the text is going to be about.
- Ask the students to read the story of Braille and find out if young people today still use it.
- Nominate a student to say the answer.

ANSWER

No. They prefer using electronic screen readers.

STUDY

2

- Read through the grammar explanation with the class and ask them to underline examples of each point in Exercise 1.
- Encourage students to compare their answers in pairs before you check them in open class by inviting different students to read out one sentence at a time and to say whether or not their sentence included an example.

ANSWERS

Blind people have restricted or no sight. They depend on their other senses in order to live independently. They use their sense of touch to read Braille. A form of Braille was used by Napoleon's soldiers so that they could communicate silently at night. But it was a French teenager called Louis Braille who developed the idea so blind people could use it. These days, however, young people prefer using electronic screen readers so that they don't have to use Braille.

in order to live, to read, so that they don't – refer to now (in general).

so that they could, so blind people could – refer to the past

PRACTISE

3

- Ask students to read the sentences and choose the correct option to complete them.
- Encourage students to compare their answers in pairs before you choose different students to read them out.

ANSWERS

1 so that 2 to 3 in order 4 so that 5 to
6 so that

Extra activity

Give students 60 seconds to memorise the sentences in Exercise 3. Ask students to work in pairs to take it in turns to test each other. One student closes his/her book and the other student reads out the first part of the sentence to see if their partner can remember the rest.

4 2.08

- Elicit from students whether they know anyone who is colour-blind and, if so, how this affects their everyday life.
- Ask students to read the conversation between Mike and Jacquie and complete it with *to* or *so*.
- Circulate and monitor students, helping if necessary.
- Play the track for students to listen and check their answers. You could stop the track and elicit the answers from different students, asking why they chose that option in order to consolidate usage.

ANSWERS

1 so 2 to 3 to 4 to 5 so 6 so

5

- Invite students to complete the sentences in their own words using *in order to/to* or *so that/so*.
- Encourage students to compare their sentences in pairs or small groups.
- Nominate different students to read out their answers.

SPEAK

6

- Divide the class into pairs to answer the questions in Exercise 6. Before they start, invite two confident students to complete and read out each of the model sentences.
- Find out students' reasons for their answers.

Homework

Ask students to make sentences using *in order to/to* or *so that/so* and these phrases: *save money; learn English; study hard; not carry a lot of money; not sunbathe too long; eat a lot of vitamins.*

LANGUAGE & BEYOND COMMUNICATE & COOPERATE

Recognise non-verbal communication *Page 56*

STAGE	TIME	FOCUS
GET STARTED		Play a game to recycle vocabulary related to the senses and present words from the lesson.
SPEAK AND READ		Communicate a phrase without speaking to your partner. Read a text about body language and discuss points that you think are true with your partner.
DO		Find examples of body language in the text and demonstrate with a partner.
REFLECT		Reflect on how body language can reveal things about us but is not always accurate.
EXTEND		Create a scene from a silent film and perform it for the rest of the class.

LIFE SKILLS

RECOGNISE NON-VERBAL COMMUNICATION

Non-verbal communication is not only important in communicating meaning, but also in building social relations. The ability to relate well to others is important throughout life and non-verbal communication plays a key role. Developing the ability to understand and use non-verbal communication can help you connect with others, express what you really mean, navigate challenging situations and build better relationships at home, at school and in the future workplace.

In order for students to get better at reading non-verbal communication, they should observe people around them and notice how people act and react to each other. Remind students that they should be aware of individual differences and that people from different countries and cultures tend to use different body language signals.

Students can train themselves to use non-verbal signals that match their words and reinforce what they are saying. They can use body language, for example, to convey positive feelings even when they are not actually experiencing them. If they're nervous about a situation, eg a job interview or a first date, they can use positive body language to signal confidence, even though they're not feeling it.

Get started

Play a game of *Articulate!* Prepare by writing some key words and phrases from the lesson on small pieces of card. Divide the class into two or more teams. Explain to students that the objective is to be the first team to correctly guess all the words that your team-mates describe in the time given. Point out that all players must take it in turns to take the top card from the pack and explain the word to their team. When a team member shouts out the correct answer, the next describer quickly takes another card and repeats the process. When the time runs out, each team counts the number of cards that were correctly guessed. Before they start, make the rules clear:

When describing a word, you *must not*:

- Say what letter the word starts with or how many letters it has.
- Say the word or any derivative, eg if the word is *time* you can't say *timer* or *timed*, etc.
- Use 'it rhymes with' or 'it sounds like' type clues.

When describing a word, you *can*:

- Choose to *pass* and not play a card – but only once each turn.
- Gesticulate, act and mime (but *NOT* mouth) the word.

Possible words and phrases for cards:

gesture, face, eye, movement, communicate, body, to tell a lie, stand, character, hide, mirror, disgusting, smell, reveal, accurate, feel, tired, quiet, hear, taste, head, wall

SPEAK AND READ

1

- Divide the class into pairs to take it in turns to choose one of the phrases in the box and communicate it to their partners without speaking to see if they can understand.

2

- Focus students on the text about body language. Ask them to read it and tick the points that they believe are true, based on their own experience.
- Ask students to compare answers in pairs before you start a class discussion by inviting different students to say which points are true for them and why.

DO

3

- Divide the class into groups and refer them back to the text to find examples of body language.
- Encourage them to take it in turns to demonstrate the body language described.
- Invite them to demonstrate other suitable examples to see if their partners can interpret them correctly.

REFLECT

4

- Focus students on the **REFLECTION POINT** and elicit whether they agree or not.
- Encourage students to discuss the questions in open class, inviting different students to answer each question.

Extra activity

Ask students to look back at the article to help them think of at least five ways they can use non-verbal communication to create a good impression.

SUGGESTED ANSWERS

Stand tall with your shoulders back.
Smile and maintain eye contact. Give a firm handshake.
Put your head to one side when you listen.
Mirror your partner's body language.

Extra activity

Ask students to talk about last weekend in pairs. In a less confident class, you could ask students to read out a conversation in the book (for example Exercise 4 on page 55). Get them to concentrate on their own and their partner's body language. After their conversation, ask students to give feedback on their partner's non-verbal communication and ask if their partner agrees with their analysis.

Extra activity

Ask students what body language they might use in these situations: *You're at a party and it's New Year. You've got a presentation in front of the class tomorrow. You've just had a fight with your friend. You've got an interview for a babysitting job tomorrow.*

EXTEND

5

- Divide the class into groups to create a scene from a silent film, following the instructions.
- Circulate and help students with any difficulties.
- Encourage students to rehearse their scene and perform it for other students to describe what happens.

Extra activity

If you have the facilities, play a silent film for students. Silent films are excellent for getting students to produce language. You could try Buster Keaton's *Nothing but Pleasure*, Charlie Chaplin's *The Kid*, *The Red Balloon* directed by Albert Lamorisse or Jacques Tati's *Les Vacances de Monsieur Hulot* and *Jour de Fête*. Alternatively, you could use more modern films like Mr Bean's *The Swimming Pool* or a Wallace and Grommit film.

Divide the class into pairs or small groups. Explain that one or two students should watch the film and describe what is happening to the other students who have their backs to the screen. Ask students to swap places every few minutes and, if necessary, write the vocabulary students need on the board as the actions happen.

Homework

Ask students to research cultural differences in hand or facial gestures. Encourage them to write short notes that they can use at the beginning of the next class to talk in groups.

SPEAKING At the chemist's

Ask for help with words at the chemist's *Page 57*

STAGE	TIME	FOCUS
GET STARTED		Recycle vocabulary to talk about common illnesses and what you can buy at the chemist's.
SPEAK		Look at photos of common health complaints and say what is wrong and what the people in the photos should do.
WATCH OR LISTEN		Watch or listen to scenes in a chemist's where people are asking for products. Practise asking for help with words when you don't know the name of something.
ACT		Role-play a conversation between a shop assistant and a customer at a chemist's.

Get started

Write these jumbled sentences on the board for students to order in pairs. Encourage them to race against each other to try to be the first to unscramble the sentences.

do / do / have / you / when / headache / What / a / you / ?
(What do you do when you have a headache?)
been / recently / sick / you / Have / ?
(Have you been sick recently?)
any / got / you / Have / allergies / ?
(Have you got any allergies?)
to / you / go / chemist's / do / often / the / How / ?
(How often do you go to the chemist's?)
buy / chemist's / can / at / What / you / the / ?
(What can you buy at the chemist's?)

Invite students to come up and write the sentences in the correct order. Drill the pronunciation of *headache* /ˈhedeɪk/. Remind students that *chemist's* is British English (in the US they say *pharmacy* or *drug store*).

Encourage students to ask and answer the questions in pairs. Choose different students around the class to say what their answers were for different questions. Elicit and write a list of products you can buy at the chemist's on the board (eg sun cream, antiseptic cream, plasters, painkillers, eye drops, etc) and save this to give students ideas in Exercise 6.

SPEAK

1

- Refer students to the photos and ask *Do these people look happy? How do you know?*
- Divide the class into pairs to answer the questions.
- Nominate different students to share their answers.

WATCH OR LISTEN

2 2.09

- Play the scenes for students to watch or listen. Ask students to note down which of the problems shown in the photos is not mentioned in the scenes.
- Encourage students to compare their answer in pairs before you nominate a student to say the answer.

ANSWERS / VIDEO/AUDIO SCRIPT 2.09

Photo c (headache) is not talked about.

1

Finn: Are you all right there?
Bella: I need something for my stomach. I've got ... I'm not sure how to say it in English. It's a pain.
Finn: You mean stomach ache.
Bella: Yes. Is this the right thing for a stomach ache?
Finn: Yes, it is.
Bella: Also, I don't understand what this means. Can you help me?
Finn: Let me see. Ah ... sunset yellow. It's a colour they use in the medicine.
Bella: I see. Does this sign mean that it is bad for you?
Finn: It can be bad for some people. Are you allergic to anything?
Bella: No, I don't think so.
Finn: Then you're probably OK.

2

Ruby: Can I help you?
Emma: Yes. I need some of that cream you put on your skin. I don't know what it's called. It's a special cream for keeping insects away.
Ruby: Do you mean insect repellent?
Emma: I think so.
Ruby: This one is very good.
Emma: What does 'light fragrance' mean?
Ruby: It means the lotion has a fragrance but it's not very strong. Here. Smell it.
Emma: You called it a lotion. What's the difference between a lotion and a cream?
Ruby: A cream is thicker than a lotion.
Emma: OK. Thank you. I'll take it.

3 2.09

- Play the scene again for students to listen and write the missing words.
- Choose different students to say the answers.

ANSWERS

1 stomach 2 stomach ache 3 stomach ache 4 skin
5 insects 6 insect

Alternative procedure: more confident classes

Encourage more confident students to try to remember and write in the missing words. Then play the track for them to listen and check their answers.

4a

- Ask the students to read the tips in the HOW TO box. Invite two volunteers to read the tips out loud.

4b 2.10

- Focus students on the phrases from the conversation and encourage them to complete any words they can from memory.
- Play the track for students to complete the phrases or check their answers.
- Play the track again for students to listen and repeat. Encourage them to pay attention to the words that are stressed (underlined in the answers).

ANSWERS / AUDIO SCRIPT 2.10

1 sure 2 means 3 called 4 for 5 difference

1 I'm <u>not sure how</u> to say it in English.
2 I <u>don't understand what</u> this <u>means</u>.
3 I <u>don't know what</u> it's <u>called</u>.
4 It's a <u>special cream</u> for <u>keeping insects away</u>.
5 <u>What's</u> the <u>difference</u> between a <u>lotion</u> and a <u>cream</u>?

Extra activity

Ask students to read out the conversations in pairs.

5

- Ask students to match the phrases in Exercise 4b to the tips in Exercise 4a.

ANSWERS

1 Say that you don't know the word.
2 Say that you don't understand.
3 Say that you don't know the word.
4 Explain what it's for.
5 Ask the other person for more information.

ACT

6 2.11

- Divide the class into pairs to complete the tasks. Encourage students to use the ideas on the board from the *Get started* activity to help them think of products you buy at a chemist's. Before they start, play the track with the expressions in the PHRASEBOOK box and encourage them to use these in their role-play. Set a time limit of five minutes to prepare and act out the scene.
- Ask students to change roles and repeat with another product you can buy at the chemist's.
- Ask students to present one of their conversations to the class.

Alternative procedure: less confident classes

In a less confident class, ask students to prepare the conversation in written form before doing this as a speaking activity. When students change roles and repeat with another product you buy at the chemist's, ask students to try to perform the role-play without their written notes.

Homework

Ask students to find four or five pictures of things that they do not know the English for. Ask them to write about these objects using the expressions in the PHRASEBOOK. At the beginning of the next class, ask students to work in pairs. Ask them to read out each description and for their partner to guess the picture it refers to.

STAGE	TIME	FOCUS
GET STARTED		Play a game to recycle language from the unit.
SPEAK AND READ		Describe a picture and talk about similar places. Read a description to match to the picture. Look at linking words to join two parts of a sentence.
PRACTISE		Link sentences together to make them more complex.
PLAN		Plan a description of a place you really like.
WRITE AND CHECK		Write the description and check you have covered the points in the plan.
SHARE		Swap your description with another student and discuss which place you would most like to visit.

Get started

Play a game of *Three in a Row* (see page 33). To win a square, teams take it in turns to choose a square and make a correct sentence linking the two items, eg *Sometimes you can find the same things in the chemist's and the supermarket.*

chemist's / supermarket	Braille / electronic screen readers	look / watch
body language / what you say	listen / hear	feel blue / see red
silent films / Charlie Chaplin	visual messages / taste buds	dictionary / history book

SPEAK AND READ

1

- Divide the class into pairs to look at the photo and describe it and tell their partner about any similar places they know. Before they start, refer students to the expressions in the PHRASE BYTES box and encourage them to use these in their discussion.
- Nominate different students to describe the photo and say if they know a similar place.

2

- Ask students to read the description and say which part of the photo doesn't match.
- Elicit the answer in open class.
- Draw students' attention to the **Get it right** box. Ask students to underline the example sentence in the text. Remind students that *quite* is a one-syllable word whereas *qui-et* has two syllables.

ANSWER

In the picture there's no forest but in the description it says there's a forest.

3a

- Refer students to the tips in the HOW TO box. Invite volunteers to read the tips out loud.

3b

- Invite students to look back at the text in Exercise 2 and underline all the linking words from the HOW TO box.

ANSWERS

Other relatives often come too, so the house ...
The house is in the middle of nowhere, and there aren't any ...
... hills to climb and a huge forest to explore. And there's the sea as well.
... wind on my face and the sand under my feet. I also love swimming ...
My gran is not only one of the coolest people on the planet, but she's also an amazing cook.

PRACTISE

4

- Focus students on the sentences and ask them to rewrite them using the words in brackets to link the ideas. Point out that some will be joined into one sentence, whereas others will still be two sentences.
- Encourage students to compare their answers in pairs before you check them in open class.

ANSWERS

1 There's a park near my house and I go there once or twice a week.
2 It's not only a good place to meet friends, but it's also a good place to do sports.
3 There are some basketball courts. There's also an area for skateboarding.
4 Once a month there's a market. They have concerts in the summer too.
5 I go there to have fun. I sometimes go there to read as well.
6 You see lots of different people there. People take their pets there too.

Extra activity

Ask students to work in pairs to write a sentence that describes each of the following words in sensory, descriptive terms: *sand*, *river*, *trees*, *house*, *birdsong*.

Encourage them to use at least two adjectives. Then ask them to note which of the five senses they have described, eg *I love the feeling of fine, golden sand between my toes.* – touch/sight.

PLAN

5

- Explain to students that they are going to write a description about a place they really like.
- Focus their attention on the **Writing plan** and go through the different points with them.
- Give students 10 minutes to write their ideas for their plan. Circulate and help students if necessary.

WRITE AND CHECK

6

- Ask students to use their plans and the model description to write their own description. Encourage them to use some of the language they have studied in this unit. Set a time limit of 10 minutes.
- When students have finished writing, encourage them to check their work.

SHARE

7

- Ask students to swap their description with a partner to read and discuss which place they would most like to visit and explain why.

Homework

Ask students to write five sentences to connect some of the ideas in the *Get started* activity using *and*, *also*, *too*, *as well* and *not only + but also*.

VOCABULARY The senses

1

- Divide the class into pairs to look at the words in the box and match the words to the five senses (touch – feel, touch; sight – look, see, sight, watch; smell – smell; hearing – hear, hearing, listening, sounds; taste – taste.
- Ask students to work individually to complete Casper Wright's introduction to his video game with the words in the box.
- Encourage them to compare their answers in pairs before you check them in open class.

ANSWERS
1 watch 2 sight 3 see 4 listening 5 hearing
6 hear 7 sounds 8 Look 9 touch/feel
10 feel/touch 11 smell 12 taste

GRAMMAR Passive tenses

3

- Write a scrambled past passive sentence on the board for students to order, eg: *invented Marconi The was by radio* (The radio was invented by Marconi) and elicit from students which tense this sentence is in and how we form the passive.
- Explain that the text is an encyclopaedia entry and ask them to complete it with the passive form of the verbs in brackets.
- Nominate different students to read the text out loud, sentence by sentence, to check answers in open class.

ANSWERS
1 was created 2 was inspired 3 was interviewed
4 will be used 5 will be connected 6 was reported
7 is played 8 will be remembered

Colour idioms

2

- Explain to students that they are going to complete the conversation from the video game with colours to make typical English expressions.
- In a less confident class, write the colour options on the board: *black*, *white*, *red*, *blue*, *green*.
- Divide the class into pairs to complete the conversation by writing a colour in each gap.
- Nominate different students to read out their answers to check them in open class.
- Invite students to read the conversation out loud in pairs.

ANSWERS
1 black 2 blue 3 white 4 black 5 white 6 red
7 green 8 red 9 blue 10 blue

(*In order*) *to* … , *so* (*that*) …

4

- Ask students to read the SensaWorld rules and complete them using in *order to/to* or *so that/so*.
- Circulate and monitor as students are doing the task. If you feel they are having difficulty, stop them mid-task and do a quick review of when we use *in order to/to* and *so that/so*.
- Check answers in open class.

ANSWERS
1 in order to / to 2 so that / so 3 in order to / to
4 in order to / to 5 so that / so 6 so that / so

Extra Resources

Go to the Teacher's Resource Centre at www.macmillanbeyond.com for:

- mid-term tests
- downloadable audio and audio scripts for the Student's Book and Workbook
- videos and video scripts
- extra vocabulary at two levels of difficulty
- extra grammar at two levels of difficulty
- CLIL lesson, with full teacher's notes
- a life skills lesson, with full teacher's notes
- Speaking Database materials
- the *Beyond* B1 wordlist
- test generator for Unit 5 testing materials (all skills)
- tips for using the Grammar Database
- and more!

Go to the Workbook pages 52–63 for further practice material

6 SELLING POWER

UNIT

IN THE PICTURE In a shop

Talk about shopping

Pages 60–61

STAGE	TIME	FOCUS
GET STARTED		Talk about something you've bought recently.
WORK WITH WORDS		Recycle vocabulary for shops and phrases to do with shopping. Listen to two conversations in a shop. Match phrases from the conversations to definitions.
SPEAK		Do a questionnaire about shopping habits.

Get started

Write these question prompts on the board: *What? Who? Where? Why? How much? Happy?* Ask students to think about something they've bought recently, either for themselves or for someone else. Divide the class into pairs to ask and answer questions about the item they are thinking of. Set a time limit of three minutes. Before they start, indicate the prompts on the board and elicit full questions.

WORK WITH WORDS

1a and 1b RECALL

- Elicit from students what you buy at a baker's, eg bread, cakes.
- Ask students to make a list of at least eight more types of shop. Set a time limit of one minute.
- Invite students to call out their answers, writing any unusual ones on the board.
- If students are unsure of the meaning of any of the words, ask others to say what you can buy there, eg
  Student A: What's a butcher's?
  Teacher (to class): What can you buy at a butcher's?
  Student B: Meat.
  Student C: Sausages.
  Student A: Ah … OK.
- Focus students on the phrases in Exercise 1b and ask them to complete them with the words in the box. Allow two minutes.
- As students finish, ask them to compare their answers in pairs before you check them in open class. Encourage students to explain the meaning of the phrases and how they differ, eg *save money* means you keep it but *spend money* means you use it to buy things.
- Ask students to do the Work with Words task on page 135.

ANSWERS

Exercise 1b

1 ask the price 2 be cheap / expensive
3 buy / pay for / sell an item 4 cost / save / spend money

2

- Focus students on the shop in the big picture and ask them what sort of shop it is and what it sells. Ask them if the shop in the picture is like the ones they buy clothes in. Invite them to say which clothes shops they like and why they like them.

ANSWER

It's a clothes shop. It sells clothes, bags, sunglasses and jewellery.

3 2.12

- Ask students to listen to two conversations in the shop and to fill in how much the two people pay.
- Play the track for students to listen and read. Ask them to fill in the amounts mentioned.
- Elicit answers from different students in open class.

ANSWERS / AUDIO SCRIPT 2.12

1 €31.97 2 €18
See Student's Book page 60 for audio script.

4 2.13

- Play the track for students to listen and repeat the phrases in orange in Exercise 3.
- Ask them to match these phrases to the definitions, drawing their attention to the example before they start. Set a time limit of four minutes.
- Encourage students to compare their answers in pairs before you nominate different pairs to each give an answer that they are confident of.

ANSWERS / AUDIO SCRIPT 2.13

2 exchange an item 3 try on clothes 4 keep the receipt
5 pay in cash 6 return an item 7 on special offer
8 in the sale 9 get a discount 10 get a refund

on special offer in the sale try on clothes
keep the receipt exchange an item return an item
get a refund get a discount pay in cash pay by card

Fast finishers
Ask students to test each other by taking it in turns to read out some of the definitions for their partner (with book closed) to say the phrase.

5a 2.14 PRONOUNCE

- Play the track for students to listen to the sounds /æ/and /ɑː/ in the words and say which one is longer.
- Play the track again for students to listen and repeat.

ANSWER / AUDIO SCRIPT 2.14
/ɑː/ is longer
See Student's Book page 60 for audio script.

5b 2.15

- Focus students on the pairs of words and ask them to circle the one they hear. Play the track for students to listen and choose.
- Encourage students to compare their answers in pairs.
- Take a poll on each pair of words before giving the answer.
- Play the second part of the track for students to listen and repeat both words.

ANSWERS / AUDIO SCRIPT 2.15
1 aren't 2 chart 3 had 4 jars 5 pack
1 ant / aren't 2 chat / chart 3 had / hard 4 jazz / jars
5 pack / park

6 THE MOVING PICTURE

- Introduce the video by explaining to students that they are going to watch the four people in the photo talking about shopping.
- Ask students which of the names are boys' names (Sebastian and Tyler) and which are girls' (Shay and Roisin). Identify the names of the people, as students will need this information to complete the listening task.
- Ask students to write each person's name in their notebooks and leave space under each one to write the answers.
- Play the video for students to note their answers as they watch.
- Encourage students to compare their answers in pairs and ask if they would like to watch the video a second time.
- Play the video again if necessary and then check answers in open class.

ANSWERS / VIDEO SCRIPT
Shay: Doesn't like shopping and gets stressed out at the shops. Prefers to shop online.
Sebastian: Doesn't mind shopping and often goes shopping with his friends, so that they can hang out and get food at the same time.
Roisin: Prefers shopping online. When going to the shops, she loves vintage shops and market stalls. Sometimes goes shopping with her mum.
Tyler: Loves going to big shops because of the variety. Doesn't like online shopping because he prefers to see the merchandise before buying anything.

SPEAK

7

- Write the word *shopaholic* on the board and elicit its meaning (*someone who is addicted to, or can't stop shopping*).
- Underline the suffix *aholic* and tell students that this suffix means 'addicted to'. Ask them if they know any other words with this suffix. Elicit or teach: *workaholic* and *chocoholic*.
- Ask students to read the shopaholic questionnaire and think about their answers. Set a time limit of two minutes.
- Divide the class into pairs to ask and answer the questions. Encourage them to give reasons or examples with their answers.
- Circulate and monitor to make corrections and keep students on task.

GO BEYOND

Ask students to do the Go Beyond task on page 135.

Extra activity
Ask students to complete these gapped sentences with a preposition:

Where can I pay ________ *this scarf, please?* (for)
Excuse me, is this jacket ________ *the sale?* (in)
These socks are ________ *special offer at the moment – you can get two pairs for the price of one.* (on)
Is there somewhere I could try this top ________ *, please?* (on)
I don't have a credit card, so I'll have to pay ________ *cash.* (in)
I'm going to ask ________ *a discount on these shoes – there's a dirty mark on them.* (for)
I hate shopping ________ *clothes … it's so boring!* (for)
I think it's dangerous to pay ________ *card all the time – you forget how much you're spending!* (by)

Homework

Ask students to choose five of the questions from the shopaholic questionnaire and to write their answers, giving reasons or examples.

READING What's it for?

Identify the tone of written comments

Page 62

STAGE	TIME	FOCUS
GET STARTED		Talk about an advert you've seen recently. Select adjectives to describe your feelings about advertising.
SPEAK AND READ		Read a website challenge and the comments people have made about the challenge. Identify the tone of comments.
REACT		Talk about your favourite adverts and whether adverts affect your buying habits. Invent an advertising slogan.

Get started

Ask students to think about an advert they can remember seeing or hearing in the last 24 hours. Ask them to recall:

- where they saw or heard the advert
- what product was advertised
- what the advert was like, eg funny, serious, annoying, etc
- what music was used (if any)
- if they liked or disliked the advert

Divide the class into pairs. Explain that each student has one minute to describe the advert they are thinking of without mentioning the product being advertised. Their partner must try to guess what the product is.

While students are talking, write these adjectives on the board: *interesting*, *creative*, *annoying*, *entertaining*, *necessary*, *fun*, *boring*, *useful*, *funny*. Ask students which adjectives they would use to describe advertising in general. Encourage them to justify their answers and to say whether they feel positive or negative about advertising. This discussion could be started in pairs and continued in open class if you feel students have a lot to say.

SPEAK AND READ

1

- Refer students to the photos. Divide the class into pairs to discuss and answer the questions. Allow four minutes.
- Elicit some ideas in open class about what the photos might be advertising.

2 2.16

- Tell students that guessing what the photos might be advertising was a challenge that an internet blogger called Zac set for his readers. Check the meaning of *challenge* (a difficult test of skill or knowledge).
- Ask students to read the blog and the comments and see if the people agree with any of the predictions and comments they made in Exercise 1. Set a time limit of five minutes for students to read the blog and discuss it in pairs. Don't play the audio at this point. Ideas for using the audio are given at the end of the lesson.

3a

- Refer students to the tips in the HOW TO box and ask what is meant by the tone of a comment. (The attitude that the person who wrote the comment wants to convey, eg positive, negative, joking, serious, critical, etc.)
- Invite volunteers to read the tips out loud.
- Ask students to cover the HOW TO box and ask them what punctuation was mentioned and what tone it could suggest (question marks for uncertainty, exclamation marks for emphasis).
- Ask students if they remember what exclamations were mentioned in the box, (*oh*, *wow*, *ugh*). Check the pronunciation of these exclamations, ie /əʊ/, /waʊ/, /ʊx/.

3b

- Invite students to read the website comments again and answer the questions. Set a time limit of two minutes.
- Encourage students to compare their answers in pairs and say why they chose the comments they did.
- Nominate different students to say the answers in open class, giving their reasons for choosing them.

ANSWERS

1 LNQ (positive comments about the challenge, eg use of *wow*; positive language, ie *great idea for a challenge;* use of smiley face)
OMG (positive comments about the second ad, eg positive language, ie *I totally love, Good choice*)
2 PT199 (use of *ugh!*; negative language, ie *totally uncool*, *awful*; use of exclamation marks)
TC (negative language, ie *Hey stupid.*)
3 angel15 (use of question mark)

4

- Ask students which tips in the HOW TO box they used to help them in Exercise 3b.

Extra activity

Ask students to find words in the text to match these definitions: *means the same as funny* – 1 word (amusing); *look at something interesting* (informal) – 2 words (check out); *the metal or plastic around the lenses in a pair of glasses* – 1 word (frames); *not fashionable* – 1 word (uncool); *a series of activities to support a social aim, eg healthy eating* – 1 word (campaign).

REACT

5

- Divide the class into pairs to discuss the questions with their partner.
- Invite different students to share and explain their points of view. Try to develop a class discussion.

Alternative procedure: less confident classes

Ask students to read the questions and make some notes for their answers. Set a time limit of five minutes. Check that students have thought about the language they will need to answer the questions well. Help students with vocabulary if necessary.

Divide the class into pairs to answer the questions.

Change pairs and repeat the task, if time.

GO BEYOND

Ask students to work individually or in pairs to write slogans for each of the photos. You may wish to give them an example, eg *Funky frames for all the family! Stop chasing those extra fruits and vegetables … you'll find them all in 5 FG Juice! Come in for our winter sale … as fast as you can!*

Extra activity

Ask students to write one or two comments about the ads or responding to the comments in Exercise 2. Encourage them to communicate the tone of their comment(s) using tips from the HOW TO box, eg

I don't think that ice desert is a good place for a holiday!!! Ugh! I think Ad 3 could be for a freezer or fridge. It looks INCREDIBLY cold.

Recorded reading text 2.16

The reading text is recorded as an extra audio track which can be exploited for various purposes.

In this lesson, play the first paragraph as a lead-in to Exercise 2. Ask students what the website is for in general and what today's challenge is.

Homework

Ask students to write about an advert that they like. Encourage them to write two paragraphs, one to describe the advert and say what the product is and the second to say why they like it. Set a word limit of 120 words.

GRAMMAR Possibility and impossibility

Make logical guesses Page 63

STAGE	TIME	FOCUS
GET STARTED		Look at comments people made about photos in the last lesson and recall the photos.
READ AND LISTEN		Read and listen to a conversation where people are looking at close-up photos of objects and making guesses about what the objects are.
STUDY		Complete grammar explanations about the use of *can't, could, may, might* and *must* to make guesses, using examples from the conversation.
PRACTISE		Practise using *can't, could, may, might* and *must* to make guesses in controlled and semi-controlled exercises.
SPEAK		Look at photos of objects from unusual angles and make guesses about what the objects are.

Get started

Write these sentences from the blog comments in the last lesson on the board:

Ad 1 must be for glasses.
No, it can't be glasses – that would be too obvious. It could be toothpaste.
Those awful clothes must be from the 1970s.
It must be for healthy eating.
It might be to do with the campaign to eat five portions of fruit and vegetables a day.
Ad 3 might be for holidays.

Remind students that these were some of the guesses that people made about the advert photos. Divide the class into pairs to recall what was in the photos and say why people made these guesses, eg *Someone thought Ad 1 must be for glasses because the whole family were wearing big glasses with black frames.*

READ AND LISTEN Grammar in context

1 2.17

- Focus students on the photos of two products from adverts. Ask them to read and listen to two people talking about the products.
- Ask students *Do they know what the products are?* (They don't: they are making guesses.)
- Divide the class into pairs to discuss what they think the objects might be. Set a time limit of two minutes for this and then ask for some ideas in open class.

ANSWERS / AUDIO SCRIPT 2.17

The objects in the pictures are a piece of Lego (left) and a games console (right).
See Student's Book page 63 for audio script.

STUDY

2

- Refer students to the aim of the lesson, *Make logical guesses*, and explain that logical guesses are based on some evidence, eg the photos in Exercise 1.
- Ask them to complete the grammar explanations with the words in orange from Exercise 1. Allow three minutes.
- Encourage students to compare their answers in pairs before you go through the explanations and ask individual students to read out the completed explanations.
- Refer students back to the conversation by asking questions like *What does Nate think the first photo is?* (the top of a cooker) *What does Maizy think it can't be?* (the top of a cooker) *Why?* (because of the colour) *What does Maizy think they must be?* (buttons) *What does Maizy think it could be?* (a gadget) *What do Nate and Maizy think the second photo might be?* (a piece of kitchen equipment).
- Ask them what verb form is used after *can't, could, may, might* and *must*, (*be* – the infinitive without *to*).

ANSWERS

may, might must can't

Extra activity

If students need help to remember which modals represent which level of possibility, draw a vertical line on the board and label the top *possible* and the bottom *impossible*.

Ask students where to place the modals *can't*, *could*, *may*, *might* and *must* (*must* at the top, *could/may/might* in the middle, *can't* at the bottom).

Tell students that *could*, *may* and *might* can all be used to say that you are not sure something is possible. It doesn't matter which one you use.

Point out that although all the examples in the conversation are with the verb *to be*, modals are also used with other verbs. Prompt students to give some examples with other verbs for these situations:

– They see a man with a trolley full of bananas at the supermarket. – *He must like bananas. He might have a pet monkey.*

– They meet a teenager who is a swimming champion. – *She must train a lot. She can't spend much time having fun with her friends.*

PRACTISE

3a

- Ask students to complete the sentences with the products from the box. Set a time limit of three minutes.
- Nominate different students to say their answers.

ANSWERS

1 car 2 ring 3 shampoo 4 spaghetti 5 mobile 6 cheese

3b

- Divide the class into pairs. Ask them to think of two products and to write very short explanations of what the products are. Point out that they shouldn't give too much detail, as other students are going to try and guess what the products are. Set a time limit of five minutes. Before they start, invite volunteers to read out the model conversation and elicit a few suggestions in open class, eg *It might be a wooden spoon. It could be a broom. It may be a ruler.*
- Circulate and help students as necessary.
- Ask pairs to form groups of four and encourage each pair to read out their explanations for the other pair to guess the products.
- Circulate and monitor, making a note of any language you wish to focus on at the end of the activity.

Alternative procedure: less confident classes

Give students some language that they might find useful, eg *It's long/round/blue/soft … ; It looks like a … ; It's got … ; It's made of … .*

4

- Ask students to read quickly through the two conversations in order to get an idea of the situation.
- Encourage them to complete the conversations with the correct modals. Point out that these can be either positive or negative. Set a time limit of four minutes.
- Encourage students to compare their answers in pairs before you check them in open class. If there is any disagreement, ask students to justify their answers, eg *I put* can't *because Anna looks outside to see if it's raining and it isn't.*
- Invite students to read out the conversations in pairs.

ANSWERS

1 might/may/could 2 can't 3 must 4 might/may/could 5 can't 6 must

SPEAK

5

- Focus students' attention on the photos. Divide the class into pairs to discuss them and decide what the objects are.
- Encourage them to use the conversations in Exercises 1 and 4 to help them and to give reasons for their guesses, especially when they are sure that something is possible or impossible.
- Monitor and make corrections as necessary.
- When time is up, or students are confident they know what the items are, refer them to page 142 to confirm their ideas.

Extra activity

Tell students you found a wallet in the street and that you are going to show them some of the things in the wallet. Ask them to make some guesses about the owner of the wallet. Prepare some 'evidence' to use, such as a business card, a train or bus ticket, a receipt, a family photo, a gym membership card, a telephone number written on a scrap of paper, etc and display it on your desk. Give students a couple of minutes to look at the evidence and then ask them to work in pairs to guess the owner of the wallet.

Homework

Ask students to write three conversations like the ones in Exercises 1 and 4 using some of the photos in Exercise 5.

LISTENING AND VOCABULARY Smart shopping

Understand the speaker's intention

Page 64

STAGE	TIME	FOCUS
GET STARTED		Recycle phrases to use when talking about shopping.
SPEAK AND LISTEN		Talk about shopping centres. Listen to an interview with a shopping centre designer. Learn how to understand the speaker's intention.
REACT		Talk about the tricks used by shopping centre designers.
WORK WITH WORDS		Learn words for people and things in a shop.
SPEAK		Design your dream shop.

Get started

Give students three minutes to make phrases of three or four words related to shopping, using one word or phrase from each of these groups:

1 *be, get, pay, keep, exchange, return, try*
2 *in, by, a(n), on*
3 *clothes, special offer, the sale, refund, receipt, item, discount, cash, card*

Explain that they can use some of the verbs more than once. Invite them to check their phrases by looking back at page 60. Ask them to take it in turns to test each other using the definitions on page 60.

ANSWERS

be in the sale   be on special offer   get a refund
get a discount   pay in cash   pay by card   keep the receipt
exchange an item   return an item   try on clothes

SPEAK AND LISTEN

1

- Read through the questions with the class. Elicit examples of services, eg bank, post office, doctor's, library, etc.
- Check the meaning of *couldn't really afford* (didn't have enough money to be able to buy).
- Give students an example answer for question 3, eg *Last summer I was on holiday and I went to a chemist's to buy some sun cream. While I was in the shop I started to look at sunglasses, trying them on just for fun. I usually don't buy expensive sunglasses because I lose them all the time, but I found a pair that I really liked, so I bought them. I didn't really want to spend that much money on a pair of sunglasses, so I felt a bit stupid when I left the shop. I lost them the next day!*
- Divide the class into pairs to answer the questions. Set a time limit of five minutes.

2a

- Explain to students that when they are listening, it is important not only to understand what a person is saying, but why they are saying it. Understanding the speaker's intention can help them make sense of a listening extract.
- Ask them to read the tips in the HOW TO box and underline key words.
- In open class, ask students which words they underlined.

2b 2.18

- Ask students to read the options and underline the verbs.
- Play the track for students to listen to the interview, focusing on the speaker's intention, and choose the correct option: A, B or C.
- Conduct a poll to see which option students chose and confirm the correct answer.

ANSWER / AUDIO SCRIPT 2.18

C

Interviewer: I'm here at Towngreen Centre with shopping centre designer James Lewis. ... James, would you mind telling us what tricks shops use to make us buy more?
James: Well, firstly, the more time you spend in a shopping centre, the more you buy. Shopping centres are often designed as a circle, like this one, so it's hard to find the exits.
Interviewer: Yes, I've already lost my sense of direction!
James: And there are no clocks, so you lose your sense of time too. Did you notice that the lifts and escalators weren't at the entrance? That meant we had to walk past a lot of shops first. It's the same reason why popular items are always at the back of shops.
Interviewer: So what's at the front?
James: Well, studies show that people nearly always turn right when they go into a shop. So that's where you find most special offers and discount items – front right.
Interviewer: What about things at the cash desk? Like the sweets at that supermarket checkout.
James: Yes, easy to put in your basket or trolley while you're waiting to pay. And look how products that children like are on lower shelves. That's so kids can take them and put them in the trolley. Whereas for adults, the most expensive items are always on the shelves at eye level.
Interviewer: So, shops play cleverly on sight. But could you tell us how they play on other senses?
James: Well, most shops use fragrances and smells – like the smell of fresh bread from the supermarket over there. Air conditioning makes the smell stronger. Touch is important too – feeling products and trying them on. Teen fashion shops often have untidy shelves – that suggests lots of people have touched the clothes, so they must be popular.
Interviewer: James, your job is to make people buy more. But don't people buy too much?
James: Well shoppers need to be smart too. You should never go shopping when you're upset, hungry or bored – you buy more then. And always ask yourself: 'Can I afford it and do I need it?' If the answer is 'no', don't buy it.

3 ▶2.18

Exam-type task

- Give students one minute to read the questions before you play the track again. Ask them to listen and choose the correct option for each question.
- Check the meaning of *trick* (an effective or skilful way of doing something).
- Encourage students to compare their answers in pairs. Ask if they would like to listen to the interview again and repeat if necessary.
- Check answers in open class. Encourage students to explain their reasons for choosing each answer.

ANSWERS
1 B 2 C 3 A 4 C

REACT

4

- Ask students to recall James Lewis' advice to shoppers (never go shopping when you're upset, hungry or bored; always ask yourself: 'Can I afford it and do I need it?' If the answer is 'no' don't buy it.) Check the meaning of *upset* (sad, worried or angry about something).
- Divide the class into pairs to discuss the questions. Set a time limit of three minutes.

WORK WITH WORDS

5 ▶2.19

- Focus students on the photos and give them two minutes, in pairs, to say what they see. Encourage them to do this without looking at the words below the photos at this stage. This will give them a chance to recall vocabulary they already know.
- Ask students to match the words to the photos. Set a time limit of five minutes.
- Play the track for them to listen and check their answers.

ANSWERS / AUDIO SCRIPT ▶2.19
a shop window b escalator c department d cash desk
e checkout f changing room g basket h trolley i shelf
j exit k customer l store detective

SPEAK

6

- Divide the class into pairs to design their dream shop. Encourage students to be as creative as they like and to follow these steps. Set a time limit for each stage to keep the activity on track.
  - Decide what the shop sells, eg football products, items relating to a favourite singer or actor, Harry Potter, etc. Suggest that they include their favourite products and/or invent products that they would like to have in their shop. (five minutes)
  - Think of an interesting name for the shop. (two minutes)
  - Make a floor plan of where things are. (10 minutes)
- Encourage students to look at the shop vocabulary in Exercise 5 and to consider how some of these items will be used (or not used) in their shops, eg Will there be a store detective? What will the baskets or trolleys look like? What will go in the shop windows? etc.
- Ask pairs to form groups of four to take it in turns to present their ideas.

GO BEYOND

Ask students to do the Go Beyond task on page 135.

Extra activity

Ask students to work in pairs and write a list of advice for people who go to shopping centres. Invite them to include an interesting title and then four or five points for consumers to consider, with advice on what to do.

Give them an example and remind them to use the expressions of purpose, eg *Decide how long you want to spend shopping before you go so that you don't waste your day.*

Homework

Ask students to think of a story about a shopping experience. It doesn't need to be true. Encourage them to include as many words from Exercise 5 as possible in their story and write at least 120 words.

GRAMMAR Indirect questions

Ask polite questions *Page 65*

STAGE	TIME	FOCUS
GET STARTED		Play a game to revise question forms and introduce indirect questions.
READ AND LISTEN		Read and listen to a conversation at a shopping centre information desk.
STUDY		Study explanations of how indirect questions are formed and when they are used. Use examples from the conversation to complete the explanations.
PRACTISE		Practise writing indirect questions. Ask and answer indirect questions using a map of a shopping centre.
SPEAK		Role-play two situations and find out information by asking indirect questions.

Get started

Play a game of *Double your Bet.* (see page 97). Write these questions on the board and explain the rules. Students have to decide if the sentences are correct or incorrect.

1 *Do you have any idea where can I find a bank near here?*
2 *Where can I find a bank near here?*
3 *Can you tell me where I can find a bank near here?*
4 *Do you know what time does the movie start?*
5 *Do you know what time the movie starts?*
6 *Do you know what time starts the movie?*
7 *Would you mind to tell me where I can try this jacket on?*
8 *Would you mind telling me where can I try this jacket on?*
9 *Would you mind telling me where I can try this jacket on?*

Set a time limit of four minutes for students to work in pairs and place their bets.

Check the answers at the end of the class, by which time students should be able to identify the correct questions.

ANSWERS
Questions 2, 3, 5 and 9 are correct.

READ AND LISTEN Grammar in context

1 2.20

- Ask students to look at the picture and say what's happening. (The boy is confused and looking at a map of a shopping centre.)
- Play the track for students to read and listen to the conversation and answer the questions.
- Check answers in open class.

ANSWERS / AUDIO SCRIPT 2.20
Electronic World, an electronics shop.
It's on level two, about five shops down after the escalator.
It closes at 7pm.
See Student's Book page 65 for audio script.

STUDY

2

- Ask students if they thought Stefano sounded polite in the conversation and why. Explain that in English we use indirect questions when we want to be polite or more formal.
- Focus students on the *Form* section of the grammar explanation. Ask students to find examples in Exercise 1 to complete them.
- Check them by nominating individual students to read them out.
- Read through the section on word order with students. Point out the following additional points:
  - After *Would you mind …* we use the *-ing* form of the verb.
  - If the direct question uses *do/does*, this is omitted in the indirect question, eg *Where does Holly live?* → *Do you know where Holly lives?*
  - If the direct question is a *yes/no* question, we use *if* in an indirect question, eg *Does the shop close late today?* → *Do you know if the shop closes late today?*

ANSWERS
any idea where I can buy a computer mouse?
tell me how I can find Electronic World, please?
showing me where it is on the map?
know if the shop closes late today?

PRACTISE

3

- Ask students to write direct questions for the other three indirect questions from the conversation in Exercise 1. Set a time limit of five minutes.
- Encourage students to compare their answers in pairs before you invite different students to come to the board and write their answers. Ask other students if they agree with the solutions on the board and make corrections as necessary.

ANSWERS
1 How can I find Electronic World?
2 Where is it on the map?
3 Does the shop close late today?

4a

- Refer students back to the phrases in orange in Exercise 1. Encourage them to use these to make the questions in this exercise sound more polite. Allow seven minutes.
- Elicit and check answers in open class.

Alternative procedure: less confident classes

Ask students to identify parts of the questions before starting, eg have them underline verbs, circle subjects and put a square around examples of *do/did*.

Remind students of the key changes they will have to make in this exercise, ie the order of the subject and verb and the removal of the auxiliary *do*.

4b

- Divide the class into pairs to role-play a conversation at the information desk in the shopping centre. Encourage them to ask and answer the questions in Exercise 4a using the map. Remind them to be polite and to use indirect questions. Set a time limit of six minutes.

SPEAK

5a

- Ask students to work in A/B pairs.
- Refer Students B to page 142 where they will find some cinema information.
- Ask Students A to use the prompts to ask indirect questions to find out this information.

5b

- Ask students to swap roles. Refer Students A to the information about a fashion show on page 141.
- Ask Students B to use the prompts to ask indirect questions to find out this information.

Extra activity

Make some sets of cards with the following 20 questions and situations:

What is the time?
What time does the concert start?
How long is the exam?
How do I get to Baker Street?
What is the teacher's name?
Where can I buy an English dictionary?
Who do I have to speak to about getting a discount?
Where are the items in the sale?
Which bus goes to the city centre?
Where is the nearest train station?
Can you tell me where the library is?
Do you have any idea what I need to do to get a travel visa?
Would you mind telling me how to download this app?
Do you know how long this film is?
Could you tell me how I can get to Charing Cross station?
SITUATION: In a clothes shop
SITUATION: At a tourist information centre
SITUATION: In the street, asking for directions
SITUATION: In a hotel
SITUATION: In an airport

Make separate sets of these indirect question starters:
Do you have any idea …
Could you tell me …
Would you mind (+ *-ing*) me …
Do you know …
I wonder if you could tell me …

Divide the class into pairs or groups of four. Give each pair/group one set of the 20 question/situation cards and one set of indirect question starters. Ask them to shuffle the 20 cards and place them face down in a pile. Next to them, they should place the indirect question starters, also face down. Students take it in turns to pick up a question/situation card.

- If it is a direct question, they should pick up an indirect question starter and make an indirect question.
- If it is an indirect question, they should convert it into a direct question.
- If it is a situation card, they must think of an indirect question to ask in this situation.

Homework

Ask students to write a conversation between a customer and a shop assistant which includes at least three indirect questions. In the next class, ask students to practise their conversations in pairs.

LANGUAGE & BEYOND *COMMUNICATE & COOPERATE*

Be assertive *Page 66*

STAGE	TIME	FOCUS
GET STARTED		Talk about how you would react and how you would feel in three different situations.
SPEAK AND READ		Read and listen to three versions of a situation. Decide which version represents passive behaviour, assertive behaviour and aggressive behaviour. Select actions from a list that show assertive behaviour.
DO		Role-play a situation in three different ways: aggressive, passive and assertive. Discuss how each role-play felt.
REFLECT		Discuss the importance of knowing what you want and acting assertively to get it.
EXTEND		Talk about how to be assertive in four different situations.

LIFE SKILLS

BE ASSERTIVE

As teenagers begin to interact more independently they are certain to find themselves in situations where they have to clearly state what they want, even if this may clash with the wishes of other people. In this lesson students will learn that there are times where it is important to know and value what they want and to be able to act assertively to get it. This is quite distinct from putting their own desires above the needs and wants of others and the tips in this lesson make it clear that being assertive is about respecting others, as well as having a healthy respect for oneself. Assertive behaviour is contrasted with the extremes of passive and aggressive behaviour and students are encouraged to explore these three ways of reacting to a variety of situations. Assertiveness is seen as an effective 'middle way' and students will learn that what we say and our body language can contribute to assertive behaviour.

Get started

Outline three situations to students and give them three minutes to talk about how they would react and how they would feel in each.

- Imagine you have bought something in a shop that was broken or damaged.
- Imagine that you have been waiting in a queue to buy tickets for a concert and someone pushes in front of you.
- Imagine that you are trying to work in class and someone keeps trying to distract you.

Invite students to share some of their ideas in open class.

SPEAK AND READ

1 2.21

- Focus students on the photos and the conversations. Ask them to read and listen to the situations and to think about how Seth behaves in each one.

- Refer them to the words and definitions and ask them to describe Seth in each situation using one of the words.
- Check answers with the class.

ANSWERS / AUDIO SCRIPT 2.21

1 B passive 2 C assertive 3 A aggressive

See Student's Book page 66 for audio script.

2

- Focus students' attention on the list and ask them to tick the actions that are assertive.
- Encourage them to compare their answers in pairs before you check them in open class.

ANSWERS

be calm and not emotional listen to other people
say what you want repeat your wishes stand up straight
make eye contact speak slowly and clearly

DO

3

- Read through the situation with students. Ask if anyone has ever experienced this type of situation.
- Explain that they are going to role-play this situation in three different ways: aggressive, passive and assertive.
- Ask students to look at the PHRASE BYTES box and decide which of the phrases could be used for the aggressive, the passive and the assertive role-plays.
- Model one of the role-play versions with a more confident student.
  Student: *Er, can you please get in the queue?*
  Teacher: *But I have to get back to my car. It's parked in a no parking zone.*
  Student: *I said, 'get in the queue', OK?*
- Divide the class into pairs to take it in turns to play both roles. If you have room in your classroom, it may help them to act out the role-play.
- Monitor and give positive feedback.

4

- Ask students to talk in the same pairs and say how they felt in each situation. Ask them if it was difficult to be assertive and invite them to give feedback in open class.

REFLECT

5

- Work through the questions with the class, inviting different students to read out each question and giving students some ideas to help them formulate their ideas (see below). Vary the dynamic for each question, eg questions 1 and 3 could be answered in pairs. Question 2 would make a good open-class discussion.
- After the discussions, invite students to read the REFLECTION POINT and say if they agree or not and why.

Suggested discussion prompts

1 Think about your friends at school or people in your family. Who is the most assertive? What makes them assertive? Can you think of any situations where they behave assertively? Maybe you think you are assertive. When do you behave assertively? Can you give any examples?

2 Ask the class to brainstorm some of the reasons why it is sometimes hard to be assertive, eg:
  - You worry that people won't like you if you say what you really want.
  - Some people might react aggressively if you disagree with them.
  - You don't want to hurt other people's feelings.

3 Give students some different contexts to think about, eg at school, at home, with friends, with the sports team, in a shopping centre, in a restaurant, on public transport, with people you don't know.

Alternative procedure for REFLECTION POINT

Copy the comments below onto strips of paper:

- *For me, an important part of the reflection point is where it says 'Know what you want'. It's much easier to be assertive in any situation when you are sure about what is important to you.*
- *I think that acting assertively is something that gets easier the more you do it. At first it's really scary, especially if you feel a bit shy, but you don't have to change your personality or anything like that. It's usually just a small change in the way you behave in situations. Give it a try!*
- *When we did the role-play in a passive way I felt really angry because the other person was being rude and I was waiting patiently in the queue but they got what they wanted! So when it says 'This will help you feel better' I think that's what it means. It's about being fair, not just to other people, but also to yourself!*
- *When you act assertively you are giving a message to other people that you respect yourself and are confident in yourself. I think this is something that is attractive to other people.*
- *I had a friend once who would never say what he wanted to do and in the end it was really boring because I always had to decide what we were going to do. I got sick of it. It's much better for a friendship if both people contribute to deciding about things to do.*
- *It's not just about being assertive all the time. Sometimes you have to decide when the moment to be assertive is. Sometimes, if something is not very important to you, you may prefer just to let things go. However it is important to feel that you can be assertive when you want or need to be.*

Explain to students that you are going to give them some comments that other students have made about the REFLECTION POINT for today's lesson. Divide the class into groups of four and give one comment to each group. Invite them to discuss whether or not they agree with the comments.

Give the groups two minutes to discuss the comment and then ask them to pass their comment to the next group. Repeat until the groups have discussed all the comments.

EXTEND

6

- Divide the class into pairs to look at the situations on page 142 and decide how to be assertive. Advise them to think about the different ways people might react in each situation and how to deal with these reactions, maintaining an assertive stance.
- Circulate and monitor, making a note of any language you would like to focus on at the end of the activity.

Extra activity

Ask students to write a conversation for one of the situations in Exercise 6 demonstrating how to act assertively.

Invite them to read out their conversations to the class and encourage other students to comment on how successful the assertive behaviour was.

Homework

Ask students to read the emails to a teen advice website (either write them on the board for students to copy or prepare as handouts before the lesson). Encourage them to choose one and write an answer, including some ideas from today's life skills lesson.

Check the meaning of *get sick of*, (get bored or annoyed with something).

> Dear Aimee
>
> I have a problem. I have a really nice group of friends, but when we are deciding about things to do, I feel too shy to make suggestions. I get a bit sick of always following along, especially as we usually end up going to the shopping centre – I'm so bored with that place ☹ I end up feeling angry with myself and with my friends but I don't know how to change things. Can you help?
>
> Marie

> Dear Aimee
>
> Recently I have had a problem with some of the guys on my football team. We used to do fun stuff like go to the cinema or go bowling but lately a couple of the guys just like hanging out and doing nothing or doing stupid things like calling out silly comments to other kids in the street. I really enjoy doing things with the football guys, but I hate just wasting time like that. The thing is, I don't want them to think I'm not cool. What should I do?
>
> Graham

SPEAKING At the cash desk

Return goods and make a complaint *Page 67*

STAGE	TIME	FOCUS
GET STARTED		Recycle indirect question forms.
SPEAK		Talk about different phrases used to return things to a shop. Say what products the phrases could refer to.
WATCH OR LISTEN		Watch or listen to four scenes where people are returning things to a shop. Learn how to be polite.
ACT		Practise being polite but assertive in a role-play about asking for an exchange or a refund in a shop.

Get started

Write these questions on the board. Ask students to work in pairs and rewrite them as indirect/polite questions.

1 *Where can I make a complaint?*
2 *What is the problem?*
3 *Where do I go to exchange this T-shirt?*

Ask different pairs for their answers and accept a variety of indirect question starters, eg *Could you tell me …* , *Do you have any idea …* , *Do you know …* , *Would you mind* (+ verb *-ing*) … .

SPEAK

1

- Focus students on the explanations people give when they take things back to a shop.
- Invite different students to read out the comments and then ask what products the phrases could be about.

WATCH OR LISTEN

2a 2.22

- Explain to students that they are going to watch or listen to four scenes where people are returning items to shops.
- Play the scene for students to note down what each person is returning and why.
- Encourage students to compare their answers in pairs before you check them in open class.

ANSWERS / VIDEO/AUDIO SCRIPT 2.22

1 A jumper because it's the wrong size.
2 A DVD player because it doesn't work, the sound isn't right.
3 A T-shirt because the customer has changed his mind.
4 A shirt because there's a hole in it.

1

Alice: I'm afraid this jumper is the wrong size. I'd like to change it for a smaller one.
Shop assistant: That's fine. Do you have your receipt?
Alice: Yes, here you are.
Shop assistant: OK … there you go.
Alice: Thank you very much.

2

Shop assistant: How can I help you?
Bella: I'd like to return this DVD player. It doesn't work. The sound isn't right.
Shop assistant: Are you sure? Maybe you haven't read the instructions properly.
Bella: I'm sure. I'd like a refund please.

3

Finn: I'd like to return this T-shirt.
Shop assistant: Is there anything wrong with it?
Finn: No, I've changed my mind. It doesn't suit me.

4

Max: I'd like to return this shirt. I'm afraid there's a hole in it.
Shop assistant: Erm ... I can give you a discount.
Max: No, thank you. Here's my receipt. I'd like a refund.
Shop assistant: Would you like to exchange it for something else?
Max: No, thank you. I'd like a refund.

2b 2.22

- Focus students on the conversations in Exercise 2a and ask them to complete them using the phrases in Exercise 1 to help them.
- Play the track for students to listen and check.

ANSWERS
1 wrong size 2 doesn't work 3 I've changed my mind
4 hole in it

3 2.23

- Ask students to look back at the phrases in Exercise 1 and to underline the words they think will be stressed.
- Play the track for them to listen and check.
- Play the track again for them to listen and repeat.

ANSWERS / AUDIO SCRIPT 2.23
1 They're the wrong size. / They don't fit.
2 It doesn't suit me. / It doesn't look right.
3 I've changed my mind.
4 There's a mark on it. / There's a hole in it.
5 It doesn't work. / It's broken.

4a

- Ask students if they thought the people in the scenes in Exercise 2 were polite, neutral or rude.
- Elicit how you can tell if someone is being polite, eg tone of voice, intonation, use of particular phrases, body language.
- Ask students to read the tips in the HOW TO box. Invite a volunteer to read the tips out loud.
- Ask students to tell you a different meaning of the phrase *I'm afraid ...*, (*I'm scared/frightened*) and explain that the two meanings are quite different.

4b

- Refer students back to the conversations and ask them to underline the polite phrases in the conversations. Set a time limit of two minutes.
- Elicit examples of each of the phrases in the HOW TO box.

ANSWERS
See underlining in video/audio script in Exercise 2a.

Extra activity
Remind students that sometimes when we make complaints or return items to a shop it's important to be assertive as well as polite.

Ask them if they can recall some of the suggestions for assertive behaviour from the Life Skills lesson. Give them prompts if necessary.

ACT

5 2.24

- Divide the class into pairs to act out two conversations. Explain that they should take it in turns to be the shop assistant and the customer.
- Before they act out their conversations, encourage them to decide what type of shop it is, what they have bought, what the problem is, if they want to exchange the item or get a refund, what options the shop assistant will offer and how the customer can be assertive and polite.
- Play the track with the phrases in the PHRASEBOOK box and invite students to tick the ones they plan to use in their conversations.
- Invite some students to perform one of their conversations for the class.

Extra activity
Ask students to read out the conversations below in pairs. Ask them if the customers get what they want (no).

Elicit why the customer didn't get what they wanted (in conversation 1, the customer is too passive; in conversation 2, the customer is too aggressive).

Ask students to rewrite the conversations making them more assertive and polite so that the customer gets what they want.

Conversation 1
Herman: Er ... sorry, but um ... there seems to be a little hole in this shirt. Um ... is there anything ... anything you can do?
Assistant: No sir. We don't normally do exchanges or refunds.
Herman: Oh. OK. Thanks anyway.

Conversation 2
Georgie: Can I speak to the manager?
Assistant: Can I ask what the problem is?
Georgie: I said I want to speak to the manager!
Assistant: I'm afraid she's not here at the moment. Can I help?
Georgie: Give me a refund on this shirt. I took it home but I don't like it.
Assistant: I can offer you an exchange but not a refund I'm afraid.
Georgie: If I wanted an exchange I would ask for an exchange. Refund! Now!
Assistant: I'm sorry, but I can't give you a refund. Perhaps if you come again later when the manager is here?
Georgie: How rude! I'm never going to shop here again!

Homework

Ask students if they can remember phrases from the lesson to match the phrases and definitions below.

Encourage them to write as many as they can without looking at page 67, and then to look at page 67 to find the rest.

1 Say that you're not happy about something
2 A polite way to introduce a complaint
3 I did want it, but now I don't
4 I'd like my money back
5 A polite way of refusing something
6 Two ways to say they're too small/big
7 I can reduce the price
8 Do you have the document that shows you paid?
9 Two ways to say it doesn't look good on me
10 Would you like to take something else which has the same price?
11 It doesn't work
12 A polite way to introduce a request

ANSWERS
1 make a complaint 2 I'm afraid ...
3 I've changed my mind. 4 I'd like a refund.
5 No, thank you. 6 They're the wrong size. / They don't fit.
7 I can give you a discount. 8 Do you have the/your receipt?
9 It doesn't suit me. / It doesn't look right.
10 Would you like to exchange it for something else?
11 It's broken. 12 I'd like ...

WRITING We look forward to hearing from you

Use polite phrases in formal emails and letters

Page 68

STAGE	TIME	FOCUS
GET STARTED		Talk about famous brands.
SPEAK AND READ		Do a survey about brands. Read a letter and say who it was written by and for. Find polite phrases in the letter.
PRACTISE		Rewrite an email to make it sound more polite and formal.
PLAN		Work in a group to plan a survey about advertising and a letter to go with it.
WRITE AND CHECK		Write the survey and letter and check them.
SHARE	Another class	Send the survey to other students and summarise their replies.

Get started

Write these names on the board: Coca-Cola, Microsoft, IBM, Google, Apple, Nokia, McDonald's, BMW, Disney, Nike.

Elicit from students what they have in common. (They are the ten most famous brands in the world.)

Check the meaning of *brand* (a product or group of products that is made by a particular company and widely recognised by its name). Ask students to say what products these brands sell and what the brand logo looks like.

Divide the class into groups to talk about any other brands that they think could be included in a list of the most famous brands in the world and any brands that are famous in their country but not as well known around the world.

ANSWERS

Coca-Cola – soft drinks   Microsoft – computers, software
IBM – information technology
Google – internet services, search engine, etc
Apple – computers, iPods, mobile phones, etc
Nokia – mobile phones   McDonald's – hamburgers
BMW – cars   Disney – entertainment
Nike – sports shoes and clothes

SPEAK AND READ

1

- Focus students on the survey about brands and ask them to read it through quickly. Set a time limit of one minute.
- Focus on the two follow-up questions to question 1 in the survey. Ask students which of the questions asks the reader to choose between two options and which asks about a wide range of options. (*What are your favourite shops and why?* = wide range of options; *Which is most important: the product or the price?* = two options)
- Ask students to underline the corresponding question words in the survey. Then refer students to the **Get it right** box.
- Divide the class into pairs to take it in turns to ask and answer the questions in the survey.

2

- Refer students to the letter. Ask them to read it and finish the sentences. Set a time limit of two minutes.
- Check the answers in open class.

ANSWERS

Class 8b, Westwood High School   a class in a different school

3a

- Check the meaning of *formal* when we are talking about writing style (suitable for official or serious tasks). Elicit the opposite of *formal* (*informal*).
- Ask for some examples of the types of writing task where formal writing is necessary, eg job application letters, letter/email of complaint, letter/email asking for information (eg about a course).
- Ask students if they think the letter in Exercise 2 is formal or informal. (It is formal.) Explain that one of the ways we can make writing formal is by using certain polite phrases.
- Ask them to read the tips in the HOW TO box. Invite volunteers to read the tips out loud.
- Ask students if they know of similar polite phrases that are used in their own language(s).

3b

- Refer students back to the letter in Exercise 2 and ask them to underline the phrases from the HOW TO box.
- Elicit how the first two phrases finish.
- Point out that the phrase beginning *We would be grateful if you could tell us …* is an example of an indirect question. Elicit that the direct question would be *What do you buy and where do you shop?*.

ANSWERS

We are writing to ask for help with a survey about brands.
We would be grateful if you could tell us what you buy and where you shop.

PRACTISE

4

- Focus students on the email and ask them to make it sound more polite and formal. Remind them to use phrases from the HOW TO box. Set a time limit of five minutes.
- Encourage students to compare their formal versions of the email in pairs while you write the model answer on the board.
- Invite students to say if their versions were different in any way. Evaluate any differences in open class and say if they are correct or not.

MODEL ANSWER
Dear Class Teacher,
We are writing to ask if your students could answer our questionnaire.
We would be grateful if they could help us.
Thank you for your help. We look forward to hearing from you.
Yours sincerely,
Class 8b, Westwood High School

PLAN

5

- Divide the class into small groups and explain that they are going to write a survey about advertising for another class and an email to go with it.
- Focus their attention on the **Writing plan** and go through the different points with them.
- Give students 15 minutes for this preparation.

WRITE AND CHECK

6

- Ask students to work individually, using the plan and the preparatory work they did in groups to write their email and survey questions. Set a time limit of 15 minutes.
- When students have finished writing, encourage them to check their work.
- Invite students to compare their emails and surveys with other members of their group.

SHARE

7

- Collect students' emails and surveys.
- Distribute a representative letter and survey from each of the groups in Exercise 5 to another class.
- When you have replies to the surveys, return them to the students who wrote the survey and ask them to write a short summary of the replies and present it to the class.

Alternative procedure

If you do not have the opportunity to send the students' surveys to another class, distribute them within your own class and ask students to fill in the survey written by another group as a homework task. As students hand in their survey answers, return them to the writers so that they can read about their classmates' opinions.

Homework

Ask students to write a short formal letter/email about something they have bought online which arrived in the post damaged or broken. Give them an outline like this:

Paragraph 1: say why you are writing
Paragraph 2: say what you bought and describe the problem
Paragraph 3: make a formal request about what action you would like the company to take
Paragraph 4: give polite thanks and say you expect a reply

Remind students to use phrases from the HOW TO boxes on pages 67 and 68.

VOCABULARY Shopping

1

- Divide the class into pairs to look at the words and phrases in the box and say what they mean. Encourage them to circle any items they don't remember.
- Ask students to work individually to complete the poster using the words in the box.
- Encourage them to compare their answers in pairs and say if they now remember the meaning of any items they circled earlier.
- Check answers in open class.
- Ask students to identify three words in the list that have the stress pattern Oo (*special*, *refund*, *discount*).

ANSWERS
1 special offer 2 the sale 3 in cash 4 by card
5 Try on 6 return 7 exchange 8 a refund
9 the receipt 10 a discount

Things and people in a shop

2

- Write this phrase on the board: *The customer is always right*. Ask if students know a similar phrase in their language(s). Elicit why a shop or business might say this, eg because they believe that if someone is going to spend money in a shop, they can behave in any way they like.
- Explain that Sid's Superstore believes in this philosophy and read through the first two sentences of the text, inserting *customer* in the first gap as an example.
- Ask students to read and complete the shop notices, pointing out that the first letter of each missing word is given.
- Nominate different students to read out each of the notices and check the spelling of their answers.

ANSWERS
1 customer 2 shop window 3 cash desk
4 escalator 5 basket 6 trolley
7 store detective 8 shelves 9 checkout
10 changing room 11 department 12 exit

GRAMMAR Possibility and impossibility

3

- Write these verbs on the board: *can't*, *could*, *may*, *might*, *must*.
- Ask students which verbs we use when:
  - we are not sure about something (*could*, *may*, *might*).
  - when we are sure something is true (*must*).
- Ask them when we use *can't* (when we are sure something is impossible).
- Explain that Lucy and Ben are having a conversation about the product in the picture. Ask them to complete the conversation by choosing the correct verbs.
- Check answers in open class. Then divide the class into pairs to read the conversation out loud.

ANSWERS
1 might 2 may 3 can't 4 could 5 must
8 might 7 must 8 must

Indirect questions

4

- Ask students to put the words in order to make indirect questions.
- Suggest that fast finishers write direct questions to match one or two of the indirect questions, eg *Where is the shoe department?*
- Nominate different students to read out their answers.

ANSWERS
1 Do you know where the shoe department is?
2 Do you have any idea how much this shampoo costs?
3 Could you tell me what time the shop closes?
4 Do you know which floor I need for the café?
5 Would you mind telling me when the sale starts?
6 Could you tell me who the shop manager is?

Extra Resources

Go to the Teacher's Resource Centre at www.macmillanbeyond.com for:

- the Speaking section of the Progress Check 5&6
- a downloadable project linked to Units 5 6
- downloadable audio and audio scripts for the Student's Book and Workbook
- videos and video scripts
- extra vocabulary at two levels of difficulty
- extra grammar at two levels of difficulty
- culture lessons, with full teacher's notes
- a life skills lesson, with full teacher's notes
- Speaking Database materials
- the *Beyond* B1 wordlist
- test generator for Unit 6 testing materials (all skills)
- tips for using the Grammar Database
- and more!

Go to the Workbook pages 64–75 for further practice material

PROGRESS CHECK UNITS 5&6

Preparing for the Progress Check

Vocabulary review

- Draw a table on the board with these headings: *The senses*, *Colour idioms*, *Shopping phrases*, *Things and people in a shop*.
- Invite students to come up to the board and write vocabulary items under each heading. For each item, check that everyone understands the meaning. The lists do not need to be complete.
- With several items in each column, refer students to the Words & Beyond pages on pages 134 and 135. Encourage them to call out any items that they missed. Students can then go through the Progress Check and see how many of the items they can find.

Grammar review

- To remind the class of the grammar they have studied in the previous two units, start a 'race', where students check the book and tell you the main grammar points from each unit. Write these on the board, asking for example sentences as students call them out. The grammar for this Progress Check is:
  - Unit 5: Passives (past, present and future); (*In order*) *to* … , *so* (*that*) …
  - Unit 6: Possibility and impossibility; Indirect questions

Optional warm-up activities

READ Exercise 1

- For students who are unfamiliar with this type of task, spend a few minutes reading through the items and the questions, pointing out that in this reading activity the texts are in the form of notes or notices.
- Direct students to the text in question 1 and ask the following questions:
  What type of text is this?
  Where would you expect to find it?
  Who would read it?
- Elicit that this is a notice in a public place and that people might read it if they were going into a library, for example.
- Then ask students to look at the question and the three answer options. Ask them to find references in the text, eg *Option A says all animals can come in with their owners but the text says no dogs or other animals are allowed, only guide dogs; Option B mentions dogs but not guide dogs; Option C mentions dogs and blind people, so C is the correct answer.*
- Go through the other texts asking the questions above about the type of text, where you might find them and who might read them. Students will then tackle the remainder of the questions with more confidence.

LISTEN Exercise 2

- Listening to a conversation can be more difficult than listening to a monologue because students have to remember who says what. With that in mind, refer students back to page 54, where they learned how to follow a conversation.
- Ask the class to tell you what audio type they are going to listen to here (a conversation between two people) and what the subject of that conversation is (the sense of smell). Remind students to use the instructions and questions to help them to predict what they are going to hear.
- Spend a few minutes looking at the questions and asking them to tell you what they are likely to hear. Prompt by asking, *If question 1 is incorrect, what might be true?*
  1 Ellen says she doesn't like / hates the smell of strong fragrances. / Ellen says she likes the smell of weak fragrances.
- Repeat for the other questions and elicit possibilities similar to the following:
  2 Ellen wants to get something at the chemist so that Kenji feels better.
  3 Kenji hasn't got a strong sense of smell. / Ellen has a strong sense of smell.
  4 There's a faint smell of cheese.
  5 Kenji agrees that the shopping centre smells bad.

WRITE Exercise 3

- Remind students that the gaps usually depend on the grammar that they have studied in the previous two units. Ask students to tell you what grammar they should expect to find in this Progress Check (passives; (*In order*) *to* … and *so* (*that*) … ; possibility and impossibility; indirect questions).
- Ask the class to look at the items in Exercise 3 and, without answering them, to note down which of them tests each of the expected grammar items.

WRITE Exercise 4

- Refer students back to the work they did on formal emails on page 68. Make sure they understand that writing for further information about a job should always be formal and polite.
- Ask students to look at the bullet points for the writing task and ask them to think about the structure of their email and which structures they will use for each bullet point. Elicit suggestions similar to the following:
  - First bullet point: opening sentence; *I am writing to ask* …
  - Second bullet point: main body; indirect questions
  - Third bullet point: closing comment; *Thank you for your help* [name]
- Ask students for suggestions for the indirect questions that will form the main body of their email. Elicit at least two different structures, eg *Could you tell me* … , *Would you mind telling me* … .

Doing the Progress Check

READ

1

- Remind students that these texts are notes or notices that we might find in everyday situations. If you have decided not to do the full warm-up, ask students to tell you what each type of text is (1 – notice in a public place; 2 – email or message to a sports coach, perhaps from a player; 3 – notice in a shop; 4 – text message; 5 – notice in a shop).
- Refer students back to the HOW TO box they studied on page 62 and encourage them to look for clues to the tone of the notes and notices in the Progress Check.
- Read through the **Exam tips** with the class and remind them to look for words and phrases in the text that correspond to those in the answer options.
- Allow 5–10 minutes for this section.

ANSWERS
1 C 2 B 3 B 4 A 5 B

LISTEN

2 2.25

- If you have decided not to do the full warm-up, encourage students to spend a minute or two looking at the questions and predicting what they might hear.
- Read through the **Exam tips** for the listening task, answering any questions students have. Refer students back to the HOW TO boxes on pages 54, 57 and 64.
- Since students will hear the conversation twice, tell them to make sure they don't lose their place in the first listening. Explain that the answers usually appear in the same order as the questions, which makes it easier to know what to listen for. If they cannot understand the answer, they should move on to the next question so that they do not miss any answers. They can then use the second listening for checking and filling in any gaps.

ANSWERS / AUDIO SCRIPT 2.25

1 B 2 A 3 D 4 D 5 A

Ellen: I'd like to go into that department store. They have some jeans in the sale. ... Oh. Oh, no! Let's go.
Kenji: We've only just come in. ... Why are you folding your arms like that? And looking so annoyed?
Ellen: The thing is ... I just see red when you're sprayed with fragrance when you go into the perfume department. You aren't even asked and they don't listen when the customers say no.
Kenji: Yes, it was strong. I could even taste it! ... Let's go back and make a complaint at the cash desk.
Ellen: No, I just need to get away from the smell.
Kenji: Are you OK? You're white as a sheet.
Ellen: Sorry, strong perfume gives me a really bad headache.
Kenji: There's a chemist over there. ... We could go in to get some ... er ... something for your headache.
Ellen: Do you mean aspirin? No, it's OK thanks. I'll be fine in a while. ... I just have a really strong sense of smell.
Kenji: Oh. What do I smell of?
Ellen: Toothpaste!
Kenji: Oh, well at least it's a good smell. I have a really good sense of hearing but I don't notice smell that much.
Ellen: Can you smell that?
Kenji: Yes, ugh! It might be the cheese in that shop near the escalator. No, it can't be cheese, it's ...
Both: Fish!
Kenji: The sushi in that sushi bar can't be very fresh.
Ellen: Basically, this shopping centre is a really smelly place.
Kenji: Although most of the smells are good, not bad. For example, the coffee from that café, the cake from the baker's, the popcorn over there. ... Mmm, I feel really thirsty and hungry now.
Ellen: I think that's the idea.

WRITE

3

- Remind students that this type of task is often grammar based. They should expect the grammar that they have studied in Units 5 and 6.
- Remind students that the meaning must be the same in both sentences and that they should check their spelling when they have finished.

ANSWERS

1 may/might be / will probably be
2 so that
3 must
4 mind telling

4

- If you have decided not to do the full warm-up, spend a few minutes going through the task with students and eliciting who they have to write to and what their message must include (the three bullet points).
- Remind them that this type of task calls for a polite and formal style. Refer students back to the work they did on this on page 68.
- Point out that it is best to begin with *Dear Ms Smith* and end with *Yours sincerely, [name]*.
- Stress that they must use correctly formed indirect questions in this task.
- Finally, remind students of the word limit and the importance of checking their spelling, grammar, etc.

MODEL ANSWER

Dear Ms Smith,
I'm writing to ask about the Saturday job in 'Top Fashion'. I'd be grateful if you could tell me what the working hours are. I'd also like to know what the hourly pay is.
Thank you for your help.
Yours sincerely,
[name]

After the Progress Check

Optional game

This game follows up on indirect questions, as well as the shop vocabulary that students have been reviewing.

- Ask students to open their books and to quickly remind themselves of the conversations on page 67.
- Put students in pairs. Explain that they are going to write conversations together, as they did in the Progress Check optional game for Units 1 and 2 (see page 64). Each pair should write four lines of dialogue and aim to include indirect questions within it. This time the conversations should be about shop situations.

Feedback and extension

READ

- Review the questions one at a time and explain to students that they are going to focus on the wrong answers.
- Put students in pairs and ask them to find reasons why each of the wrong answers is inappropriate.
- After a few minutes, discuss in open class what students have found. They should mention some of the following:

ANSWERS

1 A It clearly says 'No entrance with dogs or other animals'.
B Dogs with their owners are only permitted if the dogs are guide dogs and their owners are blind.
2 A It's possible that he wants to watch the match but he says 'we're playing', suggesting that he is in the team.
C Not mentioned
3 A/C It says 'might be available' – so we cannot say they definitely will or definitely will not be available.
4 B Not mentioned
C The frowning face symbols don't suggest excitement.
5 A/C The notice clearly says there are to be no refunds or exchanges after 30 days or without a receipt.

PROGRESS CHECK UNITS 5&6

LISTEN

- Hand out photocopies of the audio script – one for each pair – and ask students to find where they made mistakes.
- Ask pairs to underline the sections of the dialogue where they found the answers.
- Some students find listening tasks very hard. Try to encourage students who have had difficulty and stress that these tasks tend to get easier with practice.
- If the class had made a lot of mistakes, play the audio again, pausing at relevant points for students to process the information they have heard.

WRITE

- Students who had difficulty with Exercise 3 need to focus on the grammar points from the units (see Grammar review above). Write one or two example sentences on the board and then put students in groups of four to come up with more examples for each point. If necessary, ask students to write more sentences for homework.
- For students who had difficulty with Exercise 4, do a similar task, building up a model on the board. Write the following, asking different students for ways to fill in the gaps:

  Dear Ms Smith,
  I am writing to ....
  I would like to know ....
  Could you also tell me ....
  Thank you for your help.
  Yours sincerely,

- When the model is complete, ask other students to suggest alternatives. You could then rub out the previous suggestions and fill in the gaps with new ones.

GO BEYOND FOR TEACHERS

Remind students that any kind of reading they do in English will help them, including notices, notes, invitations and instructions wherever they can find them. Short texts like those in the READ section of the Progress Check are sometimes used in exams. Some sites have online tests which students can do for extra practice.

UNIT 7 TRADITION AND CHANGE

IN THE PICTURE Traditional ways

Talk about traditional and modern ways of living

Pages 72–73

STAGE	TIME	FOCUS
GET STARTED		Compare life now with life 200 years ago.
WORK WITH WORDS		Recycle vocabulary for household jobs and appliances. Learn and use words for traditional activities.
SPEAK		Ask and answer questions in a survey about traditional ways.

Get started

Write these categories on the board: *household jobs, finding information, food and eating, entertainment, clothes, transport and travel, religion.*

Divide the class into small groups and assign one or two of the categories to each group. Ask students to imagine the life of someone 200 years ago and to say how things were different then from life now. Set a time limit of three minutes. Invite each group to report back to the class about the differences they have discussed.

WORK WITH WORDS

1a and 1b RECALL

- Ask a student to read out the aim of the lesson: *Talk about traditional and modern ways of living.* Check the meaning of *traditional* in this context (the way things were done for many years in the past).
- Encourage students to start by recalling some vocabulary they know to talk about *modern* ways of living by completing the names of the appliances in Exercise 1a.
- In Exercise 1b they must explain the difference between the household jobs and add two more jobs to the list.
- Divide the class into pairs to complete both exercises. Set a time limit of two minutes.
- Check the answers in open class, asking students to spell the words in Exercise 1a.
- Ask students to do the Work with Words task on page 136.

ANSWERS / SUGGESTED ANSWERS

Exercise 1a

1 light 2 lamp 3 iron 4 cooker 5 fridge
6 dishwasher 7 washing machine 8 vacuum cleaner

Exercise 1b

1 When you lay the table, you put things on it ready to eat a meal; when you clear the table, you take things off it.
2 When you do the washing, you wash clothes; when you do the washing up, you wash dishes after eating.
3 When you sort the recycling, you put rubbish that you can recycle in different bins or bags at home; when you take out the rubbish, you take rubbish out of your house to a larger bin outside.
4 When you clean the floor, you use water; when you vacuum the floor, you use a vacuum cleaner to clean it.

Other possible jobs: make the bed, do the ironing

2

- To introduce the topic of traditional ways, go through the list of modern objects and appliances in Exercise 1 and ask students to say how people managed before these appliances were invented, eg (light/lamp) *people used candles or made better use of daylight by going to bed earlier and getting up earlier.*
- Focus students' attention on the traditional activities in the box and ask them to find eight of them in the photos.
- Encourage them to compare their answers in pairs, but do not confirm answers at this point.

3a 2.26

- Play the track for students to listen and check their answers to Exercise 2.

ANSWERS / AUDIO SCRIPT 2.26	
photo 1 – *bake bread*	photo 2 – wash clothes by hand
photo 3 – travel by horse and cart	photo 4 – knit clothes
photo 5 – sew clothes	photo 6 – make furniture
photo 7 – use gas lights	photo 8 – make your own entertainment

3b

- Ask students to say which four activities are not in the photos.
- Divide the class into pairs to take it in turns to mime these activities.
- Monitor as students are miming and check that they have understood the meaning of the four phrases. You could ask different students who are confident actors to demonstrate their mimes for the whole class.

ANSWERS

build a house chop wood grow food milk a cow

4 2.27

- Play the track for students to listen and repeat.

AUDIO SCRIPT 2.27

bake bread build a house chop wood grow food
knit clothes make furniture make your own entertainment
milk a cow sew clothes travel by horse and cart
use gas lights wash clothes by hand

Extra activity

Ask students to find verbs from the activities listed which share the same vowel sound, ie

/eɪ/ bake, make /əʊ/ sew, grow /ɪ/ build, knit, milk

5

- Elicit from students if they think we are better off nowadays than in the past.
- Refer students to the statistics in the box on page 72 and divide them into pairs to answer the questions.
- Check the answers in open class, encouraging students to give reasons for their response to question 3.

ANSWERS

1 seven billion 2 five billion 3 students' own answers

6 THE MOVING PICTURE

- Ask students to watch the video and make a list of the activities they see.

ANSWERS

wash clothes by hand, build a house, knit clothes, make furniture, travel by horse and cart, milk a cow, chop wood, bake bread, use gas lights, make own entertainment, sew clothes, grow food

SPEAK

7a

- Ask students to copy the survey into their notebooks, adding the activities from Exercise 2 in the *Have you ever …* column.
- Ask them to answer the questions for themselves by ticking the appropriate column for each activity.

7b

- Divide the class into pairs to ask and answer the questions from the survey. Before they start, draw their attention to the model exchanges and invite two students to read them out loud.
- Circulate and monitor as students are doing the task and make a note of any particularly interesting answers to highlight in open class.

GO BEYOND

Ask students to do the Go Beyond task on page 136.

Extra activity

Divide the class into pairs or small groups. Ask them to look at the list of traditional activities in Exercise 2 and say how these things are done today, eg bake bread – *We buy bread at the baker's or at the supermarket.*

Encourage them to discuss the advantages and disadvantages of the traditional and modern ways of doing things.

Homework

Ask students to do some research on the internet and to find historical photos like the ones on pages 72 and 73 which illustrate the activities listed in Exercise 2.

Ask them to save the photos to a document and to label them with the activities they illustrate.

Encourage them to add any other information about the photos that they can, eg where and when they were taken.

READING Living in the past

Make notes Page 74

STAGE	TIME	FOCUS
GET STARTED		Talk about a period of history you would like to experience and one you would prefer to avoid.
SPEAK AND READ		Make predictions about an advert based on the photographs that accompany it. Check if your predictions were correct. Make notes when you read and use them to answer questions about the text. Read about a TV series where teenagers recreate life on a farm in the 1800s.
REACT		Talk about life in the USA in 1880. Say if you would like to take part in the TV series. Study verb phrases from the text.

Get started

Invite students to imagine they had a time machine that could transport them into the past. Ask them to choose a period of history that they would like to experience and a period they would prefer to avoid. Divide the class into pairs or small groups to say what periods of history they would choose and why. Set a time limit of four minutes. Elicit ideas in open class.

SPEAK AND READ

1a

Exam-type task

- Explain that the text on page 74 is an advert from a magazine. Focus students' attention on the two photos that accompany the advert.
- Divide the class into pairs to say what they can see in the photos and what they think the advert is for.
- Don't check the answers at this point.

1b 2.28

- Ask students to read the first section of the text to see if their predictions about the photos in the advert were right. Set a time limit of one minute.
- Encourage them to talk with their partner about whether their predictions were right. Don't play the audio at this point. A suggestion for using the audio is given at the end of the lesson.

ANSWERS

The advert is for teenagers to participate in a TV programme recreating life on a farm in the late 19th century.
The first photo shows life for a modern-day teenager, buying vegetables in a supermarket. The second photo shows a teenager working on a farm in the USA in the late 19th century.

Extra activity

Ask students to cover the text and elicit how these words and numbers were used in the text: *Life-Like Productions, 1880, eight, late 19th century, 24/7.*

ANSWERS

Life-Like Productions – the production company which is making the TV series
1880 – the name of the TV series
eight – there are eight weekly episodes and eight teenagers participating in the programme
late 19th century – the series recreates life on a farm in the late 19th century
24/7 – the cameras will follow participants 24 hours a day, seven days a week

2a

- Explain to students that they are going to make notes when they read the rest of the advert. Ask them what advice they would give someone about how to make notes.
- Elicit and discuss some of their ideas in open class. Then refer students to the HOW TO box to see if any of their ideas are mentioned.

Extra activity

Write these two sentences on the board and circle the abbreviations (eg, *etc*, *sthg*, *re*, *ie*, *&*).

My grandfather did lots of tasks that we don't have to do today, eg milking the cow, fetching water, etc.

Remember to ask him sthg re traditional activities, ie tasks he had to do in & around the house.

Elicit the meaning of the abbreviations. Ask students to write a sentence using one or two of the abbreviations. Encourage them to use the abbreviations when they are making notes.

ANSWERS

eg – for example   etc – and so on   sthg – something
re – regarding/about   ie – that is   & – and

2b

- Ask students to imagine that they have a friend who might be interested in taking part. Invite them to read the whole advert, making notes about the series and how to apply for an audition. Set a time limit of five minutes.

3

- Ask students which tips in the HOW TO box they used to help them in Exercise 2b.

4 2.29

- Play the track for students to listen and answer the questions by looking at their notes, *not* at the advert.

AUDIO SCRIPT / ANSWERS 2.29

1 What can't you take with you on the series?
2 What type of people are they looking for?
3 How much experience do you need?
4 Where and when is the audition?
5 What will you need to bring on the day of the audition?
6 What's the website address?

1 You can't take your phone or other gadgets.
2 They're looking for a mix of teenagers between the ages of 15 and 19.
3 You don't need any acting experience.
4 The auditions are in New York and San Francisco on April 30th.
5 You need proof of your age and the Permissions Form signed by a parent or guardian.
6 The website address is www.lifelikeproductions.com.

REACT

5

- Refer students to the questions and give them two minutes to think about their answers.
- Divide the class into pairs to answer the questions, giving reasons for their answers. Encourage students to give extended answers.

GO BEYOND

Ask students to cover the advert text. Divide the class into pairs to try to remember what comes after each of the listed verbs in the advert. Set a time limit of five minutes, advising students not to spend too long on any one verb if they find they can't think what came after it in the text.

Invite them to check their answers in the text.

Check that students understand the meaning of each of these phrases and point out the following:

– the prefix *re* in *recreate*, means again, ie *create again* (other examples: *rewrite*, *redo*, *review*).

- the word *existence* usually refers to a way of life that is difficult
- *proof* means information or a document to show something is true
- *sign* means to write your name on a letter or document to show that you wrote it or agree with it

ANSWERS
participating in a new TV series
recreates life in the late 19th century
live without your phone, your gadgets and your social network
led a rural existence help with household jobs and farm work
be prepared for surprises provide proof of your age
signing the Permissions Form

Extra activity
Encourage students to imagine they are journalists who are going to interview a teenager who auditioned for and participated in the TV series *1880*. Ask them to write at least six questions for the journalist to ask about the audition and the series. Remind them to use the advert to help them think of questions. When they have written their questions, ask them to take it in turns to play the role of the journalist and the participant in *1880*.

Recorded reading text 2.28
The reading text is recorded as an extra audio track which can be exploited for various purposes.
In this case use the audio as an alternative for checking the answers to Exercise 1b.

Homework
Find a text of similar length to the advert from the lesson. Try to find a text related to the theme of life in the past. Ask students to make notes on the text using the tips in the HOW TO box.
In the next lesson, ask them to compare their notes in pairs and recall the text orally using their combined notes.

GRAMMAR *Used to*

Talk about habits and situations in the past *Page 75*

STAGE	TIME	FOCUS
GET STARTED		Talk about household jobs of today and in the past.
READ AND LISTEN		Read and listen to an interview about housework in the 19th century.
STUDY		Use examples from the interview to complete grammar explanations about *used to*.
PRACTISE		Practise using *used to* in written exercises. Focus on different pronunciations of the letter s.
SPEAK		Ask and answer questions about when you were six years old.

Get started

Divide the class into pairs to brainstorm a list of household jobs. Set a time limit of two minutes. Elicit some examples in open class, asking students who does these jobs in their house. Ask them if they think it's fair for parents to ask children to help around the house. Encourage students to think of any jobs their great grandparents might have done that nowadays we don't have to do, eg *fetch water, chop wood, wash clothes by hand, light a fire, feed the chickens.*

READ AND LISTEN Grammar in context

1 2.30

- Elicit the difference between *housework* and *homework* (*housework* is work involved in taking care of the home and family whereas *homework* is work that a teacher gives students to do out of class).
- Ask students what years the 19th century refers to (*1800 to 1899*). Elicit if students think people in the 19th century did more, less or the same amount of housework as we do today.
- Play the track for students to read and listen to part of an interview to check their predictions. Check the meaning of *stove* (*oven/cooker*).

ANSWER / AUDIO SCRIPT 2.30
People did the same amount of housework.
See Student's Book page 75 for audio script.

STUDY

2

- Ask students if the text in Exercise 1 is talking about single events/actions in the past or about habits and situations. Write the first two examples of *used to* from the text on the board and ask students if they are past situations or habits: *Housework in the 19th century used to be very hard.* (situation in the past) *People used to use wood stoves, for example.* (habit in the past)
- Ask students to complete the grammar explanations using the interview in Exercise 1 to help them. Allow two minutes.
- Elicit answers in open class, writing them on the board for students to check their answers.
- Point out that although *used to* is unusual because it is only used in the past, its formation is the same as any other regular past simple verb, using the *-ed* ending only for positive sentences and *use to* with the auxiliary *did* in negative sentences and questions.

ANSWERS
used to *use to* *didn't*

PRACTISE

3 2.31

- Have students look at the photo at the bottom of the page and ask them what they think the women are doing.
- Explain to students that they are going to listen to another part of the interview from Exercise 1.
- Ask them to read the text and complete it with the correct form of *used to.* Set a time limit of four minutes.
- Encourage students to compare their answers in pairs before you play the track for them to check their answers.

ANSWERS / AUDIO SCRIPT 2.31

2 didn't use to have 3 used to carry 4 used to need
5 used to make 6 didn't use to take
See Student's Book page 75 for audio script.

4

- Ask students to complete the sentences to make them true about their country. Point out that they should use the positive or negative form of the verbs in the box. Go through the example with them and elicit the negative form, ie *didn't use to wash.* Set a time limit of five minutes.
- Check the answers in open class.

SUGGESTED ANSWERS

Answers will vary depending on where students live.
1 used to wash 2 didn't use to travel 3 used to be
4 used to cost 5 didn't use to have 6 didn't use to use
7 used to write 8 used to buy

Alternative procedure

Ask students to do the task in Exercise 4 individually and then to compare their answers in pairs by taking it in turns to ask questions using *used to*, eg

A: *Did most people use to wash clothes by hand?*

B: *Yes, they did. Did most people use to travel by car?*

A: *Yes, they did.*

B: *Do you think so? One hundred years ago most people didn't use to travel by car. Only very rich people did.*

A: *Oh, yes. You're right.*

5a 2.32 PRONOUNCE

- Play the track for students to listen and repeat.
- Refer them to the written sentences and encourage them to notice the pronunciation of the underlined s in each one.

AUDIO SCRIPT 2.32

See Student's Book page 75 for audio script.

5b 2.33

- Ask students to copy the table into their notebooks.
- Play the track for them to listen and write the words in the correct column.
- Encourage them to compare their answers in pairs before you check answers in open class.
- Play the second part of the track for students to listen and repeat.

AUDIO SCRIPT / ANSWERS 2.33

music single occasionally clothes habits leisure
housework houses cost decision

used to: single, habits, housework, cost
usually: occasionally, leisure, decision
to use: music, clothes, houses

Extra activity

Play a game of *Board race*. Divide the class into three teams. Draw three tables like the one in Exercise 5b on the board. Ask students to form a line in their teams at the back of the classroom. Give the first student in the line a board pen. Explain that the student with the pen must listen to the word you say, run to the board and write it in the correct column. Others in the team can call out advice as necessary. The first student to write the word correctly in the correct column wins a point for their team. The student who has written the word returns to the end of the line and the next student takes the pen. You could mix the words from Exercise 5b with some extra words, eg

/s/: *best, most, lights*

/ʒ/: *television, pleasure, Asian*

/z/: *positive, hours, visit, physical*

6

- Ask students to use the prompts to write questions with *used to*. Set a time limit of five minutes. Before they start, read out the example and elicit how to form a question with *used to*.
- Encourage students to compare their answers in pairs as they finish.
- Appoint a student to write the answers on the board and encourage the class to tell him/her what to write. Make corrections if necessary.

ANSWERS

2 What games did you use to play?
3 Who did your best friends use to be?
4 What school did you use to go to?
5 Did you use to help with housework?

SPEAK

7

- Explain to students that you want them to remember what their life was like when they were six years old. Ask them to close their eyes, listen to your questions and visualise the answers. Ask *Where did you use to live? What did you use to like doing/playing/eating? What friends did you use to play with? What did you use to do in the holidays? Did you use to have a pet? Did you use to watch a lot of television? Did you use to help with the housework?*
- Divide the class into pairs to ask and answer questions about when they were six years old. Encourage them to start by using the questions in Exercise 6 and to keep their conversations going by asking more questions, as well as follow-up questions, to find out more information. Before they start, invite two volunteers to read out the example conversation in the speech bubbles.

Extra activity

Ask students to write four sentences about themselves using *used to*, with one of the sentences being a lie. Divide the class into pairs to read their sentences to each other. Encourage students to ask follow-up questions to try and find out which sentence is a lie.

Homework

Ask students to talk to an older person in their family about the past. Ask them to write at least four questions and answers in interview form in English. Remind them to use *used to*.

LISTENING AND VOCABULARY The pretty coloured snake

Understand the situation Page 76

STAGE	TIME	FOCUS
GET STARTED		Recycle adjectives to describe feelings.
SPEAK AND LISTEN		Make a class list of different things students listen to during the day. Learn how to understand a situation when you listen. Practise listening to understand the situation and for specific information.
REACT		Say whether you liked the story of *The pretty coloured snake*.
WORK WITH WORDS		Read a conversation between students discussing how the people in the story of *The pretty coloured snake* felt. Match adjectives describing feelings to definitions. Write sentences about when someone you know had these feelings.

Get started

Divide the class into pairs to make a list of adjectives to describe feelings. Set a time limit of two minutes. In open class, ask students how many words they have on their lists. Then, starting with a pair with only a few words, ask students to read out their list. Write the words on the board and ask other pairs for more words to add to the list, asking them to spell any tricky words. Check the meaning of any less common words as they are added. Ask students if they can see any opposites, eg *happy/sad, excited/bored*.

SPEAK AND LISTEN

1

- Write *listen to* in a circle on the board.
- Elicit from students different things they listen to during the day, eg *songs, explanations (in class), radio shows, television shows, anecdotes, jokes, stories, questions, interviews, talks,* etc, and collate their suggestions on the board.
- Divide the class into pairs to answer the questions. Set a time limit of one minute.
- Ask them if they prefer listening to fictional or true stories in general.

2a

- Elicit or explain to students that when they listen, it is important to know as much as possible about the situation that surrounds what they are listening to because this will help them to understand it better.
- Point out that when they are listening in real life or to television or video, there are lots of visual clues that can help, but when they are listening to a CD or the radio, there are certain things they must listen for to give them some clues about the situation.
- Ask students to read the tips in the HOW TO box.
- Then ask students to cover the HOW TO box and encourage them to recall the suggestions. Prompt each tip by writing on the board: *where, how, what, when*.

2b 2.34

- Explain that you are going to play the track twice. The first time they should just try to understand the situation. Ask them to read the questions before they listen so that they know what to listen out for.
- Play the track again for students to write their answers.
- Encourage them to compare their answers in pairs before you check them in open class.

ANSWERS / AUDIO SCRIPT 2.34

1 In a tent at a story-telling festival.
2 The speaker is telling the audience a story.
3 It's a traditional Native American story about a man who meets a snake.
4 The events in the story are in the past.

Hello. I'd like to start by thanking you for inviting me to the story-telling festival. It's a real pleasure to be here in this beautiful tent. I'm going to tell you some traditional Native American stories. The first one's called *The pretty coloured snake* and it's an allegory. Now, for those of you who don't know, an allegory is a story, play or poem in which the events and characters represent other things. So, at the end, let's see if you can tell me what the snake represents. OK.
Once upon a time there was a famous hunter. He was famous because he always used to come home with something good for the rest of the Nighthawks tribe to eat. One day, he was carrying home some birds that he had shot when he saw a beautiful little coloured snake. The snake was friendly but looked very hungry. The hunter felt sorry for it and gave it one of the birds to eat.
Some weeks later, the hunter saw the snake again. The snake had grown a lot bigger, but was still friendly. This time, the hunter gave the snake one of the rabbits that he had caught, and once again the snake looked grateful.
This happened a number of times. The beautiful snake always seemed friendly, but each time it had become bigger and the hunter had to give it more food to eat before the snake looked satisfied.
One night there was a dance. All the members of the tribe were there and everyone was going round the fire, dancing and singing songs. Suddenly the snake appeared and started going around the fire too. It still looked friendly, but seemed very hungry and it had grown so big that it stretched all around the people. The Nighthawks began to feel anxious and picked up their bows and arrows. They shot the snake. The arrows hurt it and it hit some people with its tail and killed them. Thank you. So, can anybody tell me what the snake represents?

3

- Ask students which tips in the HOW TO box they used to help them in Exercise 2b.

4 2.34

Exam-type task

- Ask students to look at the picture and read the notes. Set a time limit of one minute.
- Play the track and ask students to complete the notes.
- Encourage students to compare their answers in pairs before you check them in open class.

ANSWERS
1 other things. 2 a bird (to eat). 3 a lot bigger.
4 going round the fire / dancing and singing (songs).
5 they were anxious/frightened.
6 hit some people with its tail and killed them.

Alternative procedure: less confident classes
Monitor as students are comparing their answers. If you see that students have found the note completion task difficult, play the track a third time, but stop just after the answer to each note completion sentence is given to ask students what they heard. Less confident students often find the length of listening texts overwhelming and dividing it into smaller sections like this can help.

REACT

5

- Divide the class into pairs to discuss whether or not they liked the story and to say why and what they think the snake represents.
- Elicit some responses and ask what they think the snake represents.

ANSWER
The snake represents European settlers, who ate what the Native Americans gave them on the first Thanksgiving, and then grew into a monster that destroyed them.

WORK WITH WORDS

6 2.35

- Play the track for students to read and listen to a discussion of the feelings in the story. Ask them to match the adjectives in blue to the definitions. Set a time limit of six minutes.
- Encourage students to compare their answers in pairs as they finish but don't confirm the answers at this point.

AUDIO SCRIPT 2.35
See Student's Book page 76 for audio script.

7 2.36

- Play the track for students to listen and check their answers in Exercise 6.
- Play the track again for students to listen and repeat.

ANSWERS / AUDIO SCRIPT 2.36
1 ashamed 2 proud 3 sorry 4 anxious 5 upset
6 jealous 7 grateful 8 guilty 9 disappointed
10 satisfied

8

- Ask students to choose four of the adjectives and use each one to write a sentence about someone they know. Give a sentence of your own as an example, eg *My brother felt really proud last week when his team won the final of the basketball competition.*
- Divide the class into pairs to read their sentences without saying the adjective for their partner to guess the feeling.

GO BEYOND
Ask students to do the Go Beyond task on page 136.

Extra activity
Ask students to complete this quiz about the adjectives they have studied in this lesson.

1 Which is stronger? *sorry* or *ashamed* *anxious* or *upset*
2 Which of the negative feelings is the opposite of *proud*?
3 Which two adjectives are not generally used to describe your feelings about yourself or something *you* have done?
4 Which adjectives are used with these prepositions: *with*, *for*, *of*, *in*, *about*?
5 Which three adjectives form their opposites by adding the prefix *un*?

ANSWERS
1 ashamed; upset
2 ashamed
3 grateful, jealous
4 *with* – satisfied; *for* – grateful, sorry; *of* – proud, jealous, ashamed, *in* – disappointed, *about* – upset, anxious, guilty, sorry
5 (un)grateful, (un)satisfied, (un)ashamed

Homework

Ask students to fill the gaps in this gapped version of the story with one word only. For less confident groups you could give them the words in a box. In this case, add in a few extra words that they will not need, so as not to make it too easy, eg *the*, *so*, *were*, *her*.

Once upon a time (1) ______ was a famous hunter. He was famous because he always used (2) ______ come home with something good for the rest of the Nighthawks tribe to eat. One day, he (3) ______ carrying home some birds that he had shot when he saw a beautiful little coloured snake. The snake was friendly, (4) ______ looked very hungry. The hunter felt sorry for it and gave it one of the birds to eat.

Some weeks later, the hunter saw the snake (5) ______ . The snake had grown a lot bigger, but was still friendly. This time, the hunter gave the snake one of the rabbits that he had caught and once again the snake looked grateful.

(6) ______ happened a number of times. The beautiful snake always seemed friendly, but each time it had become bigger and the hunter had to give it more food to eat before the snake looked satisfied.

One night there (7) ______ a dance. All the members of the tribe were there and everyone was going round the fire, dancing and singing songs. Suddenly the snake appeared and started going around the fire (8) ______ . It still looked friendly, but seemed very hungry and it had grown so big that it stretched all around the people. The Nighthawks began to feel anxious and picked up their bows and arrows. They shot the snake. The arrows hurt it and it hit some people with (9) ______ tail and killed them.

ANSWERS
1 there 2 to 3 was 4 but 5 again 6 This
7 was 8 too 9 its

GRAMMAR Past perfect simple

Talk about things that happened before another time in the past *Page 77*

STAGE	TIME	FOCUS
GET STARTED		Recycle irregular past participles.
READ		Read a conversation about a person Petra met at the story-telling festival.
STUDY		Use the conversation to complete grammar explanations about the past perfect simple.
PRACTISE		Practise the past perfect simple in controlled exercises.
WRITE AND SPEAK		Talk about the last time you had different feelings and explain why you had them.

Get started

Draw a table with these symbols as headings: /əʊ/, /ɔː/, /ʌ/, /ɒ/, /ɪ/. Elicit or give an example of each sound and write it in the correct column, eg *go, for, but, hot, sit*. Ask students to copy the table into their notebooks. Explain to students that you are going to read a list of verbs and that they must think of the past participle and write it in the correct column according to the vowel sound it has. Students could work in pairs or individually. Read out these verbs: *cut, do, lose, build, give, fall, fly, buy, know, write, get, speak, teach, cost, hit, win, catch, wake, sing*. Check the answers in open class.

ANSWERS

/əʊ/ *go*, flown, known, spoken, woken
/ɔː/ *for*, fallen, bought, taught, caught
/ʌ/ *but*, cut, done, won, sung
/ɒ/ *hot*, lost, got, cost
/ɪ/ *sit*, built, given, written, hit

READ Grammar in context

1 2.37

- Focus on the photo. Elicit from students what they think the man (Mr Casey) is doing and where he is.
- Ask students to read and listen to the conversation and say who Mr Casey is and why Petra didn't speak to him.
- Check the answers in open class.
- Ask a few comprehension questions to check full understanding of the text: *Where was Petra when she saw Mr Casey?* (at the story-telling festival) *Why didn't she recognise him immediately?* (because he looked different – he'd shaved his beard off) *What was Mr Casey doing at the festival?* (He was speaking.)

ANSWERS

Mr Casey was Petra and Luke's first primary school teacher.
Petra didn't speak to him because he was talking when she first saw him and he wasn't there when she went back after lunch.

STUDY

2

- Tell students that the verbs in blue in Exercise 1 are in the past perfect simple.
- Read through the *Use* section of the grammar explanation with students and illustrate the explanation using this sentence: *I didn't recognise him at first because he'd shaved his beard off.*
- Ask students to complete the grammar explanations using the conversation in Exercise 1 to help them. Set a time limit of two minutes.
- Encourage students to compare their answers in pairs before you check them in open class.

ANSWERS

hadn't 'd hadn't because already

Alternative procedure: less confident classes

If your class is less confident with grammar, you might like to lead the students through an exploration of the new language before they attempt to complete the explanations.

After the students have read the conversation, write this sentence from the conversation on the board: *I didn't recognise him at first because he'd shaved his beard off.*

Ask: *What are the two verbs or actions in the sentence? (not recognise, shave). Did the actions take place in the past, present or future?* (in the past)

Ask: *Did the actions happen at the same time in the past or did one happen before another?* To demonstrate this, draw a timeline on the board showing the point in the past at which Petra failed to recognise Mr Casey. Ask a student to come to the board and show where Mr Casey shaved his beard off. Ask if it was before or after the point where Petra didn't recognise him (before).

Now ask students which of the verbs is in the past simple (*didn't recognise*).

Tell them that when we talk about things that happened before another time in the past we use the past perfect.

Highlight the form on the board: *had/hadn't* + past participle.

Ask students to find an example in the conversation of a question using the past perfect. (*Had he changed much?*)

Now ask students to complete the explanations using the conversation in Exercise 1 to help them. Leave the timeline on the board for the rest of the lesson.

PRACTISE

3 2.38

- Ask students if their grandparents like using mobiles.
- Ask them to read the story quickly, ignoring the gaps, and say why the father was disappointed and what name the grandmother used for her mobile. (The father was disappointed because he had been excited about showing his mother his new mobile but she had already bought one. She called the phone a 'pocket phone'.)
- Ask students to complete the story with the past perfect form of the verbs in brackets. Allow four minutes.
- Play the track for students to listen and check.

ANSWERS / AUDIO SCRIPT 2.38

2 had never travelled 3 had just bought 4 hadn't seen
5 had already got 6 had asked
See Student's Book page 77 for audio script.

4 2.39

- Ask students to work individually to choose the correct options to complete the conversation. Allow three minutes.
- Encourage students to compare their answers in pairs before you play the track for them to listen and check their answers.
- Focus students on the examples of the past perfect and ask them to explain what action it happened before, eg *Where had you been?* shows that the speaker means *Where had you been before you fell asleep on the bus.*

ANSWERS / AUDIO SCRIPT 2.39

1 fell 2 had you been 3 'd stayed 4 was 5 woke
6 'd missed 7 did you do 8 had already gone
See Student's Book page 77 for audio script.

Extra activity

Write this list of actions/events on the board in the order they appear in the conversation. Divide the class into pairs to order the events as they happened in real time.

a I fell asleep.
b I went to a friend's house.
c I stayed up the night before.
d I was really tired.
e I woke up.
f I missed my stop.
g I got off the bus.
h The last bus went in the other direction.
i I had to walk home.

ANSWERS

The correct order is c, b, d, a, f, e, h, g, i.

WRITE AND SPEAK

5a

- Ask students to choose three of the feelings in the box and to write a sentence about a time when they had each feeling and why. Set a time limit of five minutes. Before they start, invite two students to read out the examples.

5b

- Divide the class into pairs to tell each other the stories of how they felt and why. Encourage them to ask follow-up questions to find out more information, eg *Why hadn't you done your homework? So what happened in the end?*

Extra activity

Play a game of *Explain yourself!* Prepare a set of cards with the following situations on them: *You were crying. You were limping. You were coming out of the hospital. You were wearing formal clothes. You were wearing a wig and sunglasses. You were climbing a tree. You were laughing. You were dressed in a clown costume. You had chocolate all over your face. You were dripping wet.*

Divide the class into pairs or small groups. Each student takes the same number of cards and tries to think of an explanation for why they were in those situations that they can explain using the past perfect.

Students take it in turns to place one of their cards on the table. Their partner(s) must imagine they saw them in that situation yesterday and ask questions to find out more.

Homework

Make a handout for these tasks (1 & 2) to give to students.

Task 1: Ask students to complete the sentences using a verb from box A in the past perfect and words from box B.

Box A: lose, break, finish, forget, win

Box B: to put salt in it, his arm, my keys, my homework, the chess competition

1 I couldn't get into the house because I …
2 My brother couldn't do his piano exam because he …
3 My parents let me watch TV last night because I …
4 The soup didn't taste nice because I …
5 Everyone congratulated me because I …

ANSWERS

1 'd lost my keys. 2 'd broken his arm.
3 'd finished my homework. 4 'd forgotten to put salt in it.
5 'd won the chess competition.

Task 2: Ask students to choose the time expressions.

1 I was scared of the sea because I hadn't learned to swim already/just/yet.
2 I'd already/before/yet told my mother about the party but she'd forgotten.
3 Peter had read the book just/yet/before so he chose another one.
4 They'd before/just/yet left when you rang.
5 Had you studied English before/already/yet you came to this school?
6 My mum had just/before/yet locked the door when someone rang the doorbell.

ANSWERS

1 yet 2 already 3 before 4 just 5 before
6 just

Value your elders

Page 78

STAGE	TIME	FOCUS
GET STARTED		Check some key vocabulary to be used in the lesson.
SPEAK AND READ		Read an article about elderly people in different cultures. Talk about how they are seen in your country.
DO		Complete a profile of an elderly person you feel close to. Tell another student about this person and listen to them talk about the person they have profiled. Ask and answer questions to find out more information.
REFLECT		Talk about the importance of valuing elderly people and asking for their advice.
EXTEND	Homework	Plan to ask two elderly people for some advice. Write a report on the advice you receive and your feelings about the whole experience.

LIFE SKILLS

VALUE YOUR ELDERS

Young people nowadays are often criticised for not showing enough respect for their elders. This is often the result of a combination of factors related to the make-up of modern society and the pressures that are placed on both elderly and young people. The focus of this lesson is not on making students feel bad about how they relate to the elderly but on reminding them of what elderly people have to offer and to reflect on the value their own culture and society gives them. On a personal level, it is very likely that your students have good relationships with older people either in their families or in their communities and this lesson encourages them to share what they know about these people and what relationships mean to them. In the **Extend** section, students are asked to seek out two elderly people and ask for their advice.

Get started

Divide the class into pairs or small groups to talk about what these words mean: *wise, old people's home, retired, old age, elders, wisdom, elderly.*

Ask students to complete these sentences with the words above.

1 *When you stop working because you reach a certain age, you are* ....
2 *A more polite way of saying 'old people' is '*............ *people'.*
3 *A place where elderly people live together and are cared for is an* ....
4 *A* .... *person can give you good advice because of the experience and knowledge they have.*
5 *The time of life when you are old is called* ....
6 *The noun that comes from wise is* ....
7 *People in our community who are respected because of their age and experience are our* ....

ANSWERS
1 retired 2 elderly 3 old people's home 4 wise
5 old age 6 wisdom 7 elders

SPEAK AND READ

1

- Ask students to read the questions and give them one minute to think about their answers.
- Divide the class into pairs to answer the questions. Set a time limit of three minutes, pointing out that this activity is an introduction to the topic and that they will have time to say more about an elderly person who is special to them later in the lesson.

2

- Nominate a student to read out the first paragraph of the article, or read it yourself.
- Lead a class discussion by asking: *How do people in your country see elders? Are they respected for their wisdom? Do they teach children about the traditions and values of the culture?* Encourage students to give reasons or examples to support their views.

3

- Focus students on the questionnaire in the article. Invite them to read and complete it.

4

- Ask students to work in small groups and compare their responses. Encourage them to talk about their own experiences and to give reasons for their answers.

DO

GO BEYOND FOR TEACHERS

Sensitivity when discussing elderly people

In the next section of the lesson, students are asked to profile and talk about an elderly person they feel close to. Be aware that this may be a sensitive topic for some students if they have recently lost a grandparent or other elderly friend or relation.

5

- Refer students to the profile and ask them to copy it into their notebooks.
- Invite them to think of an elderly person they feel close to and to complete the profile with as much information as they can. Set a time limit of five minutes.

6

- Divide the class into pairs to tell each other about the person in their profile. If practical, you could let them choose who they want to work with. Encourage them to ask each other for more information. Allow five minutes.
- In open class, invite volunteers to say what they learned about the person their partner told them about.

REFLECT

7

- Give students five minutes to discuss the questions in pairs or small groups. Then open up the discussion by asking for different students' opinions in open class.
- Finish off the discussion by asking a student to read out the REFLECTION POINT. Take a quick vote to see if students agree with it or not.

Alternative procedure

Question 1 in Exercise 7 would work well as a debate, following this procedure:

Divide the class in two and reformulate the question as a proposition for debate: *People in our country generally value their elders.*

Ask one half of the class to think of arguments for this proposition and the other half to think of arguments against the proposition. Give them a time limit of 10 minutes to work on their arguments in teams of three and ask them to each decide which argument(s) they are going to present in the debate and what they are going to say. Encourage them to think of examples to illustrate their arguments.

Make groups of six students, three for and three against, and ask them to present their arguments. Point out that they should make notes about what the other side says.

After all six students have spoken, give them one or two minutes to talk with the members of their team about how to respond to the arguments of the other team.

Invite them to finish the debate by responding to the opposing team's argument.

After the debates, in open class, you could ask students what their real opinion is and if they found any of the arguments they heard interesting or original.

EXTEND

8a

- Invite students to think of some advice they would like to have from an elderly person. Encourage them to think of a topic that would be useful to them.

8b

- Ask students to do this task for homework. Encourage them to ask two elderly people they know for their advice and to write about the advice they received. (See homework task.)

Extra activity

Ask students to write a survey to find out people's attitudes to elderly people. Invite them to think of three situations and to write three possible ways a young person might react in that situation, eg:

You are watching TV and your grandmother starts to talk about her childhood.

Do you …

A Listen to your grandmother but keep watching TV?

B Ask your grandmother to be quiet because you want to watch your show?

C Listen and show interest, turn the TV off and ask her some questions?

Give students some suggestions for situations (see below) but encourage them to invent their own if they wish.

SUGGESTED SITUATIONS

An elderly person gets on the train and there are no seats.
Your uncle doesn't understand how to use his mobile.
Your elderly aunt likes to ask you questions about your life.
An elderly neighbour asks you to help her take her rubbish out.
Your grandad wants to teach you how to make a traditional dish from your country.

Homework

Ask students to write a report of 180–200 words about the advice they received from two elderly people.

Encourage them to structure their report with the following headings:

1 The problem – write what you asked for advice about.
2 The elders – say something about the two people you spoke to.
3 The advice – compare the advice you got from the two people.
4 The experience – talk about the experience of asking elderly people for advice. Was it fun? Did the elderly people seem to enjoy speaking to you? How do you think they felt when you asked them for advice?

SPEAKING At the library

Join and use a library

Page 79

STAGE	TIME	FOCUS
GET STARTED		Make a word web of words related to libraries.
SPEAK		Talk about the things you can do in your school library and in your public library.
WATCH OR LISTEN		Watch or listen to a conversation in a library. Learn questions to use to join a library. Learn how to react to information.
ACT		Role-play a conversation at a library information desk.

Get started

Draw a word web relating to the topic *Library* on the board, with the five categories: *things you borrow*, *people*, *nouns*, *verbs*, *adjectives*.

Divide the class into pairs to brainstorm words to write in each category. Set a time limit of two minutes.

Elicit students' ideas and fill in the word web on the board.

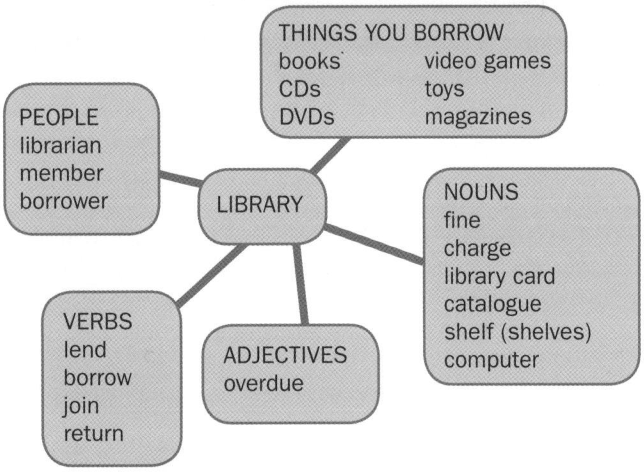

Ask students to complete these sentences using *borrow* or *lend*.

1 *If you .... something, someone gives it to you and you agree to give it back.*

2 *If you .... something, you give it to someone else and they agree to give it back to you.*

ANSWERS
1 borrow 2 lend

SPEAK

1

- Divide the class into pairs to answer the questions about libraries and the things in the box.

Extra activity
Ask students to imagine that the local council wants to close down their public library. Ask them to work in small groups to think of two possible reasons why the council might want to close the library and four good reasons why the council should reconsider. Invite different groups to share their ideas in open class.

WATCH OR LISTEN

2 2.40

- Books closed. Play the scene for students to watch or listen to a conversation in a library. Ask students to note down the two things Jack wants to do there.
- Elicit and check answers in open class.

ANSWER / VIDEO/AUDIO SCRIPT 2.40

He wants to join the library and check his emails.

Librarian: Good morning.
Jack: Hello. I'd like to join the library. How do you become a member?
Librarian: You need to fill in a membership form.
Jack: OK, and how old do you have to be?
Librarian: You can join at any age, but you need to give the name of a parent or guardian if you're under 18.
Jack: Good. And how much does it cost to join?
Librarian: It's free if you live or study locally.
Jack: Right. I'm staying with my grandmother for a month. Does that mean I can't join?
Librarian: No, that's not a problem.
Jack: Great. Could you give me a form, please?
Librarian: Of course. Here you are.

Jack: I've filled in the form. Do I have to do anything else?
Librarian: Can I just have a look? No, that all seems fine.
Jack: So can I use a computer now?
Librarian: We just need a photo for your library card.
Jack: Oh, right. Is there any way I can just check my emails?
Librarian: I'm afraid the computers are all busy.

3 2.40

- Refer students to the written conversation and encourage them to try to complete Jack's questions. Point out that they should look at how the librarian responds in order to help them decide what the questions are. Set a time limit of five minutes for this.
- Play the scene for students to check or complete their answers.
- Ask them to compare their answers in pairs by reading out the conversation.

ANSWERS
1 become a member 2 have to be 3 cost to join
4 give me a form 5 have to do 6 use a computer

Fast finishers

Ask students to find expressions in the conversation to match these: *complete a form* (fill in a form); *a person who is not your parent, but who looks after you* (guardian); *to live in the same area as something* (live locally); *only* (just)

4 2.41

- Play the track for students to listen and repeat.
- Drill the questions chorally, in small groups and individually.

AUDIO SCRIPT 2.41

1 How do you become a member?
2 How old do you have to be?
3 How much does it cost to join?
4 Could you give me a form, please?
5 Do I have to do anything else?
6 Can I use a computer now?

Extra activity

Ask students to underline the stressed words in the questions. (See underlining in audio script above.)

5a

- Explain to students that it is important to react when someone is giving you information. Ask them what might happen if they do not react at all when someone is giving them information (*the person giving the information will not know if they have understood or not*).
- Elicit what kinds of thing they say in their language(s) to react to information.
- Ask students to read the tips in the HOW TO box. Invite a volunteer to read them out loud.

5b

- Refer students back to the conversation and encourage them to find and underline examples of the words and expressions from the HOW TO box. Allow three minutes.
- In open class, invite different students to read out the examples.

ANSWERS

See underlining in video/audio script for Exercise 2.

ACT

6 2.42

- Tell students they are going to role-play a conversation at a library information desk. Divide the class into A/B pairs and ask them to read the instructions, referring Student B to the table and Student A to the information on page 141.
- Before they start, play the track with the phrases in the PHRASEBOOK box and encourage students to use these in their role-play.
- Have students role-play the situation and then swap roles and repeat the role-play. Set a time limit of 10 minutes for the whole activity.
- Circulate and monitor, making notes on any language you would like to focus on later.

Extra activity

Divide the class into pairs to do a *Lesson quiz*. Give each pair a set of the cards below for them to ask the questions on their card and check if their partner knows the answer. Point out that they should give their partner some clues if they aren't sure.

Card A

1 *What is the word for a person who works in a library?* (librarian)
2 *You want to join a library. What question do you ask?* (How do you become a member?)
3 *What ways can you react if you are happy with the information you receive?* (OK/Good/Great).
4 *I'm going to give you some information. Please ask a question to check that you understand the situation.* 'The library is open from 9am to 9pm, Mondays to Fridays.' (So + question/*Does that mean …*)
5 *What is the difference between a membership form and a library card?* (You fill in a membership form to join the library and then you get a library card to borrow items.)

Card B

1 *What is the verb meaning to take something and give it back?* (borrow)
2 *You want to know how much money you have to pay to join a library. What question do you ask?* (How much does it cost to join?)
3 *What ways can you react if you there is a possible problem when someone is giving you information?* (Right/Oh, right.)
4 *I'm going to give you some information. Please ask a question to check that you understand the situation.* 'You are allowed to borrow six books for free. There is a charge if you want more.' (So + question/*Does that mean …*)
5 *What is another way of saying 'to join a library'?* (to become a member of a library)

Homework

Ask students to write a conversation between a person wanting to join a sports club and the receptionist at the sports club. Ask them to use questions from today's lesson and to include different ways of reacting to information.

Give them the following information:

- To join you must fill in a membership form.
- If you are under 18, a parent or guardian must sign a permissions form.
- You must provide a photo for your membership card.
- Every new member must pay a joining fee* of €25.
- Cost per month is €25 or €18 if you only want to use the pool.
- You can use the club on the day you join if you pay the joining fee and first monthly payment.

fee = an amount of money you pay in order to be allowed to do something

WRITING Telling tales

Say how and when things happen in a story *Page 80*

STAGE	TIME	FOCUS
GET STARTED		Put the sentences of *The pretty coloured snake* in the correct order.
SPEAK AND READ		Think of a traditional story and tell it with your partner. Read a short version of a European story. Learn how to say how and when things happen in a story.
PRACTISE		Use words and expressions from traditional stories to complete a story from China.
PLAN		Make a plan to write a short version of a traditional story that you know.
WRITE AND CHECK		Write your version of the story and check it by looking back at the points in the plan.
SHARE		Read other students' stories and say which one you enjoyed reading the most.

Get started

Prepare copies of the story *The pretty coloured snake* cut into sentences (see below) and distribute them randomly to students. Depending on the number of students in your class, they could work individually or in pairs, with each pair having one or two sentences. (Note: if you have a small class, divide the text into fewer chunks.)

Ask them to circulate and read their sentence to classmates in order to work out the correct order of the sentences. They should then stand in line in the order of the story.

When they are ready, ask them to read out their sentences one after another and in this way tell the whole story.

Alternatively, you could cut up a set of sentences for groups of four to six students and ask them to order them correctly.

Once upon a time there was a famous hunter.
He was famous because he always used to come home with something good for the rest of the Nighthawks tribe to eat.
One day, he was carrying home some birds that he had shot when he saw a beautiful little coloured snake.
The snake was friendly, but looked very hungry.
The hunter felt sorry for it and gave it one of the birds to eat.
Some weeks later, the hunter saw the snake again.
The snake had grown a lot bigger, but was still friendly.
This time the hunter gave the snake one of the rabbits that he had caught and once again the snake looked grateful.
This happened a number of times.
The beautiful snake always seemed friendly, but each time it had become bigger and the hunter had to give it more food to eat before the snake looked satisfied.
One night there was a dance.
All the members of the tribe were there and everyone was going round the fire, dancing and singing songs.
Suddenly the snake appeared and started going around the fire too.
It still looked friendly, but seemed very hungry and it had grown so big that it stretched all around the people.
The Nighthawks began to feel anxious and picked up their bows and arrows.
They shot the snake.
The arrows hurt it and it hit some people with its tail and killed them.

SPEAK AND READ

1

- Invite students to think of three traditional stories. Then divide the class into pairs to share their story ideas and choose one of the stories to tell together. It might help if you ask them to imagine they are telling it to a third person. Encourage them to help each other to remember what happens.

2

- Focus students on the text and give them three minutes to read it.
- Ask students if they know the name of the girl.

ANSWER
She's called Little Red Riding Hood.

Extra activity
Ask a few comprehension questions to check full understanding of the text, eg *Why was Little Red Riding Hood going to her grandmother's?* (to take her some cakes) *Why did the wolf suggest that Little Red Riding Hood pick some flowers?* (so he would have time to get to grandmother's house before her) *Why did the hunter stop at grandmother's house?* (because he heard snoring)

3a

- Ask students to read the tips in the HOW TO box about saying how and when things happen in a traditional story. Encourage them to try and memorise the phrases and words. Set a time limit of three minutes.
- Then ask students to cover the box and write down as many of the phrases and words as they can remember. Elicit the words and phrases in open class.

3b

- Refer students back to the story in Exercise 1 and ask them to underline examples of the words and expressions typically used in traditional stories.

ANSWERS

Once upon a time there was a girl ... One day she was taking ... Suddenly, a wolf appeared ... Meanwhile, the wolf ran ... , then got into bed. Later, when the girl arrived, ... After that he fell asleep ... as soon as he saw the wolf, ... At first grandma looked ... but in the end she recovered ...

PRACTISE

4

- Tell students they are going to read a traditional story from China. Refer them to the picture and elicit any ideas about what they think happens in the story. Invite them to predict if it will have a happy or a sad ending.
- Ask students to read the story, ignoring the gaps, to see if their predictions were correct.
- Encourage students to complete the story with words and expressions from the HOW TO box.
- Encourage students to compare their answers in pairs before you check the answers by nominating different students to read a sentence of the text out loud.

ANSWERS

1 then 2 Suddenly 3 As soon as 4 At first
5 Meanwhile 6 In the end

PLAN

5

- Explain to students that they are going to write a short version of a traditional story.
- Focus their attention on the **Writing plan** and go through it with them. Encourage them to think individually about a story they know well.
- Give them 10 minutes to write their ideas for their plan.
- Circulate and help students as necessary.

WRITE AND CHECK

6

- Give students 15 minutes to use their plans and the model text to help them write their story. Encourage them to use time expressions to say how and when things happened.
- Monitor and give assistance as necessary.
- When students have finished writing, encourage them to check their work.

Fast finishers

Ask students to write sentences using the past perfect to answer these questions about the Little Red Riding Hood story.

Why wasn't grandma at home when Little Red Riding Hood arrived? (because the wolf had eaten her) *Why did the hunter cut open the wolf's stomach?* (because he knew the wolf had eaten grandma) *Why did grandma look ill at first?* (because she had been inside the wolf)

SHARE

7

- Ask students to swap their stories with one or two classmates and to read each other's work.
- In open class, ask students which stories they enjoyed reading the most and encourage them to give reasons.

Extra activity

Tell students that traditional stories often contain a message for their audience. Ask them to think about the two stories on page 80 and decide what the message is for each one. (*Little Red Riding Hood:* Don't be distracted by strangers. / Don't trust strangers. *The Old Man and the Golden Fish:* When you have good fortune, don't be greedy for more!)

Ask them to think of a message for the stories they have written as well.

Homework

1 Ask students to check the writing they did in class and prepare to hand it in for assessment in the next class.
2 Ask students to research and find a traditional story from a different culture. Ask them to prepare to re-tell the story in the next class.

VOCABULARY Traditional activities

1

- Nominate a student to read out the words in blue under the advert, ie *Come to Mrs Daly's Trad Camp and learn how people used to do things!* Elicit what *Trad* is short for (*traditional*).
- Invite students to say one or two things they think people might learn at Mrs Daly's Trad Camp.
- Explain that the verbs in the advert are all in the wrong place and ask students to write the correct verbs in the correct form next to the numbers 1 to 10.
- Write the numbers on the board and invite five different students to come up and write two answers each.

ANSWERS
1 bake 2 grow 3 washed 4 milked 5 knit
6 sew 7 make 8 travelled 9 used 10 made

Feelings

2

- Explain that Lidia, Albert and Alana all went to Mrs Daly's Trad Camp and wrote some comments on her website about their experience.
- Ask students to complete the comments with adjectives, pointing out that the first and last letters are given. Set a time limit of four minutes.
- Encourage students to compare their answers in pairs before you nominate different students to read out each paragraph and check answers.
- Ask other students to spell the adjectives and write them on the board so that students can check their spelling.

ANSWERS
1 anxious 2 satisfied 3 grateful 4 disappointed
5 guilty 6 upset 7 proud 8 jealous 9 sorry
10 ashamed

GRAMMAR *Used to*

3

- Write on the board: *used to / use to*. Remind students that we use these forms to talk about past habits and situations. Ask them when we use *used to* and when we use *use to* (*used to* in positive sentences and *use to* with the auxiliary *did* in negative sentences and questions).
- Ask students to complete the interview with Mrs Daly by using the correct form of *used to* with the verbs in brackets. Remind them to use *did/didn't* for short answers.
- Check answers in open class. Then divide the class into pairs to read the interview out loud.

ANSWERS
1 used to do 2 didn't use to have
3 Did you use to help 4 did 5 used to have
6 did the children use to complain 7 didn't
8 used to do

Past perfect simple

4

- Write this rule on the board: *We use the past simple / past perfect to talk about things that happened before another time in the past.* Ask students to choose which of the underlined options is correct (past perfect).
- Elicit the form of the past perfect and write it on the board: *had/hadn't* + past participle.
- Look at the rule again and ask students what tense we use to talk about *another time in the past* (the past simple).
- Ask students to complete the second part of the interview with Mrs Daly with the past perfect simple or the past simple form of the verbs in brackets.
- Encourage students to compare their answers in pairs. As they do this, write the correct answers on the board for them to check.

ANSWERS
1 started 2 had forgotten 3 Had you tried
4 didn't work 5 hadn't done 6 hadn't understood
7 were

Extra Resources

Go to the Teacher's Resource Centre at www.macmillanbeyond.com for:

- downloadable audio and audio scripts for the Student's Book and Workbook
- videos and video scripts
- extra vocabulary at two levels of difficulty
- extra grammar at two levels of difficulty
- CLIL lessons, with full teacher's notes
- a life skills lesson, with full teacher's notes
- Speaking Database materials
- the *Beyond* B1 wordlist
- test generator for Unit 7 testing materials (all skills)
- tips for using the Grammar Database
- and more!

Go to the Workbook pages 76–87 for further practice material

UNIT 8 SHE SAID, HE SAID

IN THE PICTURE In the news

Talk about people working in the media

Pages 82–83

STAGE	TIME	FOCUS
GET STARTED		Talk about current news stories.
WORK WITH WORDS		Recycle words for things we read. Learn and use words for people in the print and digital media. Identify stressed and unstressed syllables and practice the /ə/ sound.
SPEAK		Do a survey about media habits.

Get started

Prepare some pictures from one or two current news stories that you think will interest your students. Show the pictures in open class and ask students what they know about these stories. Divide the class into pairs to make a list of other stories that are in the news at the moment. After three minutes, ask pairs to form groups of four to compare their lists and to decide what is the most significant news story of the moment.

WORK WITH WORDS

1a and 1b RECALL

- Divide the class into pairs to do both tasks. Set a time limit of three minutes for the two tasks.
- Explain that, in Exercise 1a, students must complete the names of things we read by adding the two letters missing from the beginning of each word.
- For Exercise 1b, encourage them to find an example in their Student's Book of three of the things in the list.
- When the time is up, elicit answers in open class, checking the correct spelling. If there are items that students couldn't work out in Exercise 1a, give them a definition of the word to help them guess, eg *It's a list of instructions for how to cook something* (recipe).
- Invite different pairs to show the class the examples they found in their Student's Book. Elicit if the rest of the class can say what the example is of.
- Ask students to do the Work with Words task on page 137.

ANSWERS

Exercise 1a

1 cartoon 2 recipe 3 report 4 letter
5 picture caption 6 blog 7 interview 8 poem 9 profile
10 article 11 story 12 quiz 13 rules 14 survey

2 3.01

- Refer students to the table and ask them to copy it into their notebooks.
- Check the meaning of *people who work behind the scenes* (people who work in the media but are not known to the general public).
- Focus students on the jobs in the box and give them three minutes to write the jobs in the correct category.
- Play the track for students to listen and check.
- Play the track again and ask students to listen and repeat.

ANSWERS / AUDIO SCRIPT 3.01

People who write: author, blogger, gossip columnist, journalist, reporter
People who work with visuals: cartoonist, designer, graphic artist, photographer
People who work behind the scenes: editor, printer, publisher

3

- Ask students to choose the correct people from Exercise 2 to complete the sentences. Allow five minutes.
- Encourage students to compare their answers in pairs before you check them in open class by nominating different students to read out the sentences. In each case, invite students to explain why the other option is incorrect, eg *The printer doesn't own the newspaper, he or she organises the printing of it and owns the machines to do this.*

ANSWERS

1 publisher 2 reporter; journalist
3 photographer; graphic artist 4 editor 5 designer
6 cartoonist; gossip columnist; author 7 printer 8 blogger

Fast finishers

Invite students to test each other on the vocabulary. Ask them to take it in turns to read out one of the statements in Exercise 3 beginning with *Who … ?* eg *Who owns* the *newspaper and employs a lot of people*? The student answering the question should have their book closed.

4

- Refer students to the photos and elicit which of the people in Exercise 2 they can see. Allow one minute for students to discuss the question in pairs before you check answers in open class.

ANSWERS
a photographer b photographer
c author/journalist/editor/gossip columnist/blogger
d editor/designer/author/gossip columnist
e printer f designer/graphic artist

5 3.02

- Tell students that they are going to hear a designer talking about the photos. Play the track for students to listen and note down which photos she is talking about.
- Encourage them to compare their answers in pairs before you check them in open class.

ANSWERS / AUDIO SCRIPT 3.02
1 a 2 c 3 e 4 b 5 f 6 d
1 I like this photograph because we can see the reporters, journalists and photographers but we can't see who they're looking at.
2 I chose this picture because it shows that today all you need is a laptop computer and an internet connection to be a journalist, a blogger or a gossip columnist.
3 Ah! This picture was taken before the age of digital. I don't know who the person is looking at the newspaper. It might be the publisher or the editor. Or maybe it's the printer.
4 Here's a member of the paparazzi. Have you ever seen the film *Teenage Paparazzo*? It's a documentary about a real 14-year-old photographer who takes pictures of celebrities for magazines.
5 I love comics and cartoons, especially if they're funny. To be a good cartoonist you need to be a good artist but you also need to be good with words and have a sense of humour.
6 So this is a picture I included because it shows people like me, I suppose. We're the ones who make the words and images look good – the designers, graphic artists, cartoonists.

6a 3.03 PRONOUNCE

- Play the track for students to listen and repeat the word, paying attention to the stressed syllable and the /ə/ sound in the unstressed syllable.

AUDIO SCRIPT 3.03
author author

6b 3.04

- Tell students that they will hear the other words in the box in Exercise 2. Play the track for students to underline the stressed syllables and circle the syllables that have the /ə/ sound. Point out to students that not all the words have the /ə/ sound.
- Nominate different students to write their answers on the board and ask for confirmation from the rest of the class, correcting as necessary.
- Play the track again for students to listen and repeat.

ANSWERS / AUDIO SCRIPT 3.04
blogger cartoonist designer editor gossip columnist
graphic artist journalist photographer printer publisher
reporter

7 THE MOVING PICTURE

- Ask students to watch the video and say which of the people from Exercise 2 they see.

ANSWERS
editor, designer, graphic artist, photographer

SPEAK

8

- Divide the class into pairs to ask and answer the questions in the *Media habits* survey. Before they start speaking, give them two minutes to quietly read the questions and think about their answers.
- Focus students on the expressions in the PHRASE BYTES box and encourage them to use these when they are discussing the survey questions.
- Ask them which of the phrases in the PHRASE BYTES box is used to express surprise at someone's opinion (*Really? But surely …*). Explain that *surely* in this sense is used with a negative verb, eg *But surely you wouldn't want to be a reporter?*

GO BEYOND

Ask students to do the Go Beyond task on page 137.

Extra activity
Ask students to work in pairs to say what is the same and what is different about these pairs of jobs: *reporter / journalist*; *printer / publisher*; *graphic artist / photographer*; *designer / graphic artist*; *blogger / gossip columnist*; *author / editor*.

Give them some useful language, eg *They both …* ; *Both the X and the Y …* ; *The X … , whereas the Y …* ; *The X … but the Y …* ; *There are/aren't many similarities/ differences*; *For example, …* .

Homework

1 Give students this list of nouns and verbs: *blog* (n), *cartoon* (n), *design* (v), *edit* (v), *column* (n), *art* (n), *journal* (n), *photograph* (n), *print* (v), *publish* (v), *report* (v).
Ask them to write the jobs that are formed from these words using the correct suffix: *-er/-or* or *-ist*. Encourage them to do as much as they can without looking at the Student's Book and then to check their answers on page 82.
Ask them to add more jobs to the list that use the suffixes *-er/-or* or *-ist*.

ANSWERS
-er/-or: blogger, designer, editor, photographer, printer, publisher, reporter (teacher, farmer, singer, actor, waiter, …)
-ist: cartoonist, columnist, artist, journalist (chemist, receptionist, psychologist, dentist, …)

2 Ask students to write two paragraphs of approximately 50 words each to answer two of the questions from the media habits survey.

READING Media culture

Recognise formal and informal writing Page 84

STAGE	TIME	FOCUS
GET STARTED		Play a guessing game where you ask questions to discover the identity of a celebrity.
SPEAK AND READ		Talk about famous people you like and where you find information about them. Read two texts from different types of publication and distinguish between formal and informal writing.
REACT		Talk about the texts and about the issue of famous people and their right to privacy.

Get started

Play *Fame Game* with the class. Ask for a volunteer to come and sit in front of the class. Explain that you are going to give this student the identity of a famous person and that the rest of the class must ask questions to find out who he/she is. Write the name of the famous person on a slip of paper and show it to the volunteer. Make sure they know enough about the person to be able to answer questions. Tell students that the 'famous person' can only answer *yes* or *no* and that the class has two minutes to discover the person's identity. Repeat the process with a couple more volunteers.

SPEAK AND READ

1

- Divide the class into pairs to answer the questions. Set a time limit of four minutes for this.
- When they have finished, ask students to say where they find out information about famous people they like, eg *magazines, internet sites, TV shows.*
- Write *source of information* on the board and explain that a place or person that provides us with information is called a *source* /sɔː(r)s/.
- Establish that some sources of information are more serious than others and tell students that often the style of a piece of writing (formal or informal) can give us some clues as to how serious or reliable a text is as a source.

2a

- Nominate a student to read out the lesson aim.
- Refer students to the tips in the HOW TO box. Invite a couple of volunteers to read the tips out loud.
- Then ask students to close their books and ask them to tell you what they remember about the differences between formal and informal writing in terms of sentence length, vocabulary, contractions and punctuation.

2b 3.05

- Check the meaning of *publication.* Explain that it is related to the verb *publish* (to make a written document available to the public). *Publications* include different types of books, magazines, internet articles, etc.
- Explain to students that they are going to read two texts from different types of publication. Look at the three options given and check the meaning of *showbiz* (show business, the world of entertainment) and *celebrity* (a famous person).
- Ask students to read the texts and match them to the correct publication. There is one publication they don't need to use. Set a time limit of six minutes. Don't play the audio at this point. A suggestion for using the audio is given at the end of the lesson.
- Check answers in open class.

ANSWERS
Text A – 3 Text B – 2

3

- Focus students on the four possible titles for the texts and encourage them to choose the best one for each of the texts. Advise them to think about both the style and the content of the titles before they make their decisions. Set a time limit of one minute.
- Encourage students to compare their choices in pairs before you check them in open class eliciting reasons for their answers.

ANSWERS
Text A – 3 Text B – 2

4

- Ask students which tips in the HOW TO box they used to help them in exercises 2b and 3.
- Elicit some examples of the formal words and expressions from Text A, eg *On the one hand, On the other hand, however.*
- Ask students which words/phrases in Text B seemed more like spoken English, eg *By the way, Hello?, Well.*

5

- Ask students to read the sentences and circle *A* or *B* depending on which text the sentence refers to. Suggest that they underline the sentence(s) in the texts that give them the answers. Set a time limit of six minutes.
- Encourage students to compare their answers in pairs before you check them in open class, asking students to tell you what section of the text gave them the answer.

ANSWERS
1 A 2 A 3 B 4 B 5 B 6 A

REACT

6

- Ask students to work individually, first to read the questions and then to make notes to use when they are giving their answers. Set a time limit of three minutes.
- Then divide the class into pairs to exchange and discuss their opinions.

ANSWERS
1, 3, 4 – Students' own opinions.
2 Text A is probably more accurate for the following reasons:
- the author is not personally involved.
- the sources of quotes and information are stated.
- there is a more balanced approach to the issue.

GO BEYOND

Ask students to read the two texts again and find two more differences between them. Encourage them to focus on how the same events are presented in different ways.

Extra activity

Write the following words and definitions on the board, asking students to match them. Then check answers in open class.

WORD	*DEFINITION*
1 promote	*A not known to most people, private*
2 respect	*B famous person*
3 personal	*C types of mass communication like television, newspapers, etc*
4 media	*D have admiration for / treat politely*
5 celebrity	*E to help to sell something or make something/someone more popular*
6 privacy	*F a person's right to keep their personal life and relationships private*

ANSWERS

1 E 2 D 3 A 4 C 5 B 6 F

Then for each word, ask students to find two phrases or expressions in Text A that use the word, inviting them to explain the phrases in the context of this text.

ANSWERS

1 promoting his latest film; promote their careers
2 respect their privacy; respected journalist
3 for personal reasons; personal life
4 media culture; media attention; want the media to respect their privacy
5 Hollywood celebrity; celebrity children; celebrity magazines
6 respect their privacy; stricter privacy laws

Recorded reading text 3.05

The reading text is recorded as an extra audio track which can be exploited for various purposes.

As a cool-down at the end of the lesson, ask students to close their books, and play the audio again. Pause the track at various points and ask students to shout out the next word.

Homework

Ask students to read this quote from Text A:

'On the one hand, [celebrities] want media attention in order to help promote their careers. On the other hand, they want the media to respect their privacy.'

Ask students to write an essay discussing this question: *Should famous people have the right to more privacy?*

Encourage them to follow this plan:

Paragraph 1: Introduce the topic.
Paragraph 2: Talk about the reasons why celebrities need media attention.
Paragraph 3: Talk about the reasons why celebrities should have more privacy.
Paragraph 4: Give your own opinion.

GRAMMAR Reported speech

Report what people say *Page 85*

STAGE	TIME	FOCUS
GET STARTED		Write some reported sentences and guess the jobs of the people who were speaking.
READ AND LISTEN		Read and listen to a conversation containing examples of direct and reported speech.
STUDY		Use the conversation to complete explanations about how to report speech.
PRACTISE		Rewrite direct speech as reported speech. Rewrite reported speech as direct speech.
SPEAK		Exchange personal information with a partner and tell the class what you learned about your partner.

Get started

Dictate the following sentences:

1 *She said that I would need to spend a few days in bed.*
2 *He said I was going to need a filling in one of my teeth.*
3 *She said that she had been there on holiday and that she recommended it.*
4 *She said she thought the blue jacket suited me best.*
5 *She said that she had really enjoyed making the film.*
6 *He said that the soup of the day was onion soup.*
7 *She said that I had to pay a fine of 25 cents for returning the book late.*

Nominate different students to read out what they've written, writing on the board exactly what they read out and asking other students if they have written anything different.

Make sure that at the end of this process the correct sentences are clearly displayed on the board so that students can check their work. Divide the class into pairs to decide the jobs of the people who said these things.

ANSWERS

1 doctor 2 dentist 3 travel agent 4 shop assistant
5 actress/director 6 waiter 7 librarian

READ AND LISTEN Grammar in context

1 3.06

- Find out if your students have a school magazine or newspaper. If they do, ask: *What sorts of things appear in the magazine? Are you involved in producing it? If so, what exactly do you do?* If they don't, ask: *Do you think it would be a good idea to have a school magazine? What sorts of things would you like to read about in a school magazine?*

- Explain to students that they are going to read and listen to a conversation between two boys talking about a story they are doing for their school magazine with a friend called Lucy. Ask them to read and listen and say who Lucy's new photographer is.
- Elicit the answer in open class.

ANSWER / AUDIO SCRIPT 3.06

Jack is Lucy's new photographer.
See Student's Book page 85 for audio script.

STUDY

2

- Focus students on the *Use* section of the grammar explanation. Ask them what they notice about the verb tense in the two examples, ie in direct speech the verb is in the present simple and in reported speech it is in the past simple.
- Explain to students that as reported speech means reporting what someone has said at a later point in time, we usually make adjustments like this to the tense.
- Elicit what other difference they can see in the two examples. If necessary, write the sentences on the board and circle *I* and *she*. Explain that in order to make it clear who said what to whom, pronouns and other words also change.
- Ask students to read through the explanations and to complete the examples where necessary.
- Go through the explanations and check that they have completed the examples correctly.
- After checking the answers, go back to the *Use* section and highlight the difference between *say* and *tell*, ie *say* cannot be used with an direct object and *tell* must be used with a direct object. Write these sentences on the board and ask students to correct them:
  He said me that I was a good friend. ✗
  (He said that I was a good friend. ✓*)*
  My mum told that I had forgotten to brush my hair. ✗
  (My mum told me that I had forgotten to brush my hair. ✓*)*

ANSWERS

didn't want   you

PRACTISE

3

- Before starting this exercise, make sure students are familiar with the table of tense changes on page 127 of their Student's Book.
- Ask students to write the sentences from Exercise 1 in reported speech using *said*. Set a time limit of five minutes.
- Encourage students to compare their answers in pairs before you check them in open class. Invite different students to the board to write their answers up, then analyse them with the class and make any corrections that are necessary.
- Point out that although the contraction *'d* is used for both *had* and *would*, the verb form that follows makes it clear which word is being used, eg *She said she'd been. She said she'd go.*

ANSWERS

2 He said (that) they were doing a story for the school magazine.
3 He said (that) he didn't understand.
4 He said (that) he'd brought his camera.
5 He said (that) he'd tell him.
6 He said (that) he could be there in five minutes.

Fast finishers

Ask students to write two reported sentences that might be said by people in particular jobs, like the ones in the *Get started* activity. Ask them to read the sentences out to another fast finisher for them to guess the job.

4

- Write the example up on the board, lining up the two sentences so that the changes can be highlighted easily:
  Lucy told me that she didn't want to see you.
  I don't want to see him.
- Highlight the changes: *she* → *I* / *didn't* → *don't* / *you* → *him*, making sure that students understand why these changes occur.
- Ask them to write the sentences from Exercise 1 in direct speech.
- Check the answers in open class.

ANSWERS

2 I'll meet you there at seven.
3 I can talk to him.
4 I've found another photographer.
5 I'm going to do the story with him.
6 I'm waiting for my new photographer.

Extra activity

Ask students to look back at the sentences from the *Get started* activity and say what the people said in direct speech.

5

- Focus students on the sentence stems and ask them to complete the sentences about themselves. Set a time limit of five minutes.

SPEAK

6

- Divide the class into pairs to read out their sentences from Exercise 5 so that their partner can take notes. Allow five minutes.
- Nominate different students to tell the rest of the class what their partner said, involving students in correcting each other if necessary.

Extra activity

Play a game of *Reported speech football.* Draw a football pitch on the board with goals at each end, and two crosses between the centre line and the goal.

Divide the class into two teams and toss a coin to see which team starts.

Draw a ball on the centre line. The objective is to move the ball from the centre to a cross and into the goal. Say a statement out loud to the team, who then need to change it correctly into reported speech. For every correct answer the ball moves in the direction of the team who answered correctly. An incorrect answer means the ball moves in the direction of the opposite team. Teams take turns answering, regardless of a correct or incorrect answer.

A different team member must answer each time their team has a turn.

Homework

Ask students to write five sentences reporting things people have said to them during the day, eg: *My mum told me I have to go to the dentist after school. Julie said she was worried about her French exam.*

LISTENING AND VOCABULARY Picture stories

Infer meaning

Page 86

STAGE	TIME	FOCUS
GET STARTED		Play *Pictionary* to review vocabulary.
SPEAK AND LISTEN		Describe similarities and differences in a series of pictures. Listen for specific information and practise an Exam-type task. Learn and practise how to infer meaning from unspoken as well as spoken information (a listening subskill).
REACT		Act out a scene and reflect the feelings of the characters.
WORK WITH WORDS		Practise using different reporting verbs.

Get started

Play a game of *Pictionary*. Divide the class into groups of four, with the group members working in pairs.

Ask each pair to choose two vocabulary items from recent lessons in the book and write them on small slips of paper, eg items from the **Work with Words** section on page 82.

Pairs take it in turns to give one of their words to one member of the opposite pair, who must try to draw the word for his/her partner to guess. Set a time limit of one minute per word.

SPEAK AND LISTEN

1

- Divide the class into pairs to describe what they see in the pictures. Encourage them to say what is the same about the three pictures in each set and what is different.

2 3.07

Exam-type task

- Play the track for students to listen and tick the corresponding picture.
- Encourage students to compare their answers in pairs. Monitor as they compare answers to see if they need to listen to the track a second time.
- Nominate different students to say the answers in open class.

ANSWERS / AUDIO SCRIPT 3.07

1 b 2 c 3 a 4 c 5 a

1

Reporter: Hello? It's me.
Police officer: You said you wouldn't call me again, remember?
Reporter: I know. It's the last time. I promise.
Police officer: What's wrong?
Reporter: The editor wants to print the story tomorrow. I just need to check some facts. How about if we meet at the usual place at 5 o'clock?
Police officer: I can't at five. How about 5.45?
Reporter: OK. I'll see you then.

2

Reporter: Can you confirm the stories about you and rap star Dustin Dredd? Is it true that you're getting married?
Actress: No comment. Next question?
Reporter: What will you be doing next? Another western?
Actress: Ah, a real question. I'm glad you asked. Actually, my next project is going to be a musical based on the life of a famous British singer. But I can't tell you anything more at the moment.

3

Reporter: Can I check the facts again? In your original statement you claim that you saw three men but now you're saying there were two men and a woman.
Witness: That's right. I admit it sounds strange. I heard the man from the bank saying there were three men. At first, I thought he must've been right. But I had a better view of the getaway car than he did. It was definitely a woman driving.
Reporter: So the man from the bank was wrong.
Witness: Yes.
Reporter: Are you sure?
Witness: I know what I saw. There were two men and a woman.

4

Reporter: Congratulations. That was an amazing race. How do you feel?
Athlete: It's hard to describe. It's been such a long journey to get here.
Reporter: You must feel disappointed not to have come first.
Athlete: Not really. I think ... you know ... after the injury last year, it was always going to be difficult. It's hard to explain, but coming second, I still feel like a winner.
Reporter: Well, thanks for talking to us. Well done.
Athlete: Can I just add one more thing? I couldn't have done this without the support of everyone back home.

5

Reporter: So, where's the famous letter?
Source: Are you recording this?
Reporter: Yes. I always record interviews. Insurance.
Source: Anything I say now is off the record. If you use my name, I'll deny I ever spoke to you. So no recordings. Agreed?
Reporter: OK. I agree.
Source: The letter's on the bookshelf above the table. Hey! Are you still recording?
Reporter: What are you doing? Wait!

3a

- Explain that people often use tone of voice or body language to add meaning to what they say.
- Write on the board: *Yes, I'd love to come to your party!* Read it in two different ways, one enthusiastic and positive and one bored and suggesting that really you *don't* want to come to the party. Each time, ask students if they think your meaning matches the meaning of the words.
- Ask students to read the tips in the HOW TO box. Invite a student to read them out loud.

3b 3.07

- Play the track again for students to listen and choose the correct options.
- Encourage them to compare their answers in pairs before you check them in open class.

ANSWERS
1 unhappy 2 likes 3 isn't 4 very happy 5 don't trust
6 reporter's source

3c
- Ask students which tips in the HOW TO box they used to help them with Exercise 3b.

REACT

4
- Divide the class into pairs. Ask them to decide which of the scenes in Exercise 2 they liked best and to act the scene in their own words, reflecting the feelings of the characters.
- Nominate one or two pairs to act out their conversations for the rest of the class and ask the class what 'unspoken' information they could infer from the way the conversation was performed.

Alternative procedure: less confident classes
Make copies of the audio script and ask pairs to read their chosen conversation, trying to reflect the feelings and relationships of the characters through tone of voice. Having the audio script will allow less confident students to focus on conveying and recognising unspoken information.

WORK WITH WORDS

5 3.08
- Ask students to complete the sentences with the correct form of the verbs in the box. Set a time limit of five minutes.
- Play the track for them to listen and check their answers.

ANSWERS / AUDIO SCRIPT 3.08
1 promise 2 confirm 3 claim 4 admit 5 add
6 deny
See Student's Book page 86 for audio script.

Extra activity
If students are unsure about the meaning of the reporting verbs in Exercise 5, give them these definitions and ask them to match them to the verbs: *to give extra information* (add); *to agree that something is true, perhaps unwillingly* (admit); *to say something is true even though there is no evidence* (claim); *to say something is definitely true* (confirm); *to say something is not true* (deny); *to tell someone you will definitely do something* (promise).

6 3.09
- Ask students to complete the sentences with information from the stories.
- Nominate different students to say their answers in open class.
- Play the track for students to listen and repeat the verbs.

ANSWERS / AUDIO SCRIPT 3.09
1 5.45. 2 a woman and two men. 3 like a winner.
4 the recorder.
add admit claim confirm deny promise suggest insist explain agree

GO BEYOND
Ask students to do the Go Beyond task on page 137.

Homework

Ask students to report the sentences below using one of the reporting verbs from Exercise 5 on page 86 + *that*. Remind them to adjust the verb tenses, pronouns, etc.

Give them this example:
Gary: I'll clean my room.
He promised that he would clean his room.

1 Peter: I'll never tell a lie again.
2 Jonas: Oh, and another thing. I can't come to the concert on Tuesday.
3 Sally: I didn't go to the disco!
4 Hilary: I saw an alien.
5 Ben: I'll be very disappointed if I don't win the match.
6 Mr Davis: I'm definitely going to tell your parents that you didn't do your homework.

ANSWERS
1 He promised that he would never tell a lie again.
2 He added that he couldn't come to the concert on Tuesday.
3 She denied that she had been to the disco.
4 She claimed that she had seen an alien.
5 He admitted that he would be very disappointed if he didn't win the match.
6 He confirmed that he was going to tell my/his/her parents that I/he/she hadn't done my/his/her homework.

GRAMMAR Reported questions

Report what people ask — *Page 87*

STAGE	TIME	FOCUS
GET STARTED		Play a game to practise reported speech.
READ		Read a news report.
STUDY		Complete explanations about the use and form of reported questions using examples from the news report.
PRACTISE		Practice transforming direct questions into reported questions and vice versa. Write five questions to ask a famous person.
SPEAK AND WRITE		Role-play an interview with a famous person and write a report of the questions and answers.

Get started

Play a game of *Broken Telephone* (see Games page 33) to practise reported speech. In this case, the next student should use reported speech to give the previous sentence.

Suggested sentence: *The winner of the holiday competition can choose where they want to travel and when they will go.*

Reported version: *He/She said the winner of the holiday competition could choose where they wanted to travel and when they would go.*

Use the game as a chance to review some of the changes that occur in reported speech.

READ Grammar in context

1

- Focus students on the news report and ask them to read it and say what kind of job Johan has. Allow one minute.
- Check the answer in open class, eliciting which words helped them to find the answer, eg *game, club, players, pitch, fans.*

ANSWER
He's a sportsman, probably a footballer.

STUDY

2

- Ask students if the news report includes the reporter's and Johan's actual words or a reported version of what they said (a reported version).
- Elicit some of the changes that occur in reported speech, eg tenses change to the past forms of the verbs, pronouns and possessive adjectives change, etc.
- Explain that in the case of questions, there are some extra changes that have to be made when reporting. Focus students on the examples in the *Use* section of the grammar explanation and ask students what difference they can see, apart from tense and pronoun changes. (The word order changes from the question style verb-subject (*are you*) to subject-verb (*he was*).)
- Ask students to read and complete the section on *wh-* questions with examples from Exercise 1.
- Remind students that not all questions use *wh-* question words and write an example on the board, eg *Are you working today?* Remind students that these are known as *yes/no* questions.
- Write a reported version below the example question on the board, ie *She asked me if I was working that day.* Circle *if* and point out that when we report *yes/no* questions we use *if* or *whether* before the question.
- Ask students to read and complete the section on *yes/no* questions with examples from Exercise 1.

ANSWERS
the other players had reacted
he was still friends with Pepe
he had any immediate plans
club he was talking to
he could say something to his fans

Extra activity

Word order is one of the most challenging aspects of reported question form. If your students are having difficulty, give them practice at putting words in the correct order before moving on to transforming direct to reported questions, eg:

He / school / I / went / asked / to / me / which
(He asked me which school I went to.)

if / She / had / asked / I / seen / me / The Simpsons
(She asked me if I had seen *The Simpsons.*)

PRACTISE

3

- Ask students to rewrite the reported questions in orange in Exercise 1 as direct questions. Read through the example with the class and set a time limit of six minutes.
- Encourage students to compare their answers in pairs as they finish.
- Invite different students to dictate the questions to you and write them on the board exactly as they suggest. With the help of other students make any necessary corrections.

ANSWERS
'How have the other players reacted?'
'Are you still friends with Pepe?'
'Do you have any immediate plans?'
'Which club are you talking to?'
'Can you say something to your fans?'

Fast finishers

Ask students to say what some of Johan's answers would have been in direct speech, eg *He explained that it was for personal reasons* → *'It's for personal reasons.'*

4

- Focus students on the journalist's notes and ask them to write her questions in reported speech. Set a time limit of seven minutes.
- Encourage students to compare their answers in pairs before you check them in open class.

ANSWERS
2 I asked him if he could play any instruments.
3 I asked them when they would play in Britain again.
4 I asked her if she'd seen what had happened.
5 I asked him how he was feeling.
6 I asked them if they were excited about the film.

5a

- Explain to students that in the speaking section of many English exams students are asked questions about themselves. Find out if anyone has experienced this in an exam.
- Ask students to use the prompts to write both direct and reported questions. Set a time limit of 10 minutes for this. Before they start, go through the example with the class.
- Nominate different students to give their answers in open class.

ANSWERS
2 'What school do you go to?' / They asked me which school I went to.
3 'How long have you studied English?' / They asked me how long I'd studied English.
4 'Have you ever visited the UK?' / They asked me if I'd ever visited the UK.
5 'Do you like going to the cinema?' / They asked me if I liked going to the cinema.
6 'What are you doing/going to do next weekend?' / They asked me what I was doing/going to do next weekend.

5b

- Invite students to imagine they are telling someone about the exam they have just done.
- Divide the class into pairs. Ask Student A to talk about questions 1, 3 and 5 and Student B to talk about questions 2, 4 and 6. Encourage them to tell their partner about the questions too, eg: *They asked me where I was from and I told them I was from …*

6

- Set up the task by telling students they are going to imagine that they are reporters interviewing a famous person. Invite them to choose the type of reporter they'd like to be and to decide which famous person they'd like to interview.
- Ask them to write five questions they'd like to ask their chosen person. Set a time limit of five minutes.

SPEAK AND WRITE

7

- Divide the class into pairs to conduct interviews with their partner pretending to be the famous person they have chosen. Ask them to make notes on their partners' answers. Set a time limit of 10 minutes.
- When the interviews are over, encourage students to write a short report about the interview using reported questions and reported speech using the report in Exercise 1 as a model. Set a time limit of 10 minutes for students to write their interview reports.
- Invite one or two students to read their reports to the class or divide the class into small groups to read their reports to each other. If you run out of time, display students' reports around the classroom so that they can read them before or after class.

Extra activity

Ask students to role-play the interview from the news report in Exercise 1, transforming the reported speech into direct questions and answers.

Homework

Ask students to put these jumbled reported questions in the correct order and then write them in direct speech.

1 He / me / beach / if / the / wanted / to / I / asked / to / go
2 I / asked / whether /at / study / Max / me / I / thought / would / university
3 ever / I / eaten / Japanese / food / he / me /asked / if / had
4 Margot / me / how / been / long / learning / French / asked / I / had

LANGUAGE & BEYOND GET THINKING

Compare and evaluate information that you read or hear Page 88

STAGE	TIME	FOCUS
GET STARTED		Discuss a quote by Benjamin Franklin.
SPEAK AND READ		Read and listen to four people discussing the same situation. Try to decide what you think about the situation based on what you've read and heard.
DO		Examine the speakers and their versions of the situation more closely. Rank the speakers in order of reliability.
REFLECT		Talk about the importance of comparing and evaluating sources of information.
EXTEND		Write five tips for using the internet to find factual information.

LIFE SKILLS

COMPARE AND EVALUATE INFORMATION THAT YOU READ OR HEAR

We live in the so-called 'information age' and students have access to an enormous amount of information via the internet and other media. However, along with this ease of access to information comes the necessity to be able to evaluate and verify sources of information. This skill is essential for students hoping to go on to university, but it is equally important in all manner of everyday decisions, from evaluating online medical information to gathering information before making an important purchase (car, holiday, etc).

This lesson gets students thinking about the usefulness of comparing different sources of information and evaluating their reliability.

Get started

Write this quote on the board:

Believe none of what you hear and half of what you see. (Benjamin Franklin, 1706–1790)

Divide the class into small groups to say what point Benjamin Franklin is making (that you shouldn't believe what you hear or see without having clear evidence that it's true).

Discuss this idea in open class and find out if students agree. Invite them to talk about situations where what they hear or see may not be true, eg rumours, information on the internet, stories they read about in the news, photos on the internet that may have been altered, etc.

SPEAK AND READ

1 3.10

- Tell students they are going to hear four people talking about a situation that happened in a school. Ask them to read and listen to the four people and then talk to a partner and say what the situation is.

ANSWER
Laura has been accused of copying Beth's homework.

2

- Do a quick class poll to ask students if they think Laura is innocent or guilty, based on what they've read. Include a category for undecided students. Elicit a few reasons for their opinions.

DO

3

- Explain that you would like students to examine the speakers' comments more closely. Read the questions with the class and check that they understand them.
- Divide the class into small groups to discuss the questions. Set a time limit of four minutes.
- Check the answers in open class, encouraging students to explain their answers giving examples from the texts.

ANSWERS
1 Chris and Maite
2 Chris and Stefan
3 Anonymous and Stefan
4 Anonymous
5 Anonymous and Stefan

4

- Ask students to put the speakers in order from the least to the most reliable. Check the meaning and drill the pronunciation of *reliable*, /rɪˈlaɪəb(ə)l/ (a reliable person is someone you can trust to be accurate).
- Ask students to compare their lists in pairs and to give reasons for their choices. Before they start, refer students to the expressions in the PHRASE BYTES box and encourage them to use these in their discussions. Allow two minutes.
- Invite a student to read out their list and elicit from the rest of the class if they agree.

REFLECT

5

- Use the questions as the basis for a class discussion or divide the class into small groups to discuss them. In either case, give students some reflection time to think about their answers and how to express them in English before you start the discussion.
- After the discussion, focus students on the REFLECTION POINT and elicit whether they agree or not.

Extra activity

If students would benefit from more input on the REFLECTION POINT, encourage them to discuss these comments made by other students, saying whether or not they agree and giving examples of their own if possible.

1 When I'm reading about something on the internet, I usually look at a couple of different sites. Sometimes you can see that one site has just copied from another! I try to make sure I read different information about a topic so I can be more confident that the facts are true.
2 I'm on the student council at my school and I have learned that when there is a problem you have to talk to different people and get different points of view so that you have a full picture of the problem and how it affects people.
3 We did a project at school to find out who had written some of the information we found on the internet. I was really surprised that often the person was anonymous and other times the person was not really an expert but just someone who was interested in the topic. The internet is a good source of information, but after that project I always check to see who wrote the information.
4 I agree with the Reflection Point. Sometimes you hear rumours about people, but when you speak to the people involved and find out something about the people spreading the rumours, you understand that it's best not to believe everything you hear!

EXTEND

6

- Divide the class into small groups to write five tips for using the internet to find factual information. Recommend that they use the questions from Exercise 5 to help them. Set a time limit of 10 minutes.
- Invite students to circulate and compare their tips with other groups.

Homework

Ask students to use the tips they wrote to gather some information on a topic of their choice using two or more different sites on the internet. Encourage them to check for differences in facts/information, references to the sources of information, any possible reason the website might have for presenting the information in a certain way and when the information was last updated.

Ask them to write a short report of approximately 150 words to explain what they found.

SPEAKING Excuse me ...

Interrupt someone

Page 89

STAGE	TIME	FOCUS
GET STARTED		Recycle reported questions and speech. Ask and answer questions about mobile phones then report the conversation to another student.
SPEAK		Describe a picture and make predictions about the situation.
WATCH OR LISTEN		Watch or listen to two scenes and learn phrases for interrupting. Match sentences to idiomatic expressions in the conversations.
ACT		Write, rehearse and perform a continuation of one of the scenes including phrases for interrupting.

Get started

Give students one minute to write two questions for a partner on the topic of mobile phones. Divide the class into pairs and give them two minutes to ask and answer their questions. Then ask students to change partners and report the questions and their answers to their new partner, eg:

Carl asked me if I used my phone more for calling or sending messages and I told him I used it mainly for messaging. He also asked me how long I'd had my mobile phone and I said I'd had it for about two years.

SPEAK

1

- Divide the class into pairs to describe the picture and say what they think the situation is. Allow one minute.
- Elicit some ideas in open class. Don't confirm or deny students' ideas at this point.

WATCH OR LISTEN

2 3.11

- Play the first scene for students to watch or listen and check their answer to Exercise 1. Find out if their predictions were correct.
- Ask what time Leo had promised to be back (8 o'clock) and what time he arrived (9.30 – see picture).

VIDEO/AUDIO SCRIPT 3.11

Dad:	What time do you call this?
Leo:	I ...
Mum:	You promised you'd be back by eight.
Dad:	We've been worried.
Leo:	Can I say something?
Dad:	You should've phoned us and ...
Leo:	Sorry to interrupt, but I did phone you. I got voicemail.
Mum:	What? Where's my phone?

3 3.12

- Play the second scene where Leo is telling his friends about what happened. Ask students to make a note of where the phone was.
- Check the answer in open class.

ANSWER / VIDEO/AUDIO SCRIPT 3.12

The phone was in the fridge.

Ethan:	Then what happened?
Ruby:	My mom and dad are just the same.
Leo:	Hang on, let me finish.
Ruby:	If I'm late home, they get real mad.
Leo:	Wait a second. I haven't finished the story.
Ethan:	My dad is always losing his phone. It drives Mum up the wall.
Leo:	Excuse me. Will you let me tell the story?
Ruby:	OK. Keep your shirt on.
Leo:	Thanks. The phone was in the fridge!

4a 3.13

- Ask students if they noticed that in both scenes people were talking without letting others finish what they wanted to say. Ask them if they know the word in English for this (*interrupting*).
- Refer students to the phrases in the PHRASEBOOK box for interrupting.
- Play the track with both scenes together for students to complete the conversations with some of the phrases from the PHRASEBOOK box.
- Check answers in open class.

ANSWERS / VIDEO/AUDIO SCRIPT 3.13

1 Can I say something 2 Sorry to interrupt, but
3 Hang on 4 Wait a second 5 Excuse me
The video/audio script is the same as in Exercises 2 and 3.

4b 3.14

- Play the track for students to listen and repeat the phrases, paying particular attention to intonation.

AUDIO SCRIPT 3.14

1 Can I say something? 2 Sorry to interrupt, but ...
3 Hang on ... 4 Wait a second. 5 Excuse me.

5

- Focus students on the sentences and ask them to match them to sentences in the conversations with the same meaning. Set a time limit of four minutes.
- Nominate different students to say the answers in open class.

ANSWERS

1 It drives Mum up the wall. 2 I got voicemail.
3 They get real mad. 4 What time do you call this?
5 Keep your shirt on.

GO BEYOND FOR TEACHERS

Origins of idioms

Some idioms in English have interesting origins that can help students to remember their meaning. This is the case with the expression *keep your shirt on*, for example. The phrase originated in the 19th century, when men would remove their shirts for a fight as the tight collars and stiff material restricted their movements. Thus telling someone to *keep their shirt on* means *calm down*.

The origin of *drive someone up the wall* is less clear, but it most likely has a more literal meaning of escaping from someone or something that is annoying you by climbing up and over a wall.

6

- Divide the class into groups of three to practise reading out the conversations. If there's time, invite them to repeat the conversations three times, taking a different role each time. Encourage them to use intonation to express the characters' feelings.

ACT

7 3.15

- Keep students in their groups of three. Explain they are going to write and perform a conversation to continue the one in Exercise 2 and explain how Leo's mum finds her phone.
- Ask them to re-read the conversation and decide what happens next and what the people say. Before they start writing, play the track with the phrases in the PHRASEBOOK box and encourage students to use at least three of them when they write their conversation. Set a time limit of 10 minutes for students to write and rehearse their conversations.
- Invite students to perform their conversations for the rest of the class.

Extra activity

Ask students to suggest some topical issues they would like to discuss. Encourage them to talk in pairs and think of at least three issues and write discussion questions like: *Are zoos cruel to animals? Are football stars paid too much?*

Elicit some ideas in open class and write six good ones on the board numbered 1–6. Note: choose the number of issues according to how much time you have available.

Divide the class into groups of four. Give students four minutes to discuss each issue and ask them to interrupt each other (politely) using the phrases from the PHRASEBOOK box on page 89.

If you want to introduce an element of competition, tell students that they can earn points by using the interrupting phrases. Tell them that you will be monitoring, and if you think they are interrupting inappropriately, they will lose a point. Remind them that interrupting is a balance between expressing your view and respecting the views of others.

Homework

Ask students to use the idiomatic expressions from Exercise 5 to complete these sentences:

1 ______ ? We've been waiting for you for over an hour!
2 Where were you last night? I called you about six times but I only ______ .
3 I wish those neighbours would turn the music down! It ______
4 My parents ______ when I don't tidy my room.
5 Jack: Oh no! My brother borrowed my MP3 player and he hasn't returned it. When I see him, I'm gonna …
Suzie: ______ . It's here on the table.

ANSWERS
1 What time do you call this 2 got voicemail
3 drives me up the wall 4 get real mad
5 Keep your shirt on

WRITING School news

Use correct punctuation

Page 90

STAGE	TIME	FOCUS
GET STARTED		Recycle vocabulary for things you find in a newspaper. Talk about the contents of a school newspaper.
SPEAK AND READ		Order words to make newspaper headlines. Match a news story to one of the headlines. Recycle punctuation rules. Learn new punctuation symbols and how to use them.
PRACTISE		Correct the spelling and punctuation in a news story from a school magazine.
PLAN		Plan a news story for a school magazine.
WRITE AND CHECK		Write and edit a news story.
SHARE		Read other students' stories.

Get started

Write these scrambled words on the board and ask students to rearrange the letters and write nine things they can find in a newspaper. Set a time limit of three minutes.

Elicit and check answers in open class.

1 porsts wens *2 waereth*
3 rats / etaintermetnn *4 rootancs*
5 hoopts *6 rmice wens*
7 vertads *8 oopinin colnums*
9 veiwinetsr

Divide the class into pairs to say which of these things they would expect to find in a school newspaper, ie *sports news, arts/entertainment, cartoons, photos, opinion columns, interviews*. Invite students to say what recent events at their school(s) might appear in a school newspaper, eg *We had a school concert recently and we made lots of money for charity.*

ANSWERS
1 sports news 2 weather 3 arts / entertainment
4 cartoons 5 photos 6 crime news 7 adverts
8 opinion columns 9 interviews

SPEAK AND READ

1

- Focus students on the scrambled headlines. Divide the class into pairs to put the words in order to make newspaper headlines for stories they could find in a school newspaper. Set a time limit of two minutes.
- Check answers in open class.

ANSWERS
1 Spanish exam results improve.
2 School welcomes new teacher.
3 Bicycle problems continue.

2

- Ask students to match the news story to the correct headline in Exercise 1. Set a time limit of one minute.
- Check the answer in open class. Then ask students to cover the text and ask them a few questions to see how much they remember, eg *Where is the new Spanish teacher from?* (Granada, in Andalucía) *What are some of her interests?* (going to the cinema, the theatre and museums; taking photos; improving her English) *How does she feel about starting at the school?* (excited).

ANSWER
School welcomes new teacher

3

- Write the punctuation words from the box on the board and invite different students to come to the board and draw the correct symbols next to them. Drill the pronunciation of the words.

apostrophes	'	/əˈpɒstrəfiz/
capital letters	M, G	/ˈkæpɪt(ə)l ˈletə(r)z/
commas	,	/ˈkɒməz/
exclamation marks	!	/ˌekskləˈmeɪʃ(ə)n mɑː(r)ks/
full stops	.	/fʊl stɒps/
question marks	?	/ˈkwestʃ(ə)n mɑː(r)ks/

- Ask students to complete the punctuation rules with the words in the box. Set a time limit of four minutes.
- Nominate individual students to read out the rules.

ANSWERS
1 capital letters 2 full stops 3 apostrophes
4 question marks 5 commas 6 exclamation marks

4a

- Ask students to read the tips in the **HOW TO** box to learn how four more punctuation symbols are used. Check the pronunciation of the new words: colon /ˈkəʊlɒn/, semicolon /ˌsemiˈkəʊlɒn/, dots /dɒts/, quotation marks /kwəʊˈteɪʃ(ə)n mɑː(r)ks/.

4b

- Put students into pairs to find examples of the punctuation in the news story and explain how it is used.

PRACTISE

5

- Ask students to check and correct the punctuation and spelling in another story from the school magazine. Set a time limit of five minutes.
- While they are working, write the incorrect text on the board, as this will make it easier to show the necessary corrections.
- Invite some students to the board to make the corrections in a different colour. Check their work with the class and make any adjustments that are necessary. Encourage students to explain why the punctuation is necessary.

ANSWERS
This year, the drama group is going to perform a musical version of William Shakespeare's play *Romeo and Juliet*. Are you interested in acting? If you are, come to the auditions on Friday. Mrs Jones, the director of the show, told me: 'I am looking for people who love doing all these things: singing in the shower; dancing to different types of music and performing in public.'

Fast finishers
Tell students they should have corrected four spelling errors and 17 punctuation errors. Encourage them to check their work and, if they have identified fewer errors, to keep looking for more.

PLAN

6

- Explain to students that they are going to write a news story about their school for the school magazine. Encourage them to choose a suitable topic.
- Focus their attention on the **Writing plan** and go through the different points with them.
- Ask students to write their ideas for their plan in their notebooks. Set a time limit of 10 minutes for the planning stage. Circulate and monitor, asking questions to help students make the most of their planning time and to keep them on task, eg *What are you going to write about? Who are the people in your story? How are you going to include direct or indirect speech? How can you include some of the punctuation from exercises 3 and 4? Will you have a list of phrases that you could separate with semicolons? How can you make your headline attractive to the reader?*

WRITE AND CHECK

7

- Ask students to use their plan and the model news story and write their own news story. Set a time limit of 10 minutes.
- When students have finished writing, encourage them to check their work, ticking the things in the plan to make sure they have followed all the steps.

SHARE

8 Ask students to swap their stories with one or two classmates to read and discuss. Ask them if they knew about the story their classmate reported and to say if they thought the information was true or invented.

Extra activity
Set up a project where students collate the news stories according to the topics and put them together to make a real magazine. Students could work in small groups, with each group responsible either for a section, eg sports, entertainment or for a particular page. They could include visual material and extras, like cartoons, adverts, etc. At the end of the project, students could take home their class magazine to show their families.

Homework

Give students these headlines and ask them to choose one and invent a story for the school magazine: *Student wins poetry competition*; *Snowstorm closes school*; *Sports equipment stolen*; *Mobile phones banned from classrooms*.

Ask them to write 120–150 words and to include direct and reported speech. Remind them to check their spelling and punctuation.

VOCABULARY Print and digital media jobs

1

- Ask students to read the text quickly, ignoring the gaps, to tell you how many people work at the Billington Post (*one*).
- Encourage students to complete the text with the missing words that show the many different media jobs Bill does. Point out that some of the letters are given. Set a time limit of four minutes.
- Encourage students to compare their answers in pairs before you nominate students to read out a sentence each to check answers in open class.

ANSWERS
1 publisher 2 reporter 3 journalist 4 photographer 5 editor 6 designer 7 graphic artist 8 cartoonist 9 gossip columnist 10 printer 11 blogger 12 author

Reporting verbs

2a

- Explain to students that many newspaper headlines include a direct quote before the first line of the story. Write an example on the board, eg *'I'm so proud!' Clive Sithers said he was proud to win the Best Actor prize.*
- Ask students to read the quotes and headlines and choose the correct reporting verbs. Set a time limit of four minutes.
- Check answers in open class.

ANSWERS
1 denied 2 admitted 3 promised 4 agreed 5 confirmed

2b

- Ask students to match the verbs in the box to the correct definitions. Point out that there is one extra word that they don't need.
- Encourage them to compare their answers in pairs before you check them in open class.

ANSWERS
1 explain 2 suggest 3 add 4 claim 5 insist

GRAMMAR Reported speech

3a

- Ask students to brainstorm ways that reported speech is different from direct speech.
- Collate their ideas on the board and remind them of any differences they haven't mentioned.
- Ask students to write the quotes in reported speech.
- Nominate different students to read out their answers.

ANSWERS
1 He said that he'd make the world a better place. 2 He said that he was making a film in Brazil then. 3 She said that she'd seen the thief there the day before. 4 They told Bill/him that they were going to play six concerts the following week. 5 She told Bill/him that he was the best editor in the world. 6 They/The athletes told the reporters that they loved their country.

3b

- Ask students to choose the correct option to complete the sentences.
- As you check answers in open class, write these form patterns on the board – without writing the verb in brackets. Elicit which form corresponds to *say* and which one corresponds to *tell*.
  Subject + verb + *that* + sentence (*say*)
  Subject + verb + *me/you/him*, etc + sentence (*tell*)

ANSWERS
1 told 2 said 3 told

Reported questions

4

- Explain the task to students and focus on the first question with the class.
- Ask if the question is a *wh-* question or a *yes/no* question (a *yes/no* question). Elicit the words we use to report *yes/no* questions (*if* or *whether*).
- Ask students to write the reported questions.
- Check in open class.

ANSWERS
1 He asked them if he could go out that night. 2 He asked him if he'd done his homework. 3 She asked him where he was going. 4 He asked her if he had to tell her. 5 They asked him what time he'd be home.

Extra Resources

Go to the Teacher's Resource Centre at www.macmillanbeyond.com for:

- the Speaking section of the Progress Check 7&8
- a downloadable project linked to Units 7–8
- downloadable audio and audio scripts for the Student's Book and Workbook
- videos and video scripts
- extra vocabulary at two levels of difficulty
- extra grammar at two levels of difficulty
- culture lessons, with full teacher's notes
- a life skills lesson, with full teacher's notes
- Speaking Database materials
- the *Beyond* B1 wordlist
- test generator for Unit 8 testing materials (all skills)
- tips for using the Grammar Database
- and more!

Go to the Workbook pages 88–99 for further practice material

PROGRESS CHECK UNITS 7&8

Preparing for the Progress Check

Vocabulary review

- To review traditional activities, write the following on the board and ask students which words are needed to complete the phrases (suggested answers are given in brackets):
  .... *bread* (bake)
  .... *a house* (build)
  .... *wood* (chop)
  .... *food* (grow)
  .... *clothes* (knit, sew)
  .... *a cow* (milk)
  .... *gas lights* (use)
  .... *furniture* (make)
  .... *your own entertainment* (make)
  .... *by hand* (wash clothes)
  .... *horse and cart* (travel by)
- After students have made a few suggestions, see who can find the rest first from pages 72–73.
- To review vocabulary to express feelings, ask students to use an adjective they have learned in a sentence. Start them off by giving them the following example:
  I was jealous of my sister's success.
- Elicit several similar sentences.
- Put students in pairs to review vocabulary for the media. Give them exactly one minute to write down people or jobs in the media. Refer students to pages 82–83 to see if there were any they forgot. Check students' answers and, while checking, make sure they understand the meanings of the words.
- In the same pairs, students work together on reporting verbs. Students check the reporting verbs on page 137. They should then write sentences which convey the meaning accurately, eg *He admitted that he had lied to the police.* After five minutes, ask students to read out their sentences.

Grammar review

- Put students in pairs and ask them to look back at the grammar pages (75, 77, 85 and 87).
- Remind students of the grammar they have studied in these two units:
  - Unit 7: *Used to*; Past perfect simple
  - Unit 8: Reported speech; Reported questions
- To review *used to*, start a question-and-answer chain around the class. Begin by saying to Student A: *Did people use to watch television 100 years ago?* Student A then answers *No, they didn't*, before asking Student B a *used to* question. Correct any mistakes and refer students back to page 75 if necessary. Continue the chain until everyone has spoken.
- Ask the class for the rule for forming the past perfect simple (*had* + past participle). Point out that it is mainly used to express the earlier of two past actions. It is usually used in a sentence in conjunction with the past simple and it is rarely used alone.
- To review reported speech and questions, ask students to work in pairs to interview each other. One of them plays the role of a famous person, while the other is a journalist. In each pair, Student A asks three questions. They should ask the questions in direct form, eg *Do you like being a famous actress?*
- Allow a few minutes before asking students to report back what was said in the interview. Make sure you ask both Student A and Student B from each pair. This way they will practise forms like *I asked him* and *he told me*, as well as *She asked me* and *I told her*.

Optional warm-up activities

READ Exercise 1

- Tell students that they are going to practise skimming a text. Give them exactly one minute to read the text for gist. Remind students not to read it in detail.
- After a minute, ask them to close their books and tell you what they remember. Elicit the main points about the text, correcting anything students have misunderstood.
- Point out how useful it can be to skim a reading text. Explain that they will have to read more closely to answer the questions in the task but that this will be easier because they can now find the relevant sections of the text quickly.

LISTEN Exercise 2

- Remind students of the importance of reading ahead before they listen.
- Put students in pairs and ask them to look at the gaps in the news report and say which one contains the following (answers are given in brackets):
  - a job or profession (3)
  - a noun (5)
  - an activity (4)
  - a preposition and a place (1)
  - an adjective (2)
- If students generally have difficulty with the **Listen** sections, you could ask them to suggest what the answers might be. Do not, however, give any indication of the actual answers. Instead, respond by saying *It could be that* or pointing out why a suggestion is unlikely.
- Finally, point out to students how much useful information they have gathered *without* listening. They will now be much more focused when they do listen.

WRITE Exercise 3

- Refer students back to the work they did on writing stories on page 80, and ask: *How do you write a good story?* Elicit suggestions and make sure students remember that the main tense for their stories should be the past simple, which they can also combine with the past continuous and the past perfect.
- Look at Exercise 3 with the class and point out that their stories must begin with the given sentence. Point out that this sentence is an example of how the past perfect and the simple past can be combined in one sentence.
- Go through the **Exam tips** and review the HOW TO box on page 90. Remind students that there are several things they need to remember, reassuring them that it is not difficult to write a story if they follow the advice in the book.
- Put students in pairs and ask them to come up with a plot for a story based on the beginning given. Allow up to five minutes for this before asking pairs to tell you their stories. Discuss the good points of each story with the rest of the class and ask for further suggestions, focusing on the structure of the story and ensuring it has a beginning, a middle and an end.

PROGRESS CHECK UNITS 7&8

Doing the Progress Check

READ

1

- Ask students to look again at the work they have done on recognising formal and informal writing on page 84.
- Go through the **Exam tips** and invite students to say whether they follow this exact order when doing such tasks.
- Allow 10–15 minutes for this section.

ANSWERS

1 D 2 B 3 A 4 C 5 C

LISTEN

2 3.16

- If you have decided not to do the full warm-up, encourage students to spend a minute or two looking at the gaps and predicting what they might hear.
- Make sure that they understand that they have to write a word or a short phrase in each gap.
- Go through the **Exam tips** for the listening task, briefly referring students back to the work they did on pages 27, 76 and 86. Ask some students to tell you which tips were the most useful.
- Remind the class that they will hear everything twice. Students should aim to fill each gap the first time but they must be careful not to lose their place. The second listening should be for checking and filling in any gaps they have left.

ANSWERS / AUDIO SCRIPT 3.16

1 on an island 2 science fiction 3 blogger 4 knitting
5 author and publisher

Journalist: This is Karen White reporting from Paris. I've just come out of a press conference at which the film star Veronica Payne denied that she was going to stop acting. As you know, there had been rumours that she was going to give up her career, give all her money to a famous charity and go to live on an island close to Venezuela. However, she insisted that she had <u>no plans</u> to stop acting. In fact, she confirmed that she had just signed a contract to appear in the new science fiction film *Beyond*.
There were about a hundred journalists and photographers at the press conference. In fact, I think the only journalist who <u>wasn't there</u> was Heidi Williams. As you probably know, Heidi is the Hollywood gossip columnist and blogger who wrote the news story that started everything. Heidi posted the story on her blog after she had interviewed the author of *My Life*, the new biography of Veronica Payne. The author claimed that Veronica had told him that she wanted to donate all her money to the charity, live on a desert island, build her own house and live a simple life, making furniture, baking bread and knitting. <u>Yes</u>, I <u>did</u> say '<u>knitting</u>'.
Now, the problems really began when the charity, which I can't name for legal reasons, confirmed that Veronica Payne had promised to give them all her money. The charity was obviously very grateful for her donation, but now they're extremely disappointed that the film star has changed her mind. At the press conference, Veronica explained that she was very upset by what had happened. She told us that she was taking legal action against the author and publisher of *My Life*. I'm sure she'll give any money she wins from the legal action to charity.

WRITE

3

- Read through the **Exam tips** for this task. Remind students that correct use of tenses and appropriate time expressions is essential when writing a story.
- Point out that their story must begin with the exact sentence given and must follow on logically from there.
- Remind the class that the main tense they will use here is the past simple, although they can also use this alongside the past perfect, as in the opening sentence of the story, or the past continuous.
- Finally, remind students that they must leave enough time to write a satisfactory ending, as they can lose a lot of marks if their story is incomplete.
- Allow up to 20 minutes for the task, and let students know when they have five minutes left.

MODEL ANSWER

I had just got off the bus when my phone rang. It was Sami. 'What are you doing?' he asked. I told him that I was on my way home. It was a lie and suddenly I felt guilty. But how could I tell him the truth? Sami knew that something was wrong. 'What's going on?' he asked. I explained that I was with my mum but he didn't believe me. 'We used to be friends,' he said. I promised that I'd call him and hung up. Then I walked up the steps to the police station and told them what had happened. 'I have to report a murder,' I said.

After the Progress Check

Optional game

This game follows up on the work students have done recently on reported speech and reported questions.

- Ask each student to write three sentences about themselves (eg *I'm better at maths than history.*) and three questions to ask another student (eg *What is your favourite free-time activity?*).
- Beginning with the sentences, Student A tells Student B his or her first sentence. Student B then reports what was said (eg *He said he was better at maths than history.*) before saying a sentence to Student C. Continue in this way until everyone has spoken. Correct any mistakes students make using reported speech.
- Repeat the above with the questions, eg:
  Student A: *What is your favourite free-time activity?*
  Student B: *She asked me what my favourite free-time activity was. It's playing basketball. Where do you live?*
  Student C: *He asked me where I live. I live in the town centre.*

Feedback and extension

READ

- Review the questions one at a time and involve the students in the process of eliminating the wrong answers. Where there were mistakes, try to establish whether the problems were in understanding the text or the questions.
- Explain to students that they can extend their reading ability by reading articles, messages, pop-ups and instructions. Warn students that many comments that people make on websites are not written in good English.

LISTEN

- Hand out photocopies of the audio script to each pair of students. Explain that you want to see which pair is the first to circle where the answers are.
- Check their answers and deal with any mistakes students made in the **Listen** section.
- Draw students' attention to the underlined sections in the audio script. Ask them to tell you why these sections have been underlined (because they are stressed when spoken). Invite volunteers to read out these sections, stressing the relevant words and phrases. Then, play the audio again, pausing after each section for different students to repeat the intonation of the speaker.

WRITE

- Point out where students lost marks in the **Write** section, explaining the importance of:
  - correct use of tenses
  - effective use of linking devices *(so, but, then, later, after that,* etc*)*
  - effective use of time expressions *(later, after that, the next day,* etc*)*
  - a suitable progression of events
  - a satisfactory ending
- To give further practice in story writing, create a story with the class. Write a suitable story beginning on the board, eg: *I had just got to the beach when it started to rain.*
- Ask a volunteer to come to the board and write the second sentence. Continue in this way, with different volunteers until the story is completed.
- Below are some suggestions for the beginnings of new stories. You could also set one of these for homework.
  - *I had always wanted to interview my favourite singer, and this was my big chance.*
  - *As soon as I turned on the TV, I realised that something serious had happened.*
  - *Jeff had sold everything and he was ready to start a new, simpler life.*
  - *Martin had always lived on a farm and he was very happy with his life.*

GO BEYOND FOR TEACHERS

The reading text in this Progress Check is a student's essay. It can sometimes be helpful for students to read each other's written work. This may help them focus on different aspects of good writing and alternative ways of doing things. There are many sample essays online which are useful for students at this level. Ask your students to do a search for 'sample stories for EFL' online. They should find lots of examples. Ask them to print one of the stories that they like and bring it to read out in the next lesson. Tell them that they should be looking for short stories of 100–200 words.

UNIT 9 LEARNING JOURNEYS

IN THE PICTURE At school

Talk about different types of school

Pages 94–95

STAGE	TIME	FOCUS
GET STARTED		Talk about the things you like about school and the things you'd like to change.
WORK WITH WORDS		Recycle vocabulary for school subjects and education. Learn and use words for different types of school. Listen to people talking about the education systems in the US and the UK.
SPEAK		Compare your education system with the systems in the US and the UK.

Get started

Ask students to note down three things they like about school and three things they'd like to change about school. Allow two minutes. Invite students to share their notes in pairs and find out more about their partner's thoughts about school.

WORK WITH WORDS

1a and 1b RECALL

- Divide the class into pairs to complete both tasks. Set a time limit of three minutes.
- Explain that first they must make a list of at least eight school subjects. Then they must complete the word in each definition using the first letter given.
- When time is up, check answers in open class.
- Ask students to do the Work with Words task on page 138.

ANSWERS

Exercise 1b
1 exam 2 university 3 terms 4 course

Extra activity

Ask students to rank the subjects from their favourite to least favourite and compare their rankings in pairs, giving reasons for their answers.

2

- Introduce the task by telling students they are going to study the names of the different types of schools that students attend at different ages. Point out that there are two columns because the systems are different in the UK and the US.
- Divide the class into pairs to complete the table with the words in the box. Before they start, read out the example of *nursery* and check the pronunciation, /ˈnɜː(r)s(ə)ri/. Set a time limit of one minute. Don't confirm answers at this point.

3 3.17

- Tell students they are going to hear Ethan from the UK and Ruby from the US talking about their education systems. Play the track for students to listen and check or complete their answers.

ANSWERS / AUDIO SCRIPT 3.17

2 primary 3 secondary 4 nursery 5 elementary
6 kindergarten 7 middle 8 high

Ethan: In the UK, most children have to start school when they're five, and they go to a primary school. Before that, children can go to a nursery school. Then, when you're 11, you go to secondary school. In Scotland, I think primary school finishes a year later, though. Most students get a free education at a state school, but some students pay to go to a private school. Some of these are also boarding schools. That means the students live and study at the school. And then I know some people stay at home and have homeschooling, but I don't know how common that is.

Ruby: Kids in the USA often start at nursery school when they're 3 years old, but the official school system generally starts with kindergarten when you're 5. That's the first year of elementary school. You start at middle school when you're 11, and there are three grades, and then you go to high school when you're 14. Some parents pay for their kids to go to private schools, but the majority of students go to public schools. My education was different because I was homeschooled. That's because we lived on a farm that was miles from the nearest school. So my mom gave me classes at home.

4 3.17

- Ask students to read and complete the sentences about the other school options with words from the box.
- Monitor students as they are doing this task to see if it is necessary to play the track again.
- Nominate different students to say the answers in open class.

ANSWERS
1 state 2 public 3 private 4 boarding
5 homeschooling

GO BEYOND FOR TEACHERS

Public and private schools

In most parts of the English-speaking world, schools which are independent of state funding and require parents to pay fees are called *private* (or *independent*) schools. Schools which are free and funded by governments are called *state* schools in the UK and *public* schools in the US. Confusingly however, there is a small group of prestigious independent schools in the UK that are known as *public schools* although they are privately funded. This group includes well-known schools like Eton College, Cheltenham Ladies College, Harrow and Roedean.

Homeschooling, where children do not attend school but are educated at home by parents or tutors, is a form of education that is optional in many countries, but illegal in others, such as Germany. It is estimated that around 1.5 million children are educated at home in the US. Reasons for homeschooling include dissatisfaction with traditional schooling, religious or philosophical beliefs and catering for children with special needs.

5 3.18
- Play the track for students to listen and repeat.

AUDIO SCRIPT 3.18
1 nursery school 2 primary school 3 secondary school
4 elementary school 5 kindergarten 6 middle school
7 high school 8 state school 9 public school
10 private school 11 boarding school 12 homeschooling

6a
- Give students one minute to focus on the six photos on pages 94–95. Then divide the class into pairs and ask them to close their books and try to recall what was in each of the photos. Encourage them to remember as much detail as possible.
- Invite students to open their books again and discuss the questions with their partner, giving reasons for their answers, eg *I think photo three was taken in the UK because it looks like a boarding school and I think there are more boarding schools in the UK than in the US.*
- Ask students to write down the type of school they think is shown in each of the photos.

6b 3.19
- Play the track for students to listen to the messages and check their answers. Find out if their ideas were correct.

ANSWERS / AUDIO SCRIPT 3.19
1 Hello from our kindergarten in Mexico.
2 Hello, world! I'm talking to you from Los Angeles where I have homeschooling with my mom.
3 Hi. I'm recording this in my room at my boarding school in England.
4 Hello from our secondary school in Tanzania in East Africa!
5 Hi, everybody. We go to a primary school in Cuba.
6 Hello from the computer room in a high school in Brunei.

7 THE MOVING PICTURE
- Ask students to watch the video and make notes about the types of school the students go to.

ANSWERS / VIDEO SCRIPT
Leo goes to a private school for boys in London. It's quite big and he likes it.
Bella goes to a boarding school for girls in Oxford. It's not very big and she gets homesick.
Ruby goes to a mixed theatre school in London. It's not very big and she loves singing there.
Finn goes to a mixed local state school. It's big, but he likes it there.

SPEAK

8
- Divide the class into pairs to compare the education system in their country with the US and UK systems. Encourage them to say which system is most similar to theirs and what the biggest differences are. Before they start, refer students to the expressions in the PHRASE BYTES box and encourage them to use these in their discussion.

Extra activity

Ask students to think about two of the more unusual school options that have been mentioned in the lesson: boarding school and homeschooling.

Ask them to work in pairs and draw up a list of the positive and negative things about these school options.

Then ask them to change pairs and compare their list with another student, explaining their lists in more detail.

Take a quick class poll to find out how many students would like to try boarding school or homeschooling.

GO BEYOND

Ask students to do the Go Beyond task on page 138.

Homework

Ask students to imagine they have received the email below from a friend living in another country. Ask them to answer the email and write around 150 words. Remind them to use vocabulary they've studied in today's lesson.

Hi!

How are you? Hope your term is going well!

We've been asked to do a project on education systems in other countries. Could you send me some information about how it works in your country? Do you know if it's very different from the systems in the UK and US?

I really appreciate your help with this. Hope to hear from you soon!!!

Jordan xxx

READING School journeys

Understand referring words

Page 96

STAGE	TIME	FOCUS
GET STARTED		Play *Snowman* to guess three questions about school journeys.
SPEAK AND READ		Talk about your journey to school. Find out who has the most difficult journey to school. Read about students who have extremely difficult school journeys. Learn and practise how to understand referring words in a text.
REACT		Rank the journeys you read about from hardest to easiest and explain why you think so.

Get started

Play a variation of a game of *Snowman* (see Games page 33). Explain to students that they are going to guess three questions related to the topic of today's lesson: school journeys. Write lines on the board for each word of the three questions in Exercise 1.

Books closed. Invite students to suggest words. If they guess a correct word, write it in. If a word is incorrect, draw one part of the Snowman scaffold.

You could write the questions on slips of paper and give them to three different students who come to the board to lead the activity.

SPEAK AND READ

1a

- Write these gapped sentences on the board: *I get up .... 7.00. I get to school .... bus. I get to school .... foot.*
- Ask students to tell you the prepositions that go in the gaps (***at*** *7.00,* ***by*** *bus,* ***on*** *foot*). Elicit another way to say: *I get to school on foot.* (*I walk to school.*)
- Divide the class into pairs to answer the questions. Set a time limit of two minutes.

1b

- In open class, ask different students what time they get up. Ask if anyone gets up earlier than the times mentioned, continuing until you find the earliest riser in the class.
- Invite students to nominate their partner if they think he/she has a long or difficult journey to school. Encourage them to explain their partner's journey and ask the class if anyone else has a more difficult or longer journey.

2 3.20

- Tell students they are going to read about some children who have very difficult journeys to get to school.
- Focus on the title. Check the meaning of *scary* (frightening) and *school run* (the journey to and from school in a car).
- Ask students to read the article very quickly to find out where the children are from. Set a challenging time limit of two minutes in order to encourage them to read quickly. Explain that the idea of this first quick reading is to get a general idea of the content and to focus specifically on finding out where the children are from. Don't play the audio at this point. A suggestion for using the audio is given at the end of the lesson.
- Stop them when time is up and ask them to compare their answers in pairs before you check them in open class.

ANSWERS

Edison is from Ecuador. Anil and Dache are from India.
Paul and Moses are from Kenya.

3

- Ask students to read the article again, more slowly, and to write the name or names of the children to complete the sentences. Encourage them to underline the parts of the text that help them to find the answers. Set a time limit of five minutes.
- Encourage students to compare their answers and the parts of the text they underlined in pairs before you check answers in open class.

ANSWERS

1 Anil and Dache 2 Edison 3 Paul and Moses
4 Anil and Dache 5 Edison, Paul and Moses 6 Anil and Dache

Fast finishers

Books closed. Give students these numbers 0, 2, 4, 6, 14, 15, and ask them to write down or say (if they are working in pairs) in what context the numbers appear in the text.

ANSWERS

0 – Anile and Dache make their journey in temperatures that are often below zero.
2 – The River Napo can rise by two metres when it rains.
4 – Edison has to get up at 4am to get to school.
6 – It takes six days for Anil and Dache to walk to school.
14 – Edison is 14 years old.
15 – Paul and Moses live 15 kilometres from their school.

4a

- Write these sentences on the board: *Hank is 12 years old. Hank gets up at 7.00.* Ask students how they can avoid repeating the name Hank (by using *He*). Explain that we often make text easier to read by using short words like this to refer to information that has already been mentioned.
- Refer students to the tips in the HOW TO box. Invite a student to read them out loud.

Alternative procedure: less confident classes

As you go through the HOW TO box, you may find that you need to do a quick review of some of the different pronouns that are mentioned.

Draw this table on the board. Write in the words given here in bold, and ask students to fill the gaps:

Personal pronouns

Subject	Object	Possessive
I	me	my
you	**you**	your
he/she/it	him/her/it	**his/her/its**
we	**us**	our
you (pl.)	you (pl.)	**your**
they	them	their

Ask students to tell you what type of noun these relative pronouns refer to: *who/that* (a person); *which/that* (a thing); *when* (a time); *where* (a place).

4b

- Focus students on the words in bold in the article and elicit what they refer to. Do the first one in open class as an example: Ask if *ones* is singular or plural (plural). Ask if it refers to an adjective or a noun (noun). Ask students to find a plural noun in the sentence before (journeys). Ask them to replace *ones* with *journeys* and see if it makes sense (yes, it does).
- Set a time limit of five minutes for students to do the rest of the task. Ask them to underline the word or words that are referred to.
- Encourage students to compare their answers in pairs before you check them in open class.

ANSWERS

ones = (school) journeys
He = Edison
here = around the village by the River Napo in the Amazon rainforest in Ecuador
This = When it rains the river can quickly rise by two metres
him = Edison
this = a six-day trek up a frozen river or the steep, icy banks next to it
them = Anil, Dache and their father
that = (rocks and) earth
its = the school's
there = at school

5

- Ask students which tips in the HOW TO box they used to help them with Exercise 4b.

REACT

6

- Divide the class into pairs to put the three school journeys in order from the hardest to the easiest, giving reasons for their decisions. If students disagree, they should try to convince each other by explaining the reasons for their choices. Set a time limit of four minutes.
- Lead a class discussion to see if they all agree on the order and the reasons behind it.

Recorded reading text 3.20

The reading text is recorded as an extra audio track which can be exploited for various purposes.

In this lesson, use selected sentences in the audio to practise intonation. Play each sentence and ask students to repeat.

GO BEYOND

Ask students to make a list of words from the article that describe the places where students make their school journeys.

ANSWERS

... a small village by the River Napo in the Amazon rainforest in Ecuador.
High in the Zanskar Valley in northern India, ...
... a frozen river ... the steep, icy banks next to it.
the Mount Elgon region of Kenya.
... the road's made of rocks and earth that turn into mud.

Homework

Ask students to replace the underlined words in the sentences below with a personal or possessive pronoun, *one/ones*, *here/there* or *this/that*. Encourage them to re-read the tips in the HOW TO box on page 96 to help them.

1 Jack Rivers lives on a farm in central Australia. Every day Jack Rivers has to ride 50 kilometres on horseback to get to his school.
2 In the past, children used to go to small village schools. The smallest village schools had only between 10 and 15 students.
3 Bella Folson lives on an isolated island in the Scottish Hebrides. The fact that Bella Folson lives on an isolated island in the Scottish Hebrides means that getting to school is not easy.
4 Jacob Finch lives in New York. There are many different types of schools in New York.
5 My great grandfather was a farmer. My great grandfather's school days were not very happy.
6 My penfriend Susan lives in Canada. I wrote to my penfriend last week to tell her that we are planning to visit Canada in the holidays.
7 I want to go to the school we visited last week. You know, the school that has really nice classrooms.
8 I go to a big school in the centre of Bristol. Next week a theatre group is coming to the school to perform a play.

ANSWERS

1 he 2 ones 3 This 4 there 5 His 6 her
7 one 8 here

GRAMMAR Reported requests and commands

Say what people ask and tell you to do

Page 97

STAGE	TIME	FOCUS
GET STARTED		Identify errors in reported speech.
READ		Read a diary extract in which Denis describes how he gets to school.
STUDY		Complete explanations about reported requests and commands using examples from the diary extract.
PRACTISE		Practise converting direct requests and commands to reported speech and vice versa. Study and practise contrastive stress.
WRITE AND SPEAK		Write sentences about the things people ask and tell you to do. Compare and discuss your sentences in pairs.

Get started

Divide the class into pairs to correct the errors in these sentences and identify any which are correct. Set a time limit of three minutes.

1 *He said me that he had been learning the clarinet for two years.*
2 *Berta asked me if I did want to play tennis at the weekend.*
3 *He admitted that he had took the money.*
4 *He asked weather I would go for a walk with him.*
5 *The students promised they would study hard before the exam.*
6 *My father asked me if you were coming to dinner this weekend?*
7 *Gerard asked to his friends if they knew any good jokes.*
8 *The president of the club asked the players if they were happy with their coach.*

Run through the corrections quickly in open class and ask what the direct speech would be for one or two examples.

ANSWERS

1 He ~~said~~ *told* me (or *He said ~~me~~*) that he had been learning the clarinet for two years.
2 Berta asked me if I ~~did want~~ *wanted* to play tennis at the weekend.
3 He admitted that he had ~~took~~ *taken* the money.
4 He asked ~~weather~~ *whether* (or *if)* I would go for a walk with him.
5 Correct
6 My father asked me if you were coming to dinner this weekend~~?~~.
7 Gerard asked ~~to~~ his friends if they knew any good jokes.
8 Correct

READ Grammar in context

1

- Ask students what sort of things their parents ask or tell them to do in the mornings, eg *Hurry up! Don't forget your lunch! Can you wash up your breakfast plate?*
- Ask students to read the diary extract and say how Denis gets to school.

ANSWER

He normally walks to school, but he goes by car if it's raining.

Extra activity

Ask a few questions about some of the vocabulary in the text, eg *Can you find two phrasal verbs with get? What do they mean?* (*get up* = get out of bed after sleeping / *get out* = leave a place) *What expression is used to ask about going somewhere as a passenger in a car?* (ask for a lift) *What expression is used to talk about a road full of cars that can't move?* (*traffic jam*) *What adjectives are used with the nouns* rain *and* wet? (*heavy rain*, *soaking wet*).

STUDY

2

- Remind students that they studied reported speech and questions in Unit 8. Tell them that they are now going to look at reported requests and commands.
- Ask students to give you an example of a request or a command. Using their suggestions, write an example of each on the board, eg *Could you open the window, please? Open your book at page 40.*
- Underline *can/could* and *please* in the request and the imperative form of the verb in the command that you have put on the board. Remind students that we use *can/could* to ask someone to do something and the imperative to tell someone to do something.
- Focus students on the grammar explanations about how to form reported requests and commands and ask them to complete these with examples from Denis's diary extract in Exercise 1. Set a time limit of four minutes.
- Go through the grammar explanations in open class, eliciting and checking the correct examples.

ANSWERS

to eat quickly not to spend long in the shower
to go home and change

3

- Ask students to look at the reported command and request from Exercise 1 and write them in direct speech.
- Nominate different students to say the answers in open class and write them on the board. Point out that there are two acceptable versions of the request.

ANSWERS

1 Get up. 2 Could I have a lift? / Can I have a lift, please?

Extra activity

If students need further practice of the word order in reported negative commands, write the following scrambled sentences on the board for them to put in order.

me / chew / to / told / gum / He / not
(He told me not to chew gum.)

My / us / to / late / asked / be / not / teacher
(My teacher asked us not to be late.)

PRACTISE

4

Exam-type task

- Invite two students to read out the first sentence and example. Point out that both sentences have the same meaning. Remind them to use three words only.
- Suggest that they refer to the grammar explanations and examples in Exercise 2 if they are unsure of a sentence. Set a time limit of five minutes.
- Encourage students to compare their answers in pairs before checking them in open class.

ANSWERS

2 asked me to 3 not to talk 4 asked Rob to
5 told Denis to 6 to open our

5a 3.21

- Explain that in English we sometimes give extra stress to words to show that they are important for some reason. This can sometimes be to highlight that what we think is true is different to what someone else has said.
- Play the track and ask students to listen and underline the word that Rob stresses most.
- Check the answer in open class and ask why he stresses this word.

ANSWERS / AUDIO SCRIPT 3.21

He stresses *you* (see underlining below) because he is correcting Denis. Denis said 'us' in his sentence, and Rob is saying 'you, not us'. This stress makes it clear what the correct word is.

Denis: The teacher told us to be quiet.
Rob: No, she didn't. She told <u>you</u> to be quiet.

5b 3.22

- Play the track for students to listen and repeat the conversation.

AUDIO SCRIPT 3.22

Denis: She told us to bring our books on Monday.
Rob: No, she didn't. She told us <u>not</u> to bring our books on Monday.
Denis: She told us to revise for an exam on Tuesday.
Rob: No, she didn't. She told us to revise for an exam on <u>Wednesday</u>.

Extra activity – contrastive stress

Ask students to write five general knowledge statements that are incorrect. They should read them out to their partner who must repeat each statement stressing the correct information, eg *Barcelona is the capital city of Spain. No,* ***Madrid*** *is the capital city of Spain.*

6

- Ask students to write the requests and commands in direct speech. Set a time limit of six minutes. Before they start, go through the example with the class.
- Check the answers in open class.

ANSWERS

2 Stop playing computer games
3 Can/Could you make pizza for dinner, please
4 Lay the table first
5 Can/Could you pass me the ketchup, please
6 Don't eat with your mouth open

WRITE AND SPEAK

7a

- Encourage students to think about when and where their family, friends or teachers ask or tell them to do something, eg in an exam, a library, a museum, the doctor's, etc.
- Ask them to write four to six sentences about things that people ask and tell them to do. Before they start, invite a student to read out the example. Allow six minutes.

7b

- Divide the class into pairs to compare their sentences. Encourage them to say if their partner's sentences are also true for them.

Homework

Explain to the students that for homework they are going to have the chance to complain about what other people tell or ask them to do by writing four sentences using this structure:

I hate it when .... *tells/asks me to* .... *because ...*

When they have written their four sentences, ask them to write the direct requests or commands as well.

LISTENING AND VOCABULARY Circus school

Understand spoken instructions Page 98

STAGE	TIME	FOCUS
GET STARTED		Talk about things you learn and things you'd like to learn outside school.
SPEAK AND LISTEN		Look at an advert for a circus school and talk about your experiences with circuses. Listen to an interview with a student at the circus school. Learn how to understand spoken instructions. Follow instructions and learn how to juggle.
REACT		Talk about the circus school and whether you'd like to go there. Say what act you think you would be good at and why.
WORK WITH WORDS		Learn words with the prefix *self-*.

Get started

Ask students if they take any classes outside school, eg *music, sport, drama, art, dance, languages.* If so, encourage them to tell the class about them. Invite students to write down two things they would like to try learning that aren't normally taught at school. Divide the class into pairs to talk about why they would like to do these activities.

SPEAK AND LISTEN

1

- Refer students to the photos in the advert. Elicit what the advert is for (a school where you can study circus arts).
- Focus on the types of circus performers mentioned in the advert. Check the pronunciation and ask students to say what they do. (*clowns* /klaʊnz/ make you laugh; *trapeze artists* /trəˈpiːz ˌɑː(r)tɪsts/ swing high in the air; jump and catch each other; *acrobats* /ˈækrəˌbæts/ perform difficult balancing and jumping acts; *jugglers* /ˈdʒʌɡlə(r)z/ throw things in the air and keep them moving; *tightrope walkers* /ˈtaɪtˌrəʊp ˈwɔːkə(r)z/ walk on a rope suspended in the air.)
- Divide the class into pairs to answer the questions, giving reasons for their answers. Set a time limit of four minutes.

2 3.23

- Explain that students are going to listen to Emma, a student at the school in the advert. First, ask them to read the list of things she mentions.
- Play the track and ask students to make a note of the order in which she mentions these things as they listen.
- Check the correct order in open class.

ANSWERS / AUDIO SCRIPT 3.23

See underlining in audio script for answers.

Interviewer: How long have you been at the school?

Emma: I'm 15 now and I started here when I was 10, so about five years.

Interviewer: It's a long way from your hometown.

Emma: That's right. I have to stay with my aunt during the week.

Interviewer: Is it hard to be away from home so much?

Emma: No, not at all. There's a great atmosphere here and we all look after each other, so I never feel lonely. And being away from home teaches you to be more self-confident and think for yourself. You become self-sufficient. That's important, because circus performers spend a lot of time travelling.

Interviewer: What other qualities do you need to be a circus performer?

Emma: You need good co-ordination and balance, obviously. But you also need self-control. You have to stay calm and focused under pressure so that you don't make mistakes. And then there's trust. Trapeze artists, for example, do some extremely dangerous things and they have to have complete trust in each other. You also need enough self-discipline to practise circus arts for hours every day and study for your normal school subjects too – maths, history, science and so on. It's a lot of work.

Interviewer: When did you first realise you wanted to be a circus performer?

Emma: It was when my parents took me to the circus for my seventh birthday. I just knew that's what I wanted to do. Over the next few weeks, when my friends were out enjoying themselves, I stayed at home and taught myself to juggle. My parents didn't want me to come here at first, but when they saw how good I was at juggling, they changed their minds.

Interviewer: So what advice would you give someone who wants to follow in your footsteps?

Emma: At the school we're taught to believe in ourselves and follow our dreams. If you do that, anything is possible.

3 3.23

- Give students one minute to read the questions, then play the track. Ask them to listen again and answer the questions.
- Check the meaning of *self-confident* (feeling that you can do things well and other people respect you) and *self-sufficient* (able to provide everything you need by yourself without needing the help of other people).
- Encourage students to compare their answers in pairs. Monitor students as they compare their answers to gauge what level of support will be needed during feedback.
- Go through the questions in open class. If you feel students need to listen again to fully answer the questions, play the audio as you go through the questions, stopping after the answer to each question has been given.

ANSWERS

1 She lives with her aunt.
2 There's a great atmosphere at the school and the students all look after each other (so she never feels lonely).
3 Because circus performers spend a lot of time travelling.
4 Because you need to practise circus arts for hours every day and study for normal school subjects.
5 When her parents took her to the circus for her seventh birthday.
6 To believe in yourself and follow your dreams.

4a

- Ask students to read the tips in the HOW TO box about how to understand spoken instructions.

4b 3.24

- Ask if anyone in the class knows how to juggle. Explain to students that they are going to listen to Emma explaining how to juggle with two balls and that they should follow her instructions. Before you start, make sure each student has two pieces of paper.
- Remind them about the tips in the HOW TO box: listen for imperatives, sequencers, *when …* and adverbs.
- Play the track and observe students' reactions. Ask if they would like to hear the track again.

AUDIO SCRIPT 3.24

OK, let's start with two balls. First, make two balls by scrunching up two pieces of paper. When you've done that, pick up one ball and practise throwing it from one hand to the other. The ball should pass in front of your eyes. When you can do that comfortably, keep the first ball in one hand, and pick up the second ball in your other hand. Next, throw the first ball, and when the first ball is passing in front of your eyes, you throw the other ball. You will need to catch the two balls with the opposite hands. When you've mastered that, try doing it four times in a row without stopping. The next step is to add a third ball. But maybe we'll do that another day!

5

- Ask students if they heard any of the sequencers mentioned or if they heard *when* used to complete one instruction before starting another one.
- Ask students which tips in the HOW TO box they used to help them in Exercise 4b.

REACT

6

- Divide the class into pairs to discuss the questions. Set a time limit of four minutes.
- Monitor as students are talking and make a note of any errors or interesting language that you hear.
- Write three or four of the errors you heard on the board, along with any interesting words or expressions. Go through these examples in open class and ask students to help you correct the errors.

WORK WITH WORDS

7 3.25

- Remind students about the two words you highlighted in Exercise 3: *self-confident* and *self-sufficient*. Explain that there are many other words that have the prefix *self-*, meaning *related to yourself*. Point out that this prefix is used with a hyphen before the word that follows, whereas other prefixes do not have a hyphen.
- Ask students to complete the definitions with the words in the boxes. Set a time limit of five minutes.
- Play the track for students to listen and check.
- Play the track again for students to listen and repeat.

ANSWERS / AUDIO SCRIPT 3.25

1 self-confident 2 self-sufficient 3 self-conscious
4 self-taught 5 self-centred 6 self-discipline 7 self-control
8 high self-esteem 9 self-pity 10 self-defence

8

- Divide the class into pairs to take it in turns to tell each other which of the words in Exercise 7 describe themselves. Encourage them to explain why.

GO BEYOND

Ask students to do the Go Beyond task on page 138.

Extra activity

Dictate these questions: *Is there something you can do which is self-taught? Are you a self-sufficient person or do you need to have other people around? Do you have self-discipline in your schoolwork and homework? Do you know someone who you think is self-centred? Why do you have this opinion?* Ask individual students to read out the questions to check them. Ask students to work in pairs and answer the questions.

Homework

Give students a copy of the audio script from Exercise 4b. Ask them to find examples of the language mentioned in the HOW TO box.

GRAMMAR Reflexive pronouns; *each other*

Use reflexive pronouns and *each other* Page 99

STAGE	TIME	FOCUS
GET STARTED		Respond to statements about school and study and compare your opinions with other students.
READ		Read the introduction from a school website and say if it is similar to your school.
STUDY		Read and complete explanations about the use and form of reflexive pronouns and *each other* using examples from the school website.
PRACTISE		Practise using reflexive pronouns and *each other* in conversations. Use reflexive pronouns and *each other* to complete some opinions about education.
SPEAK		Decide if you agree with the opinions about education and make notes about your reasons. Talk to a partner about your opinions.

Get started

Dictate these sentences: *My friends and I help each other with our schoolwork. I like to study by myself. We study hard at school but we also enjoy ourselves. People express themselves in different ways at school. I get a bit shy when I have to introduce myself to new students.*

Ask individual students to read the statements back to you and write them on the board, making any corrections to the students' versions that are necessary.

For each statement, ask students to assign a number between 1 and 5, where 1 = *totally disagree* and 5 = *agree completely.* Divide the class into pairs to compare their answers and to explain why they gave the score they did for each item. This warmer should give you an idea of whether students are comfortable using the target language for this lesson.

READ Grammar in context

1

- Ask students to tell you what they know about their school website.
- Ask students to read the introduction from the website of Spring Hills Secondary School to see if the school is similar to their school.
- Divide the class into pairs to discuss the similarities and differences. Set a time limit of one minute.

STUDY

2

- Write these two sentences on the board: *Emma taught me to juggle. I taught myself to juggle.*
- Ask students to identify the subject in each sentence (*Emma, I*).
- Ask them to identify the object in each sentence (*me, myself*).
- Elicit why they think we use *me* in the first sentence and *myself* in the second sentence. Refer students to the explanation of the use of reflexive pronouns in the box to confirm their ideas.
- Read through the grammar explanations with students and give one or two extra examples as you go, eg *The new teacher introduced herself to the class. I sometimes enjoy spending time by myself. The students organised the party themselves. My cousin lives in another city, but we talk to each other every week.*
- You could also refer students to the sentences from the *Get started* activity for more examples.
- Focus students on the verbs that are listed and ask whether they are reflexive in their language(s).
- Drill the pronunciation of the reflexive pronouns, paying attention to the unvoiced /f/ in the singular forms and the voiced /v/ in the plural forms.
- Ask students to complete the grammar explanations with examples from Exercise 1.
- Check the answers in open class. Drill the pronunciation of the *-selves* ending, eg *themselves* /ðəmˈselvz/.

ANSWERS

themselves by himself or herself itself work with

PRACTISE

3 3.26

- Ask students to complete each conversation with the words in the boxes. Set a time limit of five minutes.
- Encourage students to compare their answers in pairs before you play the track for students to listen and check.

ANSWERS / AUDIO SCRIPT 3.26

1 yourselves; each other; us
2 ourselves; us; each other
3 each other; themselves; them
See Student's Book page 99 for audio script.

4

- Ask students to complete the opinions about education with a reflexive pronoun or *each other.* Set a time limit of four minutes. Read out the example before they start.
- Nominate different students to read out the completed opinions and check answers in open class.

ANSWERS

2 each other 3 yourself 4 each other 5 myself
6 herself

SPEAK

5a

- Explain that you would like students to decide if they agree or disagree with the opinions about education in Exercise 4. Encourage them to make notes on their reasons as they are reading. Set a time limit of six minutes.

5b

- Divide the class into pairs to talk about the opinions in Exercise 4. Ask them to use their notes to tell their partner why they agree or disagree with the opinions. Before they start, go through the expressions in the PHRASE BYTES box and model them for students. Encourage them to use these phrases in their conversations.

Extra activity

Ask students to work in pairs and write a conversation like the ones in Exercise 3.

Suggest that they write the conversation between two new students at a circus school. Encourage them to include one object pronoun, (*me, you, him, her, it, us, you, them*), one reflexive pronoun and one example of *each other.*

When they have written their conversation, ask them to blank out the pronouns and *each other* and give their conversation to another pair to complete.

Homework

Ask students to write whether they agree or disagree with two of the opinions in Exercise 4. Encourage them to write a paragraph for each opinion of around 80 words and to try to include some examples from their own experience.

LANGUAGE & BEYOND KNOW YOURSELF

Learn to be more self-confident *Page 100*

STAGE	TIME	FOCUS
GET STARTED		Play *Three in a row* to recycle words with *self-*.
SPEAK AND READ		Talk about how insecure people feel and behave in certain situations. Read an article about how to become more self-confident and match headings to the different sections of the text.
DO		Imagine how a friend who is lacking in self-confidence would respond to the steps suggested in the article.
REFLECT		Talk about how hard or easy it is to become more self-confident and what the benefits of self-confidence are.
EXTEND		Use the steps suggested in the article to help you improve your self-confidence. Keep a diary to record your progress.

LIFE SKILLS

SELF-CONFIDENCE

Teenagers can experience fluctuating degrees of self-confidence as they grow in independence and start to get a feel for their individual strengths and weaknesses. Unfortunately for some teens, bouts of insecurity can be very upsetting and have a noticeably negative effect on their behaviour. Self-confidence is often seen as something that is somehow inherent to a person's personality whereas it appears to be true that one can learn to be more self-confident. That is the focus of this lesson: to help students identify areas where they feel insecure and give them some practical steps towards improving their self-confidence.

Get started

Divide the class into pairs to write a list of words beginning with *self-*. Set a time limit of one minute and then ask them to share their lists in open class. Encourage them to look at page 98 to see if there are any they haven't included.

Play a game of *Three in a Row* (see Games page 33). Draw a 3 x 3 grid on the board with letters A–I in the squares.

To win a square, students should give you a word beginning with *self-* to complete the sentence that you read out to them.

A *If you don't need help from others, you are* ______ . (self-sufficient)
B *If you always do the things you need to do, you have* ______ . (self-discipline)
C *If you don't like people looking at you, you are* ______ . (self-conscious)
D *If you value yourself, you have high* ______ . (self-esteem)
E *If you feel that you can do things well, you are* ______ . (self-confident)
F *If you feel that your situation is worse than others, you feel* ______ . (self-pity)
G *If you learned something without a teacher, you are* ______ . (self-taught)
H *If you stay calm in stressful situations, you have* ______ . (self-control)
I *If you only think about what you want, you are* ______ . (self-centred)

Tell students that today's lesson is all about being self-confident.

SPEAK AND READ

1

- Divide the class into pairs to discuss how a person who isn't self-confident feels and behaves in certain situations. Read through the situations with them and set a time limit of six minutes for them to talk and make notes.
- Invite students to share their ideas in open class.

2

- Ask students what sorts of thing they think an article on becoming more self-confident will say and encourage them to discuss this in pairs.
- Ask students to read the article and match the headings to steps in the article. Set a time limit of five minutes.
- Encourage students to compare their answers in pairs before you check them in open class. Ask if the article included any of the ideas they predicted.

ANSWERS
1 D 2 B 3 C 4 A 5 E

DO

3

- Invite students to think of a friend or imaginary person who isn't very self-confident. Explain that you want students to imagine they are that person, and to write that person's answers to the questions in the article. Allow six minutes.

4

- Divide the class into pairs to talk about the answers they wrote in Exercise 3.
- Ask them to reflect and say if they think the steps in the article will help their friend. Encourage them to give reasons.
- Circulate and help students as necessary.

REFLECT

5

- Suggest that students work on the discussion questions in three stages: first individually, then in pairs, and finally in open class. Set a time limit of five minutes for students to work individually to make notes in response to the three questions.
- Divide the class into pairs to explain their personal responses and compare their points of view.

- Go through each of the questions in open class and nominate different pairs to contribute their ideas.
- After the discussion, focus students on the **REFLECTION POINT** and elicit whether they agree or not.

Extra activity

If students would benefit from more input about the **REFLECTION POINT**, encourage them to discuss whether or not they agree with these comments made by other students.

1. I don't think you can learn to be more self-confident. Some people are confident and other people are insecure and that's just the way it is!
2. I believe you can learn to do anything in life! Improving your self-confidence is no exception. It's like learning to swim or learning to speak a language: you get better when you practise!
3. I did an experiment the other day. I was feeling a bit down so I thought: 'I'm going to pretend I feel happy for five minutes and see what happens.' So I forced myself to smile and tried to remember what it feels like when I'm happy. I felt a bit silly, smiling crazily about nothing in particular, but after about five minutes I actually did feel a bit happier. I think you can do the same thing with self-confidence. Act as though you are confident even if you feel a bit insecure inside. Pretty soon you will notice that you really feel much more confident.
4. Talking to my friends really helps me to feel more confident. We tell each other about the things we feel insecure about. Quite often we laugh together about them and then they don't seem so important any more.
5. For some reason, when you feel insecure, it seems like you can't do anything well. At these times I think it's really important to think about all the things you are good at doing. Sometimes it's even better if you write them down. Just remembering all the things you do well helps you to feel more confident.
6. Self-confidence is like a flower! You have to give it some water every day and then it will grow. So go and look in the mirror and say something nice to yourself!

EXTEND

6

- Explain that you would like students to write answers for the questions in the article that are true for them. Use this task as a free writing activity. Encourage students to write quickly and not to worry about making mistakes. Set a time limit of 10 minutes but allow students to focus on just one or two of the questions if they wish.
- Monitor as they are writing, but focus more on content than on accuracy.
- Suggest that they keep a diary and record their progress.

Alternative procedure

You may find that your students are reluctant to write about issues like self-confidence. This may be because they lack maturity or perhaps they feel awkward about discussing personal issues. If this is the case, you could ask them to write a short text for each of the following headings:

Everybody feels insecure about something, right?
Can you become more self-confident? How hard is it?
What are the benefits of becoming more self-confident?

Homework

Encourage students to write six sentences about things they are good at and keep them in their bag or folder to give them more self-confidence when they are feeling a bit insecure.

SPEAKING Go on!

Persuade people to do things

Page 101

STAGE	TIME	FOCUS
GET STARTED		Check the meaning of *persuade* and how it combines with other words.
SPEAK		Talk about persuading and being persuaded.
WATCH OR LISTEN		Watch or listen to a conversation where someone is trying to persuade someone to do something. Learn and practise phrases for persuading and reacting to persuasion. Practise intonation for persuading.
ACT		Write and perform a conversation where a student is trying to persuade his parents to let him do something.

Get started

Tell students that the key word for today's lesson is *persuade*. Check the pronunciation of *persuade* /pə(r)ˈsweɪd/, *persuasion* /pə(r)ˈsweɪʒ(ə)n/ and *persuasive* /pə(r)ˈsweɪsɪv/ and elicit their parts of speech (*verb, noun and adjective*).

Ask students to tell you the difference between *make someone do something* and *persuade someone to do something* (*make* = to force someone to do something they don't want to do; *persuade* = to change someone's mind about something by giving them good reasons, encouragement etc).

Ask students if there is a difference in how the two phrases work grammatically:

verb + object + infinitive without *to* (*make*);
verb + object + infinitive with *to* (*persuade*).

Elicit from students which of these verbs follow each pattern: *invite, let, remind, teach, tell, see, want, watch*.

ANSWERS
verb + object + infinitive without *to*: let, see, watch
verb + object + infinitive with *to*: invite, remind, teach, tell, want

SPEAK

1

- Read through the questions in open class, or dictate them to students with books closed (see page 30).
- Highlight the pattern *persuade* + *someone* + *to do* + *something*, eg *My friend persuaded me to buy a new dress.*
- Divide the class into pairs to discuss the questions. Answer one of the questions yourself to give the students a model and to give them some time to think about their own answers.

Fast finishers
Invite fast finishers to change partners and tell each other what their original partner said.

WATCH OR LISTEN

2 3.27

- Focus on the photo and invite students to guess what Ruby is trying to persuade Finn to do.
- Play the scene for students to watch or listen to the conversation between Ruby and Finn and check if their predictions were correct.
- Nominate a student to give the answer in open class.

ANSWER / VIDEO/AUDIO SCRIPT 3.27
She persuades Finn to ask his parents if he can go to perform at the Edinburgh festival.

Ruby: We've been invited to perform at the Edinburgh festival.
Finn: Yes, I've heard.
Ruby: So are you coming?
Finn: I can't.
Ruby: Oh, come on! Be adventurous! It'll be amazing.
Finn: It's not that easy. I've got other plans.
Ruby: But this'll be a real opportunity. What could be better than performing in Edinburgh?
Finn: I'd love to go, but Mum and Dad have planned a camping holiday.
Ruby: So phone them. Tell them you're going to Edinburgh instead.
Finn: I'd prefer not to. They'll only say no.
Ruby: Don't be so pessimistic! It won't be the same if you don't come.
Finn: I'm sorry, I can't.
Ruby: OK. Will you let me speak to them?
Finn: No way! You've never met them!
Ruby: Then phone them yourself. Go on, please! What have you got to lose?
Finn: Oh, all right then. I'll try.
Ruby: Yes!

3 3.27

- Explain that there are two parts to the task. Firstly, to put the words in order and, secondly, to use the sentences to complete the conversation. Allow six minutes.
- Play the scene again for students to check their answers.

ANSWERS (IN CONVERSATION)
1 It'll be amazing
2 But this will be a real opportunity
3 Tell them you're going to Edinburgh instead
4 It won't be the same if you don't come
5 Will you let me speak to them

4 3.28

- Play the track for students to listen and repeat the sentences. Encourage them to pay particular attention to the intonation and try to copy it.

AUDIO SCRIPT 3.28
See Exercise 3 for audio script.

5 3.29

- Refer students back to the conversation and ask them to underline five different imperatives that Ruby uses to try to persuade Finn. If necessary, remind students that the imperative is the verb in the infinitive form without *to* or, in the case of a negative imperative, *don't* + verb. Allow one minute.
- Play the track for students to listen and check.
- Play the track again for students to listen and repeat, copying the intonation.

ANSWERS / AUDIO SCRIPT 3.29
Oh, come on! Be adventurous! So phone them.
Don't be so pessimistic! Go on, please!

6

- Challenge students to remember how Finn says 'no' and then 'yes' to Ruby and complete the phrases. Ask students to cover the conversation. Set a time limit of two minutes.
- Then suggest that they look at the PHRASEBOOK box to help them with any missing answers, before checking back with the conversation to confirm.

ANSWERS
1 I'd love to go, but … 2 I'd prefer not to.
3 I'm sorry, I can't. 4 No way! 5 Oh, all right then.

Alternative procedure: less confident classes
Write on the board the first letters of the words in each of the phrases, as well as the appropriate number of underscores, to show how many letters are in each word.

Extra activity
Ask students to order the expressions from definite *no* to *yes* according to how strong a reaction they express, ie:

Definite no: No way ➔ I'm sorry, I can't ➔ I'd prefer not to ➔ I'd love to go, but … ➔ Oh, all right then: *yes*

Extra activity

Ask students to write on a piece of paper something they really would not like to do, eg *go swimming in the ocean in winter, stop using my mobile phone*, etc.

Ask them to work in pairs and to show each other what they have written.

Explain that they have two minutes each to try to persuade their partner to do the thing they don't want to do. Remind them that persuasion often means giving good reasons why someone should do something. Encourage them to use phrases from the PHRASEBOOK box.

ACT

7 3.30

- Point out to students that at the end of the conversation, Finn says, *I'll try.* Ask them what he means (that he'll phone his parents and try to persuade them to let him go to Edinburgh).
- Explain that you want students to work in pairs and write the conversation that Finn has with his mother or father.
- Invite them to start by making a list of reasons for Finn to give his parents to persuade them to let him go, and a list of ways his parents might react to his persuasion. Play the track with the phrases from the PHRASEBOOK box. Encourage students to decide which of the expressions they could use in their conversation.
- Set a time limit of 15 minutes for students to write and rehearse their conversations.
- Invite students to perform their conversation for another pair or to the class.

Homework

Ask students to think of a situation in their life where they want to persuade a friend or someone from their family to do something. Encourage them to write a conversation with that person to try and persuade them.

WRITING Our school

Express reasons and results

Page 102

STAGE	TIME	FOCUS
GET STARTED		Complete sentences using *because* and *so* and compare them in pairs.
SPEAK AND READ		Talk about the information you can find on school websites. Read some information and match it to the correct section from a school website. Study how to express reasons and results and look for examples in the website sections.
PRACTISE		Complete some information by choosing the correct linking words.
PLAN		Plan how you are going to write information for two sections of a school website.
WRITE AND CHECK		Write your website sections and check that you have covered all the sections of the plan.
SHARE		Read your partner's website sections to see if there is any missing information.

Get started

To recycle using *because* to express a reason and *so* to express a result, write these sentence starters on the board:

- *I didn't have breakfast this morning because …*
- *I didn't have time to do my homework last night so …*
- *English pronunciation is sometimes difficult because …*
- *I want to study at university so …*
- *I don't like eating fish because …*
- *I sometimes spend too much time on the computer so …*

Encourage students to choose four of the sentence starters and finish them in any way they like. Divide the class into pairs to compare their answers and say if the sentences are true for them.

SPEAK AND READ

1

- Divide the class into pairs to discuss and make notes on the type of information you can usually find on a school website. If students aren't sure, suggest that they think about the type of information parents might want to know about the school. Set a time limit of two minutes.
- Encourage students to share their ideas in open class.

2

- Ask students to read the three paragraphs of information on the website and match them to the sections that appear in the navigation bar at the top of the website page. Set a time limit of two minutes.
- Check the answers in open class.

ANSWERS

1 History 2 Location 3 Canteen

3a

- Explain that in many types of written text, particularly when we are giving information, it is important to give reasons for something or explain the result of something. This is often done by linking the information with reasons or results using specific words.
- Ask students to read the tips in the HOW TO box. Invite two students to read them out loud.
- Then ask students to cover the box and to tell you the linking words for expressing the reason for something (*because, as, because of*).
- Also ask them to tell you the linking words for expressing the result of something (*so, therefore, as a result*).

3b

- Refer students back to the school website and ask them to underline seven examples of reasons and results. Set a time limit of five minutes.
- Nominate different students to read out their answers and say if each example is a result or a reason.

ANSWERS

so we are a fairly new school (= result)
because the school was so popular (= reason)
As a result, around 750 students can now study with us (= result)
it's therefore a quiet and safe place to study (= result)
Because of its location (= reason)
As most of our students stay at the school for lunch (= reason)
Therefore, our meals are all made from the highest quality, local products (= result)

PRACTISE

4

- Ask students to read and complete the information by choosing the correct options. Allow two minutes.
- Encourage them to compare their answers in pairs before you check them in open class.

ANSWERS

1 As 2 As a result 3 so 4 Because of 5 therefore

extra answer

It's from the Facilities section.

PLAN

5

- Tell students they are going to write information for two sections of a new website for their school.
- Focus their attention on the **Writing plan** and go through it with them. You could give students three minutes to talk in pairs about the sections they think they might like to write about in order to get some initial ideas.
- Ask students to make notes individually about the types of information they want to include in their sections. Allow four minutes. Invite them to ask you if they need any further information.
- Encourage them to think about who will read the website (eg parents, students, teachers, people interested in attending the school) and what information will be useful for them.
- Ask students to plan how they are going to express reasons and results. Remind them to use the tips in the HOW TO box. Set a time limit of four minutes.

WRITE AND CHECK

6

- Ask students to use their plan and the model text to help them write their website sections. Allow 15 minutes.
- Monitor and give assistance as necessary. Remind them of the importance of editing and checking their work.
- When students have finished writing, encourage them to check their work.

Fast finishers

Ask fast finishers to write some instructions for the web designer about the artwork they would like to include with their sections. Encourage them to write a detailed description, eg *Please include a photo of students acting in last year's school play. Try to choose one that includes a lot of students and that is colourful. It should persuade students that drama is fun!*

SHARE

7

- Ask students to swap their website sections with a partner. Ask them to think whether there is any other information they think should be included.
- Once they have read each other's writing, ask different students to tell the class what their partner's website section was about and what type of information it gave.

Homework

Ask students to write a section for a school website about learning English. Encourage them to start by thinking of three reasons why learning English is a good idea and three results of learning English.

Ask them to also include other information, eg what sorts of activity students do in English classes, how often students study English, any trips or excursions to do with learning English, etc.

Ask them to write around 120 words and to include different linking words to express reasons and results.

Encourage them to include pictures or photos to make their website section more attractive.

VOCABULARY Types of school

1

- Focus on the first sentence of the text and ask students what they think the expression *all-in-one* means (something that combines two or more things that are usually separate, eg *all-in-one shampoo and conditioner*).
- Invite students to read the text and complete the information with the different types of school. Point out that the first letter of each word is given.
- Nominate different students to read out the text, sentence by sentence, to check answers in open class.

ANSWERS
1 nursery 2 kindergarten 3 elementary 4 middle
5 high 6 primary 7 secondary 8 state 9 public
10 private 11 boarding 12 homeschooling

Words with *self-*

2

- Focus students on the text and check the meaning of *manifesto* (a statement of beliefs).
- Ask students to choose the correct options to complete the text.
- Encourage them to compare their answers in pairs before you check them in open class.

ANSWERS
1 self-discipline 2 self-control 3 self-pity
4 self-conscious 5 self-esteem 6 self-confident
7 self-taught 8 self-sufficient 9 self-centred
10 self-defence

GRAMMAR Reported requests and commands

3

- Explain to students that they are going to read an email from a boy who is a student at the All-In-One School. Focus on the speech bubbles and elicit which are requests and which are commands (requests – 2, 6, 7; commands – 1, 3, 4, 5).
- Explain that these speech bubbles are things that the boy and his teachers have said.
- Ask them to complete the email where he is reporting the things that have been said.
- Circulate and monitor as students are doing the task. If you feel they are having difficulty, stop them mid-task and do a quick review of the form of reported requests and commands.
- Check answers in open class.

ANSWERS
1 told us to run 2 asked him to let 3 told me not to
4 told us not to 5 told me to give 6 asked him to give
7 asked them to come

Reflexive pronouns; *each other*

4

- Elicit from students a list of reflexive pronouns and write them on the board.
- Ask them to read the things a teacher says and to complete them with the correct reflexive pronoun or *each other*.
- Fast finishers could also write the teacher's words in reported speech.
- Check answers in open class.
- If students have the wrong answers, guide them towards the correct options by asking questions like *Are there two people doing the action? Is the person doing the action to or for himself or herself? What is the subject and what is the matching reflexive pronoun?*

ANSWERS
1 each other 2 itself 3 each other 4 yourselves
5 himself 6 themselves 7 myself

Extra Resources

Go to the Teacher's Resource Centre at www.macmillanbeyond.com for:

- downloadable audio and audio scripts for the Student's Book and Workbook
- videos and video scripts
- extra vocabulary at two levels of difficulty
- extra grammar at two levels of difficulty
- CLIL lessons, with full teacher's notes
- a life skills lesson, with full teacher's notes
- Speaking Database materials
- the *Beyond* B1 wordlist
- test generator for Unit 9 testing materials (all skills)
- tips for using the Grammar Database
- and more!

Go to the Workbook pages 100–111 for further practice material

UNIT 10 CHANGING FASHIONS

IN THE PICTURE In fashion

Talk about changing fashions

Pages 104–105

STAGE	TIME	FOCUS
GET STARTED		Look at different fashions and try to guess what era they come from.
WORK WITH WORDS		Recycle clothes and accessories vocabulary. Learn words to talk about fashion details. Listen to a description of fashions from the 1970s to the 2000s and discuss which clothes you like and dislike. Practise the pronunciation of /t/ and /d/.
SPEAK		Talk about the fashions of the 2010s and 2020s.

Get started

Place some pictures around the room of fashions from different eras. Ask students to move around the room in pairs, looking at the different pictures. Encourage them to say what the people are wearing and decide what decade or century they come from. You could set this up as a competition to see which pair guesses the eras correctly.

If you have a large class that makes this sort of movement around the room impractical, display the pictures one by one at the front of the class.

GO BEYOND FOR TEACHERS

In fashion

The phrase *in fashion* is used to talk about clothing or styles that are currently *fashionable*. The opposite expression is *out of fashion* or *unfashionable*. The expression *old-fashioned* implies that something has been *out of fashion* for quite some time.

WORK WITH WORDS

1a and 1b RECALL

- Divide the class into pairs to do both tasks. Set a time limit of three minutes for these tasks.
- First, they must note down as many clothes and accessories as they can. Then they complete the sentences with the verbs in the box.
- After the three minutes, check answers in open class.
- Ask students to do the Work with Words task on page 139.

ANSWERS

Exercise 1b

1 try on 2 match 3 fit 4 wear 5 suit

2a

- Focus on the pictures on pages 104–105. Explain that when different pictures are put together like this, it is called a *collage* /ˈkɒlɑːʒ/. Tell students that this collage shows examples of Western fashion from the 70s to the present.
- Ask them to copy the table and write the labelled items and adjectives in the correct categories. Allow two minutes.
- Encourage them to compare their answers in pairs as they finish, but don't confirm the answers at this point.

2b 3.31

- Play the track for students to listen and check.
- Play the track again for students to listen and repeat.

ANSWERS / AUDIO SCRIPT 3.31

Parts of clothes: button, *collar*, pocket, sleeve
Materials: denim, leather, *silk*, wool
Fit and look: baggy, *patterned*, plain, tight

3 3.32

- Tell students they are going to listen to a report about fashion from the 1970s to the 2000s. The report summarises each decade with a key word.
- Elicit how many decades will be mentioned (four – *the seventies, the eighties, the nineties and the two thousands*).
- Play the track for students to listen and write down the key word for each decade.
- Encourage them to compare their answers in pairs before you check them in open class.

ANSWERS / AUDIO SCRIPT 3.32

70s: colour 80s: big 90s: informal 2000s: mix

In the seventies, the key word was *colour*. People wore patterned shirts and trousers and clothes in orange, green, yellow and red. Trousers had buttons high above the waist, were tight at the top but wide after the knees, and were known as 'bell bottoms'. Skirts and hair were long.
In the eighties, the key word was *big*. Hair was big, jackets were oversize with big shoulders and people wore pullovers down to their knees. Shirts were worn with the collar turned up. Trousers were baggy round the waist with huge side pockets. Lots of make-up and big jewellery was essential – and not just for girls.
In the nineties, the key word was *informal*. Jeans and T-shirts with short and long sleeves, sneakers and hoodies came on the scene and sportswear became streetwear. Hair became smooth, and plain dark colours replaced bright patterned clothes. Big-name brands hit the high street. Everybody from babies to grandparents wore denim.
In the 2000s, the key word was *mix*. People wore clothes from different decades, formal clothes with informal clothes, and expensive materials with cheap ones. Smart silk shirts and soft wool scarves were combined with jeans and trainers. People became more eco-friendly and non-leather bags and shoes and organic cotton started to appear in high street shops.

4 3.32
- Ask students to complete the sentences from the listening with words from Exercise 2. Set a time limit of five minutes.
- Encourage students to compare their ideas in pairs before you play the track again for them to listen and check their answers.

ANSWERS

1 buttons; tight 2 collar 3 baggy; pockets 4 sleeves
5 plain; patterned 6 denim 7 silk; wool 8 leather

5a 3.33 PRONOUNCE
- Play the track for students to listen to the /t/ and /d/ sounds in the words and try to explain what is different about them. Invite them to say the words to themselves with their hand in front of their mouth. Ask them which sound produces more air (/t/).
- Ask them if they use /t/ and /d/ sounds in their own language(s). If so, ask students if they are pronounced the same as in English or differently.

AUDIO SCRIPT 3.33

tight pocket denim patterned

5b 3.34
- Focus students on the five pairs of words. Divide the class into pairs to say what the words mean and encourage them to ask you if they are unsure.
- Play the first part of the track for them to listen and, individually, circle the word they hear.
- Encourage them to compare their answers in pairs and tell you if they would like to hear the words again.
- Check the answers in open class.
- Then play the second part of the track for students to listen and repeat both words.

ANSWERS/ AUDIO SCRIPT 3.34

1 coat 2 feed 3 had 4 tight 5 wide

1 coat / code 2 feet / feed 3 hat / had 4 tight / tied
5 white / wide

6
- Focus students' attention on the collage again and invite them to think about which fashions they like and dislike.
- Divide the class into pairs to exchange opinions about the clothes in the collage. Set a time limit of five minutes.
- In open class, nominate different pairs to say if they agreed or disagreed about the clothes.

7 THE MOVING PICTURE

ANSWERS

Students' own answers

SPEAK

8
- Divide the class into groups of four to look at the fashion collage again and brainstorm ideas for the fashion of the 2010s and 2020s. (If possible, bring in some current fashion magazines to help less confident students and those who are not very interested in fashion.)
- Encourage them to think about the clothes that are popular, their look and fit, what parts of the clothes are featured and the materials that are used. Remind them to use the vocabulary from Exercise 2.
- Ask them all to make notes on their ideas. Set a time limit of 10 minutes.
- Ask students to form new pairs with a student from a different group in order to compare their ideas.
- In open class, encourage different students to mention some of the things they discussed and invite other students to comment.

GO BEYOND

Ask students to do the Go Beyond task on page 139.

Extra activity

Ask students to work in pairs and design an outfit. You may find that you have some students who will take this very seriously and others who may have a bit of fun with it. Encourage both approaches. Suggest that they draw a picture of their outfit and ask them to prepare to present their design to other students and describe the clothes in detail. Encourage them to use words from Exercise 2 in their presentations. Students can present their designs in small groups or, if you have a small class, to the whole class. You could follow up by asking students to write a description of their outfit to be displayed on the classroom wall with the design drawing.

Homework

Ask students to complete this quiz.
1 What is the opposite of *patterned*?
2 What part of a shirt covers your arms and can be short or long?
3 What material needs the help of an insect in its production?
4 What part of a shirt, jacket or trousers is useful for keeping things (eg coins, keys, wallets, etc) in.
5 What material comes from the skin of a cow?
6 These are usually round with some holes in the middle. They are often made of plastic and are used to connect two parts of a piece of clothing like a shirt.
7 What part of a shirt goes around the neck?
8 What material is used to make jeans?
9 When talking about clothes, what adjective is the opposite of *tight*?
10 What material is used to make knitted clothes? (Clue: it comes from a sheep!)

ANSWERS

1 plain 2 sleeve(s) 3 silk 4 pocket 5 leather
6 buttons 7 collar 8 denim 9 baggy 10 wool

READING Fashion statements

Understand paraphrase

Page 106

STAGE	TIME	FOCUS
GET STARTED		Draw a picture of the clothing described in a dictation.
SPEAK AND READ		Talk about your opinions about fashion. Learn and practise how to understand paraphrase.
REACT		Talk about the information in the text and say what you found most interesting. Design a T-shirt slogan.

Get started

Dictate these descriptions of what people are wearing and ask students to draw what they hear.

Mary's wearing a patterned shirt with a wide collar and six buttons, and a denim skirt with two pockets. She's also wearing knee-high black boots.
Frank's wearing a plain white shirt with long sleeves, baggy jeans and leather boots. He's also wearing sunglasses and a hat.
Pixie's wearing tight jeans and a baggy jumper. She's wearing six bracelets on her right wrist and a pair of large circular earrings.

Divide the class into pairs to compare their pictures and try to remember the descriptions. Monitor and check that students have drawn the items of clothing correctly.

Ask students what type of people they think Mary, Frank and Pixie are, judging from their clothes. Ask them if they think the clothes reflect the style of any particular decade.

SPEAK AND READ

1

- Ask students to read the statements about fashion and write *agree, disagree* or *not sure.*
- Divide the class into pairs to compare their responses and explain their opinions.

2a

- Dictate these sentences to students.
  1 *I'm not interested in the latest trends.*
  2 *Your clothes make a personal statement about you.*
  3 *I want to look like the people I hang out with.*
- Ask students to match these sentences to the statements that express the same idea in Exercise 1. (1 b, 2 a, 3 c)
- Explain that using different words to express the same idea is called *paraphrasing*. Point out that in many reading tasks, particularly in exams, students may be asked to match statements or short texts to different parts of a longer text. One of the key skills for this type of task is to understand paraphrase.
- Ask students to read the tips in the HOW TO box. Invite a student to read them out loud.

2b 3.35

Exam-type task

- Introduce the task by telling students they are going to practise looking for paraphrase in a reading task. Ask them to imagine they want to buy a fashion item for the four people pictured on page 106. Point out that the short texts underneath the photos describe each person's attitude to fashion, and the texts labelled A to F describe some fashion items. Explain that the task is to match one of the items A–F to each of the people. Allow 10 minutes. Before they start, ask them to recall the procedure that was suggested in the HOW TO box. Don't play the audio at this point. A suggestion for using the audio is given at the end of the lesson.
- Encourage them to compare their answers in pairs and discuss the key words and the words they found to paraphrase them. Point out that often people select slightly different key words and this is perfectly normal.
- Check answers in open class.

ANSWERS

Luna: D Joe: E Aldo: F Ella: A

Fast finishers

Ask students to find words in the texts to match these synonyms or definitions: *prohibited* (banned – A); *advertised* (promoted – B); *objects used for fighting* (weapons – C); *fashionable* (2 words) (chic – C, stylish – D); *a large amount of money that someone owns* (wealth – E); *people who work on ships* (sailors – F); *a big success* (a hit – F).

If you want to make the task easier or quicker, tell them which text each word comes from.

3

- Ask students which tips in the HOW TO box they used to help them with Exercise 2b.

Extra activity

Write the titles of the texts from Exercise 2b on the board. Ask students if they can remember what fashion item each text was about. (A – pyjamas; B – trainers; C – belts; D – high-heel shoes; E – jewellery; F – T-shirts.)

Encourage them to work in pairs and explain the meaning of the title.

REACT

4

- Divide the class into pairs to answer the first question. Set a time limit of two minutes.
- In open class, ask if anyone knows any other interesting facts about the origin of clothes or fashions.
- Ask students to work in the same pairs to complete the gapped sentence in question 2 with three different comparatives. Point out that they must have good reasons for their comparative sentences.
- Ask pairs to join up to form groups of four and invite them to read out and explain the comparative sentences they came up with.

Recorded reading text 3.35

The reading text is recorded as an extra audio track which can be exploited for various purposes.

In this lesson use the audio track as a warmer. With books closed, play the track and ask students to write down all the words they can hear connected to clothes.

GO BEYOND

Ask students to describe a favourite T-shirt they have that has a picture or slogan on it. Invite them to explain what the picture or slogan represents.

Divide the class into pairs to design a T-shirt slogan. Point out that it can be funny or serious. Encourage them to decide what visuals they would use. Set a time limit of 10 minutes.

Then invite students to present their T-shirt slogans to other students in small groups. Ask them to vote on the best one and ask the finalists to present their T-shirts to the class, writing the slogans on the board. Take a class vote on the best idea.

Extra activity

Ask students to scan the texts to find words from the same word family as these words: *fashion*, n (*fashionable*, adj); *recent*, adj (*recently*, adv); *comfort*, n (*comfortable*, adj); *power*, n (*powerful*, adj); *style*, n (*stylish*, adj); *jewel*, n (*jewellery*, n); *origin*, n (*originally*, adv); *formal*, adj (*informal*, adj).

Homework

Ask students to do some research on the origin of jeans and hoodies. Encourage them to write a paragraph about what they found and to bring it to compare with a classmate in the next class.

GRAMMAR *So* and *such ... that*

Emphasise somebody's or something's qualities

Page 107

STAGE	TIME	FOCUS
GET STARTED		Think of adjectives to describe the qualities of certain things.
READ		Read people's descriptions of two outfits they have worn.
STUDY		Complete explanations about the use of *so* and *such ... that* to emphasise somebody's or something's qualities. Use examples from the descriptions of outfits.
PRACTISE		Practise using so and *such ... that* in written and oral exercises.
WRITE		Write a description of an outfit you used to wear. Share your description with your partner.

Get started

Ask students to write three adjectives to describe each of these: *their best friend*, *their pet (if they have one)*, *their bedroom*, *their personality*, *their hometown*.

Ask them to compare their answers in small groups and explain why they chose these adjectives.

READ Grammar in context

1

- Elicit or teach the word *outfit* (a set of clothes worn together).
- Divide the class into pairs to focus on the photos and tell their partner what they think of the outfits. Set a time limit of one minute.
- Ask students to read the descriptions and find out what their owners thought of the outfits.

ANSWERS

The boy thought his outfit was really cool.
The girl's shoes made her feel really confident, but they made her feet hurt the next day.

STUDY

2

- Ask students to be absolutely silent for one minute and to note down what they hear. Write on the board: *It was so quiet that you could hear ...* . Elicit some of the things they heard and write them on the board, eg *It was so quiet that you could hear the wind in the trees.* Ask students: *Can you normally hear the wind in the trees?* (No) *So why could you hear it?* (Because it was very quiet) Circle *you could hear the wind in the trees* and label it *result.* Ask students what word is used to emphasise the reason for the result (*so*).
- Refer students back to the descriptions in Exercise 1 and ask them to underline phrases that begin with *so* or *such*.
- Read through the grammar explanations with the class and ask students to complete them with examples from Exercise 1.
- Check the meaning of *emphasise* (to give particular importance or attention to something). Remind students that a *clause* is a part of a sentence that contains a subject and a verb.
- Invite different students to read out the completed explanations. Encourage students to think about how these examples would be expressed in their own language(s).

ANSWERS
so colourful such a cool outfit such high heels

Extra activity
In order to help to get used to using *so* with adjectives and *such* with nouns. You could do this simple drill. Prepare a set of cards which includes adjectives and nouns. Hold up each card and ask the class to say the word preceded by *so*, in the case of an adjective, or *such (a/an)* + adjective in the case of a noun. Try to move through the cards as quickly as possible so that students get used to quickly deciding between *so* and *such*. Once you have worked through the set, pick cards at random and ask students to give you a complete sentence, eg COLD (so cold) *It was so cold that the water in the lake froze*.

Students may need a quick revision of uncountable and countable nouns and/or irregular plurals so that they know when to omit the article after *such*. One way to practise this could be to give students four or five sentences, some with mistakes, and ask them to identify the correct sentences and correct the errors.

PRACTISE

3
- Ask students to read and match the two parts of the sentences. Set a time limit of four minutes.
- Encourage students to compare their answers in pairs before you check them in class by nominating different students to read out the sentences.

ANSWERS
1 e 2 d 3 a 4 f 5 b 6 c

Extra activity
Remind students, or elicit, that we use *so* and *such … that* to emphasise certain qualities. Point out that we may also give emphasis by stressing the words slightly more than usual.

Model one of the sentences in Exercise 3, adding extra stress on the words *such big pockets*.

Ask students to read the sentences out loud in pairs, stressing the *so* and *such* phrases.

4a
- Ask students to complete the sentences with *so* or *such (a/an)*. If necessary, do a quick review of the forms before they start, by asking *Which word (so* or *such) is followed by adjective + noun?* (such) *When do we use a/an after such?* (when the noun is a singular countable noun) *When do we use so?* (with an adjective, and no noun)
- Set a time limit of four minutes for students to complete the sentences.
- Encourage them to compare their answers in pairs before you check them in open class.

ANSWERS
1 such a 2 so 3 so 4 so 5 such 6 such an

4b 3.36
- Draw students' attention to the example number 1 at the end of the third sentence in Exercise 4a and point out that this is the first sentence in the story. Ask students to number the rest of the sentences in order to complete the story. Set a time limit of four minutes.
- Play the track for students to listen to the story and check their answers.

ANSWERS / AUDIO SCRIPT 3.36
The leather outfit in the shop was so stylish that I had to buy it.
The trousers were so small that I could hardly breathe.
And the jacket had such tight sleeves that I could hardly put it on.
One day, I bent over so far that I got a big hole at the back of my trousers.
It was such an embarrassing moment that I went bright red.
It's such a pity that the outfit didn't fit me. I looked so cool.

5
- Divide the class into A/B pairs. Explain that they are each going to read out some sentence beginnings that include phrases with *so* and *such*. Their partner must complete the sentences with an appropriate *that* clause.
- Write an example of a sentence beginning on the board, eg *The film was so boring …* . Nominate different students to complete the sentence with a *that* clause, eg *… that I fell asleep. / … that I left before the end.*
- Refer Student As to page 141 and Student Bs to page 142.
- Monitor as they work to check that they are carrying out the task correctly.

WRITE

6
- Explain that you would like students to write a short description of an outfit or an item of clothing that they once wore or used to have. Suggest that they use the descriptions in Exercise 1 as a model.
- Give them a minute to decide what they want to talk about. If they are finding it difficult to think of something, suggest that they think of family photos they have where they are wearing a particular outfit.
- Ask them to work individually to write their descriptions. Set a time limit of 10 minutes for this.
- When they have finished, invite them to read their description to their partner. Encourage students to ask follow-up questions to find out more about the outfit and the situation described.

Extra activity
Ask students to recall the adjectives they wrote in the *Get started* activity. Ask them to write sentences using *so* and *such … that*, eg *My best friend is so intelligent that he never has problems with exams.*

Homework

Ask students to choose a favourite photo they have and to write a description of it using some *so* and *such … that* phrases. Encourage them to say where the photo was taken, who is in it and what the situation was. Ask them to include a copy of the photo with their description if possible.

LISTENING AND VOCABULARY Materials and more

Recognise formal and informal speech *Page 108*

STAGE	TIME	FOCUS
GET STARTED		Add vowels to words to make eight words for materials used in clothing.
SPEAK AND LISTEN		Talk about whether your clothes are made of natural or man-made materials. Complete a timeline showing materials that have been used for clothes over the years. Listen to the soundtrack of a video promoting high-tech clothes. Learn to recognise formal and informal speech.
REACT		Give your opinion about wearable technology.
WORK WITH WORDS		Learn to make adjectives from certain verbs by adding *-able*.
WRITE AND SPEAK		Think of things that could be described using the adjectives ending in *-able* and compare with a partner.

Get started

Ask students to add vowels to these words to make eight materials commonly used to make clothes: *cttn, lnn, wl, nyln, lthr, slk, dnm, plystr*.

Ask students to put the materials into these categories: plant, animal, man-made.

ANSWERS
Plant: cotton, linen, denim Animal: wool, leather, silk
Man-made: nylon, polyester

SPEAK AND LISTEN

1

- Divide the class into pairs to look at the clothes they are wearing and say if they are natural or man-made materials.
- In open class, encourage students to say what materials they mentioned and write them on the board. Check that all students know the meaning of all the materials mentioned.

2

- Focus students on the timeline showing different materials that have been used to make clothes over the centuries. Elicit what material was available around 2500 BC, ie *silk*.
- Ask students what they think *wearable technology* is. Listen to their ideas and tell them they will hear more about this when they listen to the audio in Exercise 3.
- Divide the class into pairs to try to complete the materials timeline. Set a time limit of three minutes.
- Do not confirm the answers at this point.

3 3.37

- Tell students they are going to listen to the soundtrack from a video for a company that designs high-tech clothes.
- Play the track for students to check their answers from Exercise 2 and add three examples for the 21st century.
- Encourage students to compare their answers in pairs before you check them in open class.

ANSWERS / AUDIO SCRIPT 3.37

about 190,000 years ago: *animal skins*, grasses, leaves
5000 BC: linen
3000 BC: cotton
2500 BC: *silk*
2000 BC: wool
1910: the first man-made material
21st century: *wearable technology* (examples: power lights, show your status update or a video clip, charge your music player or phone)
smart materials (examples: kill bacteria and keep the air clean, break down dirt, produce fragrances to change your moods)

Nayla: Hi, I'm Nayla and I design stuff for *Future Fashion* – tomorrow's fashion today! Our clothes are dead cool but they're high-tech too. So we're gonna tell you a bit about our clothes – and the history behind them. Check this out.

Presenter: The story of clothes starts about 190,000 years ago, when people started to wear animal skins, grasses and leaves so that they could protect themselves against the weather. The first cloth was probably made by the Egyptians around 5000 BC. They were able to make linen from a plant called flax. The Egyptians used linen for clothes but also to cover dead bodies and make bandages for mummies. Around 3000 BC, people in India began making cloth from cotton. Approximately five hundred years later, around 2500 BC, the Chinese started to make silk. People were not able to use wool to make clothes until about 2000 BC.
Until the 20th century, these four natural materials – linen, cotton, silk and wool – were the main types of cloth. Production of the first man-made cloth, rayon, started in 1910. Today, we are able to buy clothes in mixes of natural and man-made materials. These mixes mean that clothes fit better, look better, and are often more affordable. In the future, however, materials will do more than keep us warm and make us look good.

Nayla: At *Future Fashion*, we're developing materials which'll be able to generate power, keep you healthy, keep the environment clean and even change your moods! Thanks to wearable technology, *Future Fashion* clothes can already power lights using energy from your body movements. They can even show your status update or a video clip on a built-in screen. How cool is that? Soon they'll be able to charge your music player or phone too. Smart materials'll kill bacteria and keep the air around you clean. And, guess what, they'll be able to break down dirt on your clothes so you won't even have to wash 'em! We're also looking at how to programme clothes to produce fragrances to wake you up, make you feel happy and help you to sleep. Pretty amazing, huh? Check out our website for this season's great styles. Everybody's wearin' em!

Presenter: *Future Fashion* – tomorrow's fashion today.

4a

- Find out if students thought the language in the listening track was formal or informal. (It was a mix of both.)
- Elicit ideas about how they can recognise formal or informal spoken English.
- Listen to their ideas and then ask them to read the HOW TO box to see if any of their suggestions are included.

4b 3.37

- Play the track again and ask students to tick the things in the HOW TO box when they hear examples.
- In open class, check answers and encourage students to identify which section of the video soundtrack is formal, giving reasons for their answers.

ANSWERS

The middle part of the video is more formal. The speaker uses long sentences and he doesn't use contractions. He uses some longer and more formal words like *approximately*, *production* and *affordable*. He speaks quite slowly and clearly.

REACT

5

- Divide the class into pairs to recall what clothes that use wearable technology will be able to do. Elicit the examples given and write them on the board (power lights using energy from your body movements; show your status update or a video clip on a built-in screen; charge your music player or phone; kill bacteria and keep the air around you clean; break down dirt on your clothes; produce fragrances to wake you up, make you feel happy and help you to sleep).
- Encourage pairs to discuss the questions.

WORK WITH WORDS

6

- Focus students on the expressions from the listening text. Explain that *-able* can be added to some words to make adjectives that mean 'you can do something'. Ask them what type of word *wear* and *afford* are (verbs).
- Read through the definitions with the class.

7 3.38

- Focus students' attention on the adjectives in the box and ask them to write down the verbs that they come from. Set a time limit of four minutes.
- Play the track for students to listen and check.
- Play the track again for them to listen and repeat.
- Draw students' attention to the word box and elicit three examples where the spelling of the verb is adjusted before *-able* is added (*recycle, rely, value*).

ANSWERS / AUDIO SCRIPT 3.38

break – breakable download – downloadable
enjoy – enjoyable manage – manageable
reason – reasonable recycle – recyclable rely – reliable
respect – respectable suit – suitable value – valuable

WRITE AND SPEAK

8

- Ask students to work individually to write a person or thing for each adjective in Exercises 6 and 7.
- Divide the class into pairs to show their words to their partner for their partner to guess which adjective goes with each word.

GO BEYOND

Ask students to do the Go Beyond task on page 139.

Extra activity

Write groups A and B on the board.

Group A: *stuff, dead cool, high-tech, Check this out!, Guess what, Huh?*

Group B: *I'm going to tell you something interesting, using the most modern technology, Look at this!, Don't you think?, things, really amazing*

Ask students to match these informal words and expressions in group A to a synonym or definition in group B.

Check answers in open class.

ANSWERS

stuff – things dead cool – really amazing
high-tech – using the most modern technology
Check this out! – Look at this!
Guess what – I'm going to tell you something interesting
Huh? – Don't you think?

Homework

Ask students to complete these sentences with informal words and expressions from today's listening.

1 ________, Mum. Our class won the first prize in the new technology competition!
2 Have you seen Chuck's new mobile? It's very ________ – got all the latest apps and ________.
3 Last week we saw some guys doing break dancing – it was ________.
4 Hey, ________! Look at this picture of Mr Jackson in the newspaper – he got married last week.
5 Did you hear that Susan's moving to Australia with her family? Pretty amazing, ________?

ANSWERS

1 Guess what 2 high-tech; stuff 3 dead cool
4 check this out 5 huh

GRAMMAR Ability

Talk about ability in the past, present and future

Page 109

STAGE	TIME	FOCUS
GET STARTED		Play a game using *can/can't* for ability.
READ		Read a blog about a fashion designer.
STUDY		Study explanations of how to use *can*, *could* and *be able to* to talk about ability in the present, past and future.
PRACTISE		Practise using *can*, *could* and *be able to* in written and spoken exercises.
SPEAK		Talk about your abilities and past achievements.

Get started

Play a game of *Hot Seat* (see Games page 33). Write on the board a person, animal or thing that students can describe by using *can/can't* for ability, eg:

bus: *Lots of people can travel on this form of transport.*
You can drive it.
You can sit or stand in it.
You can take short journeys in a city or long journeys in the country.
People can get to work using this.

snake: *It can kill you (sometimes).*
It can frighten you.
It can't run.
It can't fly.
It can eat an animal bigger than it.

Explain to students that for each word, they have one minute to help the volunteer guess.

READ Grammar in context

1

- Divide the class into pairs to discuss what a fashion designer has to be good at, eg *drawing, sewing, cutting, choosing materials, combining colours*. Set a time limit of two minutes.
- Introduce the blog of Nayla, a fashion designer. They may remember her from the listening in the last lesson. Ask them to read the blog and find out how Nayla became a fashion designer.
- Check the answer in open class.
- Ask a few more comprehension questions like: *Why did Nayla have to wear her brother's old clothes?* (Because her parents couldn't afford to buy her new clothes.) *Why did she have to borrow a lot of money?* (Because she couldn't get a scholarship.) *What does she say she can't imagine doing?* (Buying clothes in a shop)
- Encourage students to tell their partner if they would like to be a fashion designer and to say why or why not.

ANSWERS
She had to wear her brother's old clothes, so she learned how to sew and made her own clothes. Then she studied fashion design.

STUDY

2

- Ask a student to read out the aim of the lesson. Tell students that we use three different verb structures to talk about ability: *can, could* and *be able to*.
- Ask students to read and complete the explanations with the negative forms of *can* and *could*.
- Check the answers in open class and draw students' attention to the different vowel sounds in *can* /kæn/and *can't* /kɑːnt/. Drill the pronunciation of these words.
- Refer students back to the blog to find some examples of *can, can't, could* and *couldn't*.

ANSWERS
can't couldn't

3

- Focus students on the grammar explanations and the table of *be able to*. Point out that *be able to* is used to talk about ability in the present, the past and the future. Remind them that there is no form of *can* that is used for the future.
- Refer students back to the blog to find and underline examples of *be able to* (present, past and future). Set a time limit of three minutes.
- Explain that when we are talking about ability in the past, we distinguish between the ability to do something on one occasion (a specific achievement) and general ability.
- Write these examples on the board.
  I left my keys at school but I was able to get into the house because there was a window open. (specific achievement)
  When I was younger I could play piano much better because I used to practise a lot. (general ability)
- Explain that when we are talking about a specific occasion in the past, we use *was able to*, NOT *could*. Point out that this only applies for positive sentences; in negative sentences either form can be used.
- Read through the section in the box on specific achievements in the past and answer any further questions that students may have.

ANSWERS
Present: I'm able to do something I love as a job.
Past: I was able to become a fashion designer; I wasn't able to get a scholarship.
Future: You probably won't be able to guess; I hope that I'll be able to help other young designers.

PRACTISE

4a

- Ask students to complete Nayla's sentences with the correct form of *be able to*. Remind them to read all the information in the sentences so that they can decide whether the sentence refers to ability in the past, present or future. Set a time limit of five minutes.
- Encourage students to compare their answers in pairs before you check them in open class.

ANSWERS
1 was able to sew
2 'm able to stand
3 won't be able to learn
4 'm not able to speak
5 wasn't able to cook
6 'll be able to drive

Alternative procedure: less confident classes
Before they attempt Exercise 4a, ask students to underline any words that show that the sentences refer to the past, present or future.

4b
- Divide the class into pairs to say if they can do any of the things in Exercise 4a.

5
- Explain the task by telling students they are going to read about Nayla and her brother when they were small.
- Ask students to circle the orange verb forms that can be replaced with *could*. Remind them to think about the difference between general ability and a specific achievement. Set a time limit of three minutes.
- Encourage students to compare their answers in pairs before you check them in open class.

ANSWERS
1, 2, 4

6
- Refer students to the prompts and ask them to use these to write questions with *can*, *could* or the correct form of *be able to*. Set a time limit of five minutes. If necessary, go through the first one as an example.
- Invite different students to write up their answers. Encourage the rest of the class to make any necessary corrections.

ANSWERS
1 Could you / Were you able to run fast when you were small?
2 When were you able to ride a bike?
3 What two things could you / were you able to do well when you were small?
4 What two things can you / are you able to do well now?
5 What do you hope you will be able to do in the future?

SPEAK

7a
- Divide the class into pairs to take it in turns to ask and answer the questions in Exercise 6.

7b
- Encourage students to tell their partner about their greatest achievement in the past using *was able to*. If necessary, remind them that *was able to* is usually used to talk about a specific achievement on one occasion, eg *I was able to eat six hot dogs in one meal.*

Extra activity
Ask students to design a poster with the left side representing the past and the right side representing the future. Give them the following headings: *Five hundred years ago, people …* and *In 500 years, people …* .

Ask students to work in small groups and to think of five things people *couldn't* do in the past (500 years ago), eg *watch television* and five things they will be able to do in the future (in 500 years), eg *live on another planet*.

Ask them to illustrate their posters and display them on the walls of the classroom.

Homework

Ask students to write their answers to the questions in Exercise 6 and to write two more questions using *can*, *could* or *be able to*, to ask about ability.

LANGUAGE & BEYOND GET THINKING

Consider all the options *Page 110*

STAGE	TIME	FOCUS
GET STARTED		Play a game where you make spontaneous choices between two options and explain your decisions.
SPEAK AND READ		Talk about choices you have made recently. Read a conversation between two friends who are shopping for a sports bag. Make notes on the advantages and disadvantages they discuss and also on what is important to them in making their decision.
DO		Decide what is important to you when buying clothes and accessories and discuss this with your partner.
REFLECT		Discuss questions about making choices and say if you agree with the REFLECTION POINT.
EXTEND		Make a list of five decisions where you need to consider options and compare it with a partner.

LIFE SKILLS

CONSIDER ALL THE OPTIONS

Teenagers are faced with some pretty difficult decisions and often need help in making the transition from dependent children whose parents make decisions for them to independent young adults who can make decisions for themselves. This lesson introduces three important steps in the decision-making process: identifying options, weighing up advantages and disadvantages and prioritising what is important.

Later in the lesson, they are asked to list some of the more important decisions that they may face and to consider the options available to them.

Get started

Play a game of *Choices*. Tell students you are going to call out pairs of options and they must choose one of them immediately, according to their preference. If they choose the first option, they should run to the left side of the room. If they choose the second, they should run to the right side of the room. Encourage them to follow their instincts. Then ask them to explain to the person next to them why they chose that option.

Suggested options:

Australia / New Zealand, *fruit / vegetables*, *beach / mountains*, *cinema / DVD*, *cats / dogs*, *autumn / spring*, *talking / listening*, *rock / pop*, *main course / dessert*.

SPEAK AND READ

1

- Read through the tasks with students. Check the meaning of *choice* /tʃɔɪs/, pointing out that it is related to the verb *choose* /tʃuːz/. Ask students to tell you the past simple and past participle of *choose* (*chose* /tʃəʊz/, *chosen* /ˈtʃəʊz(ə)n/).
- Set a time limit of two minutes for students to think and note down some of the choices they've made in the last few days. Suggest some areas of their lives where they may have faced choices, eg *shopping, time with friends, extra activities, time with family, schoolwork, homework, daily routine, eating* or *clothes*.
- Divide the class into pairs to talk about the choices they've noted down and say which ones they found the most difficult. Set a time limit of three minutes.
- Nominate different students to report back to the class on the choices their partner spoke about.

2

- Focus on the photo of Danny and Tyson and ask students to say where they are and what choice they are making (*they are in a shop choosing a sports bag to buy*).
- Encourage students to describe the three bags in the photos and say which one they think Danny will choose.
- Ask them to read the conversation and see if their prediction was correct. Set a time limit of two minutes.
- Elicit the answer in open class.

ANSWER

b

3a

- Invite students to write notes on the advantages and disadvantages of each bag. Set a time limit of five minutes, asking students to compare answers in pairs as they finish.
- Check the answers in open class.
- Ask students to explain the meaning of the following words: *vegan* /ˈviːɡən/ – a person who does not eat or use any animal products; *eco-friendly* /iːkəʊ ˈfren(d)li/ – something that does not harm the environment; *charity* /ˈtʃærəti/ – an organisation that helps people in need; *fair trade* /feə(r) treɪd/ – making sure the producers of a product are given a fair price.

ANSWERS

c (leather bag) advantages: looks good; disadvantages: not very big
a (vegan bag) advantages: recycled materials, eco-friendly, company gives money to a charity; disadvantages: bright colour
b (fair trade bag) advantages: workers get a fair price, doesn't exploit people; disadvantages: quite expensive

3b

- Ask students to scan the text again and write what's important to Danny. Set a time limit of two minutes.
- Check the answer in open class. Check the meaning of *exploit* /ɪkˈsplɔɪt/ (to treat someone unfairly in order to get some benefit yourself). Tell students that *fair trade* was set up in order to prevent people being exploited.

ANSWERS

the product is good quality   it doesn't exploit people

DO

4

- Ask students to think about what is important to them when they buy clothes and accessories.
- Invite two students to read out the items in the list. Then encourage students to tick the things in the list that are important to them and compare their answers in pairs. Encourage them to give reasons for their answers. Set a time limit of three minutes.

5

- Invite students to decide which of the sports bags in Exercise 2 they would choose for themselves and to explain their choice to their partner. Set a time limit of two minutes.

REFLECT

6

- Divide the class into small groups to discuss the questions. Set a time limit of five minutes for this discussion. Then, open the discussion up to the whole class, asking different groups to report on what they discussed.
- Ask a student to read the REFLECTION POINT out loud. Take a class vote, inviting students to raise their hands if they agree completely, agree up to a certain point or disagree.
- Invite students who partially agree or disagree to explain their point of view to the class.

Alternative procedure

Ask students to draw a grid with four columns and copy the questions in Exercise 6 into the first column.

Ask them to start by writing in their own answers to the questions in the second column.

Then ask them to stand up and walk around the class, speaking to different students to find out their answers to the reflection questions. Point out that they should speak to two different students for each question and make a note of their answers and reasons in the third and fourth columns. In this way, by the end of the activity they should have spoken to six different students.

EXTEND

7

- Encourage students to reflect and make a list of five situations where it's very important to look at options before they make a decision. Allow five minutes.
- Ask them to compare their list with their partner to see if the decisions they thought of are the same or different.
- In open class, invite students to talk about the decisions they wrote in their lists and find the decision that was chosen by the greatest number of students.

Extra activity

Write the following list of adjectives (1–5) and descriptions (a–e) on the board.

1 Rational, 2 Intuitive, 3 Dependent, 4 Avoiding, 5 Spontaneous

a You are afraid of making decisions, so you tend to put them off for another day.
b You follow your heart and not your head.
c You just decide on the spot and don't like to think about it too much.
d You like to ask lots of other people for their advice.
e You like to analyse the situation carefully before making a decision.

Ask students to match these types of decision-maker to the descriptions. Before they start, check the meaning of these phrases from the descriptions: *you tend to put them off* (you usually postpone them); *you follow your heart* (you base your decisions on your intuition or feelings); *you just decide on the spot* (you decide without thinking too much).

Encourage students to compare their answers in pairs and tell their partner which description is most/least like themselves.

ANSWERS
1 e 2 b 3 d 4 a 5 c

Homework

Ask students to write about one of the decisions they listed in Exercise 7. Encourage them to follow this plan:

Paragraph 1: What is the decision? When do you have to make it? Why is it important?
Paragraph 2: What are the options?
Paragraph 3: What are some of the advantages and disadvantages of each option?
Paragraph 4: What is important to you about this decision?

SPEAKING You look great!

Give and react to compliments Page 111

STAGE	TIME	FOCUS
GET STARTED		Think of things that can make people feel happier without spending any money.
SPEAK		Talk about giving and receiving compliments.
WATCH OR LISTEN		Watch or listen to two scenes where people give and receive compliments. Learn expressions for giving, accepting and returning compliments.
ACT		Exchange compliments with your partner about their appearance, personality or abilities.

Get started

Divide the class into small groups to brainstorm six ways they could make someone feel happier without spending any money. Set a time limit of three minutes. Invite students to share their answers in open class and feed in some ideas of your own.

SPEAK

1

- Explain that today's lesson is about how to give and react to compliments.
- Tell students that *compliment* is both a noun and a verb.
  - As a noun it goes with the verbs *give*, *get*, *accept*, *return* and *react to*.
  - As a verb it often follows the pattern *compliment* + person + *on* + something, eg *He complimented her on her English accent.*
- Divide the class into pairs to discuss the questions. Set a time limit of four minutes.
- In open class discussion, invite students to share their answers.

2

- Focus on the photos. Tell them the names of the characters: Max and Emma in the top photo; Alice and Leo in the lower one.
- Ask them to guess what Emma and Leo are complimenting Max and Alice on.

WATCH OR LISTEN

3 3.39

- Books closed. Play the scenes for students to watch or listen to and check their ideas from Exercise 2.

ANSWERS / VIDEO/AUDIO SCRIPT 3.39

Emma is complimenting Max on his T-shirt and his hair.
Leo is complimenting Alice on being a good friend.

Emma: Hi Max. You look good today! What a great T-shirt!
Max: Thanks. I got it on holiday. I chose it because it's organic cotton.
Emma: Your hair looks nice as well. Have you had it cut?
Max: Yes, I have. I'm glad you like it. You look great too.
Emma: Thanks … So, are you going somewhere special?
Max: Erm, … You know, that top really matches your eyes.
Emma: Max, who are you meeting?

Leo:	Thanks for helping me with this homework. You're such a good friend.
Alice:	Thanks, that's the nicest thing I've heard for ages. You know I'm always happy to help.
Leo:	I'm so bad at French that I'll never be able to remember all the tenses.
Alice:	But you're good at other things. Your drawings are fantastic.
Leo:	Thanks, that's a really kind thing to say. But yes, they are pretty good!

4 3.39

- Focus students on the written conversations and ask them to find and underline all the compliments.
- Play the scenes again for students to watch or listen again and complete the expressions that Max, Alice and Leo use to accept and return the compliments.
- Encourage them to compare their answers in pairs before you check them in open class.

ANSWERS

See underlining in video/audio script in Exercise 3.

1 Thanks. 2 like it 3 great too 4 I've heard for ages
5 kind thing to say

5 3.40

- Play the track for students to listen to the compliments and responses in the conversations, paying particular attention to stress and intonation.
- Ask students to practise the full conversations in their pairs. If there's time, have them swap roles and repeat.

AUDIO SCRIPT 3.40

Emma:	You look good today! What a great T-shirt!
Max:	Thanks.
Emma:	Your hair looks nice as well. Have you had it cut?
Max:	I'm glad you like it. You look great too.
Leo:	You're such a good friend.
Alice:	Thanks, that's the nicest thing I've heard for ages.
Alice:	Your drawings are fantastic.
Leo:	Thanks, that's a really kind thing to say.

ACT

6 3.41

- Divide the class into pairs to practise giving, accepting and returning compliments. Point out that these could be about appearance, personality or ability. Before they start, play the track with the expressions in the PHRASEBOOK box and encourage students to use these in their conversations. Remind students to pay attention to stress and intonation.

Extra activity

Ask students to work in groups of six to eight and to sit in a circle. Give each student a piece of paper and ask them to write their name at the top. Ask them to hand the paper to the person on their left who must write them a compliment and then pass the paper on to the person on *their* left. Encourage them to repeat the process until their paper is returned to them. They should have written a compliment for each person in the group. Tell them that, each time, before writing their compliment they should read the compliments that have already been written and think of something *different* to compliment the person on. Encourage them to use a variety of phrases from the PHRASEBOOK box.

Homework

Ask students to practise saying the phrases in the PHRASEBOOK box at home.

Tell them that it's important that they say them out loud and imagine themselves in a real situation where they need to use the phrases.

Encourage them to record themselves if possible and keep practising until they are happy with how they sound.

WRITING For sale

Refer to two options *Page 112*

STAGE	TIME	FOCUS
GET STARTED		Play a game of *Alphabet Race* to recycle words relating to fashion and clothes.
SPEAK AND READ		Talk about buying and selling second-hand items. Read an online advert and make notes about the items being advertised. Learn linking phrases to refer to two options.
PRACTISE		Practise using linking phrases to refer to two options.
PLAN		Make a plan to write an online advert to sell two items of clothing or accessories.
WRITE AND CHECK		Write and edit your advert.
SHARE		Read other students' adverts and make a note of items you're interested in.

Get started

Play a game of *Alphabet Race.* Divide the class into small groups to try to write one word beginning with each letter of the alphabet (not including XYZ) related in some way to the topic of fashion and clothes. Set a time limit of four minutes. Explain that you will accept a wide range of words, as long as students can explain how the words are related to the topic. Tell them they will get an extra point for any new words that have been introduced in Unit 10.

Ask groups to swap lists to check their answers. Elicit answers in open class, awarding one point for each correct word and two for any new word from this unit.

SPEAK AND READ

1

- Ask a student to read out the questions. Check the meaning of *second-hand* (owned or used by someone else before you).
- Refer students to the PHRASE BYTES box and check the following words: *donate* /dəʊˈneɪt/ (to give something to an organisation that helps other people – a charity); *charity* /ˈtʃærəti/ shops (shops run by charities where they sell things that have been donated); *flea* /fliː/ markets (a market where old things are sold at low prices).
- Divide the class into pairs to answer the questions. Encourage them to use the expressions from the PHRASE BYTES box when they are answering the questions.

Extra activity

Ask students to say whether they would prefer shopping for second-hand goods online or in a flea market. Encourage them to draw up a list of the advantages and disadvantages of both types of shopping.

2

- Focus students on Jessie's advert and explain that he's going to put it online to try and sell an England football kit and boots.
- Ask students to read the advert and complete the table of notes. Set a time limit of five minutes. Let students compare their answers in pairs as they finish.
- Monitor as students are completing the table and make a note of any difficulties they are having.
- Check answers in open class.

ANSWERS

Item	Kit	Boots
size	164/one size	40 (small fit)
colour	dark blue/light blue	black with white stripes
condition	good (no marks)	good (no marks)
brand	England away	Kickit
material	cotton	leather
other details	unisex original kit shirt has short sleeves	very comfortable

3a

- Remind students that linking phrases can help a reader to understand a text and make a piece of writing more interesting and effective.
- Ask them to read the tips in the HOW TO box about using linking phrases to refer to two options.

GO BEYOND FOR TEACHERS

Pronunciation of *either/neither*

either and *neither* can be pronounced in two different ways, both of which are correct.

either /ˈaɪðə(r)/ or /ˈiːðə(r)/ *neither* /ˈnaɪðə(r)/ or /ˈniːðə(r)/

3b

- Refer students back to Jessie's advert to find and underline an example of each of the linking phrases from the HOW TO box. Set a time limit of two minutes.
- Invite different students to read out the examples in open class.

ANSWERS

Both the kit and the boots have been worn quite a lot
neither the kit nor the boots have any marks
If you want to buy either the kit or the boots separately

PRACTISE

4

- Ask students to complete the descriptions from other adverts with the correct linking phrases from the HOW TO box. Set a time limit of four minutes.
- Encourage students to check their answers in pairs before you check them in open class.

ANSWERS

1 Neither ... nor 2 Both ... and 3 either ... or
4 Both ... and 5 Neither ... nor 6 either ... or

PLAN

5

- Explain to students that they are going to write an online advert to sell some clothes, accessories or other items that they don't need. Encourage them to think of two items and make a plan for their advert.
- Focus their attention on the **Writing plan** and go through the structure of the advert with them.
- Ask them to write their ideas for their plan. Set a time limit of 10 minutes. Circulate and help students if necessary.
- Encourage them to use the language they have learned in this unit. Suggest that they use *so/such ... that* to emphasise particular qualities and linking phrases to refer to two options.
- Encourage students to compare their ideas and notes in pairs before they write their first draft.

WRITE AND CHECK

6

- Ask students to use their plan and the model advert to write their own advert. Set a time limit of 15 minutes.
- When students have finished writing, encourage them to check their work.

SHARE

7

- Display students' adverts around the class. Invite students to walk around the classroom to read different adverts and note down the items they think sound interesting.

Extra activity

Ask students to work in groups of six to give their opinions about the statements below. Point out that their objective is to use these expressions in their discussions: *All of us thought that ... ; Both ... and ... thought that ... ; Neither ... nor ... thought that ... ; None of us thought that ... .*

Discussion statements:
Fashion is only for girls. Boys are not interested in fashion.
You have to be careful when you shop online because people can cheat you.
It's better to donate clothes to a charity than to sell them.

Homework

Ask students to imagine that they have answered Jessie's advert and bought the football kit, but that when they get it they are not happy with it.

Ask them to write an email to complain to Jessie. Suggest that they structure their email as follows:

1st paragraph: Say why you're writing (*I'm writing to complain about ...*). Use phrases from page 67, eg *I'm afraid ... .*

2nd paragraph: Say what is different from the advert. Use reported speech from page 85, eg *You said that the kit included ... .* Use linking phrases from page 112, eg *Both the kit and the boots are in poor condition.* Use *so/such ... that*, eg *The socks were so smelly that I had to wash them three times.*

3rd paragraph: Say what you would like Jessie to do. Use phrases from page 67, eg *I'd like a refund.*

VOCABULARY Fashion

1

- Focus students on your clothes, if appropriate, or choose a suitable picture in their Student's Book, eg page 89, and invite students to describe them.
- Elicit words to describe parts of clothes and materials, as well as their fit and look. Write these words on the board as students say them.
- Ask students to complete the descriptions. Point out that the first letter of the word is given. For less confident classes, leave the words written on the board for them to refer to.
- Check answers in open class.

ANSWERS
1 plain 2 baggy 3 wool 4 patterned 5 sleeves 6 collar 7 tight 8 denim 9 leather 10 pockets 11 buttons 12 silk

Adjectives with *-able*

2

- Explain to students that Rob and Rosie's fashion blog advertises some rather unusual items.
- Ask them to read the list of items and choose the correct adjectives. Set a time limit of five minutes.
- Encourage students to compare their answers in pairs before you nominate different students to read out their answers to check in open class.
- Ask fast finishers to underline the stressed syllable in the adjectives.

ANSWERS
1 suitable 2 valuable 3 breakable 4 respectable 5 enjoyable 6 affordable 7 reasonable 8 recyclable 9 reliable 10 wearable 11 manageable 12 downloadable

GRAMMAR *So* and *such … that*

3

- Remind students of the expressions *in fashion* and *out of fashion*.
- Focus on the phrases in the box and elicit which two will be followed by a countable noun (*such an uncool* and *such an amazing*).
- Ask what kind of noun will come after *such big* (an uncountable or plural noun).
- Ask students to complete the fashion advice with the phrases in the box.
- Invite different students to read out a tip to check answers in open class.

ANSWERS
1 so 'in' 2 so fantastic 3 such an amazing 4 so warm 5 such an uncool 6 such big

Ability

4

- Invite students to read quickly through the text, ignoring the gaps, to find out if Lucy X is a child or a teenager (a teenager).
- Divide the class into pairs to complete the interview with the correct form of *be able to*, *can/can't* or *could/couldn't*. Tell students that if more than one form is possible, they should write both. Set a time limit of five minutes.
- Check the answers in open class. Where only one form is possible, ask students to explain why.

ANSWERS
1 were you able to choose / could you choose
2 wasn't able to pick / couldn't pick 3 couldn't wear
4 was able to choose 5 'm able to buy / can buy
6 can't wear 7 'll be able to shock

Extra Resources

Go to the Teacher's Resource Centre at www.macmillanbeyond.com for:

- end-of-course tests
- downloadable Extra reading section
- the Speaking part of the Progress Check 9&10
- a downloadable project linked to Units 9–10
- downloadable audio and audio scripts for the Student's Book and Workbook
- videos and video scripts
- extra vocabulary at two levels of difficulty
- extra grammar at two levels of difficulty
- culture lessons, with full teacher's notes
- a life skills lesson, with full teacher's notes
- Speaking Database materials
- the *Beyond* B1 wordlist
- test generator for Unit 10 testing materials (all skills)
- tips for using the Grammar Database
- and more!

Go to the Workbook pages 112–123 for further practice material

PROGRESS CHECK UNITS 9&10

Preparing for the Progress Check

Vocabulary review

- Make a table on the board with the following headings: *Types of school, Words with self-, Fashion, Adjectives with -able.*
- Invite students to come up to the board and write vocabulary items under each heading. For each item, check that everyone understands the meaning. The lists do not need to be complete.
- With several items in each column, refer students to the Words & Beyond pages on pages 138 and 139. Encourage them to call out any items that they missed. Students can then go through the Progress Check and see how many of the items they can find.

Grammar review

- Remind students of the grammar they studied on pages 97, 99, 107 and 109. Write the following on the board, asking for example sentences as you write:
  - Unit 9: Reported requests and commands; Reflexive pronouns; *each other*
  - Unit 10: *So* and *such … that*; Ability
- Make sure students give you enough examples to cover all the different forms of each grammar point, including past tenses, negatives and questions where relevant. Deal with any mistakes that come up as students are giving you examples, referring them back to the relevant pages if necessary.

Optional warm-up activities

READ Exercise 1

- Most of the answers in this task depend on the language that students have studied in the last two units. Make sure they are fully familiar with this vocabulary and grammar (see Vocabulary and Grammar reviews above).
- Tell students that they are going to practise skimming a text. Explain that skimming will give them a good idea of what the text is about, what the main points are and how the text is organised. Give them exactly one minute to read the text for gist. Remind students that they are not expected to read it in detail.
- Ask the class to look back at the HOW TO box and the work they did on referring words on page 96.
- Finally, read through the **Exam tips** with the class, making sure that students understand that they have a choice of strategies for this type of task.

LISTEN Exercise 2

- Refer students back to the work they did on understanding instructions on page 98. Then go through the **Exam tips** with the class, checking that students understand them.
- Explain to students that they should spend time on this type of task by looking at the questions and the pictures before they start listening. Encourage them to think about what they might hear in question 1 by prompting with questions such as *Where does the conversation take place?* (in a clothes shop) *What are they talking about?* (which top to buy) *What will you hear?* (either a customer talking to a shop assistant about buying a top or two people shopping for a top)
- Put the class into pairs or small groups and ask them to discuss the other items in a similar way. After a minute or two, ask questions about items 2–5, eg Item 2: *What are you going to hear?* (some instructions) *What verbs might you hear?* (*turn, push, pull*) *What nouns might you hear?* (*key, handle*)
- Finally, point out to students how much useful information they have gathered *without* listening.

WRITE Exercise 3

- Remind students that the gaps usually depend on the grammar that they have studied in the previous two units (see Grammar review above). Note that in this case, there is a lexico-grammatical item in the form of the suffix *-able*.
- Without telling you the answers, students should be able to say which grammar point is being tested in each question. Ask them which gap contains *so/such … that* (2); a reflexive pronoun (4); a reported request (3); an adjective ending in *-able* (1).

WRITE Exercise 4

- Refer students back to the work they did on expressing reasons and results on page 102 and on referring to two options on page 112.
- Put students in pairs and ask them to note down some of the things they could write for each bullet point. They do not have to write complete sentences.

Doing the Progress Check

READ

1

- Ask students to look at the title. Remind them that the title will give them an idea of what to expect.
- Encourage students to read the whole text from start to finish so that they know how the argument develops.
- Go through the **Exam tips** with students if you haven't already done so and make sure they understand the different strategies. Students will inevitably find an approach that works for them, but these tips are an excellent place to start.
- Allow 10 minutes for this section.

ANSWERS

1 B 2 D 3 A 4 C 5 D 6 B 7 C 8 A 9 B 10 D

LISTEN

2 3.42

- If you have decided not to do the full warm-up, encourage students to spend a minute or two looking at the pictures and predicting what they might hear. Ask them to think about what the pictures have in common (eg the pictures in question 1 are all of clothes).
- Make sure that they understand that they have to tick one of the pictures according to what they hear.
- Go through the **Exam tips** for the listening task, briefly referring students back to the listening they did on pages 98 and 108.
- Point out that they will hear everything twice.

ANSWERS / AUDIO SCRIPT 3.42

1 C 2 C 3 B 4 B 5 A

1

Girl: I'd like to buy a top.
Woman: How about this one? The colour really matches your eyes.
Girl: I don't know. I'd prefer one with long sleeves.
Woman: What about this one? It's made of silk.
Girl: Mmm. I don't usually wear patterned things, but this one's OK.
Woman: Or there's this shirt. It's made of denim.
Girl: It's too plain. I'll take the silk one.

2

Woman: John, listen, I forgot to tell you how to open the door to the apartment. It's one of those funny locks. You have to turn the handle up first. When you've done that you'll be able to turn the key. But turn the key before you turn the handle down again. Call me back if you can't do it.

3

James: Maria, I can't sing at your party. I'd feel too self-conscious.
Maria: Oh, go on, James. You've got an amazing voice.
James: Ask Frank to sing. He sings well and he's really self-confident.
Maria: He's really self-centred too! And he never smiles. You've got a lovely smile, but you always hide it behind your hair!
James: I don't know.
Maria: Come on, James. You'll be with friends. What have you got to lose?
James: Oh, OK then.

4

Man 1: Is that Miss Jones?
Man 2: It might be, but she looks too young.
Man 1: When was Miss Jones our teacher?
Man 2: I think it was at primary school. So ... 1990?
Man 1: No, we had her in our first year at secondary school. And that was 1995.
Man 2: Yeah, you're right. And she'd just left university, so she was probably 23 or 24.
Man 1: So, that woman can't be Miss Jones.
Man 2: No. But she *really* looks like her.

5

Teacher: Jenkins, is this your homework?
Boy: Yeah.
Teacher: Yes, sir.
Boy: Yes, sir.
Teacher: I told you to write at least 300 words. This is so short that I will not be able to mark it.
Boy: I couldn't find enough information, sir.
Teacher: I also asked you to include a photo.
Boy: I know. I couldn't find one.
Teacher: I'm afraid you will have to do this again. For tomorrow.
Boy: But ...
Teacher: No buts!

WRITE

3

- Remind students that this type of task is often grammar-based. They should be expecting reported requests and commands; reflexive pronouns; *each other*; *so* and *such ... that* and ability. In addition, the vocabulary they learned with the suffix *-able* is also tested here.
- Remind them also that spelling is important in this type of task because in a real exam they will lose marks for spelling mistakes.

ANSWERS

1 downloadable 2 such complicated 3 to help
4 myself

4

- If you have decided not to do the full warm-up, spend a few minutes going through the task with students and eliciting who they have to write to and what their message must include (the three bullet points).
- Remind them that, even if their writing is excellent, they won't get full marks if they do not include all the points.
- Explain that they shouldn't spend too long on their beginnings and endings. Suggest that they begin with *Hi Diego,* and end with *See you soon, [name].*
- Stress that the correct tenses are important. Remind them of the work they did on *either ... or* on page 112, which they will need in order to address the third bullet point.
- Finally, remind students of the word limit and the importance of checking their spelling, grammar, etc.

MODEL ANSWER

Hi Diego, I'm really happy you can come to my school. It means you'll be able to meet all my friends. They want to hear about school in the US, so you can either give a talk or an interview.

After the Progress Check

Optional game

- Students can play *Snowman* (see Games page 33). They have played this game before after the Progress Check for Units 3 and 4.
- This time, ask them to play using the vocabulary from Units 9 and 10, ie types of school, words with *self-*, fashion and adjectives with *-able*.

Feedback and extension

READ

- Ask students why they chose particular answers. If they had mistakes, make sure they understand why.
- Ask them to look at the wrong answers. Where relevant, invite them to suggest what has to change in the word order, use of grammar, etc to make the answer correct.

LISTEN

- After students have received their marks for the **Listen** section, play the audio again, this time pausing after each relevant piece of information. Ask the class to tell you why it is relevant (eg It proves that option A cannot be right, it tells you the correct answer, etc).

WRITE

- Students who had difficulty with Exercise 3 need to focus on the grammar points they have studied. Point out that lexical items can also be used here.
- Explain that in some exams, the gaps contain two elements – maybe an idiom and a preposition or a noun and an *-ing* form, etc. Students will need to make all the necessary changes.
- Write one or two example sentences on the board using the grammar points from the exercise and then put students in groups of four to come up with more examples. If necessary, ask students to write more sentences for homework.
- For students who had difficulty with Exercise 4, do another task, building up a model on the board. Write the following, asking different students for ways to fill in the gaps:

  Hi Diego,

  I'm so happy that you can come to our school because ________ .

  My class want to hear about school in the US. You could either ________ *or* ________ .

- When the model is complete, ask other students to suggest alternatives. You could then rub out the previous suggestions and fill in the gaps with new ones. Students might also suggest extra information to include. Encourage this but remind them what they need to achieve in the task and they have only 45 words in which to do so.

GO BEYOND FOR TEACHERS

The reading text in this Progress Check is known as a multiple choice cloze. There are many places to practise these online. Encourage students to search for 'multiple choice cloze' and try to find some that they can print and bring to the next lesson. Alternatively, they can write their own, producing the four options themselves. In the next lesson, they could either swap with a partner or you could photocopy some of the best for the whole class to do.

WORKBOOK AUDIO SCRIPT

Unit 1

Track 01/02

Page 8, Exercises 2, 3 and 6

A: Hey Mark! Why are you smiling? It's cold and rainy, and you failed your maths test!
B: I know, Gemma ... but I'm off to Spain. Hello sunshine! Goodbye, maths!
A: That's cool! But, er, it's not the holidays it's only the weekend. It's sorta far to go for a weekend.
B: Yeah, but it's, you know, a special occasion. I'm visiting my Spanish friend Rafa. I'm REALLY looking forward to it.
A: I believe you. What's the occasion?
B: It's his 16th birthday, and his parents have organised a BIG celebration.
A: So, when're you off?
B: Early tomorrow morning. My flight's at six!
A: Uggh! Are you ready?
B: What d'ya mean?
A: Do you have, you know, your passport and all your stuff? Is your suitcase packed?
B: Um, no! I always do things at the last minute. I can pack tomorrow morning. I don't need much – a couple of T-shirts – that's all. And a card for Rafa, of course!
A: I dunno. I think it's a bit cold there at the moment. It's March, you know, not August! Oh, hang on, there's Mr Green. He'll know. Excuse me, Mr Green, can I ask you a question?
C: Hello Gemma, what is it?
A: Is it cold in Spain at the moment?
C: Gosh, I don't know. It depends what part of Spain you are talking about. But yes, I imagine it can get fairly cold.
A: So, Mark needs to take a jumper with him to Spain for the weekend?
C: I would think so. So you're going to Spain for the weekend, Mark. That sounds lovely. As long as you're ready for the test on Monday.
B: Test? What test?!
C: I think you need to pack your history book too then Mark ...

Track 03

Page 11, Exercises 1 and 2

1
A: Hi! Pete and I are going to the cinema tonight. Would you like to come?
B: Sorry, but I can't come. I'm going to a party with Rostam.
A: That's too bad. Another time!

2
A: Hi Mac. I'm having a barbecue on the beach for our class.
B: Great! When is it?
A: It's on Saturday evening. Can you come?
B: Sure, I'd love to. I'm free that evening.

3
A: Jack and I are going on a day trip to London next Saturday. Would you like to come with us?
B: That sounds brilliant. I'd love to. Thanks for inviting me.

4
A: Hi Sami. I'm inviting some people out for a pizza tonight. Are you free?
B: Sorry. I'd love to come, but I can't. I'm going to a concert with my brother.

Track 04

Page 11, Exercise 4

Asha: Hi Hitarth, Jana and I are trying to organise a surprise birthday meal for Tina. Would you like to come?
Hitarth: That sounds like fun. I'd love to. Thanks for inviting me.
Asha: We're thinking of having it after school tomorrow at 4pm. Can you come then?
Hitarth: Oh, sorry. I'd love to, but I have to look after my little brother tomorrow afternoon.
Asha: That's OK. We can have it on Wednesday. Are you free then?
Hitarth: Sure, Wednesday sounds great.
Asha: Great. Let's meet at the Sushi House on Wednesday at 4pm. Don't be late!

Unit 2

Track 05

Page 20, Exercises 2a and 4

Message 1
Hi Brian! It's Monday morning, 7.30. We're on our way to the airport to fly to Italy for the San Remo festival and we're sitting in a traffic jam on the motorway. We've been here for half an hour and we haven't moved at all. I think a coach has broken down. It's hot and I'm bored. Some people have got out of their cars and are sitting on the grass. What a terrible start to our trip. Better go – I think we're starting to move ... at last.

Message 2
Hey. It's 11am and we're at the airport. And guess what? The plane's delayed. They say it's because of bad weather but the weather looks lovely outside. We're going to have to wait for two hours! The place is really packed – there are people everywhere! At least Dad's given me some money to buy something to eat.

Message 3
So it's still Monday – two in the morning – but the good news is we're in France! Our plane was cancelled so we collected our car from the car park and drove to the port. We got a ferry to France and we've driven all night. We should arrive in Italy at 7am. I'm so excited!

Track 06

Page 23, Exercises 3 and 4

1
A: I'm meeting my friend. She's on the flight from Paris. Where's Arrivals?
B: That's upstairs.
A: Sorry, I didn't hear that.
B: Upstairs.
A: Thank you!

2
A: I'm travelling on the 9.30 flight to Rome. Is it on time?
B: You should check the Departures Board.
A: Where's that?
B: It's over there, past check-in.
A: Can you say that again, please?
B: Yes. Go past check-in.
A: OK. Thanks!

3
A: Hello. I'm getting the flight to New York. Where's passport control?
B: Oh, you need to go to check-in first.
A: Really? Where's that?
B: It's downstairs, near the restaurant.
A: Could you repeat that, please?
B: Downstairs. Near the restaurant.
A: Thank you very much!

Track 07

Page 23, Exercise 6

/b/: toothbrush, hairbrush, bike, boat, baggage, bag
/p/: toothpaste, passport, plane, shampoo, passenger, departure

Unit 3

Track 08

Page 32, Exercises 4 and 6

Interviewer: So, tell us about you and your band.
Katya: I'm Katya from The Blackberries.
Interviewer: What kind of music do you play?
Katya: Oh – mostly pop, and some rock too.
Interviewer: OK. And do you all play instruments?
Katya: No, not all of us. Trixy and Pam play guitar. Annie's on the drums. I just stand at the front and sing.
Interviewer: So, when did the band start?
Katya: Er, at school in 2010. We played at our school concert and were so popular we started the band.
Interviewer: Have you recorded any songs?
Katya: Yes, three. You can download them all.
Interviewer: And what do you like best about being in a band?
Katya: Singing with my friends! It's so much fun.
Interviewer: Well, good luck for the future.

Track 09

Page 32, Exercise 6a

I'm Tom, and I'm a folk singer from Ireland. I like most music but especially love songs. As for instruments – I play the guitar and the Irish drum. I haven't been a singer for very long, actually. I've played the instruments for a while

– but I didn't start singing until last year. The reason I started was because I won a talent competition. I haven't recorded many songs. In fact, last month I recorded my first one, called 'Dark Hearts'. People often ask me what I enjoy about my job. I guess it's bringing music into people's lives. I think music makes people feel happy, doesn't it?

Track 10

Page 35, Exercise 2

1

Amita: Hey Malike, how was your trip to Bali with your family?
Malike: Oh, we had a really fantastic time. On the last day we saw this traditional Balinese dancing. My mum said they danced more gracefully than any ballet dancer she's seen.
Amita: Really? Why are they so good?
Malike: A lot of people say it's because they learn to dance with their hands when they're very young. Because they hear music from such an early age, they have this totally amazing sense of rhythm.
Amita: What was your opinion?
Malike: I thought the dancing was great, but I really loved the costumes. They were so colourful and beautiful. Some people think they look a bit strange, but I don't care what other people think – I loved them.

2

Amita: So, tell me more about this dancing. What kind of music do they dance to?
Malike: They dance to the gamelan.
Amita: Gamelan? What's that?
Malike: It's a kind of traditional band with things like drums, strings and flutes. My brother thought they were cool, but my dad hated it because it was too noisy!
Amita: And what about you? What did you think?
Malike: Well, I don't really have an opinion – I was so busy watching the dancers I don't really remember what the music was like.

Track 11

Page 35, Exercise 5

audience, audition, caught, concert, confidence, modern, opera, orchestra, perform, rock, song

Unit 4

Track 12

Page 44, Exercise 2a

1 Boy: Did you go to the party with Peter?
Maria: No, I didn't go with *Peter*. I went with *Ed*.
2 Boy: Are you coming round at 4 o'clock?
Maria: No, I'm not coming round at *4*. I'm coming round at *5*.
3 Boy: That girl is your sister, isn't she?
Maria: No, she isn't my *sister*. She's my *cousin*.
4 Boy: You love beef burgers, don't you?
Maria: No, I *hate* beef burgers. But I *love* hot dogs.

Track 13

Page 44, Exercise 3

Bea: You look <u>stressed</u>.
Selma: I'm not <u>stressed</u>. I'm <u>tired</u>.
Bea: Why's that?
Selma: Pierre phoned me. And not in the <u>day</u>, in the <u>middle of the night</u>!
Bea: Did he have a problem?
Selma: No, he did it as a <u>joke</u>.
Bea: That's <u>unbelievable</u>. I'd be <u>furious</u>.
Selma: Yeah. And tonight I'm going to do the <u>same thing</u>, <u>same time</u>!
Bea: Good idea!

Track 14

Page 44, Exercises 4 and 5

Karin: Hi Stefan.
Stefan: Hey Karin! What's up?
Karin: Not much ... You know, I saw Jordan's friend yesterday ... oh, what's his name ... the tall dark guy?
Stefan: You mean Brad?
Karin: Yeah. I've a *terrible* memory for names. I can remember *faces* but not *names*.
Stefan: You know, Anna, my cousin, can remember people she's seen – even just once in a big crowd. She can even remember *acquaintances* from when she was five years old. It's a special ability. People like Anna are called 'super recognisers'.
Karin: That's *amazing*. A bit like people who can remember everything they've read or every picture they've seen?
Stefan: Yes. I don't know if I'd like to be like that.
Karin: No, if you were a super recogniser, you'd get into a *lot* of trouble. Imagine going up to someone in a shop and saying 'Hi! I saw you in a museum in London six years ago!' They'd think you were *mad*.
Stefan: Gosh, yes! But Anna says it can be quite useful. The police often *pay* super recognisers to find criminals in videos of crowds. They show them a face and then the video, and they can pick out the bad guys! Like at football matches, when some fans cause problems.
Karin: I'd be happy if I could just remember people's names! Who was Jordan's friend again ... ?

Track 15

Page 44, Exercise 6a

1 *I'm* so angry
2 I'm *so* angry
3 I'm so *angry*

Track 16

Page 44, Exercise 6b

1 *Ann* can remember everything.
2 Ann *can* remember everything.
3 Ann can remember *everything*.

Track 17

Page 47, Exercise 4

1

A: Excuse me. We're here on holiday. Would you take a photo of us, please?
B: Of course ... Smile!

2

A: We haven't got a menu on our table. Would you mind if we borrowed yours for a moment?
B: Not at all. Here you are.

3

A: I'm out tonight. Do you mind doing the washing?
B: Sorry, I can't. I'm out too.

4

A: I've got to go to the bank. I won't be long. Can you tell Mum that I'll be back in time for dinner?
B: All right.

5

A: You've got some great ideas for your essay. Do you mind if I use some of them?
B: Sorry, but you should think of your own.

Track 18

Page 47, Exercise 5

Sarla: Ron – what are you doing here?
Ron: It's Marty's computer. He's having problems with it.
Sarla: Can I ask you a favour?
Ron: OK. Go ahead.
Sarla: It's my laptop. Would you check it for me? I can't get online.
Ron: OK. No problem.
Sarla: Thanks, Ron. You're a star! Another thing – I dropped my hairdryer, and it won't work now. Could you look at that too?
Ron: Sure. I'll do that after the laptop.
Sarla: Thank you so much! What would we do without you!
Ron: That's what friends are for!
Sarla: One final thing. I can't get a signal on my new phone. Can you fix that?
Ron: Sorry, I'm afraid I'm no good with phones.
Sarla: Never mind. Do you mind if I borrow your phone to call Phil?
Ron: Not at all. Here you are!

Track 19

Page 47, Exercise 7

1 **A:** If you fixed my phone, what would it cost?
B: If I fixed your phone, I'd do it for free.
2 **A:** If you had to go on stage, how would you feel?
B: If I had to go on stage, I'd feel confident.
3 **A:** If your teacher made a mistake, what would you do?
B: If my teacher made a mistake, I'd point it out.

Unit 5

Track 20

Page 56, Exercise 2b

1 Although I don't usually like wearing yellow, I think this jacket suits me well.
2 There are some times when I don't really want to go out. For example, when I've had a long day at school and I just want to relax.
3 I'm sorry, but I couldn't find the information for the project. The thing is there are so many different sites to look at, I couldn't go through them all.
4 That is SO interesting. Anyway, to get back to the subject of the survey, I thought it was really good.
5 I'd love to hear more. However, I have to go now because Tom's waiting outside for me.
6 It isn't difficult to change the settings on your computer. Basically, you need to bring up *programmes* and you'll find the instructions there.

Track 21

Page 56, Exercises 3 and 4

Interviewer: So, Tony, what's the documentary tonight about?
Tony: Basically, it's about a girl, Stella, who has a really strange problem – although some people say it's not a problem, it's an ability.
Interviewer: And what is this problem – or ability?
Tony: Well, the thing is, it isn't easy to explain. It's called synaesthesia – and don't worry, I'm not going to ask you to spell it! Basically, it's when our senses get a bit confused.
Interviewer: You're right. I'm a bit confused!
Tony: OK. For example, people with synaesthesia sometimes see colours when they hear different things – like words or music. When Stella listens to music she sees silver and gold. It depends on the type of music and the instruments.
Interviewer: That's amazing. It definitely sounds more like an ability.
Tony: Yeah – but imagine if that happens all the time. It's a very powerful feeling. And some people see colours when people are speaking to them. This happens to one man on the programme, Luke. He says that people's words are red when they're angry or blue when they're not telling the truth. Basically, his head is always full of confusing colours.
Interviewer: Right. Scary! It's strange, but sometimes words have colours for me too. When I think of the days of the week – Monday is red, Tuesday is blue ... perhaps I'm synaesth ... whatever you said.
Tony: Maybe you need to see the doctor!
Interviewer: Um, well, anyway, about the documentary. It's at 7.30 ...

Track 22

Page 56, Exercise 5b

Although most people today think of pink for girls and blue for boys, you might be surprised to learn that this is quite a new idea. Sure, it would be really weird to see a three-year-old boy dressed in bright pink walking down the street beside his mum in London today. However, in Victorian times, that wouldn't have been so strange at all! Back then, parents dressed their children in colours like pinks, blues and whites. And, even though it sounds strange now, boys in Victorian times wore dresses too – just like the girls! However, I guess things have changed a lot since then, eh?! For example, when was the last time you saw a little boy walking around in a pink dress?!!!

Track 23

Page 59, Exercise 4

1
A: Good morning. I need something for my skin. I sat in the sun too long. I'm not sure how to say it in English.
B: You mean you got sunburnt?
A: Yes. Is this the right thing for my problem? I don't know what it's called.
B: That's a suntan lotion. It protects you from the sun. You need this one if you're already sunburnt.
A: Thank you very much for your help.
2
A: Hello. I want to buy some insect repellent. What's the difference between this one and this one?
B: This one is a liquid that you put on your skin, but this one's a bit like an air freshener.
A: It says 'For external use only'. I don't understand what this means. My English isn't very good.
B: It means you spray it in the air.
A: Does that mean you don't put it on your skin at all?
B: That's right.
A: OK, I'll take this one then.

Track 24

Page 59, Exercise 5

A: Good morning. What can I get you?
B: I'd like a coffee and one of those ... I'm not sure how to say it in English.
A: You mean biscuits?
B: Yes, please, a chocolate one. And a sandwich too, please. What's the difference between mild cheese and mature cheese?
A: The mature cheese is stronger.
B: OK, thank you. Then I'd like the mature cheese sandwich, please.
A: Are you going to eat in or take away?
B: I'm sorry, I don't understand what that means.
A: Do you want to eat and drink here in the cafe or take it with you?
B: In here, please. So, that means I need something for the sandwich. To put it on? I don't know what it's called in English!
A: That's a plate. Here you are!

Track 25

Page 59, Exercise 6b

beginning of the word: blue, cloud, speak, throat
end of the word: fact, help, pink, teeth

Unit 6

Track 26

Page 68, Exercise 3

1
So Stella, I'm here today to tell you about the great new online service from Kay's supermarket. Not only can you order all your food shopping to be delivered, but you can also buy clothes and other non-food products from our website. Everything that you see in our supermarket is available on the website, including special offers and discounts. We think your listeners will be as excited about it as we are!
2
Good morning, madam. Do you have a moment for me to tell you about our new online shopping service? It's very easy to use, and it's extremely convenient. You can order everything from the comfort of your own home, and we'll deliver it to you at a time that suits you. You only have to pay a small delivery fee, so it is excellent value for money. Is it something you think you'd be interested in?
3
Hello? Is that Kay's? Yes, I'm trying to use your website to order my shopping, but there seems to be a problem. The thing is that every time I click on a product, the website puts two

of them in my basket. I also can't seem to find the fruit and vegetable page. Do you have someone there who can talk me through it?

Track ▶27

Page 71, Exercise 5

1

Waiter: How can I help?
Dahlia: I'd like to return this coffee.
Waiter: Is there anything wrong with it?
Dahlia: It doesn't look right.
Waiter: That's because it's tea. I'm so sorry, I'll change it.

2

Lars: Excuse me, I'd like to return this jumper. I'm afraid there's a mark on it.
Assistant: OK, I can give you a discount.
Lars: No, thank you. I'd like a refund.
Assistant: That's fine. Do you have your receipt?
Lars: Here you are.

3

Tara: I'm afraid I'd like to return these cakes.
Assistant: Is there anything wrong with them?
Tara: Well, they all have holes in them.
Assistant: Um. I think they're supposed to have holes. They're a kind of doughnut.
Tara: Well, I've changed my mind. I'd like a refund, please.
Assistant: No problem. Do you have your receipt?
Tara: Yes, here you are.

Unit 7

Track ▶28

Page 80, Exercise 2

1–6 [SFX]

Track ▶29

Page 80, Exercises 3a and 3b

1

A big thank you to you all for coming – and for all the great presents. It's been a fantastic day and one that I'll remember for a very long time!

2

A: Hiya! How are you doing?
B: Fine. This place is cool. Can I get you anything?

3

And over here we have an example of Monet's early work. If you look closely you can see

4

Good morning and thank you for joining me today. This morning I am pleased to welcome to the studio Harry Masters, the famous actor who has just …

5

OK. If everyone could please settle down, I'd like to make a start. So, today we are going to look at the stories behind some famous places. Firstly we're going to travel to Ireland to look at …

6

Excuse me, could I just ask you a couple of questions? It won't take long. It's about …

Track ▶30

Page 80, Exercises 4 and 5

OK. If everyone could please settle down, I'd like to make a start. So, today we are going to look at the stories behind some famous places. Firstly we're going to travel to Northern Ireland to look at the incredible tourist attraction that is called 'The Giant's Causeway'. This is a series of tall rocks that form a sort of roadway from the beach into the sea. Some of the rocks are up to 12 metres tall. They were formed because of volcanic activity about 50 to 60 million years ago. People who lived here a long time ago invented a story about the strange rocks. They said that the rocky roadway was built by an Irish giant called Fionn MacCool. He was challenged to a fight by a Scottish giant called Benandonner who lived just across the sea from Fionn. Fionn agreed to the fight and built the pathway in order to travel across the sea to meet Benandonner for their fight. One story tells us that Fionn won the fight. Another story tells us that when Fionn arrived in Scotland and saw Benandonner he was scared. He hadn't realised the Scottish giant was so big. So, Fionn ran back to Ireland. His wife, Una, wrapped him up and pretended he was her baby. When Benandonner saw the baby he became anxious. He thought that if the baby was so big, the father, Fionn, must be enormous! So he ran away back to Scotland and pulled up the rocks behind him so that Fionn couldn't follow. There are many stories about strange places like this in the world …

Track ▶31

Page 83, Exercise 2

1 **A:** It costs 32 euros a month to join the club.
B: Oh, right. That's quite a lot.

2 **A:** It costs eight euros a month to join the club.
B: Does that mean it costs 96 euros a year?
A: That's right.

3 **A:** It's free to join the club.
B: Great! I'll join now!

Track ▶32

Page 83, Exercise 4

Adam: Excuse me. Could you please give me some help?
Alana: Yes, certainly. What can I help you with?
Adam: I'd like to join the photography club. How do you become a member?
Alana: It's easy. You just fill in a membership form. We send you a membership card and give you a brochure with all the information about the club.
Adam: And how old do you have to be?
Alana: You have to be over 14.
Adam: That's fine. I'm 16. How much does it cost to join?
Alana: Well, it's 15 euros a month.
Adam: Oh …
Alana: But it's free for students.
Adam: Great! Do I have to live locally?
Alana: No. It doesn't matter where you live. You just have to show me your student card.
Adam: Here it is. Could you please give me a form?
Alana: Sure. Here you are. Fill it in and you'll be a member.
Adam: So, can I go to the next meeting?
Alana: Certainly. The next meeting's on Wednesday. Here's all the information.
Adam: Great. Thanks.

Track ▶33

Page 83, Exercise 5

1 sorry, wisdom, stove
2 mile, cameras, seem
3 decision, recognise, unusual
4 occasion, leisure, unisex

Unit 8

Track ▶34

Page 92, Exercises 2 and 3

Reporter 1: Tell us about your new film! What's it about?
Holly: All I can say is that it's a psychological thriller and …
Reporter 2: What was it like acting with Johnny Best?
Holly: Oh … he's adorable, it was a dream
Reporter 1: And what about the director? I've heard he isn't easy to work with …
Holly: Well … he's one of the most successful directors today, and … I think it's an excellent film.
Reporter 1: Was it difficult to do the action scenes? Did you do all your own stunts?
Holly: The most difficult was an underwater escape scene. I spent months training for it.
Reporter 2: Your last film was a flop at the box office, wasn't it?
Holly: Yes, well, we don't need to talk about that …
Reporter 3: Tell us about your relationship with Angus Morton? Is it true you're breaking up?
Holly: We're very good friends.
Reporter 2: But are you two having problems?
Holly: No, no problems at all.
Reporter 3: We're only trying to get to the truth. Your fans want to know!
Holly: Yes, and newspaper always print the truth, don't they?

Track ▶35

Page 95, Exercise 2

1

Teacher: Yes, so please make sure you are all here early tomorrow morning. We're leaving at 8 sharp so...
Student: Excuse me, Mr Johnson, could I ask something?
Teacher: Yes, what is it?
Student: I'm sorry, but I won't be here tomorrow – I've got to go to the dentist.

2

Student 1: So we went to the library and tried to find a book about Austria, but you know they only had books about Germany and Switzerland and nothing about Austria...
Student 2: Hang on a minute, isn't our project about Australia?
Student 1: Oh ... really! I thought it was Austria?

3

Librarian: So this is the computer centre. You can use the computers here from 9am to 9pm and ...
Student: I'm sorry to interrupt, but could you tell me if we can use the internet here?
Librarian: Yes, of course. There's free internet access for all students.
Student: Thank you.

Track ▶36

Page 95, Exercise 5

1 actor, answer, article, picture
2 camera, celebrity, singer, media
3 story, officer, newspaper, reporter
4 reader, author, cinema, survey

Life skills

Track ▶37

Page 97, Exercise 3

Dave: So how are we going to find information about a famous celebrity?
Leila: We'll look up their name on the internet?
Dave: Yeah, but which sites are we gonna use?
Leila: Let's type in the name and see what comes up first.
Dave: OK, so that first one's a celebrity magazine – I think that's gonna have all the latest information ...
Leila: Yes, but will it be accurate?
Dave: Hmm, I don't know. How about looking for articles in the newspaper as well?
Leila: That's a good idea. We can look at entertainment magazines too ...
Dave: OK, so let's make a list of things we need to find out ...
Leila: Oh, hang on a minute, look what I just found: this fan site has everything you need to know.
Dave: Nice! That makes things easy.

Unit 9

Track ▶38

Page 104, Exercise 2

Shyama: OK, so let's get started with making these paper lanterns for the party. This doesn't look too difficult, right? Look: the instructions are right here in this book.
Kevin: I've got some different coloured paper here.
Shyama: Yep and I've got scissors and some sticky tape and some coloured pencils and a ruler. Right so let's see ... so first you need to cut a strip of paper off the side. I'll draw a straight line 3cm from the side of the paper and cut along the line.
Kevin: Right, that's to make the handle. Next fold the paper in half ... like this and draw a line about 3cm in from the edge of the paper.
Shyama: Now when you've done that, turn the paper round and cut along the width of the paper from the folded edge to the line that we just drew. Cut the paper into strips about 3cm wide.
Kevin: Right, so now we can easily see how that's going to make the main body of the lantern.
Shyama: OK now, unfold the paper and refold it the opposite way round so that you can't see the pencil line.
Kevin: How about decorating the outside with some patterns or something?
Shyama: Good idea! I'm going to have flowers and stars!
Kevin: Here, use some of these pencils. I'm going to do some coloured stripes.
Shyama: Next roll the paper into a tube shape and stick the sides together with some sticky tape
Kevin: Oh, right, that's looking good!
Shyama: And finally, attach the strip of paper to both sides with sticky tape make a handle.
Kevin: That's it. OK we've done it!
Shyama: They look quite good don't they?
Kevin: Yes! Let's do another one.

Track ▶39

Page 107, Exercises 1a and 1b

1 Are you going to join a club?
2 Don't be pessimistic
3 Be adventurous.
4 What could be better than acting in a play?
5 What have you got to lose?
6 It'll be amazing.

Track ▶40

Page 107, Exercise 2

1

Mandy: I've always wanted to be on the stage! And you love acting too, don't you? Let's join this drama club.
Rita: You're joking! I'm not brave enough to do that!
Mandy: Yes, you are. It'll help your self-confidence. Go on! Be adventurous!
Rita: Well ... maybe ...

2

Parveen: I'd love to learn how to defend myself. I'd feel more confident. How about joining this self-defence class? I think that would be so useful.
Nazmi: No way ... I can't do that. I'm not sporty enough.
Parveen: Oh, come on. Give it a go. It'll be fun.
Nazmi: Oh ... all right, then.

3

Ivan: I'd really love to be a good writer, and you're fantastic at writing stories and poems. Look at this – a creative writing workshop! Let's go!
Alex: I'd love to, but I don't want other people to read my writing.
Ivan: But what have you got to lose? Maybe we can all help each other to learn?
Alex: I'd prefer not to ... I'm just not confident enough.
Ivan: Oh, you're so boring ...

Track ▶41

Page 107, Exercise 5a

1 I'm going to the film with Judy.
2 It's on Thursday at 6pm.
3 It's a cookery club.
4 We're meeting for lunch on Saturday.

Unit 10

Track 42

Page 116, Exercise 2

Presenter: Young British designers are making their mark on the fashion world at this week's London Fashion Week. It is a chance for new designers to show off their latest designs to an international audience. Fashion Week is held twice a year in the spring and in the autumn, and most important people in the fashion industry go to the shows in Paris, Milan or New York. But London Fashion Week is quickly getting a name for itself as the place to find out about the hottest trends. Can you tell us about your impressions of LFW?

Reporter: Yes, I'm a reporter here for a fashion website and ... It's crazy ... I mean there's just so much going on ... but y'know it's absolutely brilliant. There're so many new ideas. In this show, we saw a new take on the maxi-skirt. I think ankle length is definitely gonna be the new look for the autumn, and then ankle boots, they're dead cool for summer or winter - they're so wearable with any outfit. And there's a new trend in men's fashion – they're mixing checked shirts with striped trousers. It sounds strange, but somehow it just works ...!

Presenter: Thank you!
One recent development in the world of fashion is teenage fashion. Several designers have fashion shows just for teenage designs, and there are fashion stores that specialize in teenage fashion. But what do teenagers think about this? Do you watch the fashion shows to find out what to wear?

Teenage girl: No, not really! I mean, I love fashion so I read the fashion blogs and all that stuff, and it's really interesting, but I'd say that most teenagers ... well, they're usually more worried about what everyone else is wearin', and they're also developin' their own sense of style, so ... like ... I buy stuff in the fashion shops, but I mix it with things I already have and kind of make up my own look.

Track 43/44

Page 116, Exercises 4 and 5

... but y'know it's absolutely brilliant.
I think ankle length is definitely gonna be the new look for the autumn.
... they're dead cool for summer or winter.
I read the fashion blogs and all that stuff.

Track 45

Page 119, Exercise 2

1

Jasmin: Those shoes are so cool.
Leon: I'm glad you like them.
Jasmin: You've got such a good sense of style.
Leon: Thanks! That's a really kind thing to say.

2

Alex: What an amazing picture.
Pete: Thanks! I'm glad you like it.
Alex: You're so good at art!
Pete: Your picture's really good too.

3

Nita: I love your outfit.
Lily: Oh, thanks! I designed it myself.
Nita: Really! You're such an amazing designer!
Lily: Yes, it's not bad, is it?

Track 46

page 119, Exercises 3a and 3b

1 This cake is delicious!
2 You're such a good artist!
3 I love your hairstyle!

Track 47

Page 119, Exercise 5a

1 That's a very white T-shirt.
2 You're so good at writing.
3 Did you design this card?
4 Is that a new coat?
5 This sweater has tight sleeves.

Track 48

Page 125, Exercise 5a

Sofia: I liked the beginning of the story.
Alan: Me too.
Sofia: I do the same thing sometimes.
Alan: What do you mean?
Sofia: When I'm in a car or on a bus ... I look at the other people and imagine how their lives might be. Don't you do that?
Alan: No. I'm more like Martin – sleeping.
Sofia: Do you think Martin likes Kara?
Alan: I don't know. There's something strange about their relationship.
Sofia: I agree. What about Howard? He's *strange*! I think he's going to be an important character.
Alan: I don't know. I think he's a policeman and Max is a police dog.
Sofia: No way! Howard's bad.
Alan: What about the voice at the end?
Sofia: Maybe it's Howard's son.
Alan: I'm not so sure. Why does he say 'Let me go'? And how does he know Kara's name?
Sofia: I don't know. Let's read the next chapter and find out.
Alan: OK. Good idea.

Track 49

Page 127, Exercise 5

Sofia: So what did you think of Robinson Crusoe?
Alan: I ... liked it.
Sofia: You don't sound very sure. Come on, Alan. You can be honest with me.
Alan: Well ... I liked it because it's an adventure story. But the style of writing feels quite old-fashioned. I think, in general, I prefer more modern books.
Sofia: I know what you mean. The language is very formal.
Alan: And people don't go to sea anymore.
Sofia: But that doesn't matter. The story still feels relevant to me. Young people still want to leave home. I could identify with the character.
Alan: Really? I thought you wouldn't like it because there aren't any female characters.
Sofia: But that's the whole point of books. You can discover new worlds and be different people especially when the story is told in the first person.
Alan: Yes, that's true. I like stories that are told in the first person. Don't get me wrong. I didn't hate it. I think I need more time to get into the story.
Sofia: Well, I want to know what happens next. So give me back my copy.

WORKBOOK ANSWER KEY

UNIT 1

VOCABULARY 1

Page 4

1 **1** parent **2** young adult **3** teenager **4** pensioner **5** university student **6** middle-aged person **7** child **8** baby

2 **1** parent **2** child **3** baby **4** middle-aged person **5** pensioner **6** teenager **7/8** university student / young adult

3 **1** get **2** get **3** vote **4** retire **5** start/leave **6** leave **7** go **8** have **9** go **10** get

4 **1** driving licence **2** school **3** university **4** get a job **5** have children **6** retire

READING

Page 5

1 **1** all **2** information **3** start **4** words

2 different

3 **1** 5,000+ **2** get married **3** romantic **4** places **5** *Star Trek* **6** blacksmith's shop

GRAMMAR 1

Page 6

1 **1** She **2** do not/don't **3** He **4** Do **5** Yes **6** does **7** 'm **8** 're **9** isn't **10** are **11** Is **12** isn't **13** are **14** Why

2 **1** e **2** d **3** f **4** b **5** a **6** c

Page 7

3 **1** retire **2** is making **3** organise **4** are watching **5** never wear **6** stay

4a

State verbs: know, like, need, remember, think, want

Active verbs: celebrate, dance, do, enjoy, paint, prepare

5 **1** Do you need some help with that project?

2 He doesn't want to study physics next year because he thinks it's boring.

3 Freddie doesn't want to go to university when he finishes school.

4 I'm saving money to go on holiday next year.

5 Jess is getting ready to go out at the moment.

6 How often do you visit your grandparents?

6 **1** knows **2** doesn't speak **3** 'm enjoying **4** do **5** 'm not studying **6** isn't improving

7 **1** Do you like Indian food?
2 What are you doing?
3 Does your brother play football?
4 Does your dad drive to work?
5 Where are Ant and Sue going?
6 Do you like your present?

8

1 I'm cycling to work at the moment. (B) cycle
2 I cycle there every day.
3 Do you want to ask me something?
4 So … why are you calling? (C) want
5 I don't drive my car to work, (D) cycle

LISTENING

Page 8

1 **1** sort of **2** kind of **3** don't know **4** yes **5** you **6** going to **7** things **8** What do you mean?

2 Tick 1, 2, 4, 6

3 **1** Spain **2** the weekend **3** birthday (16th) **4** 6 o'clock **5** T-shirts **6** March **7** a jumper **8** a test

4 **1** gotta **2** sorta **3** can't **4** doesn't **5** um

5 **1** F **2** I What do you mean? **3** F **4** I I don't know. **5** I So, when are you off?

6 **1** Hey **2** Yeah **3** really **4** stuff **5** dunno

7 **1** I **2** I **3** C **4** C **5** I **6** I

VOCABULARY 2

Page 9

1 **1** cotton **2** enormous **3** square **4** valuable **5** plastic **6** colourful **7** tiny **8** unusual

2 **1** valuable **2** useful **3** antique **4** old-fashioned **5** special **6** colourful

3 **1** amazing wooden
2 old white
3 tiny silver
4 small traditional
5 old cotton
6 long pink

Words & Beyond

4a

second-hand: used / not new

doll: a child's toy that looks like a small person or baby

wooden: made out of wood

identical: exactly the same as something else

packaging: the paper/plastic that covers a new product before it's opened or used

4b **1** doll **2** second-hand **3** wooden **4** identical **5** packaging

5 **1** city offices **2** ceremony **3** stuff **4** diving

GRAMMAR 2

Page 10

1 **1** We **2** didn't **3** Did **4** were **5** wasn't **6** wasn't **7** Were **8** were **9** going

2 **1** was pouring **2** were preparing **3** didn't want **4** was waiting **5** gave **6** was dancing

3 **1** wasn't watching **2** was working **3** was listening **4** Did you get **5** did you send **6** sent **7** wasn't working **8** was working **9** noticed **10** didn't change

4 **1** listened **2** brought **3** was visiting **4** spoke **5** was **6** came **7** was dancing **8** fell **9** hurt

SPEAKING

Page 11

1 **1** C **2** D **3** A **4** B

2 **1** but I can't come **2** That's too bad. **3** Great! **4** Sure, I'd love to. **5** That sounds brilliant. **6** I'd love to come but I can't.

3 **1** R **2** A **3** A **4** R

4 3, 2, 7, 6, 5, 4, 1

5 **Circle:** friend, get, net, pensioner, twenty

Underline: first, person, university, work

WRITING

Page 12

1 **1** heading **2** questions **3** notes

2 **Paragraph 1** What my special day was
Paragraph 2 A detailed description of my special day
Paragraph 3 Why it was special for me

3 **1** C **2** B **3** A

4 yes

Page 13

5 **Paragraph 1** – Introduction
What was the celebration? What did you do?
Para 2 - give details
What happened?
Para 3 – Say why it was special
What event made it special? Where/ Who/When?
Connection today?

LIFE SKILLS

1 They are organising an end-of-term party.
They need to find out who is coming, book a table at a restaurant, decide on a menu, get decorations, think about music.

2 **1** b **2** b **3** b **4** b

VOCABULARY REVIEW

Page 14

1 **1** child, young adult, pensioner
2 baby, teenager, parent
3 baby, university student, pensioner
4 teenager, young adult, middle-aged person
5 child, teenager, adult

2 **Across 1** parents **2** date **3** crown **4** celebration **5** doll **6** election
Down 7 ritual **8** licence **9** ceremony **10** university **11** job

3 **opinions:** useful, valuable, unusual, old fashioned, traditional
sizes: enormous, tiny
shapes: square
ages: antique, second-hand
colours: colourful
materials: wooden, cotton

GRAMMAR REVIEW

Page 15

1 1 you're sharing **2** How's it going? **3** get **4** don't argue **5** cooks **6** are you doing **7** I'm just waiting **8** Do you want **9** we're decorating

2 1 'm looking **2** 'm preparing **3** need **4** 'm studying

3 1 invited **2** got **3** was running **4** happened **5** fell **6** cut **7** needed **8** was carrying **9** arrived **10** started

4 1 I; While I was waiting for the film to start, I bought some popcorn.
2 I; I'm sorry Mrs Rivers, but I don't understand what we have to do for homework. **3** C **4** I; Right now we're waiting for our teacher to arrive.
5 I; We were late for the wedding so we took a taxi. **6** C

UNIT 2

VOCABULARY 1

Page 16

1 Across 1 ship **5** helicopter **6** tram **7** bus **8** bike **Down 2** plane **3** taxi **4** scooter **5** horse

2 1 scissors **2** wallet **3** shampoo **4** suitcase **5** a toothbrush **6** a hairbrush

3 1 c **2** d **3** f **4** e **5** a **6** b

4 1 ride **2** fly **3** drive **4** drive **5** sail **6** ride

5 1 hairbrush **2** toothpaste **3** toothbrush **4** visa **5** sleeping bag **6** passport **7** boarding pass **8** suitcase **9** shampoo **10** backpack **11** wallet

6a Flying by plane to a different country: hairbrush, toothpaste, toothbrush, visa, passport, boarding pass, suitcase, shampoo, wallet
Taking the train to stay at a hotel in your country: hairbrush, toothpaste, toothbrush, suitcase, shampoo, wallet
Taking your bike to go camping in the forest: hairbrush, toothpaste, toothbrush, sleeping bag, shampoo, backpack, wallet

Reading

Page 17

1 headings; layout; pictures; weblinks; beginning; aim

2 Text A c Text B a Text C b

3 Text A: instruct Text B: persuade Text C: inform

4 1 C **2** I **3** I **4** C **5** C

5 1 A **2** A, C **3** B, C **4** C **5** B

Grammar

Page 18

1 1 have **2** 's **3** have **4** hasn't **5** I've **6** Where

2 1 ever/never **2** exact time **3** already/just/yet

3a underline: 've just arrived; 'm sending; 've never watched; 'm waiting; 's late; hasn't phoned; I hope; 've already bought; think I can see

3b circle: for 15 minutes; last night

4a

Infinitive	Past participle
be	been
wait	waited
travel	travelled
buy	bought
read	read
write	written
speak	spoken
catch	caught
do	done
make	made

4b been [I]; waited [R]; travelled [R]; bought [I]; read [I]; written [I]; spoken [I]; caught [I]; done [I]; made [I]

Page 19

5 1 for **2** since **3** for **4** since **5** for **6** since

6 1 I've never stayed in an expensive hotel.
2 Have you swum in the pool yet?
3 He's just unpacked his suitcase.
4 I've already been in the pool three times.
5 Have you ever been on a plane?
6 Our plane hasn't taken off yet.

7 1 I've **just** spoken to Mark. He called in the last few minutes.
2 Have you finished your homework **already**? You only started it at 5pm and it's 5.10pm now.
3 I've **never** been to Scandinavia. I'd love to go.
4 I'm afraid I haven't emailed Sarah **yet**. But I'll do it now.
5 Has Danny **ever** got more than 50% for his maths tests? I don't think so!
6 We've been here **for** two hours. Where is she?

8 1 I haven't seen Paul for two weeks.
2 Have you spoken to Kenny about the party?
3 We've bought tickets for the gig on Wednesday.
4 Sally's just got her exam results.
5 Which of these books have you read?
6 The teacher hasn't given us any homework!
7 Where have you been until now?
8 We've just won the World Cup!

9 1 We've been **2** I've already learned **3** We've eaten **4** Dan hasn't been **5** Jacky has fallen **6** Have you looked at **7** Mum and Dad have gone **8** Has Amy received

10 1 Yes, I've just finished.
2 I've already packed.
3 No, I've never been (to China).
4 No, she hasn't phoned yet.
5 I've had a pet dog for five years.
6 I've known Amy since 2005.

11 1 I've lost my passport.
2 I've already eaten
3 The taxi has arrived.
4 The weather has changed.
5 I've spent all my money.
6 I've failed my driving test.

LISTENING

Page 20

1 1 listen for the main ideas **2** listen for specific information

2a 1 they've been in a traffic jam for a long time
2 they're waiting for their plane. They've been there for ages.
3 the plane had to turn back because of an engine problem. They're still waiting.

2b 1 negative **2** negative **3** positive

3 I listened for the main ideas.

4 Message 1: 7.30 Italy motorway (in car) half an hour possible break down (coach)
Message 2: 11am airport bad weather two hours
Message 3: 2am France car 7am

5 I listened for specific information.

6 1 half an hour **2** motorway **3** bad weather **4** two hours **5** car **6** night

VOCABULARY 2

Page 21

1 1 seat **2** departure **3** arrival **4** reservation **5** distance **6** flight **7** connection

2 1 flight **2** reservation **3** distance **4** departure **5** connection **6** arrival

3 Across: 2 destination **3** passenger **5** seat **Down: 1** fare **2** delay **4** route

4a queue: a line of people waiting to do something
trip: when you go on a journey somewhere and come back again
voyage: a long journey, usually by ship
journey: the act of travelling from one place to another
passport control: the area where your documents are checked
gate: a part of an airport where you get on or off a plane
homesick: missing home when you're in another place
check in: the act of showing your ticket and giving your luggage to the staff at the airport
crew: the people who work on a plane or ship
customs: the place where your luggage is sometimes searched
take off: to begin to fly a plane in the air at the start of a flight
land: to guide a plane safely back to the ground at the end of a flight

4b

Inside the airport	On the plane	Other words
check in	crew	queue
passport control	take off	trip
gate	land	voyage
crew		journey
customs		homesick

5 **1** crew **2** queue **3** take off
4 homesick **5** gate **6** trip **7** customs
8 land

GRAMMAR 2

Page 22

1 **1** b **2** a **3** d **4** c **5** b **6** e **7** a **8** c
2 **1** present continuous **2** *will/won't* + infinitive **3** *be* + *likely to* + infinitive
4 present simple **5** going to
3 **1** are you doing **2** You'll definitely
3 We're meeting **4** is likely to be
5 You'll get **6** I'm going to ask
4 **1** does your plane leave **2** are you getting **3** Are you going to eat
4 Will you need **5** Are you likely to recommend **6** Is anybody meeting
5 **1** 'm going to have **2** 'm playing
3 'm going to relax **4** is
5 'll definitely watch **6** are likely to come
7 'll probably go **8** starts
6 **1** going to meet **2** 'll probably watch
3 aren't likely to win **4** 'll definitely be
5 'll probably score **6** aren't likely to lose **7** 'll be starting **8** 'll go **9** 'll be

SPEAKING

Page 23

1 **1** Sorry, I didn't hear that.
2 Could you repeat that, please?
3 Can you say that again, please?
4 Sorry, I don't understand.
2 **1** Gates 1-29 **2** Customs
3 Departures **4** Passport control
5 Arrivals **6** Check-in
3 Customs, Gates 1-29
4 **Conversation 1:** Sorry, I didn't hear that.
Conversation 2: Can you say that again, please?
Conversation 3: Could you repeat that, please?
5a **1** I'd like to check in **2** Can I have
3 Here you are **4** are you checking in
5 I have **6** your hand luggage
7 boarding pass **8** gate number is it
9 Gate 15 **10** a good flight
6

/b/	/p/
toothbrush	toothpaste
hairbrush	passport
bike	plane
boat	shampoo
baggage	passenger
bag	departure

WRITING

Page 24

1 **1** b **2** a **3** c
2 **1** d **2** c **3** f **4** h **5** e **6** b **7** a **8** g
3a 're really enjoying (present continuous), have had (present perfect), come (present simple), were walking (past continuous), saw (past simple), I'll be (*will*)
4a **1** At the moment **2** for 10 years
3 every summer **4** every day
5 Yesterday **6** seven days ago **7** since then **8** This evening **9** at 4.15 **10** next year

LIFE SKILLS

1 Kate was at Calcutta station. She was trying to buy some tickets.
2 It was too busy in the queue for tickets.

VOCABULARY REVIEW

Page 26

1 **1** sleeping **2** first **3** hand **4** sharp
5 university **6** passport **7** boarding
8 driving
2 **1** **passenger** – the others are all age related
2 **toothbrush** –the others are all things you need to get into places
3 **route** – the others are all types of transport
4 **homesick** – the others can all describe objects
5 **fare** – the others are things you go on
6 backpack – the others all go into a backpack!
7 **suitcase** – the others are all places at an airport
8 **vote** – the others all happen on a plane
3 **Across:** **3** teenager **5** cotton
7 colourful **9** reservation **11** scissors
12 baby
Down: **1** antique **2** connection
4 documents **6** trip **8** departure
10 money
4 **1** useful **2** square **3** old-fashioned
4 middle-aged **5** journey **6** destination
7 route **8** seat

GRAMMAR REVIEW

Page 27

1 **1** I'm working; I'll definitely be able to
2 doesn't want; doesn't have
3 has worked; loves **4** are you going; Are you likely to be **5** 're building; 's driving **6** Have you seen; were watching
2 **1** How long have you been home?
2 I've just got back. **3** The plane landed at 11.30 this morning. **4** Did you have a wonderful time in China? **5** I've never enjoyed a trip so much. **6** I took some pictures of the Great Wall yesterday.
7 I thought about you. **8** While I was walking along the Great Wall.
9 My phone hasn't worked for a week.
3 **1** has been a teacher for
2 go jogging every day **3** 's likely to rain
4 've just seen **5** while I was eating/having **6** met Tom six months ago
4 **1** has left; will take **2** are waiting; has landed **3** dropped; was drinking
4 is landing; will come **5** have not checked in; will miss

Unit 3

VOCABULARY 1

Page 28

1 opera **2** drums **3** trumpet **4** singer
5 guitar **6** orchestra **7** conductor
8 violin **9** flute **10** musician
2 **1** rock **2** performance **3** jazz
4 hip hop **5** audience **6** musician
7 venue **8** opera
3 **1** a conductor **2** the concert
3 a band **4** audience **5** musician
6 hip hop
4a **1** concert **2** venue **3** drums
4 audience **5** performance **6** singer
7 musicians **8** band

READING

Page 29

1 **1** type **2** similar **3** before **4** after
5 mean
2 and 4

Noun	Verb
audience	sing
conductor	listen
host	moaned
range	
spotlight	
standard	
Adjective	**Adverb**
classical	beautifully
fantastic	well
annual	nervously
upside down	

3 **1** yes **2** review
5 **1** Eurovision Song Contest
2 Saturday **3** Sweden **4** Denmark
6 **1** a **2** b **3** b **4** b **5** b **6** a **7** a **8** a

GRAMMAR 1

Page 30

1 **1** to go **2** to play **3** to buy
4 to become **5** to go **6** performing
7 listening **8** being **9** watching
2 **1** b, c, e **2** a, b, d
3a **1** drum/drumming, plan/planning, sit/sitting, stop/stopping, swim/swimming **2** become/becoming, create/creating, hope/hoping, take/taking, write/writing
4 Verbs followed by *to*: decide, hope, inspire, learn, plan, want, would like
Verbs followed by *-ing*: don't mind, enjoy, imagine, practise
Verbs followed by both: forget, hate, love, prefer

5 Incorrect: 1, 2, 5, 6, 8, 9, 10
1 being **2** to play **5** to play **6** to play
8 seeing **9** to be **10** to meet

Page 31
6 1 moving **2** to teach **3** playing
4 to go **5** travelling **6** to get
7 1 being **2** to be **3** being **4** to be
5 being **6** to be **7** to be **8** to be **9** to be
10 to be **11** being **12** to be
8 1 to watch **2** to join **3** listening
4 to come **5** making **6** to win **7** to write
8 to see
9 1 When did you decide to do that?
2 I don't mind helping you **3** You should learn to speak Spanish yourself!
4 I decided to learn the guitar instead.
5 I'm not planning to go until about 9pm.
10 1 to start **2** watching **3** going **4** to get **5** waiting **6** not to record
11 1 I forgot to write down the homework. **2** I prefer listening to folk than to jazz. **3** I don't mind finishing the typing for you. **4** I can't stand listening to heavy metal music.
12 1 forget to send **2** hope to see
3 enjoyed swimming **4** decided to buy

LISTENING
Page 32
1 1 information **2** Decide **3** Listen
4 notes
2 1 b **2** b **3** a **4** a **5** d **6** b **7** c **8** a
3 1 Gap 4 **2** Gap 2 **3** Gap 1 **4** Gap 5
5 Gap 3
4 1 rock **2** drums **3** in 2010 **4** three
5 singing with her friends
5 1 When they started **2** What they like best **3** Why they started **4** Instruments
5 How many songs **6** Type of music
6 6 guitar **7** because he won a talent competition **8** one

VOCABULARY 2
Page 33
1 1 extremely **2** incredibly **3** pretty
4 quite **5** really **6** terribly **7** totally
8 very
2 1 incredibly **2** very **3** a bit **4** totally
5 a lot **6** pretty **7** extremely **8** a bit
9 a lot **10** totally
3 1 extremely **2** incredibly **3** a bit
4 terribly **5** a bit **6** incredibly

Words & Beyond
4 1 stage **2** gesture **3** audition
4 confidence **5** convey **6** talent
7 criteria **8** focused

GRAMMAR 2
Page 34
1a 1 e **2** d **3** a **4** b **5** c/f **6** f/c
1b 1 good **2** the worst
2 1 the fastest **2** harder **3** most creatively **4** worse **5** the highest
6 the earliest **7** more powerful **8** better
3 1 The audience shouted more loudly for Anna than for Mark.
2 Kevin swam the fastest in the competition.
3 I didn't do as badly in maths this year as I did last year.
4 In the quiz Dave answered his questions the quickest.
5 Greta danced better than the other dancers in the audition.
6 Freddy sings the worst in the whole school.
4 1 better **2** the hardest **3** more beautifully **4** as well as **5** faster
6 better **7** as well as
5 1 Can you swim as well as Jin?
2 You need to learn to write more neatly
3 At the audition, Ahmed performed the most confidently. **4** Darina can't run as fast as Sabrina as she's only 13.

SPEAKING
Page 35
1 1 A **2** B
2 1 lot of people **2** your opinion
3 thought **4** people think **5** don't care
6 about **7** you think **8** have an opinion
3 Asking for an opinion: What was your opinion? And what about you? What did you think?
Giving an opinion: I thought … I don't care what other people think … I don't really have an opinion.
Presenting other people's opinions: A lot of people … Some people think …
4

/ɔː/	/ɒ/
audience	opera
orchestra	costume
perform	song
boring	confidence
caught	rock
audition	concert

WRITING
Page 36
1 1 but **2** although **3** even though
4 however
2 1 Although **2** but **3** However **4** but
5 However **6** Even though
3 1 Although / Even though **2** However
3 Even though / Although **4** however
5 but **6** Although / Even though
4 1 I; Although the composer Beethoven was deaf, he wrote some amazing classical music. **2** C **3** I; I'd like to be a singer, however, I get nervous in front of an audience. **4** C
5 C **6** I; The band is very famous in Europe, but no one has heard of them in the USA.

LIFE SKILLS
1 1 He's painting his room.
2 He finished his homework.
3 He thinks painting is dull and he is bored.

VOCABULARY REVIEW
Page 38
1 Across: 5 tradition **6** visa **7** orchestra
10 enormous **11** ceremony
Down: 1 valuable **2** ritual **3** colourful
4 passenger **8** drum **9** folk
2 1 customs **2** scissors **3** shampoo
4 opera **5** adult **6** trumpet **7** trip
8 passport **9** toothbrush **10** helicopter
11 route **12** election

GRAMMAR REVIEW
Page 39
1 1 Where do you like to listen to music?
2 Are you going to watch the concert on television?
3 Where were you going when I saw you this morning?
4 Have you ever learned how to play an instrument?
5 How long have you liked rock music?
2 1 decided, to get **2** will, listening
3 don't, waiting **4** planning, to play
5 being, 'll be **6** to borrow
3 1 longer **2** harder **3** quicker
4 as well as **5** the worst **6** the longest
4 1 d **2** a **3** f **4** b **5** e **6** c
5 1 Susie drives as carefully as Pavel.
2 Jacky's the best singer in/at the school.
3 I'm meeting Hugo after school today.
4 Helena has played the violin for six years.
5 I've never been to Paris before./I haven't been to Paris before.
6 We hope to have a holiday in Russia this summer.

Unit 4

VOCABULARY
Page 40
1 ambitious: having a strong wish to be rich and successful
generous: willing to be more kind, helpful or giving (with money, for example) than most people
emotional: having and expressing strong feelings
creative: describes a person who can think of lots of new ideas
competitive: wanting to win in whatever you do
cheerful: looking happy and positive
brave: not afraid of danger or difficult things

polite: not saying unkind things to people
rude: not polite: a person who says or does things that might upset or anger other people
2 **1** generous **2** emotional **3** creative **4** ambitious **5** competitive **6** cheerful
3 **1** enemies **2** neighbour **3** classmates **4** relative **5** guest **6** acquaintance
4 **1** old friends **2** team-mates **3** online friends **4** close friends
5 **1** A **2** C **3** E **4** D **5** B

READING
Page 41
1 **1** like **2** such as **3** For example **4** For instance **5** headings **6** first
2 **1** I'm quite shy with people I don't know, such as acquaintances.
2 My neighbour is really generous. For example, last week he lent me his stereo.
3 My cousin and his brother share lots of things, such as clothes and books.
4 Christo and I are very different. For instance, I love football/tennis but he prefers tennis/football.
3 **1** b **2** d **3** a **4** c
4 **1** Mae-Lin and Li **2** Kamil **3** Vi **4** Marek **5** Mae-Lin and Li **6** Marek

GRAMMAR 1
Page 42
1 **1** present **2** future **3** present **4** future
3 **1** I **2** C **3** I **4** C **5** C
4 **1** He thinks they might miss the film. **2** Greta **3** Uffi's parents will be angry and her dad will have to take Greta to the film. **4** No **5** He's going to leave in five minutes if she's not ready.
5 **1** A **2** B **2** A **4** A **5** A **6** B

Page 43
6 **1** If my sister wakes me up early tomorrow, I'll be angry.
2 We'll meet after school unless our class finishes late.
3 Harry's got tennis practice this morning unless it rains.
4 If you don't want to go shopping, I'll go on my own.
5 If you forget your key, the neighbour will let you in.
6 My dad will give us a lift unless there's a problem with his car.
7 **1** phones **2** comes **3** don't get **4** makes **5** don't talk **6** find
8 **1** If I get home early, I'll take the dog for a walk. **2** Unless I can earn some more money, I won't be able to go to Lisbon. **3** I'll wear my new dress if I go to Nori's party. **4** If we win this game, we'll be in the finals of the competition. **5** Carol will give me some advice if I ask her for help. **6** Oliver won't talk to me again unless I apologise.
9 **1** *What will you do if she says no? If she says no I'll probably cry.* **2** What will you do if I'm late? If you're late, I'll catch the bus. **3** Who will you invite to play football if Tom doesn't come? If Tom doesn't come, I'll invite Mark. **4** Where will Dave and Mike stay if they go to Tokyo? If Dave and Mike go to Tokyo, they'll stay with Yuko. **5** If Beatriz visits you, where will you take her? If Beatriz visits us, we'll take her to Madrid. **6** Will Mr Diaz be angry if I don't give in my homework? If you don't give in your homework, Mr Diaz won't mind.
10 **1** tell **2** 'll be **3** talk **4** don't tell **5** finds **6** 'll get **7** keep **8** will tell **9** won't say **10** see

LISTENING
Page 44
1 **1** important **2** stressed **3** feelings **4** up **5** down
2a **1** Peter, Ed **2** 4, 5 **3** sister, cousin **4** hate, love
3 stressed, stressed, tired, day, middle of the night, joke, unbelievable, furious, same thing, same time
4b someone they know with a special ability
5 **1** I **2** I **3** C **4** I **5** C **6** I
6a **1** b **2** a **3** c
6b **4** f **5** e **6** d

VOCABULARY 2
Page 45
1 **1** amazing, d **2** terrified, e **3** furious, b **4** shocked, h **5** ancient, i **6** exhausted, g **7** huge, c **8** awful, j **9** unbelievable, a **10** fascinating, f
2 **1** ✓ **2** ✗ **3** ✓ **4** ✓ **5** ✓ **6** ✗ **7** ✓ **8** ✗
3 **1** amazing **2** furious **3** exhausted **4** huge **5** awful **6** shocked

Words & Beyond
4 **1** ambitious **2** generous **3** emotional **4** creative **5** competitive **6** cheerful **7** brave **8** polite **9** rude

GRAMMAR 2
Page 46
1 **1** past simple **2** would **3** would **4** past simple **5** would **6** wouldn't
2 **1** an imaginary **2** past simple **3** infinitive without to **4** can **5** first or second
3 **1** had; would buy **2** changed; would move **3** would be; called **4** was; would drive **5** spoke; would understand **6** had; would move
4 **1** What would you do if you got lost abroad? **2** What would you do if you lost your homework? **3** Where would you go if you could travel anywhere? **4** How would you feel if you couldn't answer any questions in a test?
5 **A** 2; If I lost my homework, I'd tell the teacher. **B** 6; If I couldn't answer any questions in a test, I'd feel stressed. **C** 1; If I got lost, I'd ask someone for directions. **D** 4; If I could travel anywhere, I'd see the Pyramids..
6 **1** could go **2** 'd visit **3** started **4** could take **5** stopped **6** 'd visit **7** had **8** 'd fly **9** had **10** could take **11** let **12** 'd fly

SPEAKING
Page 47
1 **1** Could/Can **2** Can/Could **3** help **4** Do **5** Would
2 **1** ✓ **2** ✓ **3** ✗ **4** ✓ **5** ✓ **6** ✗ **7** ✓ **8** ✓
3a **1** Can/Could I borrow your phone? OK, All right, Sure, Of course, I'm afraid ... **2** Can/Could you give me a lift, please? OK, All right, Sure, Of course, I'm afraid ... , Sorry, I can't. **3** Would you mind helping me with this problem, please? Sorry, I can't, Not at all, I'm afraid ... **4** Do you mind if I leave early today? No, go ahead, Not at all, I'm afraid ... **5** Would you mind if I borrowed your dictionary? No, go ahead, Not at all, I'm afraid ...
3b **Circled:** Would you mind helping me with this problem, please? Do you mind if I leave early today? Would you mind if I borrowed your dictionary? Of course. I'm afraid ... No, go ahead. Not at all. **Underlined:** Can/Could I borrow your phone? Can/Could you give me a lift, please? OK. All right. Sure. Sorry, I can't.
4 **1** Would **2** course **3** borrowed **4** Not **5** Do **6** I can't **7** Can you **8** All **9** Do
5 **1** Can I ask you a favour?
2 Would you check it for me?
3 Could you look at that too?
4 Can you fix that? **5** Do you mind if I borrow your phone to call Phil?
7 **1** **a:** If you fixed my phone, what would it cost?
b: If I fixed your phone, I'd do it for free.
2 **a:** If you had to go on stage, how would you feel?
b: If I had to go on stage, I'd feel confident.
3 **a:** If your teacher made a mistake, what would you do?
b: If my teacher made a mistake, I'd point it out.

WRITING
Page 48
1 **1** d **2** a **3** b **4** c
2a Definition 1: lie (Verb 2); Definition 2: bear (Verb 2); Definition 3: frank; Definition 4: relay

3a 1 fly – sky **2** city – pretty
3 cruise – choose **4** abroad – afford
5 flight – sight **6** trip – ship
7 friend – lend **8** plane – train
4 1 simple **2** no **3** no **4** no
5 friends and relatives **6** cities and sights, different cultures and people
7 eat wonderful food and take lots of photos **8** happy and relaxed

LIFE SKILLS

1 She has to decide what she's going to do during next week's holiday. She decides to stay home and revise, and then go away with her parents for a couple of days.

VOCABULARY REVIEW

Page 50

1 1 E; patient **2** A; orchestra
3 D; stage **4** B; heavy metal
5 C; traditional
2 1 huge **2** online **3** friendships
4 acquaintances **5** date **6** reminds
7 celebrations **8** stuff **9** homesick
10 miss **11** distracting **12** focused
3 Across: 4 valuable **8** retire
10 suitcase **11** rhythm **12** reservation
Down: 1 wallet **2** venue **3** queue
5 scissors **6** classmates **7** passenger
9 audition

GRAMMAR REVIEW

Page 51

1 1 invited **2** won't get **3** will land
4 were **5** told **6** agree
2 1 take **2** 'll be **3** wear **4** were
5 'd explain **6** doesn't understand
7 wouldn't worry **8** cared
3 1 have you been **2** joined **3** chatting
4 to join **5** to practise **6** Do you have?
7 more confidently **8** better **9** 's calling
10 you'll be **11** wants
4 1 We'll have the party outside if it doesn't rain. / We wont have the party outside if it rains. **2** Jas writes more neatly than Mason. **3** I hope to travel abroad after my exams. **4** While the band was playing, many of the audience left. **5** We're likely to be late so let's meet inside the restaurant.
6 I don't mind rock music, but I prefer heavy metal.

Unit 5

VOCABULARY

Page 52

1 1 shoulder **2** neck **3** hand **4** face
5 back **6** leg **7** knee **8** toe **9** foot
2 1 smell, nose **2** taste, mouth
3 touch, finger **4** hearing, ear
3a 1 touch **2** taste **3** smell **4** sight
5 hearing **6** hearing **7** hearing **8** touch
9 sight
3b 1 feel **2** taste **3** smell **4** see, look
5 listen **6** hear, sound **7** hear **8** touch
9 watch, see
4 1 watch **2** tastes **3** sounds **4** smells
5 hear **6** feels **7** see **8** look **9** listen

READING

Page 53

1 1 Before **2** visuals **3** connection
4 style **5** when
2a 1 a **2** b **3** b, c, e
3 1 C **2** C **3** C **4** I **5** I **6** C
4 1 a **2** b **3** a

GRAMMAR 1

Page 54

1 1 are **2** isn't **3** subject **4** was
5 weren't **6** will/'ll **7** won't **8** be
2b 1 no **2** the action **3** yes
2c 1 don't know **2** not as important as
3 very obvious
3 1 P **2** P **3** A **4** P **5** A **6** P **7** A **8** A
4 were taken, was opened, were brought together, is written, was damaged, will be repaired, will be sent back, was built, is still lived in
5 Present passive: is written, is still lived in; Past simple passive: were taken, was opened, were brought together, was damaged, was built; Future passive: will be repaired, will be sent back

Page 55

6 1 Too much food is thrown away these days. **2** Most food is bought in supermarkets, not in markets.
3 The pizza was delivered just one hour after I ordered it. **4** In the future, more vegetables will be grown in people's gardens. **5** We were told by the manager that the restaurant was closing. **6** Some of the best products are made by small companies.
7 1 made **2** was launched **3** isn't delivered **4** is fitted **5** is controlled
6 travels **7** was designed **8** will take off
8 1 is served **2** is delivered **3** were taken **4** isn't cooked **5** are given **6** is built **7** are given **8** will be opened
9 1 This delicious sauce was first made in the Caribbean. **2** Then it was brought to England by immigrants in the 1950s.
3 It wasn't liked very much by English people at the time because it was too spicy. **4** Then it was developed by a company and made less spicy.
5 Today the sauce is enjoyed everywhere in the UK. **6** It is used in many everyday meals. **7** Next year it will be sold in the Caribbean. **8** Will it be bought there?

LISTENING

Page 56

1 1 an important point **2** examples
3 contrasting information
2a 1 3 **2** 2 **3** 1 **4** 3 **5** 1
2b 1 b **2** e **3** a **4** c **5** d
3 a
4 1 I **2** I **3** C **4** C **5** C **6** I
5 1 Although/Even though **2** however
3 For example/instance **4** although/even though **5** However **6** For example/instance

VOCABULARY 2

Page 57

1 1 once in a **blue** moon **2** see **red**
3 get the **green** light **4** as **black** as night **5** out of the **blue** **6** tell a **white** lie
7 as **white** as a sheet **8** be in the **red**
9 black and **white** **10** feel **blue**
2 1 j **2** b **3** f **4** a **5** c **6** d **7** h **8** e **9** g
10 i
3 1 g **2** h **3** e **4** i **5** b

Words & Beyond

4 1 crisps **2** pale **3** tongues
4 complaints **5** ban **6** chemist
7 perfume

GRAMMAR 2

Page 58

1 1 order **2** to **3** so **4** that **5** so **6** so
2 1 in order to/to **2** so that **3** so that
4 in order to/to **5** so that **6** so that
3 1 c **2** b **3** e **4** f **5** d **6** a
4 1 In order to/To **2** In order to/To
3 So that **4** so that **5** In order to/To
6 So that **7** so that
5 1 We met at the café so that we could have a good chat. **2** I organised a party in order to celebrate my birthday.
3 I studied hard in order to do well in the test. **4** We left early so that we would be in good time for the flight.
5 I chat to an online friend in Canada in order to improve my English.

SPEAKING

Page 59

1 1 When you don't know the name of something **2** When you don't understand a word
2 1 I'm not sure how to say it in English. **2** Does that mean … ?
3 I need something for …
4 Is this the right thing for … ?
5 I don't know what it's called. **6** What's the difference between … ? **7** I don't understand what this means. **8** I need some of that … **9** It's for …
3 Explaining what you need: I need something for … ; It's for … ; I'm not sure how to say it in English.; I don't know what it's called. ; I need some of that …
Asking for help: Does that mean … ?; I don't understand what this means.; Is this the right thing for … ?; What's the difference between … ?

4 1 need something **2** how to say it
3 Is this the right thing for **4** what it's called **5** What's the difference **6** what this means **7** Does that mean
5 Correct order: 4, 6, 1, 7, 2, 9, 5, 8, 10, 3, 11
6b Beginning of the word: cloud, blue, throat, speak; **End of the word:** teeth, pink, help, fact

WRITING
Page 60
1 1 and **2** as well **3** after **4** end **5** true
2 1 and **2** also **3** too **4** also **5** also **6** as well
3 1 We always go camping and I love sitting outside listening to the birds singing.
2 I not only like to go sightseeing, but I also like to visit the places that local people go to.
3 We usually go to the park. We go to see our relatives in the city as well.
4 My cousins always come on holiday with us. My aunt and uncle sometimes come with us too.
5 My friends and I rent a small house in the mountains, and we go walking every day in the fresh air.
6 I not only stay at home for my holidays, but I also do nothing for a week. It's so relaxing!
4 1 and **2** Not only **3** also **4** also **5** as well / too **6** as well / too
5 A 3 **B** 4 **C** 1 **D** 2

LIFE SKILLS
1 She was at Laura's party. She was talking to Charlie.
2 She had her arms folded.

VOCABULARY REVIEW
Page 62
1 eye, ear, nose, back, mouth, face, hair, wavy, good-looking, big, small, straight, hearing, watch, taste, sound, smell
2 eye – big/small – watch; ear – big/small –hear, sound; nose – big/small – smell; mouth – big/small – taste; face – good-looking; hair – wavy/straight
3 1 sheet **2** back **3** blue **4** hard **5** night **6** common
4 1 emotional **2** competitive **3** ambitious **4** furious **5** blind **6** homesick **7** enormous **8** valuable
5 1 complaint **2** flute **3** invisible **4** stuff **5** aid **6** community **7** venue **8** relative **9** extremely **10** pensioner

GRAMMAR REVIEW
Page 63
1 1 were invented **2** are made **3** drank **4** are **5** think **6** is claimed **7** will continue **8** will be sold
2 1 I watched the documentary so that I could learn more about memory.
2 Sam gets better marks than his brother because he works harder.
2 My friends came round today in order to say Happy Birthday! **4** Janice talks more loudly than anyone I know!
3 1 I can see more clearly with these new glasses. **2** I wanted to visit the new pizza place, but it was closed. **3** Sam enjoys learning the guitar in her spare time. **4** You must listen more carefully in class. **5** I was inspired to start writing because of my love of books. **6** Ben speaks Spanish better than anyone in our family.
4 1 b **2** d **3** f **4** c **5** a **6** e
5 1 not likely to say **2** 're hoping to go **3** 'd like to **4** didn't forget to send **5** better than **6** If you come

Unit 6

VOCABULARY
Page 64
1a 1 doll **2** mobile phone **3** boots **4** bread **5** suntan lotion **6** magazine **7** chicken **8** cat food **9** tennis balls **10** dictionary
1b

Newsagent's	magazine
Sports shop	tennis balls
Pet shop	cat food
Toy shop	doll
Bookshop	dictionary
Chemist's	suntan lotion
Electronics shop	mobile phone
Shoe shop	boots
Baker's	bread
Butcher's	chicken

2 1 price; buy **2** save; cheap **3** expensive; pay **4** spent; cost
3 1 f **2** e **3** a **4** i **5** j **6** c **7** b **8** h **9** d **10** g
4 1 by card **2** a special offer **3** return **4** keep
5 1 boots **2** expensive **3** special offer **4** the sale **5** shoe shop **6** tried **7** card **8** receipt **9** return **10** refund **11** exchange **12** discount **13** electronics

READING
Page 65
1 1 uncertainty **2** emphasis **3** wow **4** positive **5** comments
2 1 d **2** d **3** c **4** a **5** b
3 1 c **2** a **3** d **4** e **5** b
4b 1 a **2** d
5 1 Mikey and Harvey **2** Kimmy55 **3** HannaB

GRAMMAR 1
Page 66
1 1 not sure **2** possible **3** impossible
2 1 logical **2** infinitive (without *to*) **3** the same **4** sure **5** sure
3 1 B **2** A **3** C **4** A **5** C **6** B
4 1 c **2** f **3** e **4** d **5** a **6** b
5 1 D **2** S **3** D **4** D **5** S **6** S
6 1 could **2** can't **3** must **4** could **5** can't **6** must
Page 67
7 1 a ii b i c iii **2** aii b i c iii **3** a iii b ii c i
8 1 can't **2** must **3** must **4** could/may/might **5** could **6** must **7** could **8** must
9 1 The burger bar can't be open.
2 She must be sick. **3** There might be a sale. **4** She might be at the cinema with Sami. **5** it must be on tomorrow night.
6 That can't be Elisa at the door.

LISTENING
Page 68
1 1 Listen for the main message.
2 Listen for expressions that give an opinion or suggestion.
3 Decide what you have learned and/or how you feel after listening.
2 1 b **2** d **3** c **4** a
3 1 c **2** b **3** a
4 1 c **2** a **3** c

VOCABULARY 2
Page 69
1a 1 basket **2** trolley **3** customer **4** checkout **5** store detective **6** cash desk **7** changing room **8** department
1b

People in a shop	Different areas of a shop	Things you put your shopping in
customer store detective	checkout cash desk changing room department	basket trolley

2 1 escalator **2** window **3** store detective **4** changing room
3a brand: the name/make of something for sale
slogan: a short, easy-to-remember phrase used to help sell a product
advertising: trying to persuade people to buy products
campaign: a group of connected actions done for a specific reason, ie advertising campaign
amusing: funny
product: an item for sale
afford: have enough money to pay for something
shopaholic: a person who loves shopping
3b 1 advertising **2** campaign **3** amusing **4** brands **5** products/product **6** slogans **7** shopaholics **8** afford

Words & Beyond

4 **1** b **2** a **3** c **4** b **5** b **6** a

GRAMMAR 2

Page 70

1 **1** any **2** mind **3** tell **4** polite **5** before **6** after

2 **1** I **2** D **3** D **4** D **5** I **6** I

3 **1** Do you know when the new shopping centre is going to open? **2** Do you have any idea how much Dave paid for the tickets? **3** Could you tell me where Mandy and Kenny live? **4** Do you know what kind of clothes Keira likes wearing? **5** Would you mind telling me when the concert starts? **6** Could you tell me what today's date is?

4 **1** c Can you tell me why it isn't working? **2** b Do you know how I can find the registration page? **3** a Would you mind telling me how I can save my details for next time? **4** e Could you tell me how I can search for a specific book? **5** d Do you have any idea how long it takes for books to be delivered?

SPEAKING

Page 71

1 **1** like **2** much **3** afraid **4** thank **5** I'd like to speak to the manager, please. **6** I'm afraid there's a problem with this. **7** Thank you very much. **8** No, thank you.

2a Polite: 2, 4

3 **1** M **2** C **3** R **4** T

4 **1** I'd like to buy some flowers, please. **2** I'm afraid this phone isn't working well. **3** No, thank you (I don't want a discount). **4** Thank you very much.

5 **1** can I help **2** I'd like to **3** It doesn't **4** I'm afraid **5** give you **6** your receipt **7** anything wrong **8** changed my mind **9** Do you have **10** you are

6 **1** d **2** b **3** a **4** e **5** c

7 /ae/ advertising, bag, brand, cash, challenge, map, shampoo
/a:/ card, department, father, guitar, large

WRITING

Page 72

1 **1** I am writing to ask **2** I would be grateful if you could **3** Thank you for your help. **4** I look forward to hearing from you. **5** Yours sincerely

2 **1** F **2** I **3** F **4** F **5** F **6** I

3 a 3 **b** 4 **c** 5 **d** 6 **e** 1 **f** 2

4 **Polite phrases:** I am writing to ask for your help. I ... would be grateful if you could fill it in ... Thank you for your help. We look forward to receiving your questionnaire. Yours sincerely;
Indirect questions: Would you mind telling us what you think is important for a good online music store?

LIFE SKILLS

1 They are on a train. People are sitting in their seats.
2 passive

VOCABULARY REVIEW

Page 74

1 **1** department **2** sale **3** card, cash **4** changing **5** polite **6** queue **7** huge **8** distracting **9** very

2 **1** ambitious **2** shocked **3** generous **4** noisy **5** exhausted **6** allergic **7** assertive **8** blind

3 **1** gave **2** left **3** went **4** got **5** get **6** have

4 **1** violin, piano **2** tram, underground, **3** scissors, hairbrush **4** customer, conductor

GRAMMAR REVIEW

Page 75

1a **1** Could you tell me where Miss Turner is? **2** Do you know when the film starts? **3** Do you know what time Brian is leaving? **4** Would you mind showing me where the tablet computers are? **5** Can you tell me what colours you have this in? **6** Do you know why Teresa is angry with me?

1b **a** is teaching **b** to leave **c** you're going **d** has already started **e** have **f** don't know

1c **1** a **2** d **3** b **4** f **5** e **6** c

2 **1** This dress was designed in France. **2** These cars are made in Russia. **3** These sweets aren't produced anymore. **4** Was this jacket returned yesterday? **5** The thief was arrested by the police this morning. **6** Will Tim be seen by the doctor later today?

3 **1** I was buying a sandwich in the café when I saw Vanessa. **2** I don't like shopping in the sales because it always gets very busy. **3** Did you buy this lotion in the supermarket? I didn't see it at the chemist's yesterday. **4** They didn't/wouldn't give Sari a refund when she asked because she had bought the dress on special offer. **5** We have just been to the new shopping centre, and we spent far too much money! **6** It's going to rain so I need to buy an umbrella.

4 **1** unless **2** in order to **3** working **4** can't **5** would spend **6** might

Unit 7

VOCABULARY 1

Page 76

1 **living room:** computer, lamp;
kitchen: fridge, kettle, iron, dishwasher, vacuum cleaner, cooker, washing machine;
both: clock, phone, radio, light

2

For cleaning things:	For making or keeping food and drink:	For work, leisure and games:
vacuum cleaner dishwasher washing machine	cooker fridge kettle	computer phone radio
For clothes:	**For telling the time:**	**For helping you to see clearly:**
iron washing machine	clock	lamp light

3 **1** d **2** e **3** g **4** j **5** h **6** c **7** a **8** b **9** f **10** i

4 **1** chop **2** bake **3** build **4** knit **5** make **6** grow **7** travel **8** use **9** wash **10** make **11** milk **12** sew

5 **1** milk the cows **2** chop wood **3** bake bread **4** wash clothes by hand **5** sew; clothes **6** make their own entertainment **7** travel by horse and cart **8** use gas lights

READING

Page 77

1 **1** information **2** headings **3** important **4** abbreviations

2a why it was built, the people who built it, the difficulties they had

2c **1** very **2** difficult **3** people **4** including **5** approximately **6** building

3 The job is to be a storyteller.

5a **1** next year **1** in many capital cities **2** how the men built the tunnels, how the trains were developed, learn about the most beautiful stations, hear stories about the underground **3** 15–19 **4** interested in history, enjoy talking to people, like acting, strong speaking voice, can do regional accents **5** parents' permission **6** by contacting them at undergroundex.com

GRAMMAR 1

Page 78

1 **1** used **2** use **3** use **4** did

2 **a** 2 **b** 1 **c** 2 **d** 1

3 **1** used **2** use **3** did **4** used to **5** rain **6** use

4 **1** We used to go camping every summer. **2** Jake didn't use to play computer games. **3** Did you use to travel to school by bus? **4** How often did you use to play tennis? **5** Where did your grandparents use to work? **6** I didn't use to do much sport.

5 **1** I used to have a dog called Nala. **2** I didn't use to drive a car. **3** I didn't use to use a computer. **4** I used to listen to the radio. **5** I didn't use to eat meat on Fridays. **6** I used to argue with my brother. **7** I didn't use to play a lot of sports.

Page 79
6 **1** Who used to take you to school? **2** How did you use to travel to school? **3** What household jobs did you use to have to do? **4** Did you use to have a bike? **5** What did you use to do in the evening? **6** Did you use to have a computer?
7 **1** did you use to live **2** used to live **3** Did you use to play **4** didn't use to have **5** used to have to **6** used to work **7** used to help **8** used to clean **9** used to chop **10** didn't use to spend
8 **1** used to live **2** used to be **3** didn't use to be **4** used to buy **5** used to work **6** used to love **7** Did you use to know **8** used to talk

LISTENING
Page 80
1 **1** clues **2** conversation **3** talk **4** interview **5** adjectives
2 **Situation 1** d **Situation 2** b **Situation 3** f **Situation 4** a **Situation 5** c **Situation 6** e
3b **1** Situation 2 **2** Situation 6 **3** Situation 4 **4** Situation 1 **5** Situation 5 **6** Situation 3
4 a
5 **1** C **2** I **3** I **4** C **5** I **6** I

VOCABULARY 2
Page 81
1 **1** upset **2** jealous **3** ashamed **4** proud **5** grateful **6** disappointed **7** guilty **8** satisfied **9** sorry **10** anxious
2 **1** ashamed **2** proud **3** upset **4** jealous **5** guilty **6** satisfied **7** disappointed **8** grateful **9** sorry **10** anxious
3 **1** grateful **2** jealous **3** guilty **4** proud **5** disappointed **6** anxious **7** ashamed **8** upset **9** satisfied **10** sorry
4a **1** for **2** about **3** of **4** for **5** of **6** about
4b **1** jealous of **2** anxious about **3** upset about **4** sorry for **5** grateful for **6** proud of

Words & Beyond
5 **1** genuine **2** take part **3** rural **4** snores **5** statistics **6** fetch **7** wisdom **8** tribes

GRAMMAR 2
Page 82
1 **1** had/'d **2** hadn't **3** past participle **4** hadn't
2 **1** before **2** simple
3 **1** hadn't revised; didn't do **2** had finished; went **3** had practised; passed **4** had rained; was **5** 'd already spent; didn't buy **6** had finished; got
4 **1** e **2** d **3** f **4** c **5** b **6** a
5 **1** had … joined **2** had been **3** had entered **4** hadn't read **5** had … forgotten **6** had … sat **7** had gone **8** had ended
6 **1** took **2** 'd had **3** What had you done **4** had just finished **5** Hadn't you eaten **6** had done **7** decided **8** had finished **9** What had you said **10** had ordered

SPEAKING
Page 83
1 **1** Great **2** right **3** So **4** mean
2 **1** right **2** Does that **3** Great
3 **1** I'd like to join the photography club. **2** How do you become a member? **3** How much does it cost to join? **4** How old do you have to be? **5** Do I have to live locally? **6** Could you please give me a form? **7** Could you please give me some help? **8** Can I go to the next meeting?
4 **1** Could you please give me some help? **2** I'd like to join the photography club. **3** How do you become a member? **4** how old do you have to be? **5** How much does it cost to join? **6** Do I have to live locally? **7** Could you please give me a form? **8** can I go to the next meeting?
5 **1** wisdom **2** seem **3** recognise **4** unisex
6 /s/ sorry, stove, seem, unisex /ʒ/ decision, unusual, occasion, leisure /z/ wisdom cameras, miles, recognise

WRITING
Page 84
1 1 Once upon a time **2** One day **3** then **4** later **5** as soon as **6** suddenly **7** meanwhile **8** at first **9** in the end
2 3, 6, 1, 7, 5, 8, 4, 2
3 **1** Once upon a time **2** One day **3** As soon as **4** Later **5** At first **6** Meanwhile **7** Suddenly
4 **1** Once upon a time **2** As soon as **3** Later **4** one day **5** suddenly **5** Then
6 Paragraph 1: c Paragraph 2: b Paragraph 3: a
7 **Paragraph 1:** 2 **Paragraph 2:** 3 **Paragraph 3:** 1

LIFE SKILLS
1 **1** 1 grandson and grandad **2** He thinks he's won first prize in a competition. **3** He should check out the company carefully and read the email again because it looks like a trick.
2 Suggested answers: He is not respectful – he doesn't listen to his grandad's advice. He is also rude and patronising to his grandad – he says he doesn't know what he's talking about and knows more about the Internet than him. He also uses rude words: Don't be stupid, grandad; You're so old-fashioned.
3 Suggested answers: He should listen to his grandad's advice in the future. He shouldn't be rude and disrespectful to him.

VOCABULARY REVIEW
Page 86
1 anxious, ashamed, disappointed, grateful, guilty, jealous, proud, satisfied, upset, sorry,
2 load the dishwasher, grow food, bake bread, chop wood, knit a jumper, travel by horse and cart, sort the recycling, tidy the room, do the washing up
3a **1** discount **2** trolley **3** patient **4** receipt **5** amusing **6** classical **7** generous **8** creative **9** keyboard **10** audience
3b **shopping:** discount, trolley, receipt; **music:** classical, keyboard, audience **describing people:** patient, amusing, generous, creative;

GRAMMAR REVIEW 1
Page 87
1 used to live **2** used to travel **3** used to take **4** had earned **5** used to fly **6** had left **7** had completed **8** didn't use to give **9** Neil Armstrong
2 **1** hadn't done **2** told her **3** had been **4** had taken **5** believed **6** had told **7** had forgotten **8** had gone
3 **1** was listening **2** knocked **3** were standing **4** asked **5** are asking **6** was making **7** Have we met **8** had known **9** hadn't seen **10** moved **11** were driving **12** will be
4 **1** act as well as Francis **2** 20 euros, I could buy **3** was designed in the USA **4** (that) I could chat **5** must be really difficult **6** visiting the museum

Unit 8
VOCABULARY 1
Page 88
1 **1** e **2** a **3** f **4** c **5** b **6** d
2 **1** news article **2** survey **3** recipe **4** cartoon **5** picture caption **6** quiz **7** letter **8** interview
3 **1** printer **2** author **3** reporter **4** designer **5** editor **6** blogger **7** cartoonist **8** photographer
4 **1** cartoon **2** profile **3** recipe **4** interview **5** reporter **6** report **7** publisher **8** journalist

READING
Page 89
1

Formal writing	Informal writing
longer sentences	contractions (*I'll, don't*)
full verbs (*I will, do not*)	shorter sentences
formal phrases (*However*)	spoken phrases (*well, anyway*)
correct punctuation	extra punctuation (!)

2 3
3 A I B I C F
4 **1** A, B **2** C **3** A **4** C **5** A, B, C **6** C
5 **1** d **2** c **3** e **4** a **5** b
6a **1** F; Longer sentences, formal phrases, full forms
2 F; Formal words and phrases
3 I; Shorter sentences, spoken English phrases
4 I; Shorter sentences, contractions, extra punctuation to add emphasis
5 I; Shorter sentences, spoken English phrases

GRAMMAR 1

Page 90

1 **1** have **2** were **3** didn't **4** would **5** can **6** had asked
2

Subject	Object	Possessive
I	me	my
you	you	your
she	her	her
he	him	his
it	it	its
we	us	our
they	them	their

3 **1** told **2** told **3** said **4** told **5** told **6** say **7** said **8** tell **9** told **10** told
4 **1** They/wouldn't/him: They said they wouldn't give him any more money.
2 He/had printed/him: He said that they had printed a story about him that wasn't true. **3** She/they/were,/her/her: She said that they were going to interview her about her book. **4** She/she/could/them: She said she could phone them from the station.

Page 91

5 **1** were **2** would **3** wasn't **4** wanted **5** loved **6** would **7** had **8** had **9** thought **10** was **11** was **12** hoped
6 **1** was; him; his **2** were; their **3** him; wanted; him **4** would; him/her **5** had printed his **6** hadn't spelt his
7 **1** I'm very disappointed. **2** The other player's much better than me.
3 I haven't been playing well because of my injured knee. **4** I'm thinking of retiring from tennis soon. **5** I want to spend more time with my family.
8 **1** Jack said he was going to be late. He told Jim that he would meet him at seven.
Jim said that he would wait for him in the coffee shop.
2 Rachel said she hadn't gone to school because she had been sick.
Emma said she hadn't been there either because she had been to the dentist.
3 Sam said they had gone skating at the weekend and they were going again on Saturday.
Sue said she didn't have any skates but Sam said he would ask his friend to lend her his skates.

LISTENING

Page 92

1 **1** how **2** tells **3** think **4** relationship **5** directly
2 A film star and some newspaper reporters.
3 **1** excited about **2** got on well **3** didn't get on well **4** always **5** disappointed with **6** not happy **7** is **8** doesn't trust
4 **1** I **2** C **3** I
5

The film star wants to talk about	But she doesn't want to talk about
her new film	the director
her stunts	her boyfriend
her co-star	her private life
	her last film

6 **1** confirmed **2** denied **3** claimed **4** added **5** promised **6** admitted

VOCABULARY 2

Page 93

1 1d 2c 3b 4f 5a 6e
2 **Across** **2** confirm **3** admit **4** deny
Down **1** promise **2** claim **3** add
3 **1** confirmed **2** claimed **3** admitted **4** added **5** denied **6** promised
4 **1** insisted **2** explained **3** suggested **4** agreed

Words & Beyond

5 **1** witness **2** victim **3** celebrity **4** paparazzi **5** sources **6** privacy

GRAMMAR 2

Page 94

1 **1** was **2** I **3** had **4** was **5** would **6** had **7** could
2 **1** a **2** b **3** b **4** a **5** b **6** a
3 **1** was **2** had been **3** had inspired **4** had watched **5** had liked **6** would be
4 **1** What is your new film about?
2 What was the most difficult scene?
3 What inspired you to become an actor?
4 Have you watched any films recently?
5 Did you like them?
6 What will your next film be?
5 **1** He asked me what my name was.
2 He asked me where I was from.
3 He asked me how long I was going to stay.
4 He asked me when I had last visited England.
5 He asked me if I was on holiday.
6 He asked me if I would stay with friends.

Speaking

Page 95

1 e **2** f **3** c **4** a **5** d **6** b
2 **1** teacher / student **2** student / student **3** school librarian / student
3a Conversation A 3, 1, 2
Conversation B 3, 2, 1
5 **1** article **2** celebrity **3** story **4** survey

WRITING

Page 96

1 **1** I like swimming, art and photography.; comma **2** My teacher's name is Mr Edwards.; apostrophe
3 Can you guess the title?; question mark **4** 'I'm not going to retire,' he said.; quotation marks **5** He's doing concerts in Paris, Rome and London.; capital letters **6** Our summer camp has a wide range of activities: water sports, skateboarding and climbing.; colon
2 **A** a, 4, 8 **B** b, 2, 5, 6 **C** c, 1, 3, 7
3 **1** 'We're extremely happy with our exam results and hope to do even better next year,' said deputy headmistress, Suzanne Wilks.
2 Alan Gardner, school advisor, said, 'The website is run by students and is an excellent way for them to discuss their school experience.'
3 Exam results at Gillingham School have doubled for the second year in a row.
4 School students will take part in a lot of exciting new projects: planting trees to prevent soil erosion; setting up recycling bins all over the school; starting a vegetable garden in the school yard.
5 Students at Fernlea School have designed a new website for their school.
6 Students can do a number of things on the website: evaluate canteen food and make suggestions for improvement; discuss opinions about what teaching methods help them to learn the most; discuss problems at school and offer suggestions and advice.
7 A survey of students and teachers revealed the reasons for their success include: increased access to computers and the internet; individual advice in the academic support centre; peer mentoring with older students.
8 This term, Greentree School has started a new environment club.

LIFE SKILLS

3 They mention the following websites: a celebrity magazine, a newspaper, entertainment magazine, fan site.
They have forgotten to look at multiple sources.
4 **1** Text 3 **2** a F b NK c T

VOCABULARY REVIEW
Page 98
1 **1** anxious **2** upset **3** knit **4** gas lights **5** reporter **6** photographer **7** promise **8** claims **9** receipt **10** escalator
2 **1** A journalist writes articles.
2 A cartoonist draws cartoons.
3 A poet writes poems.
4 Some reporters write gossip.
5 You usually feel guilty if you have done something wrong.
6 You usually feel proud if you have done something fantastic.
7 You usually feel grateful if someone helps you.
8 You usually feel disappointed if you don't get something you expected.
3 **1** editor **2** checkout **3** sight **4** incredible **5** acquaintance **6** orchestra **7** passport **8** enormous

GRAMMAR REVIEW
Page 99
1 **1** I asked him why he'd become a journalist.
2 I asked you what the worst thing about your job was.
3 I asked you if you'd interviewed a lot of famous people.
4 He said he loved writing stories about people.
5 I said I wasn't at home very much.
6 I said I didn't earn a lot of money.
2 **1** I used to write poems when I was young,
2 When I was at school I didn't use to like sports,
3 While I was in the supermarket doing my shopping,
4 I had left my passport at home
5 Could you tell me
6 There are a lot of gossip
7 so that I wouldn't/didn't get burned
8 Sam must be at home
3 **1** being **2** followed **3** in order to **4** must **5** had never **6** are you doing **7** haven't been **8** to go **9** might **10** I'll phone

Unit 9

VOCABULARY 1
Page 100
1 **1** geography **2** maths **3** languages **4** music **5** art **6** science **7** information technology **8** PE (physical education)
2 **1** e **2** a **3** f **4** b **5** d **6** c
3 **1** elementary **2** high **3** public **4** private **5** kindergarten **6** nursery **7** primary **8** secondary **9** state **10** homeschooling
4 **1** term **2** subject **3** university **4** exam **5** course

READING
Page 101
1 **1** c **2** e **3** b **4** a **5** d
3 **1** I **2** C **3** I **4** C **5** I **6** I **7** I **8** C **9** C **10** I **11** I **12** C
4 **1** pupils **2** subjects **3** travelling from place to place **4** children **5** Bangladesh **6** schools
5 **1** The school is run by the students. Teachers don't tell **them** what to do.
2 Students can go the same classes or they can go to different **ones.**
3 Siberia is in northern Russia. It's very cold **there.**
4 The teachers travel with the children and teach **them** in their homes.
5 The boat picks the students up, and **it** takes the children back home.
6 There is a lot of heavy rain in the monsoon season. **This** / **It** causes a lot of damage to buildings and roads.

GRAMMAR 1
Page 102
1 **1** be **2** told **3** not **4** to
2a **1** A **2** B **3** C **4** D
2b **1** Could you stop talking, please? **2** Could you not look at me like that, please? **3** Turn to page 5. **4** Don't talk so loudly!
3 **1** She told us to open our books.
2 She asked him not to talk to her.
3 I told you not to stay up late.
4 We asked them to turn down their music.
5 You told me not to phone.
6 They asked us not to wait for them.
4 **1** He asked me not to make any noise.
2 He told her to tell him her name.
3 They asked us to share our books.
4 They asked them to turn off their mobile phones,
5 She asked him to carry her books.
6 He told me not to phone him again.
7 He asked them to meet him at 6pm.
8 She told me not to forget to give her back her book.

Page 103
5 **1** 'Get a haircut.' my mum told me.
2 'Can you help me wash the car?' my dad asked me.
3 'Please can you help me with my computer?' my sister asked me.
4 'Don't be late for dinner.' my mum told me.
5 'Can you help me get dinner ready?' my mum asked me.
6 'Don't wear that T-shirt. It's too cold' my dad asked me.
6 We had a test yesterday. First, the teacher told us to be quiet. Then she told us not to talk. Next she told us to sit down. After, she told Jenny to put away her mobile phone. Then, she asked Fiona to hand out the test papers. After that she told us to write our names on our paper. Finally, she told us to start writing.
7 **1** My mum told me not to eat quickly.
2 My mum told me to tidy up my room.
3 My mum told me to clean my shoes.
4 My mum told me to finish my homework.
5 My mum told me not to play too many computer games.
6 My mum asked me to go and buy some milk.
7 My mum asked me to make a cup of tea.
8 My mum asked me not to talk so loudly.
8a **1** She told us not to bring our mobile phones.
2 They asked us to send her an email.
3 We asked them not to turn on the TV.
4 He told us to open out books.
5 You told him to answer the questions.
6 I asked her to help me with my homework.

LISTENING
Page 104
1 **1** you **2** next **3** When **4** comfortably
2 **1** Get some paper, scissors, sticky tape and some coloured pencils.
2 Draw a line using a ruler and pencil.
3 Cut off a strip of paper.
4 Fold the paper in half.
5 Draw a line 3cm in from the edge.
6 Turn the paper around.
7 Cut strips from the folded edge to the line.
8 Unfold the paper.
9 Refold the paper the other way round.
10 Decorate he paper with coloured pencils.
11 Roll the paper into a tube.
12 Stick the ends of the tube together.
13 Stick the strip of paper to both sides.
3 **1** Get some paper, scissors, sticky tape and some coloured pencils.
2 Decorate the paper with coloured pencils.
3 Cut off a strip of paper.
4 Cut strips from the folded edge to the line.
5 Stick the strip of paper to both sides.
4 **1** You **2** First **3** Next **4** When **5** Finally

VOCABULARY 2
Page 105
1 **1** self-confident **2** self-conscious **3** self-taught **4** self-centred **5** self-sufficient
2 **1** d **2** a **3** b **4** e **5** c

3 **1** self-confident **2** Self-pity **3** self-centred **4** self-defence **5** self-esteem **6** self-sufficient
4 **1** compulsory **2** trip **3** mud **4** steep **5** icy **6** trek

Words & Beyond

5 **1** pessimistic
2 juggler
3 adventurous
4 clown
5 insecure
6 tightrope

GRAMMAR 2

Page 106

1 **1** c **2** a **3** d **4** b
2

Personal pronoun	Reflexive pronouns
I	myself
you (singular)	yourself
you (plural)	yourselves
he	himself
she	herself
it	itself
we	ourselves
they	themselves

3 **1** c **2** a **3** a **4** b **5** b **6** c
4 **1** ourselves **2** us **3** each other **4** ourselves **5** each other **6** myself
5 **1** each other/ we can't do our **2** looked at each other **3** enjoy ourselves **4** their money/themselves **5** talk/myself **6** went to Grenada/myself **7** kept his problems/himself **8** cried / herself

SPEAKING

Page 107

1 **1** c **2** e **3** b **4** f **5** a **6** d
2 **Conversation 1** C **Conversation 2** A **Conversation 3** C
3 **Conversation 1:** I'm not brave enough.; Go on! Be adventurous!
Conversation 2: I'm not sporty enough.; Come on.
Conversation 3: What have you got to lose?; I'd prefer not to.
5 **1** film; a **2** 6pm; b **3** club; b **4** lunch; a

WRITING

Page 108

1 **1** b **2** e **3** c **4** d **5** a
2 **1** because **2** As **3** so **4** As a result, **5** therefore
3 **1** b **2** a **3** d **4** e **5** c
4 **1** what students eat at school; sports facilities **2** not having enough free time; performance in exams
3 the atmosphere in class; technology students can use

LIFE SKILLS

1 Paragraph 1 d Paragraph 2 b, e Paragraph 3 c Paragraph 4 a

VOCABULARY REVIEW

Page 110

1 **1** confident **2** pity **3** centred **4** sufficient **5** taught **6** defence
2 **Across** **3** university **5** exam **7** homeschooling **8** private
Down **1** kindergarten **2** boarding **4** secondary **6** term
3 **Travel items**
backpack
passport
sleeping bag
suitcase
visa
Music words
conductor
opera
orchestra
performance
trumpet
Personality
bad-tempered
brave
creative
generous
patient
People and relationships
acquaintance
enemy
neighbour
relative
teammate
Appliances
cooker
dishwasher
fridge
iron
lamp

GRAMMAR REVIEW

Page 111

1 **1** to talk; each other **2** us to; ourselves **3** them; themselves **4** me; myself **5** them; themselves **6** had made; themselves
2 **1** wasn't **2** would **3** was **4** could **5** I'll **6** so that **7** write **8** you'll
3 **1** a **2** a **3** b **4** a **5** b **6** b
4 **1** He asked me what time the train left.
2 I never travel by myself.
3 I used to play football …
4 I was told by him …
5 I can't imagine ever leaving this place.

Unit 10

VOCABULARY 1

Page 112

1 silk dress **2** short sleeves **3** leather boots **4** small buttons **5** patterned dress **6** wide collar **7** denim jacket **8** big buttons **9** baggy sweater **10** wide sleeves
2 **1** trying on **2** wear **3** suit **4** baggy **5** fit **6** match
3 **1** leather **2** baggy **3** plain **4** pockets **5** belt **6** wool
4 **1** sleeves **2** belt **3** plain **4** pockets **5** baggy **6** leather **7** wool **8** collar **9** boots **10** dress

READING

Page 113

1 **1** main **2** important **3** synonyms **4** family **5** category
2 fashion problems that people have
3 **1** B **2** C **3** A
4 **1** B **2** C **3** A **4** B **5** A **6** C
5 **1** f **2** d **3** e **4** b **5** a **6** c
6 **1** f **2** c **3** d **4** a **5** e **6** b

GRAMMAR 1

Page 114

1 **1** was **2** that **3** so **4** such **5** an **6** were **7** such
2 **1** I, such **2** C, **3** I such **4** C **5** I such a hot day/so **6** I so **7** I so **8** C
3a **1** They were such uncomfortable boots that …
2 It was such a warm coat that …
3 They were such tight jeans that …
4 The dress was so beautiful that …
5 The T-shirt was so baggy that …
6 The jacket was so large that …
3b **1** d I never wore them
2 c I didn't need a sweater.
3 b I couldn't put them on.
4 a everyone admired it
5 e it came down to my knees.
6 f it looked like a coat.

Page 115

4 **1** baggy; baggy jeans **2** tight; tight shoes **3** expensive; an expensive watch **4** high; high heels **5** big; a big hat
5 **1** The coat was so expensive that he couldn't afford it. It was such an expensive coat that he couldn't afford it.
2 The shoes were so large that she kept falling over. They were such large shoes that she kept falling over.
3 The jeans were so tight that I couldn't sit down. They were such tight jeans that I couldn't sit down.
4 The dress was so delicate that she was afraid to wear it. It was such a delicate dress that she was afraid to wear it.
6a **1** The shop had such loud music that I got a headache.
2 The shop assistant was so rude that I decided not to go back there again.
3 It was so crowded in the shop that I had to wait for ages.
4 I was such a warm coat that I wore it every day in the winter.
5 They were such fashionable jeans that everyone asked me where they were from.
6 The bag was so expensive that I was afraid of losing it.

LISTENING

Page 116

1 **1** longer **2** full **3** formal **4** careful **5** shorter **6** contractions **7** simpler **8** less

2 **1** Paris, Milan, and New York **2** twice a year, in spring and autumn **3** maxi skirts, ankle boots, checked shirts, striped trousers **4** maxiskirts, ankle boots **5** She doesn't think that teenagers follow them.

3 **1** F **2** I **3** I **4** F **5** F **6** I

4 **1** y'know **2** gonna **3** dead **4** stuff

5 **1** F **2** I **3** I **4**F

VOCABULARY 2

Page 117

1 **1** enjoyable **2** downloadable **3** affordable **4** valuable **5** reliable **6** recyclable

2a **1** manageable **2** suitable **3** reasonable **4** rechargeable **5** recyclable **6** unbreakable **7** enjoyable **8** reliable **9** downloadable **10** suitable **11** wearable **12** affordable

Words & Beyond

3 **1** labels **2** exploit **3** cruel **4** chic **5** outfit **6** fair trade **7** sacrifice **8** eco-friendly

GRAMMAR 2

Page 118

1 **1** Can **2** couldn't **3** aren't **4** Are **5** was **6** weren't **7** Was **8** will **9** won't **10** Will

2 **1** present **2** past **3** future **4** be able to **5** was/were able to **6** couldn't **7** will be able to

3 **1** am/'m not able to swim **2** aren't able to play **3** weren't able to ride **4** Were you able to cook **5** were you able to study **6** Was he able to dance **7** will/'ll be able to ride **8** won't be able to go

4 **1** could **3** could **4** could **5** could **6** could **7** couldn't **8** could

5a **1** was able to swim **2** couldn't run **3** was able to swim **4** was able to win **5** can join **6** will be able to enter **7** will be able to compete **8** can win

SPEAKING

Page 119

1 **1** c **2** f **3** a **4** e **5** b **6** d

2 **1** so **2** them **3** such **4** kind **5** an **6** glad **7** good **8** too **9** love **10** thanks **11** amazing **12** bad

3a **1** a **2** b **3** a

3b **1** This cake is delicious! **2** You're such a good artist! **3** I love your hairstyle!

4 **1** i **2** ii **3** i **4** ii

5 **1** white **2** writing **3** card **4** coat **5** tied

WRITING

Page 120

1 **1** b **2** c **3** a

2a **1** Both **2** and **3** either **4** or **5** Both **6** and **7** either **8** or **9** neither **10** nor

3a **1** Either **2** or **3** neither **4** nor **5** either **6** and **7** either **8** or **9** neither **10** nor

3b **1** I **2** I **3** I **4** C **6** C

LIFE SKILLS

1 Suggested answers:
1 What's it made from? **2** Does it have a guarantee? **3** Are they unbreakable?

VOCABULARY REVIEW

Page 122

1

Picture A	
Girl	**Boy**
patterned T-shirt	tight jeans
short sleeves	narrow collar
pockets	four buttons
Picture B	
Girl	**Boy**
plain T-shirt	baggy jeans
long sleeves	wide collar
no pockets	three buttons

2 1valuable **2** affordable **3** comfortable **4** downloadable **5** recyclable **6** enjoyable

3 **1** retire **2** enormous **3** departure **4** audience **5** straight hair **6** shy **7** enemy **8** customer **9** disappointed / dissatisfied **10** deny

GRAMMAR REVIEW

Page 123

1 **1** such **2** such a **3** so **4** so **5** such **6** so **7** such **8** so

2 **1** yourself **2** can't **3** buying/to buy **4** used to **5** you could **6** are you **7** must **8** I'd **9** will you be able **10** to be

3 **1** This camera was made in Korea. **2** We went to a boutique to buy some T-shirts. **3** Could you tell me what time the show starts? **4** He asked me to lend him my dictionary. **5** I used to have long hair when I was younger. **6** She asked me to take some pictures. **7** He said he had never seen such beautiful clothes. **8** They said they were going to study art and design.

4 **1** b **2** b **3** a **4** b **5** a **6** a **7** b **8** b

EXTRA READING Owl Hall

Page 124

1a **1** wasn't **2** didn't know **3** some problems **4** didn't like **5** evening **6** bad

3 **1** her dad **2** She felt like she could see all the way down his throat to his stomach. **3** She could feel someone watching her **4** The place was called Owl Hall and something didn't feel right.

4 **1** yawn **2** caravan **3** creak **4** bumpy **5** track **6** kick

5 **1** Alan and Sofia like **2** Alan does **3** Alan and Sofia aren't **4** Alan thinks **5** Sofia says **6** Alan and Sofia want

EXTRA READING Robinson Crusoe

Page 126

1 **1** I **2** C **3** I **4** I **5** C **6** I

2 **1** One of Robinson's older brothers was killed in the war. **3** His mother didn't think he should go and refused to speak to his father. **4** Robinson's first day at sea was a terrifying experience. **6** Robinson decided not to go back to his family in Hull.

3 **1** The style of writing is formal.

4 **1** going to sea **2** being at sea **3** his friend and his father **4** his mother and father **5** the sea **6** the other men; the storm **7** on the shore

5 Sofia

6 **1** e **2** c **3** f **4** a **5** d **6** b